THROUGH LIFE AND ROUND THE WORLD

THROUGH LIFE AND ROUND THE WORLD:

BEING THE STORY OF MY LIFE

RAYMOND BLATHWAYT

AND

MORTIMER MENPES

GYAN

Published by

Gyan Publishing House
5, Ansari Road
Daryaganj, New Delhi-110002
Phone: 011-47034999, 9811692060
E-mail: books@gyanbooks.com

Distribution Network
gyanbooks.com
India, USA, Canada, UK, Australia

ISBN: 978-93-7014-101-8 (PB)

First Published, 1917

2nd Impression 2025

Printed at: Gyan Press, Delhi.

THROUGH LIFE AND ROUND THE WORLD
Author: RAYMOND BLATHWAYT and MORTIMER MENPES

Photo by] [*Swaine, New Bond Street.*

THROUGH LIFE AND ROUND THE WORLD

BEING THE STORY OF MY LIFE

By RAYMOND BLATHWAYT

WITH ILLUSTRATIONS BY MORTIMER MENPES

1917

TO

HERBERT BEERBOHM TREE

AND

HARRY DE WINDT

TWO OF MY OLDEST AND DEARBEST FRIENDS

I DEDICATE THIS BOOK

CONTENTS

ILLUSTRATIONS

THROUGH LIFE AND ROUND THE WORLD

CHAPTER I

UNDER THE OLD OAK-TREE

Tityre tu patulae recubans sub tegmine fagi,
Silvestrem tenui Musam meditaris avena.

THE housemaid danced with Pedro the murderer, the nursemaid footed it lightly enough with Godfrey the forger, "Cookie" looked smilingly on from the kitchen door, I laboriously turned the handle of the barrel-organ, whilst my little brother played with the tiny red-jacketed monkey, and the wearied Italian organist slept the sleep of the just beneath the great oak-tree that so delightfully overhung our lawn, and beneath the dancing shadows of which I used to lie and dream and weave the golden threads which lend such enchanting romance to the innocent days of childhood. That is almost the earliest incident that arises to my mind from among the dim and half-forgotten memories of an unusually crowded past.

For my dear father, who was a country clergyman, had, some years before the occasion to which I refer, been presented to a convict chaplaincy by my mother's cousin, Sir George Grey, a famous Victorian Secretary of State and the grandfather of Viscount Grey of Fallodon, who was, indeed, mainly brought up by him; and hence it was that all my earliest associations were connected with that curious convict system with which, fortunately for them, so few of the English people are in any way acquainted whatever. And yet though my earliest memories are of long lines of grey-clad, broad-arrow-stamped men, heavily tramping along the lovely sunlit roads of an unusually wild and beautiful part of England, they are not sorrowful memories, nor are they in the least soiled or tainted with suggestion of crime, or wickedness, or evil-mindedness. It is a remarkable fact that these convicts appeared to have realized for themselves the old classic adjuration, *Maxima honos pueris debetur* ; for never once—though owing to the inevitable carelessness or indifference of the ordinary nursemaid I was thrown into constant association with the men, specially chosen and well-conducted men, however, who formed what was known as the garden gang, and who were assigned to the leading officers, such as the Governor, the Chaplain, the Deputy-Governor, and the two doctors, assigned to them in somewhat the same fashion as convicts were assigned to the earlier settlers in Australia—I can never once remember any single one of those men making use of a bad word in my hearing. On the contrary, it was Godfrey the forger who taught me a little child's prayer which I have never forgotten, and which ran as follows :—

And now I lay me down to sleep,
I pray the Lord my soul to keep ;
And if I die before I wake
I pray the Lord my soul to take.

It was Pedro, the South American Spaniard, who had stabbed a man to death in London, but who escaped the death penalty to which he had been sentenced owing to certain extenuating circumstances, who first revealed to me the fact that Mary was the Queen of Heaven, a piece of theology which much startled and horrified my father, who was, of all Evangelicals that I have met, absolutely the most strict and undeviating, and it was that same occurrence which led to a much sterner supervision on the part of my pastors and masters than I had previously been subjected to. It is a curious and pleasant reflection, however, that I can remember nothing but what was good and pure in my quite unavoidable association with those poor convicts. As a matter of fact, it was an association very much on a par with that of Eton and Harrow boys with their fathers' grooms in the stables of a big country house, and really fraught with neither more nor less evil than that is. Many of this garden gang were quite elderly men, though Pedro and Godfrey, my special friends, were comparatively young men, and some of them had known a far different existence in the outside world.

One I remember was a famous baronet, of whom his friends—and they were legion—had nothing to say but what was wholly admirable ; another, a splendidly handsome, white-haired old man, who used, as a special privilege, to act as clerk to my father in the chapel, and who, as a still further privilege, was allowed to wear his own pince-nez, had been mayor of a great city in the North, and had actually entertained Queen Victoria and the Prince Consort to luncheon at his own house ; whilst a third, who played the organ in chapel, was a Public School and University man. It will therefore be understood that such men could behave themselves, in a general way, quite as well as, if not better than, many free and happy men outside. O'Donovan Rossa—though he came many years later—was another of these unfortunates, and he, though a very convinced and resolute Fenian, was in many respects a really fine fellow ; whilst Michael Davitt, whom I met thirty years later at a Cabinet luncheon in Australia, was one of the most charming men I ever knew.

Pedro and Godfrey, between them, made me a beautiful little garden, "all to my very own self," as Godfrey told me ; and he dug out a tiny little lake in it, and then went into the woods that lay so thick around the garden—a kind of primeval forest which was crammed with wild North American Indians, and centaurs, and lions, and South Sea savages, and the most fearsome dragons—and cut me some bulrushes, out of which he fashioned some little boats, which he sailed upon the water for me. Godfrey was very good to me and really one of the heroes of my childhood, and so what more natural than that I should help him to escape when I was asked to do so!

He was quite innocent! He told me so himself, so of course it was true; and "Cookie," who had a very soft spot in her heart for the big, handsome, good-natured young man, whose real and undeniable good looks and natural charm of disposition no cropping or shaving or dressing up in hideous garb could possibly disguise or do away with, determined one day she would help him to escape. So, with her finger on her lips to ensure my silence, having previously conjured me by the most blood-curdling oaths to deathless secrecy, she flew upstairs one memorable November evening and returned with a long black clerical coat and a pair of old black trousers, which my father had discarded, and flung them to Godfrey, with: "Go into the pantry, Jem, me darlin,' and put 'em on there, and look your sharpest." And Godfrey disappeared for five of the longest minutes I have ever known; and then out came a tall, very handsome curate, and I said, "Oh, Godfrey, you *do* look nice!" And Godfrey crammed some bread and cheese the housemaid had got ready for him into his pocket and said, as he kissed us all one after the other: "Good-bye, Cookie, I am off. Good-bye, Master Raymond dear; I'll do the same for you one of these days, you see if I don't. And don't you forget to say that little prayer I taught you every night, and keep some salt always in your pocket and let me know if you ever catch a bird with it." And he was off into the dark night and down the dark, wet hill that led him to the canal and to the railway station, safe for London Town.

And I sat by the kitchen fire and read stories in the red-hot coals, and almost thought I saw a giant behind the pantry door; and then I nodded, and I think I must have fallen asleep, when suddenly I was wide awake, and the housemaid said in a thrilling voice, "Hark! what's that?" And my heart beat till I was nearly suffocated, and the great prison bell clashed and clanged in the foggy winter night, and I heard the warders dashing by; and suddenly a gun went off, and "Cookie" began to cry hysterically. And then the nursemaid took me upstairs and brushed my hair, and I went down for the usual few minutes before dinner, and my bedtime, to look at picture-books in the drawing-room. And then my father came in. "Godfrey's escaped," he said; "I'm afraid he'll get the 'cat,' poor wretch, if they catch him." And then I went up to bed, perfectly ill with excitement and anxiety. I was only six after all, and I cried myself to sleep; and when nurse woke me in the morning she said: "They ain't caught poor old Godfrey, Master Raymond, and pray they never will, nasty beasts!" But, alas! a week after my father opened *The Times*, and after a moment or two he read us out a piece which said that a young policeman had met a man walking in a street in London, and he went up to him and said, "You are James Godfrey—you've got to come with me." And oh, how "Cookie" and all of us cried! And "Cookie" said: "There, Master Raymond, you 'aven't caught your bird yet, but they caught poor old Godfrey."

One curious and really rather dreadful part of it was that my aunt, Mrs. Charles Blathwayt, who was staying in the house with us at the time, was the sister of the then Secretary of State for the Home Department, Mr. Gathorne-Hardy, afterwards Earl of Cranbrook, who was actually, *ex officio*, the head of the whole Convict Department! This momentous fact I was, of course, too young to realize at the time, but the servants and I kept our dark secret so well that it was not till I told my dear father the whole story in 1901 that he realized to the full the appalling but not wholly unhumorous significance of the occasion.

I have said that we lived amidst beautiful surroundings, and I rather desire to emphasize that fact, for no one can estimate to their fullest extent the value and importance of early associations and surroundings. My childish memories are of wonderful summer days, when never a cloud dimmed the sky and the scent of the pine-woods was always in the air, and the sun used to set behind a vast range of dark blue hills, which were frequently dotted with the white tents of soldiers engaged in the great summer and autumn manœuvres which began to be so popular in those far-off days. We were a singularly happy family, though we were always very poor, and I never even went to a pantomime until I was well over twenty years of age. Our greatest treat, on our very rare expeditions to town, was a visit to the British Museum, the National Gallery, Madame Tussaud's, or the Christy Minstrels. I don't suppose my father ever had more than £500 a year at any time of his career, and I am quite sure he had never dined in a smart restaurant in all his life—for one thing, I don't think they existed for anybody in those days, and for another, he would have loathed them and all their associations and their inherent vulgarity. For he was a great gentleman, in the most splendid meaning of that ridiculously wrongly used and absurdly abused word to-day. He was so aloof from, and, to my childish idea—and, indeed, to the idea I hold almost as strongly to-day as I did then—so far above, the ordinary run of people that I cannot imagine him in connection with them at all ; he was simply a scholar, an omnivorous reader, an artist, an exceedingly fine preacher, and, with his brothers, a certain Captain Jennings-Bramley, who was Governor of the prison, and the late Lord Leconfield, whom we knew in later years, far and away the most distinguished-looking man I have ever seen—and that in a day when "distinction" was a much commoner thing in the streets of London than it is to-day. It is a curious thing that whilst women have enormously advanced and improved, physically as well as mentally, men as a rule have just as curiously deteriorated. But my father and his brothers were extraordinarily distinguished to look at. People always turned to look after them in the street. I remember once, when I was about ten years of age, I had come up to town as a special treat with my father, and I walked down Piccadilly with him and my Uncle Charles, and we suddenly met Mr. Disraeli, as he was then, and my father whispered to me, "Look, Raymond, here's Mr. Disraeli."

And as the great man passed us, with a very scrutinizing gaze at the two tall and stately clergymen, I turned to look at him, and lo! he had turned also and was gazing hard at us. That was my one and only glimpse of that splendidly picturesque Victorian figure, and a glimpse I shall never forget.

I was walking the other day with Captain Harry de Windt and Miss Elaine Inescort, the charming actress, and as we crossed St. James's Square we passed a singularly distinguished-looking man—all of the olden time—and our fair friend said—

"What a splendid-looking person! He's a regular Colonel Newcome!"

"There, Harry," I said, "isn't that true? He is exactly the type of man we used to see by the dozen in the sixties and the seventies, and that you never see nowadays save and except as a sort of dim survival."

I hope no one will laugh at me for saying all this, though if a son may not admire his own father, I don't know whom he may admire.

Of my mother I will say no more—at present, at all events—than that she is the greatest memory I have. There are people and memories too sacred for words, and my memory and thoughts of her are of that nature. With my father, of course, it is somewhat different. He stands, and will stand for all time, so far as I am concerned, as quite one of the most remarkable men I have ever known. I have known far cleverer men, of course, and in certain respects much more lovable men, but I have never known, among all the wonderful and remarkable and distinguished men I have met—and I have met more than most—I have never known one who stood so strikingly apart from his fellows as he always did. Very cold and proud and very aloof and reserved—so reserved that I hardly ever knew him to lunch or dine out with a single living soul in all my life, and so proud that he would never ask a favour of any of our relations, several of whom held very high office in the country—he nevertheless was characterized by perfect simplicity of manner and address. Either he or his brother Charles could easily have been bishops had they chosen to exert themselves but ever so little, for they possessed exceptional qualifications for high dignity ; but they were simply too proud and too indifferent and too unambitious ever to move a finger to help themselves or any of their family. And I like to think of it, even though we were in our family so really poor that sometimes, with one son at Oxford and another at Cambridge, it was hard work to make both ends meet. My uncle Charles had married money, and, with some other of my more worldly-wise relatives, represented what was to our simple ideas the really wealthy side of life ; indeed, I believe one of my aunt's brothers was one of the few millionaires England had produced before the American and South African Crœsuses had begun to flood our shores. So we grew up in a world of simplicity of which the modern day knows little or nothing, and which, I suppose, it would heartily despise. My father began teaching us Greek and Latin at an age when the modern boy hasn't even begun to tackle his English Grammar, and I was caned for a false quantity before I was eight. And it did me all the good in the world too. And another thing : my father was never what is known as a "pal" to his children, and that, too, in my estimation, was all to the good. I don't believe one bit in the modern system of calling your father "old chap." Heavens ! I wonder what would have happened to me if I had so appallingly forgotten myself ! I don't wish to bear unduly hard upon the present system ; I am sure it has its good points, just as I am equally certain it has its bad, but I simply neither like it nor believe in it. Sometimes, indeed, it is nothing less than disastrous in its results.

A year or two ago, I was lunching with some friends and their son, a boy of fifteen or sixteen, home from a very famous Public School for the holidays.

"Let me have some champagne, mother," he said.

"Oh no, darling, I can't ; it's too early."

"Oh, don't be a fool, mother ; let me have some."

"No, darling ; I really don't think it's good for you."

"*You filthy swine!*" he cried, his face black with passion.

There was a dead silence. I looked at his father, earnestly hoping that he would then and there break every bone in his body. Oh no, not the "pal" father! Not a bit of it!

"Oh, Harry, you shouldn't talk like that to your mother, you know." That was all he said.

I leaned over towards the brute and I said, "My father would have killed me if I had said that to my mother!"

Some of my modern readers will marvel at my emotion on this occasion. Well, they may. I can only say that there are times when one could commit murder and be justified in committing it. That was one of them for me.

I don't pretend for a moment that all the youths of to-day are like that—the very reverse is the case. I cannot emphasize this fact too strongly, and not to do so would be grossly unfair. Nor would I suggest that the "pal" father is always so criminally forbearing. But at the same time there is far too much of that kind of thing about. Twice within the last three years I have seen supposedly well-bred children, in a towering passion, fling a pack of cards in their parents' faces—one a boy who actually cut his mother's lip open with the violence of his passion, and the other a girl who dashed all her cards full into the face of her father. And in each case the children, each of whom was over fourteen years of age and who ought to have been most severely punished, were not even reprimanded!

Well, all this is to say that though my father was very severe, very often too harsh with us, and sometimes hardly just in his punishments, yet he always commanded and merited and retained for life our admiration and respect, and this to his dying day, which occurred only a few days before the death of King Edward; and it must indeed be rare to find a large family of children which was so proud of, and so devoted to the very last to, a father who never in the best sense of the word failed them when they required him most.

And in a way—though I am ignorant enough now,

Heaven knows!—he and my dear mother educated us so splendidly. Our Latin and Greek lessons never bored us, because we learned the story and the romance and the history and the geography of them at one and the same time; and when I was only seven years old my mother used to read to me such a book as Motley's "History of the Dutch Republic," or Prescott's histories of the Mexicans and the Peruvians. But it was not so much the actual lessons or the subjects she chose as the whole tone and spirit of her instruction, and the refinement which, like a halo, encircled it all, leaving behind an undying memory of indefinable charm and the most delicate romance. And it was she who used to read to me that wonderful Dream, that classic of English literature, though I was too young to appreciate anything more than its stories of the giants, Bunyan's "Pilgrim's Progress"; it was she who initiated me, later on in my childhood, into the delicate beauties of George Herbert's "Temple" and Shakespeare's "Tempest" and Spenser's "Faerie Queene." I can never hear of Clovis, or Charlemagne, or St. Louis of France without thinking of mother's lessons to me from Mrs. Markham's famous French histories, with their pretty steel and wood engravings; nor can I even to-day witness Martin Harvey's beautiful performance in "The Only Way," without recalling her simple recital of Dickens's famous "Tale of Two Cities," with which she accompanied Mrs. Markham's account of the French Revolution. And when she read me the "Tales of a Grandfather," she would also give me her own personal memories of Sir Walter Scott, whom she knew when she was a very small child, and she would try and adapt his Scottish stories, where they fitted in with the particular piece of history she was reading, to my childish understanding.

And talking of Scott reminds me I may as well break off for a moment to enlarge upon what I can recall of her memories of the greatest man Scotland has ever produced. I recall the wonderful enthusiasm that Sir Herbert Tree aroused in Edinburgh one night at a grand dinner which was given to him by the Pen and Pencil

Club ten or twelve years ago, when I sat next to him, and he, at the end of his speech, which was quoted in full in all the Scottish papers next morning, read them an extract from my mother's letter which she had written me, all unconscious that it would ever reach others' eyes or ears than mine, though, of course, she had not the slightest objection to my dear old friend thus making use of her stories, which came in with extraordinary appropriateness in a speech dealing so charmingly and sympathetically with Edinburgh's literary and artistic associations and reminiscences.

"You must let me bring that into my speech to-night, Blathwayt," said Tree. "Wire to your mother and ask her permission."

"No," I replied; "that would frighten her into a fit. There's no earthly harm in your doing so, and I'll send her the *Scotsman* the morn's morn"—Tree and I always speak broad Scots in Edinburgh and with the most violent brogue when we are in Dublin, as we sometimes are together. My mother, in begging me to go to a certain square in Edinburgh where my grandfather had lived, and where Scott often dined with him and such Scottish celebrities of that day as the Duke of Buccleuch, the eccentric Earl of Buchan, and the Constables, re-told, and told it accurately, the famous story of Mrs. Siddons at my grandfather's dinner-table. The footman had brought her a glass of water, and, looking at him very solemnly, the great queen of tragedy said, in her most impressive style, "I said 'porter,' young man, not 'water'!"

There is a well-known engraving which depicts Sir Walter Scott giving a reading of one of his new books at Abbotsford, with, amongst other Scottish worthies of the day, the Etterick Shepherd, James Hogg, seated at Scott's feet, and John Gibson Lockhart and my grandfather seated at the end of the table.

A few years ago I was staying in Cardiff with that delightful Scotsman Sir John Duncan, the proprietor of the *South Wales News*—alas! that he has quitted a world that was always the happier and better for his genial and noble presence—and he told me of an aged "brither Scot," wellnigh a century old, who was living out at Roath, and advised me to go and see him, as he was full of stories of Sir Walter, who had been his father's friend and whom he himself also remembered distinctly. So I went to see the dear old man, and I am glad now I did. I had no sooner told him who I was than he said: "Yes, I remember now. And I remember I was walking out to Abbotsford when I was a big boy one day and your grandfather passed me driving in his phaeton and he gave me a lift out to Sir Walter's, and when we got there we found Sir Walter reading in the library, with your dear mother and her sister playing with the dog on the hearthrug—they couldn't have been more than five or six at the time."

Piercing through that wonderful golden mist of memories and romance which always enshrouds the far-off past of my childhood's days, it seems to me that everything centres round that beautiful old oak which dominated our whole garden. The sound of its leaves fluttering in the breeze was the first sound that greeted me on waking in the morning, and it was beneath its shadow that I first realized the golden arrows shot by the early sun, and after my lessons I used to fall asleep to the eternal music of the wind among its branches. Shadowed by its protecting care, I read the first book I ever read all by myself—Marryatt's "Masterman Ready," a book that not only coloured all my after-life, but that added tenfold to the interest of those wanderings of mine through the after-years all over the world. To this hour I can never behold the palms bending to the strong sea breeze on the scented shores of Ceylon or in some little West Indian forest without recalling the delightful pictures in "Masterman Ready," any more than I can behold the magnificent architectural glories of a sunset in the Indian Ocean, with all its marvellous outline and its exquisite translucency of atmosphere and its gorgeous colouring, without thinking of that other favourite of my childhood, R. M. Ballantyne's "Coral Island." So extraordinarily vivid and powerful are one's earliest memories and associations that one can never get wholly rid of childhood's past, and if you are fortunate enough to have had such a childhood as mine you never want to. And then it was under that tree that I read my first two novels—surreptitiously, of course—Mrs. Radclyffe's famous "Mysteries of Udolpho," with that thrilling and delightful sentence which has lingered with me all my life, "*The castle clock struck one!*" and the other was "Lady Audley's Secret," by Miss Braddon, all of whose books were my joy for years and years of my early life.

I have maundered on a long time about this same childhood, but it is not without its special meaning and significance. Upon your childhood, to a very great extent, depends all your after-life. And what is so sad a feature of to-day is that to a very great extent children, and especially the children of the upper classes, appear to have no childhood at all, for they are absolutely robbed of it. They are little mannikins only too often, going out to restaurants and theatres and parties and the Lord knows what! Simple pleasures don't appeal to them in the least. Little simple pleasures—the simpler the better—that even to-day delight Herbert Tree and myself bore the young people stiff. And the heart that has lost its simplicity is dead indeed.

But I must hurry on, or this immensely lengthy chapter will never come to an end. Poor as we were, of course Eton, Harrow, Winchester, and Rugby, to which so many of one's friends and relatives went, were hopelessly out of the question for me and my brothers, so we went, some of us—for we were a pretty large family, of which I was the eldest—to a very admirable private school, run, on Public School lines as far as possible, by the Rev. C. W. Arnold, a near relative of the famous Arnold of Rugby, and, like him, a very prince among men. I can see him now, tall and very upright, clad in cap and gown, striding into the school hall to take the Sixth Form in their Greek play; I can see him, as clearly as I could then almost, batting at the wicket and scoring more runs sometimes than even the famous professionals Pooley,

Jupp, and Julius Cæsar, who used to come down and play at our annual match. He it was who took hold of my brother John and made such a fine cricketer of him that some years after Lord Harris wanted him to play in the Kent Eleven. It was under him that I first heard of a wonderful young cricketer, who in the early 'seventies had already become famous, named W. G. Grace.

Ah! those wonderful initials "W. G."! Surely the most marvellous, the most romantic, and the most memory-evoking initials that were ever known! Where on earth has "W. G." and his score not been talked of, and by how many eager generations of boys has not his personality been regarded as almost more divine than human! I have heard him discussed at messes in India, on battle-cruisers in Hongkong and Jamaica; I have talked him over with veld farmers in South Africa and with hard-working Cabinet Ministers in far Australia, and wherever willow is king "W. G." has been, and almost still remains, monarch of all he surveys. To this day I can never hear the thud of the bat, upon a hot summer noon, without a flashing memory of the heroic figure and the bearded face of the genial giant as he would stride across the pitch at Lord's, or of that famous morning in 1892 when, at long last, I sat and talked with the hero, the classic, fabled hero of my boyish days, and he, revolving many memories, like the sporting Sir Bedivere that ho was, told me the story of his vast and wandering life.

I am always glad that my old headmaster was the famous cricketer he was, for it was at his hands I first learned what little of the game I know. He was an ideal man for boyhood's impressionable days: very tall and upstanding, with light, rather curly hair and a noble forehead; a distinguished preacher, and altogether a notable personality as he stood in the pulpit of the tiny school chapel and preached those simple and yet stirring sermons to us boys, which were so curiously suggestive and reminiscent of those other sermons preached forty years before in Rugby Chapel by his illustrious relative, and the memory of which has been for ever immortalized by Tom Hughes in his classic schoolboy story, "Tom Brown's Schooldays." And well can I remember his coming into the school one June morning, just before the great Franco-Prussian War burst like a thunder-cloud upon the Continent, and saying to us all: "Boys, you will be sorry to hear that Charles Dickens died yesterday." All the same, however, my most vivid and my most sacred memories cling round, and are associated and linked up together with, the rustling leaves and the darting rays of sunshine always flashing through that old oak-tree upon the garden lawn.

Underneath that tree, as I have already said, I read my childhood's favourite works, the works so popular in that day—"Ivanhoe," and "Pickwick," and "The Wide, Wide World," and "Uncle Tom's Cabin," and "The Heir of Redclyffe," and "East Lynne," and all of Ballantyne and Marryatt and Mayne Reid that I could get hold of. It was here that I used to lie and dream of other worlds than that which I then knew, and here that as a little boy I sat and listened, one very far-off day, to my father and Frederick Denison Maurice and Charles Kingsley discussing a series of popular lectures for the unfortunate convicts, all part of a plan for ameliorating and reforming their dreary lives, but a plan which, being too charming and ideal for the official mind, was speedily trampled under foot by the authorities. And yet how the poor wretches enjoyed those lectures they were afforded the opportunity of hearing! Even now, after more than fifty years, their cheers as they listened to Charles Kingsley's stirring words, or to the charm of Tom Hughes's simple eloquence, are ringing in my memory.

But my days beneath the old oak-tree were, all unconsciously to myself, drawing to a close, and a summer day came when I woke to hear its gentle murmuring for the last time, and for the last time the sun shot his golden arrows through the shimmering leaves upon the grass at my feet. For my father had been appointed British Chaplain in Boulogne, and thither we went in the late summer of 1872 and my childhood's days were over for ever, surely the most golden childhood, because so simple and so perfectly natural a childhood, that I have ever heard of; and I bade good-bye to the old oak-tree for good and all. I went and sat beneath that tree only a few weeks ago; it hasn't changed a bit. But those who sat there and played with me, where, indeed, are they to-day? And when they read these words, those of them who still wander midst these glimpses of the moon, what will their memories be of the days that will never come again?

I can never forget the tumultuous morning of our departure—the brilliant sunshine, the sinister walls of the great prison outlined against an azure sky, the sparkling drops of dew still bedecking the scented roses, and then the long line of uniformed warders, many of them heroes of the Crimean War, standing at strict attention, as my father and mother and all of us drove by in a huge wagonette hired for the occasion, and which all my life nearly had carried me on our little picnics and excursions; and then the great burst of cheering, started and led by that splendidly handsome, gallant soldier Captain Bramley, the Governor, as we slowly passed down the line. Even the stern lips of my father quivered, and my mother was quite undisguised in her emotion. A turn in the road, and my childhood was swept out of my life for ever.

CHAPTER II

BOULOGNE AND THE ISLE OF WIGHT

BOULOGNE in the seventies was a charming town, and I can never forget my first impressions of it as the dome of the cathedral sprang into view from the steamer's deck and one caught one's first glimpse of the far-famed Column of Napoleon and the still better known lighthouses at the end of the two piers, between which the steamer, storm-tossed and wave-worn sixty seconds before, glides so smoothly and so calmly to her berth in the odorous harbour. And Boulogne then was more picturesque by far than it is to-day, and much more choice in its summer visitors and immeasurably more interesting in its all-the-year-round English residents. The Cockney tripper practically knew it not at all, and the perfectly poisonous holiday-makers from Lancashire and Yorkshire had probably never even heard of it. Some people will find fault with my vigour of phraseology: all I can say is that he who has seen the Lancashire and Yorkshire tripper at his or her worst, as I have seen them time and again, will agree with me that the adjective "poisonous" is absolutely a mild term to apply to them. I speak of them as I have seen them before the war. I rejoice to think that in the battle line they are very Paladins. For the matter of that, I can well imagine that the heroes of Crécy and Agincourt may have been quite distasteful in the piping days of peace. But Boulogne in the seventies was specially interesting to a very young fellow, only seventeen, like myself, from other points of view beyond the merely pictorial, though its wonderful old ramparts, and its pretty avenue of trees in the Tintelleries, its glorious old churches and the walls of the Haute Ville so redolent of the stormy days of Godfrey de Bouillon, and the belfry and the beautiful old château at the corner of the ramparts, appealed to my sense of the romantic and historic to a quite remarkable extent. At the same time, I frankly confess it was the social aspect of the place that so attracted a boy who had hitherto been brought up in a comparatively lonely country district.

As the children of the British Chaplain we naturally got to know most of the very large British colony pretty quickly, and we were asked out here and there and everywhere. Even to-day I recall the names of my friends and companions of those golden far-off days. Colonel Webster-Wedderburn, with his sons and his beautiful daughter Violet, who subsequently became Lady Savile of Rufford Abbey, who died only a few years or so ago, were amongst the people we knew best; and then there were Colonel and Mrs. Darling and their son Ralph, a great pal of mine, and Grace, their handsome, golden-haired daughter; and the really wonderfully good-looking family the Snows, one of the girls of which family subsequently married Mr. Royle, of Cairo and Port Said, and who was long famed, and deservedly so, as the most beautiful woman between here and India; and then there were the Traill-Simpsons, one of the daughters of whom married the present Lord Lauderdale. There was Lady Cecil Gordon, whose daughters used to stay with us and make up a very merry party at what served us as our very quiet vicarage in the Rue de la Paix. I must not forget the Wellesleys and their daughters, one of whom became Mrs. Arthur Wilson, of Tranby Croft (or was it Mrs. Charles Wilson, now Lady Nunburnholme?); and, of course, the Hanbury-Williams girls. One very interesting couple consisted of old Sir William Hamilton and his wife, whom he had married when he was released from the French prison in which he had been interned as a British prisoner of war during the Napoleonic wars, his bride actually and most romantically being the daughter of the gaoler of the prison. He was acting as British Consul in the days of my father's chaplaincy. I recall the men about the place—a wild, harum-scarum crew some of them were, but all splendid fellows, and, of course, years and years older than myself: handsome Stewart-Muirhead; Jerry Pocock, whose elder brother, Sir George Pocock, the Crimean hero, died only a few months ago; Lionel Darell; Ernest Prothero and his brother the Admiral; Jemmy and Tony Safe; Hayes-Sadleir; and, amongst the older men, Lord Clarence Paget; Colonel Coventry; Sir Seton Gordon; Colonel Ross, of some place or other in the Highlands (not Bladensberg, I know); Sir Gerald Fitzgerald, the Knight of Glin; a delightful person, and an Irish dean whose name I forget, with a lovely daughter, who subsequently became the wife of the well-known soldier Sir William Gatacre. And there was one wonderful man there, whom I will not specify further than by saying that he was the Honourable ——, brother of the Earl of ——, one of the most romantic, if perhaps somewhat eccentric, personages that I have ever met. I can never forget one remarkable incident in which he was concerned. My father had to take a funeral, and he bade me accompany him in the carriage. Seated by father was Lord Clarence Paget, and, on the seat opposite, this gentleman, whom I will not name, and myself. My father was in his surplice and Cambridge hood, and my companion was clad in the costume of a Cavalier of Charles II's time, which was the garb he almost invariably walked about in: wide hat and drooping scarlet feather, wonderful frills and ruffs, and elaborate black silk stockings. We had to call at the house for the body. Arrived there, my father got out and walked into the house, a very ancient building in a very poor quarter of the town. He came down a few minutes afterwards and said: "There will be no funeral to-day. The authorities have arrested the body for debt." And then he turned to me and said: "You never heard of Crockford's, the great betting-place in St. James's Street—you are too young; but that poor man was the son of the famous Crockford, and he inherited a large fortune from his father. A sad ending to such a life and inheritance!" The cavalier nodded his scarlet plume, practically blinding me for the moment, as he remarked: "Yes, it's enough to put any one off ever making another bet in this world."

Let me break off here for a moment. When Sir H. B. Tree produced "The Last of the Dandies" in 1901 at His Majesty's, he gave a very realistic stage presentment of Crockford's Betting Rooms in what is now the Devonshire Club, and I told him one night of the above incident. Just as we finished talking—we were in his sitting-room at the theatre—a very old lady was shown in, and Mr. Tree, as he then was, said as he shook hands with her—

"What is it you wish to see me about?"

"Well, Mr. Tree," she replied, "your death scene of Count D'Orsay is all wrong."

"Oh, I beg your pardon, my dear lady, it is not; I have made all inquiries, and I assure you it is correct in every detail."

"Nevertheless, Mr. Tree, it is not correct."

"Well, really, madam," very gently replied the famous actor-manager, "I can assure you I am right and I speak with authority."

"Possibly, Mr. Tree," answered the old lady; "and yet I ought to know. *I am Count D'Orsay's daughter, and he died in my arms!*"

However, let me get back to the seventies and to Boulogne.

The Cavalier was an object, naturally enough, of wonder and admiration wherever he went. In addition to wearing love-locks and drooping feathers and silk stockings and laces galore, he always enamelled his face most carefully, so as to hide the ravages of time, I presume; but he was most sensitive to any comments upon his appearance, and as he was six feet two inches in height and a magnificent boxer, people were usually very careful not to offend his not unnatural susceptibilities in this direction. Once, however, he let himself go with a vengeance. He was walking down the front when three or four English sailors, just landed off a merchantman in the harbour, made some jeering remark about his bizarre appearance. One by one he took them on, and in less than five minutes the whole lot of them were flat on their backs in the dirty Boulonnaise gutter, while he walked unconcernedly on, airily dusting his soiled fingers with a delicately laced handkerchief.

You never can judge by appearances!

It was a somewhat queer *milieu*, take it altogether, for my scholarly father and my saint-like mother; but they kept always wholly aloof from it, though with some of the more sedate and elderly residents of the British colony they were naturally on terms of cordial friendship, whilst my father's singularly beautiful voice and preaching always crammed our church both summer and winter. Boys don't listen to sermons much—frankly, I think they would be rather prigs if they did—and I was no exception to the rule, but one sermon of my father's at this period I do remember. A friend of ours, a beautiful girl, the granddaughter of a certain General Douglas-Hamilton, died, and my father preached her funeral sermon, and I faintly recall his allusion to her grandfather, who, as a very young subaltern, had gone unscathed through the smoke and battle of Waterloo. It seemed, naturally enough, so historic and far away to me that it was difficult to realize his charming grandchild had actually been one of our own playmates.

And then there were the picnics out at Pont de Briques and the tennis parties at the Château d'Hardelot, where the Guys lived, one of whom, I fancy, has since developed into "Guy d'Hardelot," the writer of those charming songs with which we are so familiar to-day. Just about the middle of the seventies came the great rage for Moody and Sankey, and their tuneful, jingly hymns "Hold the Fort," "There were Ninety and Nine," "The Great Physician Now is Near." Well, these famous evangelists in 1875 created such a stir and such a sensation as never was known in London. The Prince and Princess of Wales and half society and pretty well all the Cabinet of those days used to flock to hear them, and every one, in drawing-rooms even, and certainly in the streets, used to sing and hum their famous tunes, and their fame reached over even to Boulogne. And it came in this way: One day my father went downstairs, and there seated in the drawing-room were Mr. Stevenson Blackwood—afterwards Sir Stevenson Blackwood, Financial Secretary to the Post Office—and his wife, the Duchess of Manchester, who were the parents of one destined to be far more famous than ever they were—Algernon Blackwood the author, of whom I will have much to say later on. And with them was their brother-in-law, Captain Charles Hobart, a son of the Earl of Buckinghamshire and brother of the famous Hobart Pasha, Admiral of the Turkish Fleet, and Mrs. Charles Hobart and their son Gus, who speedily became my great friend, and who also, incidentally, became engaged shortly afterwards to my sister, then a girl of sixteen. Now it so happened that Captain Hobart (afterwards Hobart-Hampden) had, with his brothers, been at school with my father and the Tennysons, and he speedily brought himself to father's memory; and then he proposed that under my father's auspices they should hold a series of revival meetings in Boulogne—and not, perhaps, before they were required, for some of the British residents were a pretty hot lot in those days. So the meetings were held, and Mr. Blackwood and Captain Hobart and Sir Samuel Anderson, the Crown Solicitor of Dublin, and my father used to give the addresses. Whether the meetings did any good or not I really cannot say; but they are memorable in my mind for the reason that they constituted a link, as it were, in the chain of association and reminiscences which joined up Lord Tennyson and his brothers and my father and his brothers and the Hobarts in school and college friendships right through nearly the whole of the last century—certainly from 1815, when the Battle of Waterloo was fought, to Wednesday, July 19, 1916, when I sat and talked with Algernon Blackwood, Sir Stevenson Blackwood's son, and cousin of my dear old friend Gus Hobart, who after all never married my sister, owing to the tragic fact that he went straight from Sandhurst to India in 1876, where he died in Madras a year later from a sudden attack of cholera, the very place where his uncle, Lord Hobart, was Governor.

About this time, of course, I was frequently in London, which, from many points of view, was a very different place from what it is nowadays. It certainly was a much gayer place, though there were no restaurants hardly, or smart hotels, or music-halls, as we know them now, and only a very few theatres ; and telephones and taxis, of course, were not even invented. But silly, irritating little restrictions were not so painfully in evidence as they are to-day, and the somewhat grandmotherly rule of the L.C.C. had not overwhelmed a vastly more joyous city than that of which the present generation can have any idea, though I quite believe that in many respects we have progressed enormously. There was much more drinking in those days than one can imagine now, and extraordinary stories are told of the prowess of men in that direction in the seventies. I know of one case where a certain distinguished man asked a friend of mine, still hale and hearty, to dine with him.

" Can you drink ?" said the would-be host.

" Yes ; I think I can do my share," replied my friend, who told me this incident only a few days ago.

On the night in question, when he arrived at his host's house he found he was the only guest. Opposite the master of the feast's seat stood in solemn array six bottles of port, and the same number of bottles stood opposite his own seat. Before they quitted that table, at somewhere about three o'clock the next morning, those two heroes had consumed every single drop of the wine between them !

" Disgusting ! " some of my readers will say ; and I agree, though I think that total abstainers are sometimes inclined to intemperate addiction to the more solid pleasures of the table. But such an incident, though very rare even in those days, helps to illustrate and accentuate the tremendous gulf that yawns between the social life of the seventies and that of to-day. People were at once far more lax and far more rigid than could be even imagined nowadays. Take modern Nonconformity, for instance. How extraordinarily that element of the community has widened and broadened out from that very rigid, cast-iron, and intolerant system which so characterized the latter half of Queen Victoria's reign! To-day we find Free Churchmen of the type of Mr. A. K. Yapp, the secretary of that aforetime almost incredibly narrow-minded religious body known as the Y.M.C.A., actually hand-in-glove with Roman and High Anglican priests and arranging for Sunday evening sing-songs for our homeless soldiers with the leading lights of musical comedy—and more power to his elbow, I say, for so doing. But such laxity in the religious world would have been absolutely unthinkable in the seventies and eighties of last century.

London is both better and worse than it was when I was careering through its sunny, golden streets in the days of which I write so wistfully and affectionately. And assuredly young men were far more exposed to temptations of many and varied kinds than I imagine they are or can be to-day—though at my age, of course, I know little or nothing of the life a modern young man about town leads or of the temptations to which he is exposed. I imagine they are rather more "shepherded" than we ever were, or than we would ever have consented to be. At the same time, though I gladly realize that the drinking habits of the community are greatly modified from what they used to be, I am bound to acknowledge that even to-day the men who accomplish the greatest work for the Empire, and the men I most admire, are emphatically not teetotallers.

But in the early seventies I was very young and very heedless, and I don't suppose I shirked my "whack" any more than did my comrades, although nowadays and for many years past I am and have been almost a teetotaller. Amongst my friends in that far-off period was a kind of cousin of mine, a certain Captain Glynne Turquand, in the Guards—a very smart person indeed (and, by the by, it was in 1872 that I first heard the word "smart" used to describe ultra-fashionable society, so the word is not quite so modern as some people imagine), who frequently figured as the hero of some of Ouida's famous novels. Glynne Turquand was a very outstanding figure in London society just about that period, as also were "Charlie" Buller, of the 2nd Life Guards, and Charles Chase Parr, the Harrow cricketer, and Chandos-Pole; and these men, with many others whom elderly men to-day will well remember at Jem Mace's boxing-saloon in St. James's Street, were in evidence all over the town and at every available function. I remember one well-known man about town, a connection of my own, bearing an historic name, who walked into a certain bar, and, catching a glimpse of a big picture of Queen Elizabeth, he said: "Oh, that's the old girl who beheaded my ancestor," and taking a revolver out of his hip-pocket, he forthwith put a bullet clean through the virgin Queen's right eye! And then there were the Argyll Rooms, which were open for dancing all night long; and Barnes's famous "Blue Posts" in the Haymarket, a very fashionable resort for the young men of the period, when Piccadilly was crammed all night long with innumerable "soiled doves" —and very lovely women many of them were too—and everybody went home with the milk and a frightful headache. Not that I myself ever "painted the town red"; I was far too delicate, and also far too reticent and reserved, even then, for such joyous episodes, but most of my friends were great artists at it. And it was just about this time, two or three-and-forty years ago, that I recall first hearing Miss Vesta Tilley singing at some place—I can't say where it was now—and I heard her only the other night, and, upon my word, she hardly looked any older than she did then.

Temperance as regards drink has, thank goodness, made tremendous headway amongst men, though I really think the drink craze is far worse with women than ever it was when I was young. But the temperance of to-day is due rather to an appreciation of the laws of hygiene than to the absurdly fanatical—although I must, in fairness, own really earnest and well-meant —strivings of the typical teetotallers, many of whom, though devoted persons of lofty character, have told me quite frankly that they would far sooner let a wife or a friend or a child of theirs die than give them that drop of brandy which would save their lives. That I can only characterize as the most mistaken fanaticism. I honour them for the strength of their principles and the staunchness of their convictions, but I would draw the line at their literally murdering other people in order that their own souls, and possibly the souls of their unfortunate victims, may be unstained. There is no doubt, however, that the sobriety of to-day is a vast gain to the community, especially when one compares the condition of the streets of to-day with what it was in the early seventies.

And this brings me to the Isle of Wight, where, in the year 1875, my father was appointed to the living of Totland Bay, near Freshwater—another charming and beautiful home, and where the people, as they were in Boulogne, were of the most kindly and interesting description that one could possibly desire.

To begin with, there were, first and foremost, the Tennysons. Alfred Tennyson was then, I think I may say with truth, incomparably one of the stateliest, most romantic, and most interesting figures in the whole world—not in England only, not only in literary or social circles, but absolutely the most interesting, the most famous, the most sought-after figure in the whole world. And I can think of no exception. He was a classic figure, almost as though he had stepped out of Homer or the Æneid, or out of the pages of the Bible. I am not exaggerating. It was as one of the greatest figures of her own marvellous era, crowded with historic personages as it was—"the old Duke," Faraday, Kingsley, Gladstone, Disraeli—that Queen Victoria, who dearly loved him, regarded her Poet Laureate. What wonder, then, was it that to my youthful imagination he was, as he remains to-day, incomparably the greatest person I had then or have ever since met! The Tennyson household was remarkable and interesting, and I am quite sure the present Lord Tennyson, from whom I received a beautiful letter on the death of my own dear father six years ago, will not mind my referring to it.

It was a household consecrated by the love of two devoted sons for a very wonderful father and a very exceptional mother. I have spoken of the love and devotion of my own family for our parents. It was more than equalled by the devotion of Hallam Tennyson and his brother Lionel—now long dead, alas !—for their father and mother—something too sacred to be spoken about almost, though I just hint briefly at it in these pages. Lady Tennyson was always very delicate, and I always picture her, as I last saw her, when my mother and I called on her one day, lying on the sofa, where her son was always in close attendance, and where her poet-husband used to come when he wearied of smoking and writing in his study upstairs. It was from their beautiful garden—" a careless-order'd garden "—at Freshwater that one caught the glimpse of that " noble down " and the ship " glimmering away to the lonely deep " of which the poet speaks so charmingly in his invitation to his old friend Frederick Denison Maurice : " Come, Maurice, come ; come to the Isle of Wight."

And the great poet would come into the drawing-room and talk to his wife's guests. We were all dreadfully nervous, of course, and awfully frightened of him, but I think we always felt, as an American lady said to me one day as he left the room : " Well, I may never see him again ; but talk of 'one crowded hour of glorious life,' the last five minutes have been worth all the rest of my life put together ! " and she turned away to hide the tears that *would* come. It was very much the same with Henry Irving when he stayed with Tennyson. He would meet princes and ambassadors without giving them a second thought, but even he experienced a nervous tremor when he first encountered the world-renowned poet. I recall him as clearly as a figure etched in sepia against a white horizon—the splendid dome-like head, the noble forehead, the handsome, rough-hewn features and straggling beard and moustache, the organ-like voice, the loose, easy grey suit, if I remember right after all these years. And vividly also do I remember his taking hold of my sister once, before a whole drawing-room full of people, and turning her blushing face to the full light and saying, "You are a pretty girl, my dear!" I recall that incident as though it were yesterday, and yet it is upwards of five-and-thirty years ago! Another memory I have of him: I came in from my walk one windy November evening and I found Lord Tennyson sitting over the fire with my parents, and he was recalling memories of his old schooldays with my father—or, rather, with my uncles, for he was a little too old to have been actually at school with my father, though they had passed under the same headmaster—and the poet was alluding to the present-day system of kindness as opposed to the tremendous severity of his and my father's schooldays.

"Why," he said, "old W—— thrashed a boy more unmercifully for a false quantity than a modern head-master to-day would thrash a boy for the worst offence of which schoolboys could be guilty. It was a cruel age, and yet I believe poor old W—— meant well by us. Don't you remember that poor boy he flogged so dreadfully for not having his lessons done that the child was in bed for six weeks afterwards? And very often I couldn't hold my knife and fork for days together after one of his canings. What awful trouble he would get into nowadays!"

And then the poet got up and put on his glasses to look more closely at a steel engraving of the very head-master he had been criticizing, which hung over the mantelpiece. A grim old figure enough, clad in cap and gown, a typical University don of ninety years ago or so. And then sitting down, I remember, he took up his cup.

"That's a pretty bit of china, Mrs. Blathwayt!" he said to my mother.

"Yes," she replied; "and to me as interesting as it is pretty, because both Sir Walter Scott and Tom Moore have drunk tea out of this set at my dear father's house in Edinburgh. And," she tactfully but very sincerely added—for nothing on earth would have induced my mother to have said anything that was not absolutely sincere—"and now it will be more interesting and valuable than ever."

And then the splendid old poet, in high good-humour, donned his flowing cloak and his famous wide-brimmed hat, and bidding us a gruff good-night, he disappeared into the windy night. He was gruff, yes ; but what a heart of gold, what tenderness, what kindly consideration beneath all the surface roughness !

To us in the Isle of Wight in those long-dead golden days, to the whole Empire, to all the world, Alfred Tennyson was then, as he remains to-day, the most splendid figure of all that splendid Victorian era !

And then there was Tom Hughes, the illustrious author of "Tom Brown's Schooldays," who lived about equidistant from the Tennysons and ourselves—a notable figure, a fine upstanding man, with keen, well-cut features and sandy whiskers ; and his beautiful and charming sister, Mrs. Nassau Senior, and his brother, Hastings Hughes, and his family. "Tom Brown," as every one called him, was a great athlete, and he gave my two little brothers their first swimming lessons in Totland Bay. And I mustn't forget a very marvellous old clergyman, born with the nineteenth century, who lived close to the vicarage, and who used to preach for my father, and who in his ninetieth year could walk twelve miles a day. He was the Rev. Christopher Bowen, the father of two famous sons ; one, Edward Bowen, the Harrow master, of whom Dr. Butler, when he was the headmaster of the great school on the Hill, used to say, "What would Harrow be without Edward Bowen?"—Edward Bowen who, with Dr. Farmer, the school organist, compiled that famous book of Harrow songs, which includes the deathless "Forty Years On" ; it was Edward Bowen also who brought Dr. Butler, just about the time he became Master of Trinity, to preach for my father at the little church in Totland ; and it was his brother who was so famous in after years as Lord Justice Bowen, a distinguished and pleasing figure whom every one in the parish liked and admired.

I recall, too, the charming and gracious personalities

of a certain Prince and Princess Ion Ghika, the Rumanian Minister, who used to spend the summer in our parish ; and the Princess, I remember, wanted to take my sister back with them for a long visit to Rumania. There was also Sir Samuel Baker—the discoverer, was he not, of the Victoria Nyanza ?—and his wife, who were great friends of ours. An interesting coterie, take them for all in all.

And then, of course, there was Mr. Wilson Carlile, the head of the Church Army, who used to take my father's duty year after year ; a singularly pleasant, genial man, loved by every one, whose only weakness was, and still is, his quite extraordinary affection for people with titles, but a man who, for all that, has devoted a very splendid and self-sacrificing life to the succour and salvation of the most suffering, the most destitute, and the most absolutely hopeless people that the world has ever known.

It was a charming home-life, and the Isle of Wight provided a lovely and romantic background for all that was most delightful in our youthful memories.

CHAPTER III

THE WHEELS OF CHANCE

SOMEWHERE pretty early in the seventies I wandered to the Western World, and, after varied experiences, I found myself in a little country town in Connecticut—a quaint, queer, typical, bitter-souled, appallingly narrow-minded little New England town, commoner perhaps in the seventies than would be possible to-day: a place where prohibition was rife, but where secret drinking was still rifer; where the cruelty of the saint towards the sinner, the horrible and unbelievable lack of charity, the incredibly poisonous chatter of gossiping scandal-mongers, and the prurient vision of disappointed and impossibly acid and acrid old maids surpassed anything of which I have ever had experience before or since. The town was religion mad and ruled, or perhaps I had best describe it by calling it "terrorized," by a couple of ministers, very rigid, unbelievably bigoted, though possibly thoroughly sincere men, who, with their deacons, made life very difficult for those who were not of their way of thinking. You will scarcely believe me when I say that to smoke a cigar in the street, or a pipe, of course, or any form of tobacco was accounted an absolute sin, and I cannot remember that any native of the town ever dared do so, although I myself, despite my extreme youth, being a Britisher, did not hesitate to smoke whenever I wanted to. In fact, it was a perfect joy to me, silly boy! to puff by the ministers' houses like a factory chimney in full blast. I had got a little money with me, very little, and I was in the company of two other Englishmen, one a man about my own age, the son of a

General officer, an Eton boy, a handsome, devil-may-care sort of chap, whom everybody loved, and the other a queer, quaint, delightful person, many years older than either of us, whom we always addressed as "George." His other name was Atkins, but we never called him by it, and to the end of our journeying and sojourning together he was always "George," pure and simple. Carew and I followed admiringly in the wake of "George," who also had been at a Public School—Rugby, I believe—before we were either of us born or thought of, and who could and did turn his hand to anything that came along, and a pretty queer job he made of it sometimes.

We all three lodged together in a sort of boarding-house, and of course we were the only Englishmen in the town; indeed, I doubt if in those days there were many Englishmen in Connecticut at all. They were far more scarce then than now, and in consequence we were a mingled source of joy and admiration to the simple-minded natives, and especially to the feminine element, Carew and I particularly because, as they said, we were so like the Englishmen they had read about in books, and they loved to hear us call "pie" "tart," or "larf" instead of "laff," or any other old thing to which they didn't happen to be accustomed. My eye-glass, too, which I have worn all my life practically, immensely delighted them, and of course the younger portion of the community were much impressed by our absolute ignoring of all the ridiculous conventions and absurd restrictions in which and by which all of them were held in such hopeless bondage. Not that we deliberately or of *malice prepense* set ourselves in opposition to the ways of the community: we simply didn't know they existed, and by the time we had fully realized the actual state of affairs we had so established our own method of existence that we were left in peace to our own devices. I suppose we were considered too hopelessly abandoned for reformation to be even possible.

I don't suppose English people as a rule, save and except perhaps some of the old-fashioned Dissenters, can even begin to realize such a condition of affairs as was quite common in the small towns and villages in Maine, Connecticut, Vermont, and the New England States generally. Worse than the old Puritanic conditions prevailed, worse because whilst they were undistinguished and unilluminated by the noble and all-purifying influence of a deep and searching spirituality, they were characterized by downright cruelty and tyranny: the letter had absolutely triumphed over and murdered the spirit. And there was something pathetic in the manner in which the total abstainers sincerely believed they had crushed the demon of drink—as they termed it—the while he raged more furiously in that little town than I have ever seen before or since. For, of course, secret drinking prevailed to a perfectly horrible extent.

Well, to this town there came one day, to our inexpressible joy, albeit to the horror and indignation of the unco' guid, a travelling circus and menagerie, and as the prima donna, or the leading lady, or whatever they called her, and three or four of the feminine members of the "fit-up," came and stayed at our boarding-house, we three Englishmen saw a very great deal of that circus—in fact, for the time being, we were established as sort of *ex-officio* members of it, and a high old time we had of it altogether. To begin with, the prima donna and Carew fell violently in love with each other, and that started things humming. It was a burning summer that year, and those two used to sit out on the veranda—the stoep it was always called—and make love to one another so hot that it scorched the begonias in that little back garden, and surprised even the rattlesnakes in the neighbouring potato-patch. She was an awfully pretty girl and as plucky as they make 'em, and we four were inseparable, and the minister's wife used to toss her head when we passed her window on our way to the circus where "Maimie" had to do her "stunts" every night.

And while she was "stunting"—riding bare-backed round and round the tan, or jumping through a hoop, or twisting on a trapeze-bar—I would sit and smoke and chat with the clowns and the grooms, the dagoes, the niggers, the Mexican greasers, and the stablemen at the back of the performers' tent. And a queer and amusing and reckless, good-hearted lot they were, too. I fairly loved them. There was one old chap there they used to call "Elephant Bill," and of whom they used to relate a very funny yarn. In earlier life, not so many years before, he had been an artist's model, and as he was a very handsome and dignified old chap, with a bald head and a long white beard, he used often to sit for biblical personages. Well, it chanced that a certain artist was painting a New Testament scene, and he engaged old Bill to sit for him as the Apostle St. Matthew. Some years afterwards the artist was walking in the New York Zoological Gardens when he ran up against his old model.

"Hullo, Bill!" he cried. "What on earth are you doing here?"

"Well, sir," replied Bill, "I aint doin' much. I'm engaged in these 'ere gardins a-cleanin' out the helephants' stables. A nice sort o' occypation for one o' the twelve apostles, aint it, sir?" he bitterly added.

We had a great excitement one day. It was billed all over the town in advance, and for a week previously nothing else was talked of in the place; even the two ministers were excited about it. For it was announced in all the local papers and on every wall in every street that on a certain evening the Rev. Thomas Q. Venning would read the marriage service over a certain couple in the lions' den at the circus. The Rev. Venning was a minister in the next town; he must have been rather a sport I should think, for I own such a feat takes some doing, and Carew and George wanted to bet me that he would funk out of it at the last moment. Well, the night came, and so did the Rev. Venning and the bride and bridegroom. The two men looked a little pale about the gills, and I offered to stand the parson a drink at the nearest chemist's, where I knew I could get varied "poisons" under the name and in the aspect of bottles of medicine. However, he wasn't taking any, and the girl laughed at the bare idea of such Dutch courage. She didn't mind a bit. Of course there was an enormous crowd, and I began to be anxious less there should be a scene and the animals be frightened.

At eight to the minute the band started in with the wedding march and the lions' trainer and the keeper stepped into the den—a very big one—with their gigantic rhinoceros-hide whips, and then the bridal pair and the parson stepped in behind him, the band playing for all it was worth.

The parson, looking very white, began a very abbreviated form of the marriage service, and he hurried along at a rate which would have allowed him to give any man as far as "Pontius Pilate" in the Creed and then romp in ahead of him, but he couldn't get any speed on the bride. She actually delayed taking off her glove till the parson bade the groom put the ring on her finger. She didn't even glance at the lions, who were obviously getting restive, the more especially that the wretched bridegroom was one of the plumpest and most appetizing-looking men—from a leonine point of view—that one could possibly imagine.

At last, at long last, infinitely to the relief of every one in that heated and excited audience, the minister came to the final Amen and the bridal procession filed out again, but not before the irritated and long-suffering lioness had made a grab at and torn clean away from her the floating ribbon the little bride wore round her waist. And do you know, that plucky little woman wanted to go and get it back from the outraged animal! And there was no swagger or pretence about it either: she simply didn't know what the word "fear" meant. The bridegroom, on the contrary, fairly collapsed, and the minister confessed to me that he wouldn't do it again for all the dollars in the United States.

And then one day it was announced that Miss Mamie Collins—that was Carew's mash!—who, according to the time-honoured announcements, "had appeared before all the crowned heads in Europe," would ascend in a balloon "ten thousand feet into the blue empyrean"—that was how the bills phrased it—and would then descend to earth again in a parachute. And it was our turn to be anxious, and a pretty sickly time of it we all had. For, of course, it was all new to us, and the thought of that dear little woman jumping down ten thousand feet was too horrible and ghastly for words, and we did all we could to dissuade her from so mad a project, as we considered it, but all to no purpose. She didn't worry about it one little bit, not she; she was as plucky as the bride, and pluckier, for she knew her risks, which the other hadn't done. It was then, I think, that I realized, what I have often experienced since, how frequently women are far braver than men.

It was an anxious week, as I have said; but it came to an end at last, and the morning of the day dawned when Maimie was to do the "Elijah stunt," as she irreverently termed it, and go up to heaven in a balloon instead of a chariot of fire. A lovely day it was as she and I walked down the street and out of the town and on to the great wide-stretching field whereon the circus tents were pitched and from which the balloon was to ascend.

Things were all ready for her and the meadow was crowded with a very excited throng, and Maimie went into her dressing-tent to get into her tights—those same tights, by the by, constituted a terrible rock of offence in the eyes of the ministers' and deacons' wives, though, as a matter of fact, they were nothing very out of the way. Well, out she came, looking very jolly, for she had a charming figure, which the tights displayed to its very fullest advantage, and the crimson light which was cast by her Japanese sunshade—a great rarity in those days, and especially so in a New England village—was immensely becoming to her lovely face, and into the basket she stepped, kissing her hand to us three standing anxiously by as she did so, and then the word was given to "let go," and in a minute, so it appeared to me, she was far above our heads. It was a dead still day, and, to judge from the very stationary appearance of the balloon, there were no upper currents of air at all. We had hired a sort of buggy, and we started out in the direction in which it would appear likely that she would descend, and we got as far away from the crowd as we possibly could, keeping our eyes fixed all the time upon the balloon. Up and up it soared, and down and down our hearts sank. I had a very powerful glass with me, so I could keep a pretty good eye on all that was occurring in that terrific blue so awfully far away. At last I discerned a kind of movement. I made out a figure stepping over the side of the basket, sliding down a rope, it appeared to me, and then there was a kind of upward spring of the balloon and a solitary speck falling, falling in that marvellous blue space. "By God! she's coming down!" I ejaculated, and then it appeared to me something opened out and expanded and the downward rush became a gentle inclining to the earth. We all three breathed more freely, and there came across those sunny meadows and borne to us from afar upon the scented summer breeze the faint far-off cheering of a vast multitude. Down and down and down towards the blessed earth that brave, pathetic little figure came dropping through the summer day, and I drove like Jehu for the spot whereon I quickly realized she would fall, and at last I saw her touch the ground and then she appeared to collapse. I pulled up just outside a gate, tied the horse up, and then we vaulted the gate and flew over the lush grass to where we could see her stretched flat upon her back, our hearts in our mouths the while. As we got up to her she raised a smiling face to Carew.

"Say, Jack, have you got a match?"

"Oh, hang the match!" said Jack. "Are you all right? That's all I'm worrying about."

"Why, of course, I am, you dear old silly; never better!"

And indeed I don't believe she ever was. But we all swore we wouldn't go through that hour again for all the diamonds in Golconda. I don't think any of us have ever forgotten it, although I don't think I have ever spoken of it to any one; but to this day Jack tells me he sees her in his dreams, dropping, dropping, dropping through the sunlit air, and he wakes to find the cold sweat breaking out upon his forehead. It was an immensely plucky thing to do, although she always used to declare it was "as easy as old boots."

I shall never forget that circus and that menagerie. Even now I can sniff the pungent tan and sawdust and the still more pungent smell of the lions, all delightfully mixed up together with the smell of that powerful "twist" tobacco with which they filled their black cutties and meerschaums. The life was always full of subdued excitement, for it was a careless kind of menagerie altogether, some said too careless—for they were always "mislaying," as they used to term it euphoniously, one of their charges—an elephant, maybe, or a python, or a tiger, or a crocodile; they weren't particular one way or the other.

One day, just after breakfast, I peeped in at the messroom door. There was a full-grown tiger licking the jam and bacon off the plates. "Oh, I beg your pardon!" I ejaculated as I hastily shut the door. A moment after I met Jack, the tiger's keeper.

"I can't find that tiger nowhere," he said to me. "I guess I've mislaid the ornary old critter."

"You have," I icily replied, for I was a good deal annoyed with the danger I had so narrowly escaped. "You'll find him in the messroom licking the plates."

"Thank you, mate," he said as he lazed away in the direction of his missing friend, humming to himself—

> "Jack Sprat could eat no fat,
> His wife could eat no lean,
> And so between them both
> They licked the platter clean."

An hour after I overheard the proprietor asking his little son if he had washed up the breakfast dishes.

"Hadn't no need to, Pop; the tiger licked 'em like he knew they wanted cleanin'"

I didn't go to lunch *that* day!

Another day I had to drop myself down off the balustrade to give place to the python, which was coiling itself up the stairs, and Carew jolly near sat down on the crocodile, which was hidden away in the deep grass near the river.

I asked the proprietor once why he mixed up menageries and circus dancers in the way he did.

"Well, young feller," he said, "it's like this. Pretty often round about these ornary old New England towns the people are so religious they wouldn't go to a circus noways. But a camel or an elephant or a serpent—well, you'll find them all in the Bible. Behemoth, he's a elephant, and the camel goin' through a needle's eye, and, of course, the serpent in the Garden of Eden. Well, I always bring in them scriptooral references, and they know what they're up against, and they think tights ain't so wicked 'longside of an elephant or a camel."

I have referred to the "carelessness" of the men in dealing with their animals, though I fancy much of that carelessness was assumed, and beneath lay intimate knowledge of the ways and wiles of their charges, and they weren't really taking all the risks they appeared to be taking, and their carelessness was nothing compared with the instances of which Carl Hagenbeck used to tell me some years ago. It always amused me, though, to see the serpent-keeper dash down three or four pounds of python or cobra upon a marble slab as a grocer might dash down a slab of butter. "Pound of cobra, madam? Yes, madam, and the next article?"

Well, after a while we parted company with the circus, and Carew and Maimie bade one another a wild and despairing farewell. Carew, of course, is still going strong. Indeed, I believe he's a Colonel at the Front, and I read this chapter over to George only the other day. Maimie I have never even heard of since we all separated, and I should think the dear old circus proprietor has long since departed this life, for he wasn't very young then; he must have been at least sixty.

He told me one incident that immensely amused me. I related it thirty years ago in a London paper, but I daresay it's forgotten by now. He had a blue-faced baboon once which drew the whole countryside to the menagerie. One morning early he was sitting outside the tent when a man and his wife—a regular Farmer Hayseed—approached, followed by twenty young people.

"Say, mister," said the old chap, "we want to see your baboon, so I've brought my family along; only I want to do a deal for the lot."

"All them your children?" said the boss. "One father and one mother?"

"All mine and all hearn," replied Farmer Hayseed, with a backward gesture towards his wife.

The boss gasped.

"Say," he said, "you all just stop right here, and I'll bring that old baboon out to see *you*. He ain't had much excitement lately, but I guess you and your family will cheer him up and give him something to think about winter nights."

George and Carew and I drifted on, always travelling "very light." As a matter of fact we had no choice in the matter. Heavens! we were hard up, but always in the best of spirits and generally in fits of laughter, even when we were so hungry that, as George put it, we could easily have eaten a lion, with a whole regiment of cavalry inside him, jackboots and all. One day we arrived in a village, and as we were very nearly at the end of our tether George declared we must get some "chores" to do. So, having made a few inquiries and got certain information, we started off for a kind of farmer and carpenter and wheelwright and odd-job sort of man we heard of, and when we got there George marched into a lumber-yard as bold as brass, Carew and I following close upon his rear, and a man came up and George said to him—

"Are you the boss?"

"Wal, I guess I fit in thar," was the reply.

"Well, look here, boss," said George, "do you want any help?"

"Yaas, I reckon I du. Kin you make wheels, you fellers?"

"Wheels!" replied George. "Wheels! Why, I've been at the job all my life."

I shook my head. Carew stepped manfully forward.

"Wal, I'll give you fifteen dollars a week each to start with and a room and board. Is it a deal? Can you do chores about the house, young feller?" he said to me.

I "guessed" I could, and he, saying he'd tell his "darter" to find me some work, turned into the house, whilst Carew and I tackled George on the extraordinary position in which he had placed himself.

"You can't make wheels, you old humbug," said Carew, "can you?"

"Never made a wheel in my life, not even a watch-wheel," replied George; "but I'm going to have a jolly good try right here and now, and so are you, Carew, my boy."

They both stripped for the fray, and having each got hold of an adze, they started in upon some planks of wood that were lying in thick profusion about the yard. And just at that moment the boss returned.

"Wal, thar you are, boys; thar's the wood and the toolhouse is up yonder, so get a push on you; and you come with me," he added, turning to where I stood rather disconsolately, and, following him into the house, I left George and Carew and started on my own adventurous career. The "darter" turned out to be a pretty little thing enough, and as we were about the same age and full of life and I was the first Britisher she had ever seen, much less talked to—and Lord! as old Pepys says, how she "laffed" when I did start in to speak—we were very soon regular old friends. She pinned a big apron round me, and screamed when a few minutes afterwards I returned with a bucket of water from the well and tumbled over that infernal apron and spilled all the water over the kitchen floor. I was sufficiently awkward and unhandy, but I contrived to show her, or to tell her, how to make an omelette, of which up to that moment she had never even heard.

About two hours later the boss came in, and he said to me: "You been helpin' my little gal, eh? That's right. Well, come along, and we'll see how them other chaps are gittin' along and bring 'em back to have some supper." Though I think if I remember right he called it "lunch," which they often do in country districts in America. Well, when we reached those two fellows they had evidently been working like mad, to judge by the chips that lay about, and there were some nicely "dressed" planks of wood all ready to be worked up into wheels; the boss seemed thoroughly satisfied, and he said: "Well, boys, come along and we'll have supper and then a smoke. I guess you are ready for a rest."

The evening passed all right. George sang "Tom Bowling," and the boss said "it was a damned dismal sort of ditty, anyway"; and we all went to bed and slept like tops. In the morning I turned out early and lit the kitchen fire and put the kettle on, and wished Glynne Turquand and the other Guardsmen could have seen me—how they'd have laughed! And then George and Carew went out to the wheelyard and I went and did my "chores." Look at my portrait now and imagine me sweeping the room and making the beds, etc., though I must confess I was always a dab at blacking boots, which, of course, was just the one thing they never dreamed of doing there, right out in the wilds. About eleven o'clock I knocked off, and, nodding to the "darter," I went out into the yard and joined the others, George shouted out to me as I came up—

"We've started wheelmaking in earnest now! What do you think of *that* for a wheel?" And he held up an absolutely incomprehensible affair in wood, held together by a few nails.

"Good heavens!" I said. "Why, that's not a wheel; it's a problem in Euclid!" and I laughed till I was feeble with laughing. And then up came the boss himself for the first time that morning. He looked at George's wheel, and then he looked at George and George looked at him.

"What's that?" said the boss.

"It's a wheel," said George as bold as brass.

"A wheel!" screamed our employer. "Why, darn it all, man, it's an eight-day clock! That thing will never be round, and it'll never *go* round either, not on your life!"

"These are wheels that my friend and I are making," replied George with all the gravity and dignity that he could summon to his aid; "but they're not the kind of wheels that you are accustomed to in this country. It's a wheel they use for the roads in Russia."

"But doggone it all, man," said the boss, "we're in Connecticut, not in Russia!"

"It's an octagonal wheel," obstinately continued George, "which you will find admirably suited for your corduroy roads here. A wheel like *that*," he continued with ill-concealed pride in his handiwork, "will last you a lifetime, and *then* you can hand it down to posterity as an heirloom. You'll find the farmers hereabouts for hundreds of miles will make a run on your yard for these wheels."

The boss, who was absolutely one of the best, burst into a roar of laughter.

"Well," he said, "you'll have to make a run *out* of the yard; for a week of you and your friend would about ruin me." And as he spoke he thrust a fifteen-dollar bill into George's hand, another into Carew's, and a ten-dollar bill into my hand. "I suppose you'll want to go with them?" he said to me.

George protested. "Look here, boss," he said, "we can't take this money if you are not satisfied. You must take it back, and we'll try our luck elsewhere."

"Not a bit of it," replied the boss. "You chaps have made me laff as I never hoped to laff again. Any ornary old cuss can make wheels, but, darn it all, it takes a man to make *that*!" And, pointing feebly at George's "problem in Euclid," or "eight-day clock," as he called it, he sat down upon a tree-trunk and laughed till he was too weak and exhausted to laugh any more.

And then we made for the *dee*pot and once more

were on the road, and the wheels of chance lay far in our rear. I daresay they are in a dime museum now. I have seen freaks I have laughed at less than I laughed at George's corduroy wheels.

Here I end my very early days. Henceforward my records deal with the rather strenuous work and career of manhood. But I am glad I went through the experiences I then went through. They did me good; they enabled me to realize something of what life really meant, even our little adventures in the circus. They help one to see life and to see it straight and see it whole, and I made none the worse an East End curate that I had seen a little bit of real life and of life in the rough and done a few "chores" in a New England farmhouse—for I had more than one experience of that kind when out in America in the seventies. And oh, by the by, I wouldn't have lost the experience of that boarding-house where I met Maimie for anything on this wide earth! I think the lady who kept it was the most absolutely amusing, the most shiftless, the most feckless, and the most good-natured person I ever met in my life—and always mislaying everything. She had a husband, a horrid little man whom we all detested, a sneaky little fellow, always prying about and poking his nose into household affairs, a regular "kitchen colonel," as they call them in America. But she was a rare good sort, with a heart of gold and a head like a sieve.

I remember one night we had pork and beans for supper, and we were to have had potatoes, too, but when the moment arrived for them they could nowhere be found.

"Why, I declar' to goodness I put them taters all out ready in the dish agin you all come in to supper!" cried the puzzled and distressed landlady.

"Perhaps the cat has eaten them," suggested Carew.

"Eaten the potatoes, Jack!" cried Maimie. "Why, that cat's got all she can do, laffin' at you and Ray talkin', ever to find time to eat potatoes! No, we've got to do without any potatoes to-night, I guess."

After that we went into the parlour, as they always called it, and Maimie made to sit down on the sofa. Suddenly she gave a frightful screech. "For the land's sake!" she screamed, "I'm sittin' down on a rattler's nest, sure!"

I flew to her side and pulled her up. Hanged if she hadn't gone and sat plump down on the potatoes, which by some mischance the landlady had banged down on the sofa and then clean forgotten what she had done with them! Carew and Maimie and I laughed for one solid hour over that episode, and indeed I once nearly laughed at it in the middle of the Litany one day, years and years afterwards, in a stately West End church here in London!

Well, as I say, these little experiences are good for one; they are very innocent really, and they keep you from crystallizing into a prig, anyway, which many young Englishmen are only too apt to do in the very early days of their career. Maimie was a girl in a thousand, though I suppose they would look askance at her in a deanery. She had a heart of gold and such courage as I never saw in mortal man or woman in my life; and if we three young men did run a little wild—well, the young man who never makes a mistake very rarely makes anything else, except, perhaps, an infernal ass of himself, and it all helps to make you more human and more sympathetic and more understanding. At all events, I not only don't regret my early experiences, but I believe they did me far more good than harm, and I look back upon that period of my life as upon the golden days of youth.

CHAPTER IV

A GLIMPSE INTO A CURATE'S LIFE AND MIND

"Now, Mr. Blathwayt," said the Rev. Canon Henderson, a handsome, white-haired, thoroughbred little man of the world, and extremely popular with the students of the Dunchester Theological College, of which he was the Principal, and whither I was sent in the middle seventies, for the parental funds did not then allow of University fees, and where I remained for two whole years reading for the Church—"now, Mr. Blathwayt, just read this passage out of Æschylus, will you, and let me see what you make of it. Read the Greek first and then translate it."

I must remark, in parenthesis, that I had gone up to be examined for entry into the college.

By all that was fortunate the Canon had struck upon one of my father's favourite pieces, the opening lines of "Prometheus Bound"—at all events, the famous lines where Prometheus bewails his fate—

> ὠ δῖος αἰθὴρ καὶ ταχύπτεροι πνοαὶ
> ποταμῶν τε πηγαι ποντίων τε κυματων
> ἀνήριθμον γέλασμα . . .

I rolled out the Greek as well as I could, and, thanks to my father's training, quite correctly, and then sailed in with the English of it.

"'Oh, godly atmosphere——'" I began.

"Hum!" said the Canon; "that's a little bald. Hadn't you better say, 'Oh, atmosphere divine'? However, go on."

—"'and ye swift-winged gales,'" I continued, "'and

you the fountains of the rivers, and thou the innumerable ripple of the ocean's waves.' "

"Can't you put it a little more poetically, Mr. Blathwayt?" said the Canon. "Ah, yes! that's better; very good indeed—'many twinkling smile of ocean.' That's enough. You'll do."

"Have I passed?" I joyously inquired, having been busily engaged in fagging up at least half a dozen subjects for the previous year in preparation for this very exam. about which I had been hideously anxious and which I had been dreading for months.

"Oh yes," replied the Canon; "I can always tell whether a man will do or not within ten minutes of his coming into the room. The chief thing with me is that he should be a gentleman; all the rest will come as a matter of course. I think you'll be very happy here. There are some very nice fellows. You play cricket, I suppose? That's right! Well, we've got quite a good Eleven in the college; indeed, one of the men got his cap at Oxford only last year. You had better see about your rooms to-day, now you are in Dunchester, although the term doesn't begin for another eight weeks," he continued, as he handed me a list of authorized "diggings," from which I was at liberty to make my selection.

And thus I started on my heavenward path via the Anglican Church. I may as well cut a long story short and say that I passed out of the college and into the Church itself very nearly as easily as I had succeeded in doing with Canon Henderson, whose soul God rest! He was a delightful person, a little worldly, perhaps, but a scholar and a gentleman and a sportsman to his finger-tips. He loved you if you were enthusiastic over a game, but he would have been dreadfully uncomfortable if you had shown any anxiety about your soul. "My dear fellow, really you must forgive me, but we don't talk about that kind of thing in a drawing-room," he once said to a clergyman who asked him his opinion about Moody and Sankey, who just then were creating a great sensation throughout the land.

On another occasion a young man who was mightily perturbed about his soul, so he said, and who had "doubts," as he expressed it, went to the Canon in great distress. Canon Henderson looked at him for a moment, and then, thoughtfully fingering his chin with his left hand, as he had a habit of doing, he peered quizzically at him over his spectacles and said: "Have you ever tried Carter's Little Liver Pills, Mr. Jones? Just take two to-night at bedtime and try to get a couple of hours at the nets every morning, and come to see me again in a month's time."

Jones, I may add, is to this day a capital wicket-keeper, and a really hard-working and very much respected rector of a large town parish in the Midlands.

The ultra-earnest and unco' guid sincerely detested Canon Henderson's methods, and I quite understand that now and again they gave occasion to the very orthodoxically judicious to grieve considerably. All the same, I wish there were a few more of his type going about to-day. He may not have been very spiritually-minded—deep spirituality, as a rule, is not a very prominent characteristic of the Anglican clergy—but he was, in the best sense of the word, a Christian and a gentleman, and so I say again, God rest his gallant soul!

I went straight out to Trinidad on leaving Dunchester, which exactly suited my restless and roving disposition; and there, in the handsome old cathedral church of that gorgeously beautiful island in the Windward group of the West Indies, I was ordained a deacon in the Anglican Church.

I can never forget the ordination service in that far-off tropic church, with the palm-trees clashing in the strong sea-breeze just outside the great open windows; the curious impression produced upon one who saw it for the first time of a vast congregation, men and women alike, white, black, and brown, all vigorously fanning themselves in a vain endeavour to keep cool; the white-faced clergy and the coal-black choir; and above them all and over them all the noble and inspiring presence of Bishop Rawle, one of the most remarkable and one of the most splendid specimens of humanity I ever met. And in the Governor's pew sat the Governor, Sir Henry Irving, with his guest, Lord Ailsa, who was a great friend of my cousin Glynne Turquand, the two owning and racing together a famous yacht—the *Bulldog*, if I remember rightly. I was the only person ordained that day, and I may here remark that for a few months I was the youngest Anglican clergyman in the world; and I remember somebody suggested at the time that I ought to be photographed in company with Canon Beadon, who was then over a century old, and, naturally enough, the oldest priest in the world. What I didn't like was putting on the clerical coat for the first time. It seemed to cut me off from the rest of the world; it gave me, at all events, a very uncomfortable feeling of unnaturalness. I hated being different from other young men, and to have people apologize to me if they said "dammit," as though I were a lady. I wasn't ashamed of my uniform—far from it. I am saying nothing against it; it is absolutely necessary and desirable that it should be worn. I am simply recording the impression it made on my young mind when I first put it on. I disliked its rigour, its difference from that worn by every one else, its suggestions of super sanctity. I disliked it much as a British officer dislikes—or, at all events, up to 1914 used to dislike—his uniform off the parade-ground or wearing it when off duty. I realized what is indeed the fact, that the clerical coat cuts a man off from his fellows to a quite remarkable extent. And always underneath was the feeling—of which I shall speak later—that I was not quite the type of man to wear the parson's habit.

Beside the Bishop, the cathedral clergy consisted of the Archdeacon of Trinidad; a certain Canon whose name I forget; the Rev. Archibald Burrows; and the Rev. Isaac Keay.

Mr. Burrows was a splendid type of man altogether, and little less than worshipped by the parishioners—a great, tall, broad-shouldered man, with a waving beard and a voice like a storm-trumpet—he had been a captain in the Merchant Service before he took his degree at Trinity College, Dublin—a laugh that was so infectious that every one who heard it within a mile radius would join in it, and a smile that won every mother's and baby's heart in the island ; and such a tender heart ! I have never met a more lovable man. His own worst enemy—and, indeed, himself his only enemy, for there were men and women in Trinidad who would have died for him in those days—and never a soul who could endure to hear a word against him. I was twenty years his junior, and he took me completely under his wing, and never a man was kinder and dearer to another than he was to me. I am sure my old friend W. J. Locke—then an immensely popular schoolboy at the great Trinidad College—will support me in this, for well do I remember Burrows taking me to see Mr. and Mrs. Locke, who were among the best known and most popular people in Port of Spain, and our meeting the charming, rather delicate-looking schoolboy who, all unknown to any one of us, was to develop into one of the finest novelists and stylists that England has ever produced.

Mr. William Isaac Keay, a brother of Sir Seymour Keay, a well-known English M.P., was a totally different type of man, but a man also of the very highest character, and a very remarkable man too. He had been in business for many years before his ordination, but, though inclined to dryness in certain aspects of life, he was scholarly to a rather exceptional degree, and with a curious fund of humour. He was a fine preacher, especially to any one of a thoughtful temperament. He wasn't so popular as Burrows, not nearly ; and I don't think he liked me much ; but he was an exceptionally fine type of cleric, and would have done honour to any position in the Anglican Church. He is still in Trinidad, or he was there when I visited the island a few years ago, though by now he must be at least eighty years of age.

Of Bishop Rawle, what can I say but that he was one of those men who stand apart from their fellows altogether. He was an unforgettable experience in a young man's life, a worthy, spiritual descendant of George

Herbert, Bishop Andrewes, or Archbishop Laud. He was a regular pioneer bishop, and admirably suited for the West Indian blacks, amongst whom he had worked—first as Principal of Codrington College, Barbados, and then as Bishop of Trinidad—for many long years. In addition to great gifts as a preacher, he was the typical missionary bishop, and was a first-class carpenter—I am sure he would have turned out a far better wheel than George Atkins could ever have accomplished—and a really admirable architect and surveyor. I remember well helping him build a little wooden church in a part of the island known, I think, as the High Woods. I didn't do much of it, I fear—I couldn't, but he worked like a Trojan, and with the sureness of touch of the practised expert.

Shortly after my ordination I was appointed, amongst other duties, to the Anglican chaplaincy of the great leper hospital which lay some three miles out of Port of Spain. That was an experience I can never forget—a terrible vision of unspeakable pain and horror and suffering, which came as a blow to a very young man who had never really witnessed anything but the bright and light-hearted side of humanity in all his life ; and yet it was an experience that I would not now have missed for a good deal, because I consider that all experience—except, of course, that of the vile side of life—helps to deepen character and widen one's whole vision of and outlook upon the world.

I think I will describe my first visit to and glimpse of this terrible home of suffering humanity, and let that suffice for the rest. The leper hospital was totally isolated from the surrounding neighbourhood, whither it was reached by a long country road, bordered and shaded on each side by the most magnificent palm-trees that one can see anywhere in the tropics. The road, for a great distance, runs parallel with the Caribbean Sea, and down to the waterside the land consists of mangrove swamps, very beautiful, very mysterious, creeping with unimaginable horrors, and deep in mud in which lurk malaria and fevers and the very shadow of death itself. More than once I have crept carefully down to the water's edge and gazed, fascinated, upon that old-world sea wherein Drake's and Raleigh's caravels must often have sailed, and upon the far horizon of which I would sometimes catch a glimpse of some white-winged ship, glimmering in and out of the sunshine and the shadow, as it took its way to the lonely deep, whilst just above my head the great palm-branches clashed and clattered in the strong trade winds. It was like a chapter out of one of Marryatt's or Ballantyne's fascinating tales, and almost one could fancy Captain Kidd or Morgan, the fierce buccaneer, stealing into those little land-locked harbours with a pirate ship laden from stem to stern with the red gold and the diamonds and the jewels and the rich wines they had captured from some luckless ship in oceans away on the other side of the world. In the far, dim distance the mountains of Venezuela rose blue upon the misty, sunlit horizon, and a blazing sun burnt into one the realization that these were the tropics with a vengeance.

And then I would retrace my steps to the road, and suddenly I would find myself in an Indian village, surrounded by Indian coolies and by women from Bengal and Bombay, who, with arms and legs laden with bangles glittering in the brilliant sunlight and tinkling ever as they walked, with easy, graceful abandon, presented a vast contrast to the sturdy negro wenches who, with magnificent carriage and incredibly stately port and grinning, meaningless cackle, would go chattering down the tropic road ; or I would meet a couple of sad-faced, cryptic, silent Chinese laundrymen coming out of the barrack-square wherein one caught a glimpse of white-clad British soldiers, towards whom for the nonce I acted in the capacity of chaplain. The colouring of the whole scena was almost beyond imagining : the dark green of the foliage of the splendid old cotton-trees, with their grey, massive trunks, that must have been old in the days of Elizabeth ; the graceful forms of the palm-trees, sharp outlined against a sky of bronze, deepening into purple upon the exquisite range of tropical mountains in the not very distant rear ; the picturesque shacks of the negroes, apparently for the most part manufactured out of withered palm-branches ; the far-stretching fields of sugar-cane or bananas, waving green beneath the blaze of sun and clashing here and there in the vigorous sea-breeze ; the exquisite hues of the humming-birds, flashing back all the myriad tints of a hundred rainbows as they hummed and hovered over a flower in the little forest ; the blazing, brilliant scarlet flame of fire that is the flowering of the dust-laden cactus-hedges upon the roadside ; the swoop of the scavenger vultures or bald-headed crows, foul but useful birds of prey upon which it is penal to fire a shot—for they, indeed, are the angels of health and cleanliness, as they are so described by Michelet in that exquisite book of his (my delight as a child), " L'Oiseau " ; and here and there a pariah dog would snap and snarl from its hiding-place in the little Hindoo village, wherein upon certain days and at stated hours you would catch glimpses of the turbaned coolies and the women, with their immemorial robes of incredibly artistic colouring—reds and greens and blues, never crude, but soft and harmonized as by the hand of a prince of colourists, reminiscent of the most glorious days of mediæval Cairo, Delhi, or Bagdad ; you would, I say, catch glimpses of them stealing away through the shadows of the tropic wood to do *puja* in the little temple, wherein they preserve in a far land the religion and the romance and the memories of long-forgotten days upon the Ganges or beneath the shadow of the green and snow-clad Himalayas.

You may imagine how entrancingly fascinating it all was to a young man fresh from the prosaic surroundings of an English provincial town like Dunchester—even though there the grey, historic old cathedral reared itself stark and stern, with its memories of Norman conquest, Plantagenet rule, and Tudor triumph. But in those days, though I was the most romantic youth it was possible to imagine, I had not learned to harmonize and correlate the splendour of Empire with the far-reaching and multi-coloured history of the nation that had preceded the welding together of the tropics, East and West, in one magnificent accomplishment of statecraft and strategic and military effort combined. And so I would pass down a sun-flecked, shadow-stricken roadway, across which one would watch the little green lizards ever running to and fro, and whereon one would very rarely catch a glimpse of the deadly little crimson coral snake pursuing its sinuous and devious course, leaving its slimy trail in the white dust, until I arrived at those grim, fast-closed doors over the portals of which, I always felt with aching heart, might well have been inscribed Dante's inscription of terror :—

All hope abandon, ye who enter here.

And once inside, you find yourself in a vast, a very vast, enclosure, beautiful with the dread, vague beauty of the tropics, as outside the palm-trees made loud music in the breeze, and the shadows fell refreshingly upon the burning ground, and in the far distance the mountains reared their splendid heights into the tropic sky ; nothing but perfect beauty so far as Nature met the eye, and nothing but horror indescribable and terror unimagined and suffering beyond all conception when one gazed upon the crowd of leprosy-stricken men and women and children which always gathered round the chaplain on his entry into those disease and sorrow-laden premises. But what, perhaps, tried me most, and over which I could never obtain the mere physical mastery, was the indescribable odour of leprosy, which, once experienced, can never be forgotten, but which haunts one through life. After a lapse of between thirty and forty years that appalling odour is still in my nostrils, pungent, sickly, and unescapable.

The lepers dwelt, and still dwell, in long, low buildings, which are practically, all day and all night long, open to all the winds of heaven that blow, so that at all hours the strong sea-breeze sweeps through those dim corridors of disease and death with a sensation of purity and of cleansing that is indescribably grateful to people visiting the hospital, like myself, for the first time. I am not exaggerating when I thus dwell upon the nausea that overtakes almost every visitor to a great leper hospital. At his own earnest request I once took in with me a young officer from the barracks whom I had known at Sandhurst—poor G. P. Williams-Freeman, who died only a few years ago, Chief Constable of Shropshire—and he had not been in the place ten minutes before, overcome by the appalling sights and that terrible, faint, disease-laden effluvia, he fainted dead away. More than anything else it was the thing that affected me most, and more especially in conducting service in the tiny chapel, when I would be surrounded on all sides by men and women in every stage of this fell disease.

There they would stand, a congregation of figures of death, such as not even a mediævalist monastic artist could have conceived in those curious pictures of death and hell they would execute in their old missals, and they would sing faintly and feebly, the while some of them could scarcely turn over the leaves of their prayer-books with fingers from which the decaying flesh would crumble away even as they kneeled in prayer. It was a sight that would have overcome a heart of chilled steel, that would have brought tears to the eyes of a Prussian general. Never have I witnessed anything more pathetic than or anything so absolutely heartbreaking as the little schoolroom wherein those tiny leper children would do their daily meed of lessons, taught them by a young black schoolmaster, himself far on the way to the leper's hideous and unspeakable end. Dear little things they were some of them, little Hindoo boys and charming little West Indian negroes —for as quite children their charm and fascination are undeniable and irresistible—and one little English boy, isolated for ever from his parents and his brothers and sisters, who eagerly used to lie in wait for me on my return to Port of Spain, in order that I might tell them how little Charlie was going on. Some of the children were so ill and some were so far gone in the disease and their fingers were so unspeakably sore they could scarcely hold the pencil wherewith they wrote their exercises or did their sums upon their slates. And yet I never once heard a murmur from their lips. Indeed, as a matter of fact, both they and their splendidly heroic teacher loved the hours of school, though one like myself realized sadly enough that they would never grow up to receive any benefit from their lessons. And though sometimes the rare, unwilling tears, squeezed out of them by the unbearable agony of their sufferings, would steal down their cheeks, usually they were the happiest, the brightest, the best behaved, and the most easily amused and kept-in-order children that I ever met—and I have had an enormous lot to do with school-children all my life.

In many respects, though the memory of that little pain-haunted schoolroom comes to me through the long years with something of a heartache, it is nevertheless an oasis in a desert of the arid selfishness that only too often characterizes and disfigures the lives of people into whose hearts no sorrow and no suffering, unfortunately for them, has ever entered. For I have lived long enough, and I may add painfully and sorrowfully enough, to realize that the perfectly easy and the selfishly comfortable life is of all fates the one that is most to be dreaded upon this earth.

And then I would quit the schoolroom and, accompanied by some of those devoted Roman Catholic Sisters of Mercy, who had left their own country and all their friends to come to work in this house of death, whence they never again emerged into the world, I would make my round of the wards in which the dying lepers were confined to the end.

I can see those long-drawn aisles of suffering now as I write. In many a ward the sufferers would sit at their bedsides with a sheet or a blanket enshrouding them for ever from human view—mere lumps of decaying humanity, with not even strength to groan left within them, with nothing but an unspeakable and unspoken longing for the kindly touch of death. And through the door of the ward at one end I would catch a glimpse of the verdure-clad mountain-top, with all its suggestion of health and wind and long views across the mysterious ocean and its memories of the spacious days of great Elizabeth; and through the other door a glittering, sparkling vision of the sea, as it tumbled, a snowy-tipped breaker, upon the silver sands, would send a message to me of life and youth and hope eternal. And then I would raise my eyes to the lintel of the doorway facing the mountains, and I would behold, hanging down from the woodwork, the huge, wonderfully architectured nest of the jack-spaniards, an incredibly terrible form of hornet, a swarm of which was ever humming and hovering about the door, and a sting from one of which meant almost certain death. I never realized why that nest was not destroyed. No one seemed to mind it, though to me it was a veritable nightmare, for a jack-spaniard is to a hornet what a hornet is to a wasp, so you may imagine it was not altogether a desirable companion!

One of the memories of my life comes to me, surrounded with the gloom and mystery of a picture by Rembrandt. It was a typical tropic evening. Over the sea the sun was declining upon the dark purple of the horizon, with a magnificent pageantry of gold and silver and green and crimson, with an architecture of the sky that one can only see in England in the gorgeous cloudlands of Turner or of Gustave Doré, and with domes and temples and pinnacles that outlined themselves in glittering lines of fire upon the azure blue of the heavens; and landwards the rich tropic foliage and the indescribable hues of the forest took upon themselves new intensity in that curious half-light which is so characteristic a feature of the sunset hour in those far climes. And in the little leper cemetery beneath the lonely hills I was conducting the funeral of one of the sufferers set free at last. And with a sudden pang I realized that I was the only non-sufferer there, the only person there who was blessed with health the only one of all that crushed and smitten crowd who knew not the meaning of pain.

The dying rays of the sun fell upon men and women

no less surely dying, and it was with an indescribable sensation that I listened to their voices raised upon the evening hymn, and almost as I listened the purple tropic night descended upon the scene, the stars rushed out, and the fire-flies glittered here and there in the sudden gloom; the pungent odour from a wood fire in the Hindoo village hard by floated down upon the breeze with a wonderful sense and suggestion of cleansing purification, and I took my homeward way with, though I knew it not then, a memory engraved upon my heart that will never fade away this side of the grave.

People at home imagine that a clergyman's life in the West Indies is the life of a missionary; but, of course, it isn't so. The people there are as Roman or as Anglican or as Nonconforming as they are at home, even more so perhaps, for faith is harder in dying in those far lands than it is here in the heart of the world's civilization. And though here and there among the negroes linger traces of the old Voo-doo worship and faint memories of the mystic terrors of the religions and fetishes of the dim and death-haunted forests of Central Africa, and though, scattered sparsely throughout the villages and little towns of Trinidad, the Hindoo temple bells summon the Hindoo faithful to their orisons, yet, as a rule, religious faiths and practices are precisely there what they are here to-day. And the parish system is as much in vogue as it is among the villages clustered at the foot of the Wiltshire Downs. And though the prayers and Litanies are so reminiscent and so colourful of the good old golden days when Charles was king, and though they must sound with faint puzzlement upon the ears of people whose forefathers beat the tom-tom and sacrificed upon the banks of the Niger or in the indescribably dread and horror-stricken forests of the Congo, yet I doubt if they meant either more or less or conveyed either more or less of comfort and consolation to the simple-minded West Indian negro than they meant or convey to the villagers in the neighbourhood of Salisbury Plain or the smart-frocked lady in a church in Mayfair. To all of them alike the magnificent English of the Elizabethan homilists comes with the deadening effect of habit and long use, and scarcely one among them ever stops for one moment to consider the import of the glorious words that trip so easily and so thoughtlessly from their tongues.

> My words fly up,
> My thoughts remain below,
> Words without thoughts
> Never to heaven go.

And that is to a great extent the whole tragedy of the Anglican Church, and very possibly, for aught I know to the contrary, the tragedy of all religions. With only too many it is carried on and perpetuated in sheer unintelligent thoughtlessness. If people but paused a moment to think, and made a habit of so pausing, religion would either go under altogether or, which I infinitely prefer to believe, it would be so absolutely revivified that it would become what it was originally intended to be—the soul and spirit of life and the salt of the material world. It is the lack of vital faith that is responsible for the decay of the Anglican Church.

It was as a young curate in Trinidad that doubt first assailed my soul. I mention this because it was doubt in the end that sealed my career as an Anglican clergyman—the utter inability I experienced to believe implicitly all I was required to teach, and the hopelessness, the misery, the impossibility of remaining in a calling which every tradition of honour and honesty and every vestige of decency and good feeling demanded I should abandon once and for all. But it took me seven years to reach a final decision and to arrive at the moment when, penniless and without a single earthly prospect, I threw off my black coat and white tie and emerged once again in the world a free man. All this, of course, I will describe later ; for the present I will endeavour as best I can to describe the actual working life as well as the mental condition of a man into whose heart and mind was gradually creeping a doubt as to the possibility, let alone the probability, or the truthfulness or otherwise of the dogmas and doctrines he was required to teach, with behind him that very infallibility at which even the Anglican clergy jeer when they denounce it as it thunders out its decrees from the papal chair of Rome.

In a way, so far as my ecclesiastical education was concerned, I had never had a chance. The whole scientific basis of religion is spirituality. For without spirituality religion simply cannot exist. Now, spirituality is the one thing which is rarely even hinted at by your spiritual pastors and masters when you are preparing for ordination. It is quite understandable why it is so, though scarcely perhaps why it should be so. With the Dissenting ministry I believe it is very different. From the first they are encouraged to liberate their whole souls upon matters spiritual; they come, for the most part, of a class which does not cling to the delicate reserves that are so typical and characteristic of the English upper classes, to whom the soul is a mystery only to be unveiled and glanced at for a moment in the Holy of Holies and then carefully wrapped up and hidden away again. With Dissent it is much more a matter of everyday life and experience No one—always excepting, of course, my own father, but that is beside the question: he was not my tutor or my instructor; I refer now entirely to the system and to those who were appointed to carry it out—no priest or bishop or tutor ever asked me about my soul or even hinted to me that I had one; they never pointed out to me the mystery or the solemnity or the earnestness or the reality of the Ordination Service. I was left to worry it all out for myself—and I didn't! And from my own very intimate experience of the Anglican clergy, I should say that at least half of them take upon them their vows and their Orders as carelessly and thoughtlessly as I did.

Now, honestly, though I don't like them as a rule, and though socially they are not often quite all they might reasonably be desired and expected to be, yet from certain points of view, and notably the spiritual point of view, the Dissenting minister is far better prepared and suited for his ministry than the Anglican. And yet somehow or another the Anglican Church has time and again proved itself to be one of the most formative influences that have ever been evolved in the long history of humanity. I can scarcely imagine a system better calculated to influence and educate and refine a nation than the Church of Andrewes, Laud, George Herbert, Charles Kingsley, Frederick Denison Maurice, and—yes, the present Bishop of London. Even those very reticences and delicate reserves touching the spiritual sources and wellsprings of its whole life and functions, even those apparent defects, all go to the formation of a lofty type of national and individual character. The very Catechism which irritates the unthoughtful and unthinking person of the modern day, with neither grace nor breeding nor tradition behind him, and which I frankly confess is responsible for much of that long-descended snobbishness which enters almost unconsciously into the heart and life and the innermost being of every single man and woman born and brought up upon English soil, even that very Catechism inculcates and is responsible for a type of character which you will find nowhere else on earth, and which has resulted in an England than which no country on earth is nobler or more deservedly blessed.

Therefore it will readily be understood that I am not presuming to gird at the Church of my fathers and at the altars of which, ever since it was re-founded and re-established as the National Church, three or four hundred years ago—and I pray forgiveness of my High Anglican friends who would fain make it coeval with Rome herself—my ancestors have served as priests, I only venture to point out and explain and perchance excuse myself for having at length discovered that to preach its doctrines and its dogmas in their entirety in these modern days became to me an absolute spiritual impossibility.

Splendid as Anglicanism undoubtedly is, and endowed with many of those essential qualities of mind and spirit which go to the formation of the highest type of character, yet it is curiously unconvincing as a distinctly spiritual force, partly perhaps because it is so pre-eminently an outcome of compromise. It is a Church without a saint or without a martyr, so far as I know, of its own, and that lacks the saving grace of fanaticism. Some one pronounced its fate and its distinctive characteristic when he declared that it was the only Church for a gentleman, and that, which I think was the dictum of Sydney Smith, absolutely describes it and absolutely damns it. Half the secret of that failure to rise to the present hideous occasion of tragedy and disaster, of which failure we hear so much to-day, is due, I think, to the fact that with a large number of the clergy faith in the old dogmas is stone cold. A great many of these men ought not to be in the Church at all. Both they and the Church would be the happier and the better for their quittance of an office which has become to them, as it became to me thirty years ago, absolutely unendurable. I doubt if the ordinary laity has any conception of the extent to which unbelief has invaded the hearts and minds and souls of a large proportion of the Anglican clergy—and that, too, in the very highest ranks.

Some years ago my friend the Rev. Forbes Phillips, the Vicar of Gorleston, who had dramatized Mr. Guy Thorne's "When It Was Dark," declared in an interview to the *Daily Express* that, though he had dramatized the book, he was by no manner of means in sympathy with the author of the book; "and for this reason," said he: "I don't for one moment believe that all those hideous tragedies that Mr. Thorne describes, as the inevitable outcome of a supposed discovery of the body of our Lord in the tomb, would have resulted. I don't think any tragedy at all would overtake the world, for the simple reason that I don't believe the physical body of our Lord ever rose from the grave at all. I honestly believe that if we could discover that tomb and excavate it we should find the dim remains of the Saviour of the world still there. And this belief doesn't cause me the least unhappiness, nor does it tend to weaken my faith in the slightest degree ; rather it tends to deepen my assurance of the spiritual resurrection of Jesus Christ. To me it is reducing the spiritual splendour and beauty of the Resurrection to a base materialism to assert that Christ rose with his body unchanged. The whole value and beauty and efficacy of that miracle of the Resurrection lies in its intense spirituality."

Well, naturally, this interview created a great sensation both in the religious world and in the outside world. Mr. R. J. Campbell preached on it at the City Temple, and one of the great London dailies demanded Mr. Phillips' expulsion from the Church, and the bishops foamed at the mouth. Indeed, the word went round that Archbishop Temple had determined on calling a meeting of the episcopate with a view to a kind of Anglican banning by bell and book and candle of the so greatly daring Vicar of Gorleston.

Somehow or another the whole episode crumbled away in silence, and we heard no more about it at all. One day, a year or two afterwards, Mr. Phillips told me that he went to his diocesan—Bishop Sheepshanks of Norwich—and asked him why he had not been summoned before the episcopate

"My dear Mr. Phillips," replied the good old man, a saint if ever there was one on earth, "I grieve to tell you that when it came to the point half the bishops on the bench declared that they held the same views about the Resurrection that you had declared you held."

I have alluded to my growing lack of faith. This does not necessarily refer to the main doctrines of the Christian faith so much as to my utter inability to give credence to the rigid Anglican interpretations of the Christian rule of life, which frequently, to my mind, result in the manufacture of sins which are no sins at all in the sight of God. For instance, I got into great trouble once, years after I had left Trinidad, because I dared to remarry in a church an unfortunate lady who had been forced to divorce a cruel, unfaithful, and drunken husband.

"But what was I to do?" I said to my vicar. "The

poor woman was no more to blame than you are for her unfortunate position."

"On the contrary, Mr. Blathwayt," was his perfectly sincere and honest reply—"on the contrary, it was so wicked of her to divorce her husband that I would not hesitate to refuse to admit her to the Sacrament."

"Well," I replied, "I would gladly marry even the guilty party in divorce, let alone the innocent."

"It is horrible to hear you say so," answered the vicar; "for in my opinion such people are too wicked even to argue with."

And nothing could move him from this attitude, which appeared to me to be absolutely devoid of reason, common sense, charity, and Christianity. And yet what a splendid man he was! An ultra-High Churchman, and, like most of his party, self-sacrificing and devoted to the last degree. But his views on these matters appeared to me to be absolutely contrary to the whole teaching of the Master. It was a quenching of smoking flax which Christ would not have quenched, a breaking of a bruised reed which He would not have broken, an adding to the already lengthy list of human sins and frailties another item which was not a sin at all. It is the assumptions of Catholicism in these particulars which so deter men like myself from what in many respects is a supreme and a superb faith. And it is curious that it is just the most devoted section of the Church which is the most active in the promulgation of these, what I cannot help calling pernicious, doctrines. For I don't think it can be reasonably denied that the High Anglicans, as a rule, have done more to commend their Church to the general populace, especially amongst the very poor, than any other section of the Christian community—that is, in England, of course.

But I think honestly that the one man who shook my faith most of all was Bishop Forbes, of Brechin, in his book on the Thirty-nine Articles which I was given to read up for my Priest's Orders later on in my clerical career. Now, I can perfectly understand the simple, straightforward doctrine of transubstantiation which is boldly, and to a certain extent logically, put forward by the Roman Catholics ; and I can appreciate and sympathize with the finely spiritual theory of Zwinglius and the Genevan Reformers generally, who, denying the sacramental efficacy of the Last Supper, affirm that it is merely a very solemn and a very sacred memorial feast, a ceremony which I believe Arnold of Rugby maintained could be administered by every father of a family at the conclusion of the evening meal ; but the subtle, involved evasions and illusions and delusions and intricacies of Bishop Forbes's theories were absolutely as beyond and above my understanding and comprehension as they were opposed to all reason and common sense, as I understand the terms, and to the simple, ordinary teachings of Jesus Christ.

Bishop Forbes deliberately disbelieved and rejected the doctrine of transubstantiation and the alleged Lutheran doctrine of consubstantiation, in place of either of which perfectly understandable doctrines he substituted theories and dogmas of his own which I confess were hopelessly beyond my understanding and comprehension when I was required to read them up for my priest's examination. I must be pardoned for dealing with very sacred matters and details of this kind in a book which is not intentionally either theological or controversial. But I wish to make my standpoint and the reason of my quittance of the Church perfectly clear. It was not a case of a young man setting up his own rash and ill-considered opinions in opposition to those of his seniors and his infinitely spiritual superiors ; it simply was that, whether these dogmas were true or false, they were such as it was absolutely impossible for me to subscribe to in their entirety. And the Bishop himself would have been the very last man to have required me to do so. Nor, indeed, did any so require me. I had quite sufficient knowledge of theology, and discrimination enough, to realize the wonderful scholarship, the extraordinary patristic learning of the Bishop, as well as I possessed sufficient delicacy of feeling to appreciate and warmly to admire and envy the rare refinement and the deep spirituality which characterized every line of his remarkable work on the Thirty-nine Articles; but the more I read and studied it the more completely did I realize the hopelessness of honest agreement and conformity on my part. I felt that I could not honestly lay my hand upon this book and declare that I subscribed to its theses and its doctrines with my whole heart and soul. As a sudden flash of lightning it displayed to me, vividly and beyond all hope of evading or shirking the issue, how far removed from what it ought to have been was my attitude of—I will not use so harsh a word as "infidelity," or even "unbelief," but I will say, non-acceptance of doctrines to which I could not subscribe in any sense or form. And I believe I was right, though a good many of my friends at the time considered that I was overstraining the whole position. But with heart, head, and conscience alike urging me to abandon an attitude and a position which absolutely crippled all one's efforts for good, and which went far towards nullifying all one's feeble attempts to instruct others, I felt I had no option but to surrender my Orders and start life afresh—in short, it was my bounden duty to my conscience and my Chuch.

As I say, I am convinced that Bishop Forbes himself would have been one of the first to have commended my action. This I was told by his immediate successor, Bishop Jermyn. Many years previously—about twenty—Bishop Forbes wrote to Mr. Gladstone: "The present condition of Anglicanism is not only essentially provisional, but eminently perilous. The two issues now are rationalism or catholicism. The Anglican bishops, unfortunately, know so little of precise theology that one cannot tell what they may do." No one penning such words as these but would be compelled to acknowledge that resignation in such a case as mine was the only possible course of action for a man with any decency of feeling or rectitude of character in him whatever.

The truth of the matter, to be quite frank, was that I possessed no particular gift of faith, no particle of real spirituality, which is the whole essence and which is, if I may so describe it, the only possible and scientific basis of the religious life ; and, though always possessed naturally of the spirit of reverence, and that to a marked degree, I had no real aptitude for religion whatever, and I never have had. And that I suspect is the case with hundreds, possibly thousands, of the clergy to-day, who are otherwise thoroughly good fellows. Well, my contention would be that such men ought, in fairness to themselves and to their Church, to abandon a profession for which they are not fitted in certain essential respects.

I remember Dr. Boyd Carpenter once, when I was staying with him in Ripon, told me that one of his vicars confessed quite frankly that he never dreamed of reading his Bible except on Sundays at the lectern. Well, that, of course, is a hopeless condition of affairs. And it is quite remarkable how very few of the young curates of to-day know anything, even by name, of the great classics of the English religious literature—Bunyan, or the Elizabethan homilists, Milton, Baxter, or even the great modern divines, such as Charles Gore or Canon Illingworth, Newman, F. W. Robertson, and many others, all of whom are sealed fountains to them. And, of course, as to literature, outside their Church, or literature that deals with science, modern thought generally and the like, poetry and biography, they appear curiously indifferent even to its very existence. It is impossible for them to attempt to lead people with whom they cannot even hope to keep abreast in the ordinary avenues and byways of modern thought.

Well, this has been a tremendous digression which really does not belong to this part of the book at all. But somehow or another it has forced itself in here, and as the book appears to be writing itself, I haven't much choice in the matter.

My life in Trinidad was extraordinarily interesting quite apart from my work. The whole surroundings were so exceptional. I lived with the Bishop, which in itself was an education, for he was so delightfully well-read a man and so fine a scholar, with such delicate perceptions of life, that one's vision was constantly being not only widened and deepened, but also illuminated, lit up at times as a landscape is for a moment startlingly lit up and elucidated by a flash of lightning. An Anglican bishop, as a rule, takes a lot of knowing, whether you regard him, as some do, as a blot on the landscape, or, as the ladies in the suburbs invariably regard him, an ornament to any society.

But Bishop Rawle was a splendid character, and in common with that fine scholarship which most of our bishops possess, or certainly did possess thirty years ago, he was distinguished also by a readiness of wit and a sense of humour which I am bound to acknowledge is one of the redeeming features in the episcopal make-up.

As a class they are men whom it is almost impossible to surpass in any other class of the community. I rank them with our judges and our headmasters. They are men of whom not only the Church but the whole country may well be proud; they are exceptionally interesting—far more so than the top men in almost any other profession you may like to mention.

At the same time, much as I admired the Bishop and interested and fascinated even as I was by his pungent and outstanding personality, I used to be glad to get away now and again into society which didn't keep me always so terribly on the *qui vive*. No one who hasn't tried it can even begin to imagine how difficult it is to be always up to concert pitch with an Anglican bishop. They take a lot of living up to! Maimie and the circus were far less exhausting, even the tiger and the crocodile. By the by, how Bishop Rawle laughed when I told him of that circus! He and I happened to run up against a huge python in the High Woods one day, and I said, "Oh yes, that reminds me——" And then I stopped dead short, suddenly remembering to whom I was talking. However, he had the whole tale out of me, wheels and all, in less than no time, and I thought he would never stop "laffin'."

Well, as I say, I used to get away from the episcopal *ménage*—I was nearly writing "menagerie"!—and sometimes I would wander down to the quayside and go and have lunch on board his ship with some wandering skipper—and what interesting men they were! and the crew, burnt nearly black by the suns of many oceans, and with great gold earrings glittering against their glistening black locks—and I would sit on deck under the awning and watch the sun dropping down behind the mountains of Venezuela, and I would sit fascinated by the spectacle of the long line of pelicans flying home low down upon the water and exquisitely etched against the crimson sunset, and I would lazily lie and listen to the water lapping against the vessel's prow—a perfect idyll of the tropics. And on another occasion I remember I joined a small party of the officers at the barracks, and we took a launch and steamed out to a little desert island, or almost desert, whereon an old soldier, who had fought in India and at the Crimea, entertained us, and gave us of all dishes that you can think of, whalesteak! And that reminds me that years afterwards I was one of a small luncheon-party of very interesting people—for the most part: Sir H. M. and Lady Stanley, one of the most entirely charming, as well as one of the handsomest, women I ever met; Mons. Cambon, the French Ambassador; the Marquis de Soveral; and Sir Henry Thompson, the famous physician, and looking exactly like his portrait which hangs in the old English room at the National Gallery. The conversation turned upon rare dishes, and I can remember how much Mons. de Soveral amused us all by his vivid description, accentuated by the piercing gaze of his black eyes, of an old historic Portuguese dish. And then Sir Henry Stanley, with that quiet, gentle voice of his, recalled a quaint bird he had once eaten in Africa; and Sir Henry Thompson declared he believed he had eaten everything it was possible for a human being to eat. But I stumped him with the whalesteak I had eaten years before on the little lonely island of Monos.

And sometimes, of course, I would go up-country

and stay with a sugar-planter, and that was always interesting. What I enjoyed in Trinidad was its perpetual sense of the cosmopolitan. There is but little that is provincial in the islands. Surrounded by the wide world, as it were, and the resort of the world to a great extent, you are never bored with a sense and with the almost horror of the provincial as you are here in England. Trinidadians, to begin with, are an amalgam of English, French, Spanish, Portuguese, Danish, negro, and half-caste, to say nothing of the vast number of Hindoo and Chinese coolies who have resided in the island for several generations. And the ships come in from the great deep and to the great deep they return; and there is a sense of life and movement and perpetual change and a romance and a charm which are quite indescribable, but absolutely understandable to all those who have ever lived in the tropics.

You are much nearer death, but you live your life more abundantly than it is ever possible to live it in more temperate climates. And in the end the climate did for me. I found it impossible to keep up with the work and keep in health at the same time, and so after a while, with great regret, I resigned my position, bade my farewells, and sailed for England once again.

THE DESK IN THE LIMEHOUSE WINDOW WHERE CHARLES DICKENS MADE HIS RIVER-SIDE NOTES FOR "OUR MUTUAL FRIEND."

CHAPTER V

A GLIMPSE INTO A CURATE'S LIFE AND MIND (*continued*)

On my arrival in England from the West Indies, still in my middle twenties, I obtained a curacy in the Southern Counties, and here, for the first time in my life, I experienced in its entirety the whole inner meaning of the phrase "truly rural," as it is termed; and I learned something of the loneliness of the Anglican cleric's existence, a loneliness which I should appreciate far more to-day than, as a very young man, I did then, and a loneliness which is responsible in part for many an unknown and unsuspected tragedy. I learned also, very gradually, and as is the way with young people, without knowing or realizing that I was learning, something of the influence, and the reasons for and the explanation of that influence, that is exercised over the English people, through the succeeding generations, by their national Church. There is nothing else quite like it in the history of humanity, though I suppose the quiet, all-pervasive, and all-pervading influence of the French abbé or curé is of a somewhat similar nature. Some one has said, and with a certain amount of truth, that if the Church of England has done nothing else, she has at least placed a gentleman and a scholar in every parish in the land. This is to take a too roseate view of the Anglican Church to-day, I fear, for breeding and scholarship are no longer the *sine quâ non* they once were; but, roughly speaking, the saying contains a pretty general truth. Frequently enough, for miles round, in a widespread country district the parson is the only person with any education or pretensions to refinement whatever, and therefore and naturally he must exercise the influence that mind always exercises over matter. Trollope, who knew the English country parson better than most, has left us some fine pictures of the mid-Victorian cleric, in whose vicarage or rectory were often to be found the only evidences of literary or artistic civilization for miles round a wide-spreading district.

Five-and-thirty years ago country life in England was very much what it must have been in the days of the Stuarts, and I don't think that the mental vision or aspirations either of farmer or of labourer differed in any essential respects from what they were in those far-off picturesque days. I myself have seen and talked with old women who have dragged through life under suspicion of being witches, and who have actually undergone torture for it; and I remember once, in preaching a sermon on the leprosy of Naaman and referring to my own experiences a year or two previously in the West Indies, one Wiltshire farmer was heard to observe to another as they wended their way through the church porch: "'Tis disgraceful o' thikky young feller talkin' about them lepers; it's all popery, that's what un is!"

People sometimes find fault with the country parson for his lack of vision, of imagination, of intellect, but he is better without them almost amid such surroundings than with them. A man cursed with imagination in the English country lanes and by the hedgeside were almost better dead, so like a leaden weight upon the soul presses down the dead unintellectuality, the hopeless animal materialism, and the unutterable lack of imagination of the country joskin. There is nothing so hopelessly impenetrable in the world, though now and again one is confronted unexpectedly by a vision of elemental nature and passions which are quite startling and terrifying in the glimpse they give you of the fires burning unsuspected and unimagined beneath.

Hall Caine and Eden Phillpotts lift the lid from off the rural pots and kettles sometimes. The life of a village, far more than that of London or Liverpool, can sometimes reveal unimagined spectacles of revolting cruelties, the meannesses that belong to, and are the outcome of, souls that are but little removed from those of a world of apes; and to see naked humanity at its dead worst thirty years ago or so you had but to go and live in an English village. And this in any part of England. Ask James Blyth, the author of those remarkable stories of the Norfolk and Suffolk peasantry, if I am not right; talk to Hall Caine or Eden Phillpotts, and you will almost certainly find that they will tell you exactly the same. And, of course, in Wales conditions are infinitely worse, as witness the terrible stories of "Caradoc," many of which, I know from my own experience, are absolutely photographic statements of well-known facts.

But it would be folly, and worse than folly, to deny that there is also an immense and an indefinable charm in the rural life of England, and the country parson's lot is often one to be envied. It is a curious life they lead, many of them; it is existence, vegetation, rather than life; there is little movement in it, no change; but, like a stagnant pool, it is frequently picturesque and alluring by its very quiescence. I remember one dear old clergyman who had lived beneath those Wiltshire Downs without ever sleeping out of his vicarage one single night for hard upon sixty solid years! Now, you've only got to think what that means, and of the kind of mind and life that such an existence implies. He had actually left Oxford in the twenties of the last century, and there in that parish he had lived, first as curate, then as vicar, for sixty years without moving out of the parish for one single night. When he first settled down there railway trains were not so much as thought of; Waterloo had been fought and won only some eight years previously; and during his life in that lonely country district George IV and William IV had reigned and died and Victoria had succeeded them, and the Crimea had been stormed by our cannon, and the Civil War of America had finally settled the Slave Question, and the great Franco-German War had established Bismarck as the foremost man in the Councils of Europe, and half a hundred other happenings had thrilled the civilized world, and he knew practically nothing of them whatever. He only read the county paper once a week, and once a week he perused the pages of the *Guardian*, without, I fancy, ever comprehending or being seriously interested in what he read. He used to leave me breathless now and again with delighted astonishment, or black in the face with ill-suppressed giggles, by declaiming against such ridiculous, new-fangled notions as railway locomotives and telegraph-wire messages and penny postage, which last, he declared, was more bother than it was worth. Sometimes he forgot all about the railway. Once I said to him—

"I've been up to London since I saw you, Mr. Welford."

"Lord bless my soul!" said he. "You must have found it very heavy going, didn't you, with all this wet and mud about?"

All this in the early eighties, when, of course, railway travelling was precisely as it is to-day, neither better nor worse.

Of course, I don't pretend for a moment that this dear old man was typical even then of the country clergy; still, he was not so exceptional as to be in any way singular. I have known elderly vicars, grey-haired and worn, looking forward to the annual choir treat with the eagerness and simple-hearted pleasure of a boy; for, as a matter of fact, with many of them it was frequently the only outing they were able to afford themselves year in, year out. To me such pleasure, such excitement, over so trivial an event was fraught with unutterable pathos; it told such a tale of death in life. And yet, in a way, it was not, perhaps, wholly unenviable.

The marvel to me is that the country clergy are what they are, considering the tragedy of loneliness and poverty, material and spiritual, physical and mental, that is so often their unhappy lot. But then again, of course, and quite as frequently, the rural rectory is the centre of culture, refinement, scholarship, and quiet social charm, which you could not rival anywhere else on earth.

Some of the most delightful men and women I have ever known, or that I could hope or wish to meet, have been country vicars and their wives and daughters.

Here in these delightful old rectory gardens you will see English life at its purest and best; and in these picturesque, red-roofed, Tudor-chimneyed old rectories you will find the indefinable charm of existence which you associate with George Herbert in his garden at Bemerton, hard by Salisbury Close, or with John Inglesant in the closing days of his eventful life beneath the grey old Norman towers of Worcester Cathedral. And what can be more reminiscent or more suggestive and eloquent of the long story of the English race and nation than to pass with one of these country rectors from the tennis or the croquet match upon his wide-spreading lawn to the hushed and immemorial quietude of the village church, wherein the fathers of the hamlet have worshipped for almost unnumbered generations, and wherein the Knight Crusader's tomb, or the memorial of the Elizabethan statesman, with the stiff crimped and starched ruff round his neck, and with his wife and family dutifully kneeling in a row behind him, testify to the enduringness and the unchanging character of the life and history of our English countryside? And you meditate upon the stateliness of the Anglican prayers and the sonorous splendour of the Bible language as it has echoed and re-echoed through those long-drawn aisles for centuries before you were born or thought of, and you begin, however thoughtless and unimaginative you may be, to realize something of what the Church of England is, and what it means to, and what it has accomplished for, and the nature of its mission to, the English nation first and then, widespread over the whole world, to the British Empire at large.

Of course, I never realized all this when I was a curate; I was young and thoughtless, and I didn't think much about anything, and I knew even less. It is only in after-years that the meaning and intention of any great phase of national life really penetrate one's mind and soul. At the time, quite candidly speaking, I suppose the life rather bored me, stifled me with its utter uneventfulness and its extraordinary lack of promise or hope for the future. And, mind you, what I have been describing as my own experience of thirty years ago is precisely what is taking place to-day. There is no change whatever in the conditions or circumstances of the country parson's life, and but curiously little in country life generally. I know this as a fact, because I am constantly staying with squires and clerics all over the country. And, despite motor-cars, telephones, and cinematographs, Shakespeare's and George Herbert's England still lives for those who have the seeing eye and the understanding heart.

You will perhaps wonder why I "spread myself" so much—to use an inelegant but expressive phrase—upon England and her national Church. Well, it is but natural: I had had so much to do with it, and I am still so intimately connected with the Church, and I have seen it in so many phases and avatars—if I may use the phrase—all over the world, that I have come at long last to realize that, together with the Roman Church and the British Empire, it is one of the greatest political facts—using the word "political" in its widest and most comprehensive sense—that the world has ever produced.

The Church with its temples, broadcast o'er the Empire, preserves and incorporates and tells the story of our race as nothing else can ever do. It is England in miniature and at its most inspired moments. I have sat in the church at Delhi, with its records of the tragedy of the Mutiny tabulated upon the walls; and I have read something of the discovery of the "vext Bermoothes" by Sir George Somers in Shakespeare's day over the altar of St. George's Church, Bermuda; and I have stood beneath the memorial tablets to the Servants of the Honourable East India Company in Cape Town Cathedral. I have listened to the intoning of the Prayer for the High Court of Parliament in Ottawa and in Melbourne, and I have watched the Anglican priest going hither and thither upon his mission in the streets of Canton and Tokyo, and I have realized that a Church which is so regally Imperial as is the Church of England must possess within itself qualities of supreme excellence, with which, perhaps, the unthinking and the careless are by no means prepared to credit it. But I think that the spirit and meaning of the Church are best known and appreciated and expressed by the little grey, Norman-towered, ivy-clad buildings which have made themselves so absolutely part of the English landscape that without them England could scarcely be said to exist. There is no more binding link between the Motherland and her daughters overseas than that which is afforded by the Anglican Church, and the sonorous English of Elizabeth's spacious days finds its echo in many a little tabernacle in the West Indian forest, or hidden away in the Australian bush, or upon the lonely South African veld.

It is sometimes the one and only thing that keeps the homesick emigrant upon the Canadian prairie in touch with all he held dearest in the far-away Wiltshire village or Yorkshire moor. And this lengthy screed in 1916 is the outcome of my acceptance of a curacy in Wiltshire away back in 1880. And of my work in that curacy I really have naught to tell, which of itself is eloquent. It was an absolutely uneventful life, and yet probably full of formative influences of which I knew and recked nothing at the time.

One had pleasures and distractions, scanty enough at the time, but the memory of which, through the long years, recurs with a curious, thrilling pungency. I recall the lovely golden September days when one would start out in the early misty morning, when the hedges, glittering with the dew-spangled spiders' webs, gave promise of a brilliant day, and the partridges rose with a startling whirr from the stubble just over the hedge ; or one went rabbiting with the dogs, and one realized how difficult and how baffling the scurry of even a rabbit could be until one had got one's hand well in, though not near so baffling as the towering in the air and the flight, almost straight at one, of a wild old cock pheasant. And a breeze would rise later in the day and chase the mist away, and great white clouds would come sailing over the Downs, casting purple shadows over the land, which would chase one another in never-ending ripples, like the waves upon the sea. And one would pause a moment to drink in the wonderful and unmatchable beauty of the English scene, with the grey tower of an old Norman church just peeping out from the green trees ; and the red and grey and green lichen of an old, old wall, encompassing some quaint, old-fashioned Elizabethan garden would tell you a story of quiet romance and of the charm of the Old Country such as you had never dreamed or realized before. Even the gun upon your shoulder and the fox-terrier at your heel speak of a life such as you will not find lived to such perfection as it is in the charming countryside of old-world England, which is one reason why I love all those delightful, old-fashioned coloured sporting prints painted in the thirties and forties of the last century, and which you see now and again, with wonderful coaching and hunting scenes in the Midlands, in many an old print-shop in the West End. All these things speak of England at its very best—of an England which is, I fear, fast passing away, and of which probably the old-fashioned country clergyman, gentleman and sportsman *au bout des ongles*, knows more, and which he loves more devoutly, and of which he is more typical and reminiscent and actually representative, than any one else on earth.

Well, that kind of thing ameliorates the otherwise rather dull life of the country curate to an extent that the mere townsman would find it impossible to understand. Or there would be a morning's fishing on the deep, swift-moving stream at the bottom of the Vicarage garden : the dull, warm morning, with the clouds low down in the sky, and the fish jumping for all they were worth, and the heavy scent of roses is in the air, and the grass is damp beneath your feet. Charles Kingsley has told it all so delightfully that I fear to tread where he has gone before me with such knowledge and such discrimination and such wonderful love and sympathy and appreciation. All these things made a country curacy more than endurable to me.

Curiously different was my next curacy, which was in

the extreme east of London. Here one saw life, and saw it abundantly, and, I may add in passing, sometimes rather disgustingly, for what an East End curate does not know or has not experienced of the shady side of life, and the miserable and the utterly hopeless and degraded, is not worth knowing. And he who has never worked among the London poor doesn't know and cannot imagine of what patience and self-sacrifice and unbelievable splendour of character our poor and much-abused humanity is capable.

I don't think that, in their way, there are more charming poor people in England than you meet in East London. They were and are immeasurably preferable to the country poor. And they are so full of humour !—the old women most of all. And I am an authority on old women—or, rather, I was.

Being junior curate in this gigantic parish of twenty thousand souls, I was allotted to the old women's almshouses, in addition to which most of the mothers' meetings fell to my lot—an odious duty, concerning which decency and a regard for my women readers' blushes forbid my entering upon unsavoury and unappetizing details. Curates ought to be "shooed" out of mothers' meetings—not that I can ever imagine any curate in his seven senses ever intruding upon one of his own initiative. But vicars' wives, and sometimes, I grieve to add, their daughters, insist upon the attendance of the unfortunate curate ; and I attended them, until at last one tragic but wholly indescribable incident solved the problem of my attendance for ever. Wild horses, nor even wilder vicaresses, would not drag me into one to-day.

The old women at the almshouses were the joy of my life. One of them was ninety-five years of age, exactly seventy years my senior, and she ruled the clergy, and especially myself, with a rod of iron. She would send for me on any or no pretext, at any hour of the day or night, never mind what the weather might be. One snowy midnight I received an urgent summons to her bedside, and I hastened thither, fully expecting she might be dead by the time I reached her. Nothing of the kind.

"A nice time you've been, Mr. Blackpool"—they never could manage my name, and never seriously tried to, anything with a B and two syllables served their purpose—that was her greeting. "I want yer to wind that there eight-day clock o' mine."

"What, at one in the morning!" I indignantly cried. "Drag me out of bed into the snow to wind up your confounded old clock! Really it's too bad of you, Mrs. Johnson," I went on, though inwardly I was consumed with joyous laughter at her supreme impertinence. I revelled in it.

"Nice langwidge for a parson!" she ejaculated, raising her eyes to the heavens with irritating piety. "Yes, Mr. Brassplate, wind up my clock: them's my very words. The vicar says 'isself the very last time he was 'ere you was to do anything I required. Them's his orders, and well you knows it, Mr. Blackpool! So there's no good swearin' about it, wich I don't 'old with parsons usin' such disgustin' langwidge in my 'ouse."

Of course, one wasn't not only one little bit angry with the dear old soul, but as a matter of fact, I absolutely enjoyed her violent denunciations of me. She was one of the many bright spots of humour in my East End life, and she really liked me at the bottom of her heart. As she very truly used to say—

"I allus tells a servant-gal wot I thinks of her, straight and done with it, and I allus tells a curick the same; then you know where you are!"

Another old lady, feeling her end drawing near, stipulated that her own pet curate, Mr. Dunstan, was to bury her.

"I want to go alongside o' my old man," she whimpered, "and I know that there Blackpool—wich Black 'e is by name and black 'e is by nature!" she viciously added—"'e'll go and put me alongside o' some other ooman's 'usband, just out o' spite like!"

"Well, Mrs. Smith, what cheer with you to-day?" I said to another old lady one day.

"Cheer!" she bitterly replied. "'Ark at 'im! A lot o' cheer about me, I reckon, with my poor old limbs as full of rheumatiz as that winder's full of 'oles"—which indeed it was and a hint to me to get it mended, which I did. "I wish you young curicks would think a little more and talk a little less, and then—— Oh, thank ye kindly, Mr. Blackpool, wich I says to old Mrs. Brown—wich 'er tongue goes nineteen to the dozen, wich I says to 'er only this morning, I says, 'That there Blackpool's got a kind 'eart if 'e ain't got anything else,' and she says, 'Kind!' she says, 'wich e's never given me cause to say e's kind. Never had but one 'orspital ticket out o' the man all the time e's been 'ere'; wich I allus says, sir, there's no pleasin' some folks, try as you may."

The poor are at times curiously callous. I well remember once saying good-bye to a dying man. He was as conscious as I am now at the present moment. As I let go of his hand his old wife said quite casually—

"What day'll suit you for the funeral, sir?"

"Ain't she in a 'urry, sir!" whispered the poor fellow, with a smile.

But an East End curate's life isn't made up of old women only; it's a position of infinite variety, and there is no known use to which you may not put a curate—if he submits to it. I've known long-suffering, greatly forbearing men in my time to be used as nursemaids for the vicar's youngest children. I remember once an exact case in point with regard to myself. There was a big meeting being held at the Vicarage, at which the whole parish—the responsible part of it, that is—was gathered together in solemn conclave regarding a great bazaar we were going to hold in the Vicarage gardens; churchwardens, curates, district visitors, teachers—we were all there.

"Mr. Blathwayt," said my vicar, a tall, dignified, singularly handsome man, whom everybody, including his curates, loved and honoured, "what shall we give you to do?"

"Oh, Mr. Blathwayt must look after Peggy," struck in the vicar's wife, who was really a very charming woman and who knew well what friends little Peggy and I really were.

"My dear," said the vicar very crushingly, "I engaged Mr. Blathwayt as my curate, not as your nursemaid."

Curates have been used to do the Vicarage marketing. One curate I knew of used to have to go and get pork chops every Saturday morning for the vicar's Sunday dinner. I have known a wealthy squire send a dish of dubious mushrooms down to the curate's lodgings. If he survived the meal, well and good; if not—well, the squire and his relations *did*! You can use the curate to cut the bread and butter at a school feast. He's used for and used *to* everything. Nobody worries about him, nobody heeds him; and yet he's almost invariably the most popular person in the parish. I've never known a curate shirk his job, even at its most dangerous, and it can be as deadly almost as Ypres or Verdun.

I remember once there was a terrible epidemic of smallpox in a huge district, and the senior curate and I had been all day long going in and out of the stricken houses. In one house, indeed, we had been obliged to put a dead man into his coffin, as even the undertaker's men shirked the job. His head actually came off as we laid him to rest, he was so appallingly rotten. Well, we were walking back to our "diggings," feeling rather sick at what we had seen and very done up, when we came across a sort of Socialist meeting, with a man ranting away in the centre. As he caught sight of us he yelled out—

"Look at them two b—— parsons! Idle, lazy, good-for-nothings I calls 'em, livin' on the likes o' you and me!"

My friend pushed his way through, jumped up on to the little platform or whatever it was, flung the man on his back as easily as I would throw a doll on the floor, placed his foot on his stomach, "just to keep him quiet a bit while I tell you a few home truths," he said, and then he addressed the crowd.

"'Two lazy, idle, good-for-nothing b—— parsons,' eh?" said he. "That's what our friend calls us, is it? Keep still, you brute!" he cried as the man tried to get up. "Keep still until I've finished, or I'll send you home so that your own mother won't know you! Now look here," he went on, boiling with rage and overwrought with our terrible day's experiences, "I am getting sick of the manner in which you cowardly, scoundrelly Socialists are always running down men a thousand times as good as any of you could ever be! Yes, I mean it!" he vociferated—"a thousand times as good! My friend and I started work at five o'clock this morning, and we shall finish about eleven if we've any sort of luck. During that time we've visited sixteen smallpox cases, and I should think this fellow under my foot may very possibly make the seventeenth! Now, all I say is this: which one of you is willing to do the same for £2 10s. a week and your own board and lodging to find? Don't all speak at once!"

And then he cleared off with their cheers ringing in his ears.

I always feel indignant when I see the curate mocked at on the stage. The stage curate is almost invariably represented as a mere figure of fun, an unworthy caricature, which by now I should have thought the best-class actor would have been tired of depicting, as tired as he must be of being beaten by him every year at football and cricket. Do you realize that the finest cricket eleven or football fifteen or rowing eight and some of the most accomplished boxers in the kingdom are to be obtained from among the ranks of the despised curates? I suppose that, as a body, there is no class of men that can surpass them in sport and athletics and games generally. And yet the poor dear old stage goes wearily on making game of men whom they really love and admire; for there is a very strong bond of union, if not indeed of actual affection, between stage and Church, which become more and more united as civilization progresses and men in each profession realize that their mission to humanity is curiously allied in object and intention.

East London is a curiously fascinating part of the world. To the casual passer-by it is a vision of despair; it is a nightmare of horror; it possesses not one redeeming quality. To the thoughtful and the loving worker it is full of endless interest; it reeks with the history of the past; it is saturated with real romance. All the way from Whitechapel to Barking the story of the past is written so that he who runs may read. There is, or rather up to the beginning of this year there was, a doctor, still in the fifties, whose whole life and that of his father's before has been spent in tending to the physical welfare of the East Enders, and Dr. Frank Corner is a household word from St. Paul's Cathedral to Ilford Parish Church. A tall, splendidly built, clean-shaven, handsome, massive-faced and broad-shouldered, genial giant, he divides with Will Crooks the honour—and it is a great honour—of being the best loved, most looked-up-to man in the whole of the East End of London. He and his charmingly dainty little wife kept open house for many years in Poplar, where they would frequently receive some of the most distinguished people of the day; for every one knows Frank Corner, as they knew his fine old father, who more than once refused a knighthood from the Premiers of his day.

Dr. Frank himself is a supremely fine doctor, with a knowledge of his profession and a dexterity in his craft and a delicate intuition in his diagnosis which I have never known surpassed. However, he'll hate all this. I have brought him in because, not only is he a great East London celebrity but because he, better than any one else I know, has East London at his fingers'-tips, and so with him we'll wander round certain districts together, and I'll be bound, at the end of our walk, you'll say you have learned more of East London than you had imagined was possible all your life before.

The whole scenery of East London is so marvellously varied, so wonderfully picturesque, so full of story, if you possess but the seeing eye and the understanding heart and the knowledgable brain. In the district where I was curate for three long, delightful years one would catch a glimpse of the glittering Thames flowing through the low marshlands, with Woolwich on the one side and Barking on the other, and a loneliness and a wildness of scene which would give one the impression of the wolds of Lincolnshire or of Yorkshire, instead of being only ten miles or so from Charing Cross. And upon a summer day the breeze would blow in, almost with the salt freshness of the sea, and I would watch the great sails of a solitary mill near East Ham turning rapidly or slowly and lazily, as the case might be, and I would fancy myself a boy again as I listened to their old-world creaking; for there is nothing so reminiscent of the past of old England as a windmill and its uneasy, groaning, creaking sails. And the grey old Abbey Church tower, whence William the Conqueror dispatched the orders for his coronation at Westminster Abbey, stands in the quiet sunshine, as it has stood for unimagined centuries, and as it may indeed have stood almost as a landmark to the invading Danes; it still stands to-day dominant over the wide-stretching marshlands, a witness to the history of a bygone day.

And then, coming nearer to London proper, one finds oneself in the romantic regions of dockland, and one is haunted with memories of Marryatt and Clark Russell and the historians of London's most eventful days. In the East India Road district you behold those splendid old mansions which were built two hundred years ago by the nabobs who had enriched themselves in the service of "John Company," and you find yourself in the centre of that vast shipping world which once sent out the most splendid merchantmen the world has ever seen—those magnificent clippers, with their white sails towering up to the blue heavens and melting away in the dim horizons which passed them on, one after the other, on their way to China and the farthest East. And you can go into some of these beautiful old houses, and there you will find exquisite fireplaces or gorgeous ceilings or wonderful old stairways, redolent of the days when Charles was king and the man who had been plucky enough to go buccaneering returned rich enough to fit out one of these little palaces for himself and his wife to grow old and to die in. Walter Besant tells you about these houses in his "All Sorts and Conditions of Men." The docks are lonely and deserted now, compared with what they once were, but they have a splendour and a beauty that is incomparably their own; and sometimes as the sun has been sinking in the west and I have caught the sparkle and glitter in the distant towers and roofs of the Crystal Palace, and I have watched a great liner coming in from Melbourne or Bombay, and the lights have begun to glimmer in the dock lamps and the buildings are outlined stark and rigid against the summer blue, I have come to the conclusion that, from the strictly artistic or Whistlerian point of view, East London is one of the most really beautiful places in the world. And then you wander on until you get to the mysterious region of Rotherhithe and Wapping Old Stairs. Here you are in Dickens's land and in a queer, old-fashioned district wherein, Dr. Corner told me, there lived only seventy years ago or so, if as much, a set of people who owned their own little ships, upon which they and all their families perpetually lived and in which they used to wander off to any and every part of the world, never mind how far away it was. One family, whom in later days Dr. Corner himself knew, used to load their ships up with toys which they would take with them and sell at a tremendous advantage to the Falkland Islanders.

"And now," said Corner, "you are in Ship Alley. Look at the overhanging eaves and the narrow causeway. This place was full of pressgang crimps and harlots and the like, all living, and living well, too, on the sailors in from the seas just off a long voyage, men who had not been home for six years and who landed at last with five or six hundred pounds in their pockets, which, poor devils! they would 'blue' in a week or less. And worse than that," continued the doctor, pointing to a rickety old house, "beneath the floor of that house sixteen bodies of full-grown men were discovered in 1870. Why," he went on, "there used to be an old girl here—I knew her well—who would take £70 a night in drinks—champagne chiefly—and take it for weeks and months on end. You have no idea of the money some of the people would make here. There's Swedenborg's old church, and there," he went on, pointing to a desolate little burial-ground, "is where Swedenborg was buried. Here is Ratcliff Highway, where Captain Cuttle used to come and think; and here, as you can see, is the Chinese quarter." A quarter, I may observe, in which you will see at least fifty Chinamen for every Englishman. It is as completely Chinese in that long street as it is Chinese in China Town, in San Francisco. The doctor also pointed out to me the old house in which Captain Kidd spent his last night on earth before his execution in Execution Dock hard by, an ancient building with a lovely staircase dating back to James I's day, which any one may see for himself who chooses to pay a visit to Wellclose Square.

"And now," said Dr. Corner, "I will take you into the house of a very old friend of mine, whose family, the Waters, have certainly lived here ever since the days of Henry VII. The Waters of to-day will give you any amount of memories of Charles Dickens, who used to come and sit in that old bow-window there, hanging over the river, and write about Rogue Riderhood in his 'Our Mutual Friend.' All that part of the novel was done at Mr. Waters's desk in Mr. Waters's house, for Dickens took no end of pains to get all his local colouring perfectly accurate." So we entered the house, climbed the very old-fashioned staircase, and found ourselves in a bright, sunny old room, with a bow-window such as you might get in an old Elizabethan country house in Devonshire, and there sat a hale old fellow, well over seventy, though very young and vigorous in voice and movement, so young that one altogether forgot his increasing years.

"Yes," he said, "Mr. Dickens used to sit in that very chair you are sitting in now, Mr. Blathwayt, at that very desk, and write away for dear life, just lifting his head now and again to ask my father some question about the life on the river or to make a note of something that was taking place on the river, just as you are doing now."

The scene from the window was very animated, as it was in Dickens's day; the sun shone and light clouds floated in the summer sky; a steamer was fussing down the centre channel and great barges slowly moved down in its troublous wake; a few white-winged seagulls, with their shrill screams and their rapid movements here and there, gave a wonderful sense of life and movement to the whole scene.

"Mr. Dickens," continued Mr. Waters after a while, "used to come down to visit the girls and boys in a workhouse here in which he was interested. Now, it so happened that in the yard of that workhouse there was a biggish schooner rigged up, just as you can see at Greenwich Hospital to-day, where an old chap named Pereira used to teach the boys sailing and manning a ship. You see, it was a good size, big enough to hold fifty boys at a time. Well, one day Mr. Dickens—whom Pereira hated because he had called him in some article he had written 'a mahogany-faced, amphibious sea-dog with a glazed hat'—came down to see the boys, and as they were at exercise on board the ship he went on board, too, to watch them. Well, as luck would have it, Pereira stepped off the ship on to the pavement to give some order. Mr. Dickens, who was always fond of his joke, at once yelled out, 'Hi! hi! Man overboard!' and he snatched up a great coil of rope and threw it so hard at Pereira that he knocked him down. Of course, the old chap was furious. He never forgave Mr. Dickens, who, naturally enough, was quite upset at what he had done; but Pereira never forgot it, and his last words to me about Mr. Dickens were, 'I hate the sight of the man.' A good many years after that Mr. Napier Hemy, the artist, came down to make a picture of the river and the scenery of 'Our Mutual Friend,' and he had just said to me, 'Was old Rogue Riderhood a real character?' and I said to him, 'You lift your eyes and look straight in front of you, and you'll see the very man doing exactly what Dickens describes him doing in "Our Mutual Friend."' Mr. Hemy looked up, and there was old 'Nasty Dick,' as we always called him, pulling his boat into the old inn so wonderfully described by Dickens under the name of the 'Six Jolly Fellowship Porters,' and I called out to old Dick, 'Have you got a stiff un?' and sure enough he was towing a dead body he had found, just as Dickens had described him in his book—a body for which he would receive five shillings—and he was pulling in to the inn to get a drink on the strength of that five shillings, the while the poor body lay swishing to and fro in the tide."

Mr. Waters further told me that he had himself been to school with Joe Gargery, the well-known character in "Great Expectations," another of Dickens's most popular works. I feel ashamed to add this, but it is almost necessary in these days when so few of the younger generation know even the most classic of Dickens's books or heroes by name.

What a curious life that was in the East End! The slum I myself was obliged to live in—how horrible it was! I remember my bedroom was right over a very low-class butcher's shop, and each time he hung a half-bullock or took it down from the great hook in the ceiling he would jar the whole room. It was a most uncanny sensation, and outside, day and night, a scene of drunken ribaldry such as no Hogarth scarcely could paint and which would tax a Kipling to describe; with the scent of fried fish floating in upon the hot, foul, fœtid summer night breeze, and the atmosphere sulphurous, not only with oaths and curses of the most lucid and lurid description, but literally and pungently sulphurous with the fumes from the great chemical works down by the river and unspeakably disgusting in addition, with a hundred other unnameable and unimaginable stinks and odours, and factory-girls, swinging down the narrow street, arm-in-arm, pushing every one aside, except, of course, the "curick."

"'Ullo! 'ere's Mr. Blackpool comin'! Give 'im room, gals! 'E's a b—— good sort!"

And they would say it of all the curates, only they knew me best because I lived—I had to—right down amongst them, and as a matter of fact I had a large class of factory girls for reading and geography and the like, and so they knew me well.

CHAPTER VI

A GLIMPSE INTO A CURATE'S LIFE AND MIND (*continued*)

I TRUST I am not giving too trivial a view of the ordinary curate's life; I can only assure my readers it is, at all events, an absolutely truthful one, viewed from the standpoint of a man to whom the humorous side of humanity invariably and insistently presents itself. The other side is always poignantly there, and there is little need to emphasize all its horror and misery. As curate of an East End parish, with twenty thousand of the poorest people in London, as a daily frequenter for nearly a year of the unspeakable slums of a great Scotch manufacturing town, as a chaplain of a leper asylum, as one who has worked much in hospitals all over the world, my readers will readily understand that there are few phases of human sickness and suffering of which I have not had an intimate and very painful experience. But it is unnecessary, especially in such a period of sorrow and tragedy as the present, that I should harrow my readers' feelings with descriptions of what were daily experiences, and which I never shirked for the curious reason that, apart from the dishonour and unmanliness of it, I always had a superstitious feeling that to do so would bring down an avalanche of sorrow upon my own head. And I have already had enough of that—one way and the other. So in this book I will confine myself, as far as possible, to the brighter side of the clerical life, assuring my readers that a curate's life can be very bright, if he chooses to make it so.

Amongst the duties which, as junior curate, fell heavily to my share was one I much disliked and dreaded—I

REV. R. J, CAMPBELL.

mean baptizing babies. St. Paul contending with the beasts at Ephesus can hardly have suffered such anxious miseries as some of his children in the Faith are called upon to endure in the discharge of the clerical offices. I have christened as many as fourteen children at a time—it's an awful job sometimes; struggling with a lusty boy of four years of age, held in your left arm, whilst you are dipping the right hand in the font, is not half so easy as it sounds. One wretched curate I know once let a six-months-old child fall bang into the font. Can I ever forget the appalling splash and the father's face as he hissed out at the deeply abashed cleric: "Butter Fingers! that's wot I calls yer! Butter Fingers!"

Another amusing incident occurred when a proud parent, replying to a curate who had complimented her on the charming behaviour of her little one, said: "Well, you see, sir, it's like this. 'Is father an' me's been practisin' on 'im for the last three weeks with a pail o' water." And then the answer made by an East End godmother to the curate who had asked her the usual question—

"Do you, in the name of this child, renounce the devil and all his works, the pomps and vanities of this wicked world?"

And she gaily replied: "Oh yes, *I recommend them all*"!

Incidents like these are rays of sunshine athwart the gloomy pathway of the cleric who threads his life along the slimy slums and alleys of our great cities.

An East End lady, a towering, bullying virago, presented herself to the vicar one day—

"My name's Jane Brown, and you married me to Peter Simmons a year ago, Vicar."

"Oh yes, Jane; I remember. Well, what is it?"

"Well, Vicar, I thought I'd look in and tell you *Peter's escaped!*"

The vicar's wife had, for the second time during their brief married life, presented her husband with twins. A stranger clergyman, who knew nothing of what had happened, took the service the day after the lady's second confinement, when all the parish was ringing with the news. Ascending the pulpit, he gave out his text, chapter so-and-so, verse so-and-so, "Two are better than one." A subdued snigger ran round the church. The clergyman frowned, looked threateningly round the building, and then declaimed once more, very vigorously and emphatically: "Two are better than one." And I regret to say the church simply rocked!

A curate, one day in East London, having several couples to marry, accidentally united two bridegrooms to the wrong brides. Here was a pretty kettle of fish! He sent hastily round to the vicar, who flew to the vestry post-haste.

"Have they signed the registry yet, Mr. Evans?" said he to the curate.

"No, sir."

"That's all right, then; I'll marry them again."

At that moment one of the bridegrooms struck in—

"Well, sir, we've been talkin' it over like, and we've made up our minds to keep as we are!"

A clergyman had, by the aid of the deaf-and-dumb alphabet, just married a deaf-and-dumb couple, when a lady came up to him and said—

"Did you notice the bridegroom had an impediment in his speech?"

The parson said—

"What on earth do you mean, Mrs. Johnson?"

"Well, the top of one of his fingers was missing"!

The mistakes that clergymen inevitably make at times, either in preaching or in reading, afford much innocent amusement. The Rev. H. B. Chapman, Chaplain of the Savoy, recently had a telephone number assigned to his house, and for a week he used to go about saying it over to himself, with the result that on Sunday he requested the congregation to sing hymn "Three-double-eight, Gerrard."

Then there was the classic and really brilliantly clever though unintentional mistake of the Vicar of Gorleston, who had been spending the week supervising the rehearsal of one of his plays in London, and who, on the following

Sunday, gave out the following notice: "There will be evensong in this church every day this week, with matinées on Wednesday and Friday."

I once myself was guilty of a slip in the pulpit which caused amusement for many a long day after. I was, perhaps, rather nervous owing to the somewhat exceptional nature of the congregation, which consisted, among many others, of the late King Edward, Queen Alexandra, and the then Canon Brooke Foss Westcott, afterwards Bishop of Durham, one of the most distinguished scholars and ecclesiastics of his day. I was only twenty-five years old at the time, and I was naturally much perturbed at the idea of preaching in the presence of so distinguished a man. My text was "A good soldier of Jesus Christ." And after a while I said, or meant to say: "And thus you see how the disorderly, selfish recruit is changed into the well-disciplined, self-sacrificing soldier." Instead of which, I electrified my hearers and immortalized myself by announcing: "And thus you see how the disorderly and selfish *curate* . . ."!

Another great pleasure in my clerical life was my work in the schools. East End children are often delightful: charming natures and frequently quite astonishingly charming manners. And, as a rule, they love the "curick." Whenever I got depressed and wearied with the misery of the slums, I used to turn into the schools. There I was certain of delightful distraction, and it was complete rest and happiness to lose one's own life in that of the children around one. I never had so many and such dear friends as I had in those simple days!

The answers of some of these children are quite wonderful—whether intentionally so, or whether they are only happy flukes, it is impossible to say.

"Now, boys," said the vicar one day to a class of bright little fellows, "I have to divide four potatoes fairly and equally between five boys. How shall I do it?"

Dead silence, until at last one little fellow held up his hand: "Mash 'em, sir!"

The teacher heard two very tiny little girls talking together one day.

"You don't know what we've got in our 'ouse," said one of them to the other.

"What is it?"

"A new baby brother," was the impressive reply.

"My! Is he going to stay with you always?"

"I don't know; but I 'spect he is. He's got all his things off"!

"What's your father, my dear?" asked a vicar once of a little girl.

"Please, sir, when 'e's at work 'e's a bricklayer; when 'e's out of work 'e's a teetotaller"!

A clerical friend of mine, vicar of a large parish, went into his schools recently and found a number of children drawing from the life; a dear little girl, in the classic costume of Cupid, standing as their model. Suddenly the teacher, a young woman of about twenty years of age, called out—

"Now, children, draw a soldier."

After a few moments the curate, who had been looking over the children, hurriedly approached the teacher and, overwhelmed with embarrassment, said to her—

"Hadn't they better dress their soldiers?"

The teacher, with scarlet cheeks, sprang up and rapped loudly on her desk.

"Children, attention! *All soldiers in uniform!*"

But, of course, it is the women really who, as a rule, give one the greatest cause for thankful joy and joyous thanksgiving, and frequently owing to their almost divine capacity for inconsequence. I could tell you many a long story apropos of this characteristic of theirs, but I really have no time or space to do so. I will summarize the whole genus in a perfectly charming little anecdote which is told, I believe, by Miss Maude Valerie White, whose delightful songs can only be surpassed by her amazingly clever and delightful stories. To her one day came one of these East End ladies, very indignant and irate, and thus she relieved her soul—

"Wich I never 'eard nothink like it all my born days,

wich 'e spoke to me just as I was startin' for church, as no 'usband would never 'ave done. 'Is language was—well, there! *An' me with my bonnet on!*"

While I'm on the topic of these delicate little distractions in the clerical life, I would fain make a passing reference to a story that was told of the archdeacon of our district. When this special archdeacon of whom I speak was married, he started out on his honeymoon with a face bearded like the pard—you could scarcely see any archdeacon at all. His bride had frequently bewailed his beard and whiskers, which she detested. So on the third night of their tour he quietly slipped out, after she had gone very early and very tired to their bed in the hotel. He came back an hour afterwards with a face as bare as a billiard-ball, and, of course, absolutely unrecognizable, and, undressing quietly, he lay down beside his unconscious spouse. In the morning, the bright sunlight streaming in upon the bed, Mrs. Archdeacon woke, and then turned to wake her spouse with the usual archidiaconal kiss. To her unspeakable horror she beheld a clean-shaven stranger at her side. Trembling with terror, she crept out of bed, gathered up all her frills and flounces, and was creeping on tiptoe out of the room when suddenly she heard a voice from the bed—

"Ellen, Ellen! Come back, and I will explain everything!"

A very amusing incident occurred in one East End parish which I know. There was a certain old organ-blower who would, despite all remonstrances, persist in blowing when the organist had finished playing, thereby greatly upsetting the congregation with the horrible sounds in the empty pipes. One Sunday the organist wrote him a note, which he dispatched by one of the choir boys. Unfortunately, the wretched boy, misunderstanding his instructions, climbed the pulpit stairs and handed it to the vicar, who had just given out his text, and who, to his extreme indignation, found these words written in the letter—

"Will you stop when I tell you to! People come

here to listen to my music, not to your horrible noise."

Another very good story about this same organ-blower, who, I may add, was a regular character, known far and wide for his eccentricity as well as his extreme illiteracy. The vicar was away, and the locum tenens, on his arrival in the vestry on the first Sunday, found this nondescript creature awaiting him.

"Well, what is your exact position here, my man?" asked the clergyman.

"Well, sir," was the reply, "some folks calls me a sextant, some says as I'm a beetle, but the vicar 'e always calls me a virgin!"

You may perhaps say, why did I leave the East End if I was so fond of it? Well, I may reply, it was because I got ploughed for an examination for priest's orders. You see, I worked so hard whilst in the East End that I literally had no time for reading, which is the form of study, I regret to say, I had always detested, in addition to which I had no fancy or taste or appreciation of theology in the slightest degree. I worked hard at the practical part of my profession, for I really was very fond of it. I liked poor people, and I had an aptitude for them. I think I can honestly say I never got in their way, or trod on their corns, or forgot to take my hat off in their houses. The greatest compliment I ever had paid me in my life was after I had left my London curacy. Shall I be guilty of bad taste in telling it? Why not, after all! My vicar, walking down the street one day, met an old woman.

"Well, Mrs. Smith," he said, "and so Mr. Blathwayt's gone at last."

"Yes, Mr. Vicar, sir, and I'm main sorry for it. I don't 'old with curicks as a rule, well knowin' wot an infernal noosance they are to every one in the place, but I will say this for that there Blackpool, *'e allus know'd wen it was washin'-day!*"

And let me say it's something to know that much in a big East End parish. It's worth a whole Greek play, and, indeed, it's a great deal more practical. The poor detest a man who always muddles about. I don't think I ever did. I think it's so far due to myself to say so much. And then again I think I was always popular in the pulpit. I knew how to talk to poor people and how to interest them. And they love that. I venture to say so much as this because I feel, after all I have said about my unfitness for the vocation, people might well ask why on earth I went into it at all. Well, my success in a huge East End parish, if I may so far describe the result of my efforts, answers that question. I was really fond of poor people and they were fond of me. I know I can say that without fear of contradiction. I think I owed it mainly to my sense of humour. However, that sense of humour didn't help me in my exam., at which I did, I frankly own, about as badly as it was possible for me to do, especially in the strictly theological papers. The question, however, which stumped me, which fairly put the lid on my efforts —to use a very modern and a very expressive phrase—was—

"Give the ten plagues of Egypt in their order."

It not only stumped me but it annoyed me; it annoyed me so much that instead of answering it I quitted the Examination Hall, and when I got home I wrote a note to Canon Churton, the examiner, in which I asked him plainly what was the good of such a question. I was then thirty years of age, and I felt justified in asking him what possible usefulness there could be in such a piece of knowledge. By return post I received a letter—

DEAR MR. BLATHWAYT,

The Bishop would like to see you at his London chambers on Monday, and he will then probably answer your question.

So up to town I travelled on the Monday, and I was charmingly received by old Dr. Claughton, a very handsome, courtly divine of the old school. He was then Bishop of St. Albans.

"Well, Mr. Blathwayt," he said, "you've done very badly at your examination. Can you tell me how it is?"

"Well, my lord, I'm very sorry to hear it," I replied. "I am still more sorry to say it's not the first bad examination in my life. In fact, I've no faculty for exams. at all, and I never show at my best at them."

"But I can't understand it. Canon Churton says your paper on the Prayer Book would—— Let me see. What *does* he say? Oh yes; here it is—'would disgrace a Board School teacher.' Those are his exact words. Well, I can't have clergy like that in my diocese. He says your Greek Testament is good and you appear to possess more than average intelligence. But a man who can't give the ten plagues of Egypt in their order is hardly fit to minister to the spiritual wants of a great London parish."

I confess I felt a little nettled, but, I need scarcely add, I hid all manifestation of feeling beneath a perfectly icy and unmoved exterior. At the same time, I wasn't going to give in without putting up something of a fight.

"Well, but, my lord," said I, "may I ask you very respectfully who is advantaged by such an apparently extraordinarily useless piece of information. Honestly, my lord, it appears to me neither historically, nor spiritually, nor practically useful. I can't see what purpose it serves. Surely it doesn't matter whether I put the blood first, or the lice, or the hail-storms! They must have all been equally unpleasant. I have worked hard for a good many years in a very difficult parish. I have never spared myself once, and I believe you will find all the people are on my side—from the vicar and the churchwardens downwards. And yet I must leave a place where I am trying to do good work, and where the people like me, because I cannot give the ten plagues of Egypt in their order! I think it's very hard, my lord."

"Dear Mr. Blathwayt," said the good old man, as he put his hand on my shoulder, "I know it's hard, but I've no choice in the matter. You see, rules and regulations and discipline must be kept up or the whole cosmos goes to rack and ruin. And examinations, I may remark, are intended to be passed. Go and start again somewhere else. I'll help you. You are sure to do well, though now things may look a little black for a time. I myself will give you a special letter of recommendation to your new vicar."

Well, there was nothing for it. I had to return to my parish and tell my vicar, who was disgusted and didn't hesitate to say so. And I had to say good-bye to my poor people, whom I honestly loved. And my last farewell was as follows. There may be those who will laugh at it as a piece of curate sentimentality. Well, they may. It's a scene, however, I have never forgotten.

I was always very fond of the children in my district, and I knew every one of them and they knew me. One of them was a dear little girl about ten years old. She was dying of a kind of decline. Her home was indescribably miserable; her parents were scarcely human in any of their attributes; their degradation was unspeakable. On what turned out to be the last day of her life I went to see her, and on my way I bought her a bunch of flowers. And, by the by, that is one of the charming and redeeming features of poor-class Londoners—their love of flowers and of animals, a love which you rarely find in country districts. When I entered the room where the poor child lay panting out her last moments on earth, I found both her father and mother in a vociferously drunken slumber upon the bed in the corner of the room. Three or four noisy children played, and quarrelled, and shouted, and screamed, and jumped round about and on to the bed where this darling child lay. I bent down and kissed her, and then I gave her the bunch of roses and sweetpeas. Her sweet face flushed with pleasure.

"Oh, but are they really for me? Oh, dear Mr. Blaffwayt, I do love you so much!" she said, as she pressed them to her lips in a perfect rapture.

I couldn't speak, so I stole away from the room as swiftly as I could.

Next day, as the sun was setting, I went to see her. She lay like a marble statue in the evening light, life's fitful fever passed; but the flowers were still pressed against those pallid lips, her comfort to the end!

And next day I had left the parish for good and all.

Here is one curious little peep into Anglican methods which is typical of a hundred English parishes, where the vicars consider their bishops more, perhaps, than they do their Bibles. A rector under whom I once worked said to me one day—

"Mr. Blathwayt, let me have your list of Confirmation candidates this afternoon."

"I haven't got any, sir," I replied.

"Not got any candidates for Confirmation, and the Bishop coming in six weeks? How disgraceful!"

"Well," I said, "I'll put that right as soon as possible."

Next morning I rose at five and started on my round: up one slum and down another, to this terrace and that row, till I had exhausted my whole district—and myself. I would enter a house, say to the boy or girl: "How old are you?" "Fifteen." "Let me put you down for Confirmation." And down they would go accordingly. At five o'clock that evening I turned up at the Rectory, tired out but triumphant.

"Well, Mr. Blathwayt, what is it?" said the rector.

"I've got my Confirmation candidates, sir," I replied.

"Already!" said the astounded cleric. "How many?"

"Eighty, sir," I answered.

"Oh, good man!" he said. "Well bowled!"

Well, that kind of thing speaks for itself. So much of it is show—all show; figures and statistics. But that doesn't build up a Church. That's not the kind of foundation upon which to build your hopes for eternal life; not upon such shifting sands can one find the assurance of salvation. It was that kind of thing that used to shake my faith in the reality of the whole thing.

On leaving my London curacy I proceeded to Scotland, where, through the influence of my late vicar, who was very indignant at my enforced departure, and whose memory is one of the most delightful of my life, I had obtained a curacy in the Scottish Episcopal Church, under a very famous dignitary of that Church.

A remarkable man this, quite self-made, I believe, a northern Scotsman to his finger-tips, hard-headed, shrewd, with a wonderful gift of wit and humour, a combination which is not quite so frequent as people imagine. Irishmen are usually witty, Scotsmen humorous, purely English people very rarely either; but this Scotsman was both, to a quite remarkable and exceptional degree. A very charming character, and immensely popular with all classes of the community. A very sturdy, broad-shouldered, thick-set man, with a massive, clean-shaven face, with eyes that were always twinkling with merriment, and a temper and a disposition of the very sweetest nature it is possible to imagine. Not a very good preacher, but a wonderful organizer and an indefatigable worker; a very advanced Churchman, with the appearance and the peculiar mode of speech, and a certain method of carrying himself, that allied him so closely to the Roman priest that none could ever differentiate between them. He detested Romanism, however, almost as much as he did Presbyterianism, out of which he had originally sprung himself. His parishioners could not make enough of him, and I was as much fascinated by his wonderfully compelling personality as was everybody else, for the man was irresistible, and as good and genuine and devoted to his work and vocation as he was popular. Peace to his ashes! for he has long been dead.

Of course, he had his little defects—he wouldn't have been as popular as he was if he hadn't. But they took a lot of digging out. And he had his preferences and his antipathies, the same as every one else. He and I got on very well for a time, though as a rule he had no overwhelming love for people from so far over the Border as I hailed. Still, my Scotch blood on one side and my genuinely artistic appreciation of his sense of humour, which he never needed to emphasize or explain, as he told me he generally had to do with Englishmen—and especially Englishwomen—stood me in good service throughout my sojourn in his parish. But all the same, the advanced ritualism of the services and the extremely stringent view I was expected to put forth and promulgate from the pulpit, concerning the doctrines and dogmas of the Church, were too much for me in the end. I simply couldn't, in common honesty, subscribe to what was to me no less than hopeless superstition and the most impossibly rigid theories concerning divorce and the re-marriage of divorcing or divorced people. To my new rector and to my brother clergy, without exception, the mere thought of divorce was abhorrent. To me it appeared to be the only right and moral escape from a hideous *impasse*, though I quite realized, as I do now, that it ought to be availed of only as a last resource. To deny the Sacrament to a faithful but dishonoured wife, or to a husband who has been deserted for another man, and who have done nothing more monstrous than avail themselves of the law's sympathy and humanity, I considered nothing more or less than degrading to the teaching of Christ, and I said so definitely and vigorously.

Well, my rector and my brother clergy, in all honesty and sincerity, took up the very reverse position. They would vigorously refuse the Sacrament or the hope of re-marriage in church to any one, however innocent themselves, who had been driven to divorce by either an erring husband or wife. And they would hear of no exceptions. And upon this rock, as also upon their, to me, almost impossibly advanced sacramental teachings, absolutely sincere and genuine on their part, and put forward by them with the greatest charm and the most winning spirituality, we came to a final and irrevocable decision to part, I determining at the same time to quit a Church whose doctrines I no longer believed and taught, as in common honesty I was bound to believe and teach them. Though, I am bound to own, I disliked and had no personal sympathy with doctrines and instructions which appeared to me to be indefensible and illiberal and uncharitable in the highest degree, yet my admiration for those who held and taught those doctrines was unbounded.

The clergy of the Scottish Episcopal Church are a remarkable set of men; they are men of whose value and exceptional mental qualities and spiritual worth few people—even in Scotland itself—outside their own parishes and churches and congregations have any idea whatever. They are extraordinarily devoted, and, like most of their countrymen, remarkably well educated. Deeply read, and with all the tendency to metaphysics that so characterizes the Presbyterian ministry, as it also does the ranks of the Jesuits, to each of which body they bear a strong family resemblance, the Scottish Episcopal clergy are intellectually—and very often spiritually too—far in advance of their Anglican brethren on the southern side of the Tweed. At the same time, I am bound to confess that their ecclesiastical and episcopal claims and pretensions are much resented by the official Church of Scotland, which is, of course, rigidly Presbyterian, and over which the reigning monarch presides as titular head, as he does in England as head of the Anglican Church. In indirect but in somewhat amusing fashion, this high political fact led to my final undoing.

To speak quite frankly, the late Queen Victoria, whose memory is dear to the hearts of most Britishers, was extremely unpopular with the majority of the Scottish Episcopalian clergy, who could scarcely endure the mention of her name—my own rector absolutely hated her. And for this reason—very unfairly, as I think: As official Head of the Established Church of Scotland, Queen Victoria very properly considered it her duty when at Balmoral, to attend the services of the parish church, just as when in England she, as Head of the Anglican Church, attended the services of the national Church of England. And she greatly resented the presence of an Episcopal Church in Scotland, and would not recognize its existence in any shape or form—never, for instance, dreaming of inviting a Scottish bishop to dine and sleep at the Castle, as she, every week almost, invited the leading ministers of the Established Church of Scotland to Balmoral. Well, it so chanced that it fell to me to preach the sermon one summer Sunday in the church of which I was a curate in Scotland. And as it was the anniversary day of the accession of Queen Victoria to the throne, I quite unthinkingly ascended the pulpit and, much to the pleasure of the general congregation, who idolized the Queen and knew and recked nothing of the little ecclesiastical jealousies and prejudices of their clergy, delivered a vigorously loyal and enthusiastic discourse upon the many and glorious virtues and attributes of Queen Victoria and her glorious reign. Well, all went well so far as the congregation was concerned, but when I got back to the vestry, my word! there was an explosion! My rector completely lost his self-control, and my brother clergy were little better. Dashing down his biretta and flinging off his stole, as though it had been contaminated and defiled by the theories I had promulgated from the pulpit, my rector cried out to me—

"How dared you preach about that old woman, who, you know perfectly well, hates our Church, in my pulpit!"

"Really, sir," I protested very respectfully, "really, you must forgive me, but my duty to my Queen precedes even my duty to my rector."

"No, sir, it does not!" was the instant and very indignant reply. "Your duty is to me. Queen Victoria despises our Church, and never loses an opportunity of slighting our bishops and clergy. I forbid you to mention her name in my pulpit again. If you do you quit my curacy!"

"Well, sir," I replied, rather nettled at the manner in which he considered it fit to treat me for a perfectly innocent and inoffensive sermon on my part, "in that case there is no more to be said. I shall make no promise one way or the other. But if you do dismiss me for saying a good word about your own Queen in the pulpit, it's almost sure to get to her knowledge, and I don't think she'll be very pleased."

"Then she must be angry!" replied my rector. "And much good may it do her! The Queen has no jurisdiction over this Church, at all events, thank goodness; and it is immaterial to me what she may think or say or do in the matter, which doesn't concern her in the slightest degree!"

As a matter of fact, I thought myself it concerned her very considerably.

Two days afterwards I received an invitation to luncheon from the Bishop, who was an Englishman, and, I knew, very much in sympathy with my views, on these matters at all events. He met me with a smile.

"Well, Mr. Blathwayt," he said, "I hear you have been doing battle for your Queen, like the good Cavalier you are."

"Well, my lord," I replied, a good deal relieved at the manner in which he appeared to regard my "contumacy," "I ventured to break a lance on her Majesty's behalf. Not that I think it will do her any good, or that it has greatly advanced the cause of the Empire—so far, at all events, as St. ——'s Church is concerned."

"Not a bit!" replied the Bishop, with a hearty laugh. "Not a bit! On the contrary, I believe you have endangered the Succession, *and* the Constitution. But seriously, why didn't you leave well alone and keep the peace among her Majesty's loyal subjects? Surely it would have been wiser."

"Exactly, my lord. But to tell you the honest truth of the matter, I had no idea the rector felt so keenly on the matter. I never realized it for a single second, or I would never have dreamed of making his pulpit a sort of coward's castle for preaching my own views. As a matter of fact, it was the very sermon I preached last year in my last curacy, and I didn't give the matter a second thought until I came down from the pulpit and met the rector in the vestry."

"And after that the Deluge, I suppose?" smiled the Bishop.

"Yes, my lord, and the Judgment Day too!" I replied.

"Oh, well," he answered, "I'll write and tell the rector that you acted thoughtlessly, and had no idea of annoying him or hurting his feelings. It's always difficult for an Englishman to grasp the prejudices of a Scotsman, or even to appreciate the fact that they exist. You see, they resent things which we don't even notice. And it's much worse in Ireland even than it is here. Well, good-bye; and for the future, if you are advised by me, you'll let our good Queen fight her own battles. I am sure she's well able to defend herself."

And so the affair passed off.

I hope I haven't given my readers the idea that I was throughout my clerical career a battlesome and contumacious shaveling, always defying my spiritual pastors and masters. For the direct contrary was the case. Out of my six rectors, only one was thoroughly unsatisfactory, and no curate was ever known to stay with him for longer than six months except myself, who contrived to endure him for a year. My rectors and my vicars and my bishops were, as a rule, men who would have been distinguished in any walk of life, men whom to know was a privilege and an education, whom to associate with was to love and admire. This very Scotch rector of whom I have just been speaking was, as I have already hinted, one of the very finest men one could possibly meet in any country or in any profession, and I am delighted to think I served under him, under a man whose life and teaching, and whose whole example, come to me even now as an inspiration and a benediction.

And of many of my old clerical companions I retain the most delightful memories. I often think, for instance, of a certain Mr. Wallace Duthie, beneath whose charming eloquence I have more than once seen such a keen literary judge and critic as Dr. W. L. Courtney, the editor of the *Fortnightly Review*, sitting quite entranced. A very witty man, as well as one of the finest preachers I ever heard, it was impossible ever to get the better of him. On one occasion I was sitting with him, and his churchwarden was shown into the room.

"I can't do anything with Smith"—referring to one of the choirmen—said the visitor. "When I went to ask him on Wednesday night to come to practice he said he was putting in his peas, and last night he had entered for a billiard tournament."

"Oh, well, it can't be helped," replied Duthie. "There's one good thing about him, at all events," he continued. "He evidently *minds his peas and cues!*"

On another occasion a very indolent and dissolute sort of fellow came up to him before a number of people in the smoking-room of a great Australian liner, and, pointing to the little gold cross on his chain, he said, very brutally—

"I suppose you wear that to advertise your profession?"

"Yes," replied Duthie, calmly and coolly. "It marks my calling, just as your nose marks yours!"

I preached my last sermon, as a curate, in that Scotch Episcopalian church—and it wasn't on Queen Victoria either! And then I quitted the Church professionally for good and all. I have remained friends with and kept in touch with all my old clerical friends, as far as possible, and with as many as have lived up to the present day. I bade good-bye to them, bishops and all, with the utmost friendliness and cordiality. They all sympathized with my difficulties and approved of my course of action, and not even the highest churchmen amongst them ever resented my action in the slightest degree.

I have purposely been explicit on this matter, though not tediously so, I trust. For I rather resent the attitude some lay people are apt to take up with regard to a man who feels it his duty to abandon his Orders. On more than one occasion it has been somewhat ill-naturedly hinted behind my back that I was unfrocked, whatever that mysterious ceremony may imply.

Well, I am sorry to disappoint these good people—but I was not!

As I say, my chief reason for giving it all up was not only my inability to subscribe to, much less teach and preach, dogmas and doctrines in which I had no real particle of belief, and which, in my opinion, actually militated against the whole life and teaching of the great Founder of Christianity, but my honest conviction that neither spiritually nor temperamentally was I fitted to be a priest in a Church demanding, in these respects, the very loftiest type of man. And this question is at the bottom of all ecclesiastical attempts at reorganization to-day.

What, of course, is essential, as I have already hinted at, is a vast improvement in the quality of the clergy themselves—not only from the spiritual point of view, but from the purely intellectual. They are not nearly so well educated as they used to be, although their congregations are more intellectual than ever, and, considering that a Church, to be of any use to the community whatever, must be a *teaching* Church, that its influence must first and foremost be exercised in an educative capacity, this is deplorable, and in itself explains the failure of the Establishment to fulfil its duty towards the State, to say nothing of its far higher spiritual mission to the souls of men.

Preaching is sadly at a discount in the Anglican Church to-day, partly because it calls for a calibre of mind and a capacity for thought which are absolutely lacking in the average cleric, and partly because many of the clergy themselves have ceased to believe in what they are called upon to preach. Where there is an able, thoughtful preacher you will always get a large and eager attendance at church, not because people are naturally spiritually-minded or "hungering and thirsting after righteousness"—they are not, but simply because, quite independent of doctrine or dogma whatever, they love, men and women alike, something that really stirs their imagination and makes them think. Now, a large proportion of our clergy, being unable to think for themselves, having probably, indeed, never been taught to think, are wholly lacking in the ability to make other people think. And a Church that neither thinks nor teaches is really worse than no Church at all. We shall probably hear a good deal of this in the very near future. I am writing these words on September 15, 1916, and the much-talked-of National Mission will be over by the time this work is published. What I feel is that the Mission ought to be directed first and foremost towards the clergy themselves, and it ought to result, not only in a great clerical regeneration, but also and chiefly in a great combing out of the ineffectives. I cannot help feeling that what is essential is an absolute transformation amongst the clergy, spiritually and intellectually. We sadly require some great inner society—a kind of Anglican Order of Jesuits—to take this matter remorselessly and relentlessly in hand. We want an order of men who shall flame through the land, afire with zeal and earnestness and seized with the infatuation for reality. No great cause was ever carried through to success without a fanatic, and the cry of the Church of England to-day is, or ought to be, for a fanatic, though it makes one smile to think of fanaticism and State Anglicanism in the same breath.

In Sidney Smith's day the Church of England was like to die of dignity. To-day, alas! it frequently hasn't even vitality sufficient to be dignified. And yet in many respects its possibilities were never vaster, its best hopes never so near to realization, if only the best men were allowed to have their chance. And fully one-half the clergy realize this. What so many of them complain of, and complain bitterly, is that convention forbids their insistence upon the things that really matter, their condemnation of the sins that really stain, the compulsion that is laid upon them to preach doctrines that have long since crumbled into the dust of dead and gone days.

Only yesterday one of the best known and most popular bishops on the Bench said to me—

"This is the day of realities, and yet half my time is spent in trying to get old ladies of either sex to look facts in the face. If I tell them, for instance, that evil-minded gossip and blasting scandal is worse in God's sight than a young fellow, in the heat of love and youth, committing what is called 'the worst sin of all,' they hold up holy hands of horror, and for ever after I am looked upon with doubt and suspicion. But until we can get straight vision our Church is doomed. And, to be quite frank, Nonconformity, in these respects, is blinder even than we are. Both Church and Dissent spend too much time in manufacturing new sins, which really aren't sins at all."

In my curate days I possessed a dim realization of all this, and the impossibility of putting such ideas into force so weighed upon me that, as I say, I threw up the whole thing in disgust. And, frankly, I have never regretted having done so since. A curate can hardly ever dare to speak the truth, the real, straight truth, in the pulpit for fear of giving irreparable offence. I remember once, in a sermon on the "woman taken in adultery," a curate friend of mine gave expression to a truth so self-evident that it was an absolute platitude, but it pretty well did for him in the end. "In many a woman's life," he innocently cried, "her own plain face has been her own best friend, and to it she owes the preservation of the most precious thing in life." I don't think his feminine hearers ever forgave him—certainly not the plain ones! Unfortunately, curates are not encouraged to think, and they are hardly ever permitted to say what they really believe and would wish to say.

What is much to be desired is, if I may so express myself, a more definite alliance between spirituality and intellectuality. This is only reasonable. The one great objection I formed to the Salvation Army, when I first came into contact with it, as a young curate, upwards of thirty years ago, was that it appeared to consider it necessary to degrade religion in order to make it attractive to the masses in the slums. Well, apart from the fact that a religion which must be vulgarized to be effective is not worth having, my own experience had taught me that the poor people preferred to have something offered to them to which they could look up. They are quite sufficiently intelligent, and have quite sufficient power of idealization, to prefer an image radiant in the sunlight above them to an idol in the mud beneath their feet.

And that is a truth, I think, that is universally applicable. The clergyman of the future, if he wishes to exercise a great moral force, must realize that humanity possesses a mind as well as a soul, and his appeal must be directed as much to the one as to the other, and in the blending of the two he will find, so far as he himself is concerned, a keen intellectual joy.

There is scarcely a subject on earth which lends itself more readily to the keenest exercise of intellectuality than does the theology of the Christian religion; for, widely regarded, it touches the whole of human life, it leaves unexplored no avenue of human thought, and, as a matter of fact, it opens up undreamed-of vistas in human effort and energy that call forth all the intellectual possibilities and potentialities of the Christian preacher and teacher. And when we reflect that every work of man's ingenuity, be it a watch or a warship, is the outcome of the spiritual world, the materialization of an idea, the outward, tangible manifestation and fulfilment of a thought, a movement in the human brain, we realize at once all the immense intellectual possibilities that confront the really thinking and spiritually-minded priest. But in order to be able to think a man must first of all read, and he must agonize—to use the old Greek term—before he can either think or teach. Therefore my urgent plea for a far more highly educated and intellectual order of clergy.

There is no profession in the world in which the execution of its duties is not either much helped or much hampered by the personality and individuality of its members, and this is immensely true of the priestly office. Napoleon's personality and that of Wellington, the wonderfully acute and penetrating personality of Lord Nelson—these are the qualifications which contributed mainly to the success of their armies during their lifetime, and to the undying memories which are now attached to their glorious names.

It is the personality of the man himself. And in the Church, I honestly believe, personality tells more than in any other walk of life: partly for the reason that the priest is related, by his very office, in an extraordinarily intimate manner to his fellow-beings, and partly owing to the fact that the man's life preaches an infinitely more eloquent sermon, and one that influences the world immeasurably more than any spoken or written words from the pulpit could ever hope to do. And the Anglican Church is curiously dependent, for its influence, upon the personalities of its ministers. All this is so obvious as to be a trite commonplace. And in looking back on the many clerics I have known, I recall a score of remarkable figures—men, that is, capable of impressing themselves and their theories, their whole conceptions of life upon the people to whom they have been called upon to minister, and whose whole influence is due, not nearly so much to the creed they preach as to the character they possess.

Let us take two very remarkable men, great personal friends of my own, and you will realize the truth of what I have been saying; two men who, by a happy concatenation of circumstances, are now engaged together in guiding and controlling the religious fortunes and destinies of one of the most populated and progressive cities in the world—I refer to Birmingham, wherein two of its leading and most distinguished citizens are embodied in the singularly charming and amiable personalities of Bishop Russell Wakefield and the Rev. R. J. Campbell, a really wonderful and clever combination. I don't think you could possibly hit upon two men more thoroughly adapted to commend their office and their Church to widely differing classes of the community than these two. Simply because in themselves they possess absolutely charming natures, and it is personal charm which invariably, and sometimes most unjustly and unfairly and undeservedly, carries all before it, absolutely apart from the fact as to whether the possessor of it really deserves or merits the popularity that, unsought and unasked on his part, is invariably showered upon him.

I am almost afraid I shall be accused of exaggeration in what I say of these two priests. The Bishop I have known more intimately almost than any one else of my numerous friends (or enemies) and acquaintances. I have stayed with him time and again, and left him after each visit marvelling afresh at the sweetness of a nature which never sees but the good side of any one and never by any chance loses an opportunity to do a friend—or an enemy if he has one, which I greatly doubt—the best turn in his power ; and, utterly unspoiled by success, as simple-minded and as good-hearted, though always the thorough man of the world, as when he was a hard-working town curate.

Clean-shaven, broad-shouldered, with a handsome, kindly face, upon which a smile is almost always curving round a well-cut mouth, a perfectly devoted father, and the most sympathizing and human prelate that ever walked this earth, what wonder that Russell Wakefield wins affection wherever he goes ! Just ask the men in the trenches what they think of the cheery, kindly bishop who sat with them when the shells were flying fast and thick, and who never failed to see and understand the pathos of their position and the cheerful pluck and endurance of the poor fellows under tragic and terrific circumstances.

Well, it is because he is a man with a man's heart that he speaks with such conviction to the hearts of men wherever and whenever he is thrown in contact with them. It is not scholarship, to which he makes no pretence, or eloquence, of which he possesses a certain degree, or marvellous capacity for organization, or a taste or distaste for milk-puddings, that constitutes Dr. Wakefield one of the most popular prelates of the day ; it is his endearing personality, his quite exceptional charm.

Frankly, as one may well understand, I think that there are other qualities more essential to the making of the ideal bishop than any he possesses. I would prefer more scholarship and a greater capacity for insight and for vision. I think that a certain element of hardness, the hardness and yet the flexibility of highly tempered steel, would add to rather than detract from his value as a spiritual force in a community of which he is the religious head ; but I am fully conscious that such a quality might possibly endanger or nullify those characteristics to which I have given such prominence.

I think it is very probable that the hard-headed

merchant and business men in Birmingham might re-echo this sentiment of mine, and those who recall the exceptional scholarship of Bishop Gore, and his penetrating vision into the mystic world of spirit by which we are all enshrouded, must now and again regret that their present chief pastor remains only the most delightful man they have ever met.

They must reflect, however, that the Church, like humanity, is made up of all sorts, and that in Bishop Wakefield they possess, not only a devoted prelate and a high-bred gentleman, but also a man who will always, and as a matter of high principle, put their needs and requirements before his own prejudices or preferences.

Whilst the Bishop, to my way of thinking at all events, is lacking in certain important ecclesiastical and episcopal qualifications—such, for instance, as a really lofty standard of scholarship, and a certain indefinable but quite definite ecclesiastical mode of thought, a more directly sacerdotal attitude and vision, if I may so venture to express myself—he is pre-eminently, and with great naturalness, a real Father in God, not only to the people in the diocese but more especially so to his clergy. And that is one of the things in which, in the past, the Anglican episcopate, at all events, has been only too frequently lacking. I have seen too much of it not to know what I am talking about. Hitherto bishops have been apt to hold themselves far too much aloof, and when they have met their clergy they have been in the habit of encountering them too much in the style and manner of the drill-sergeant on parade. They have not been fathers to them, let alone Fathers in God. I make no doubt that their position is frequently a trying one, and that curates and even vicars are at times a source of worry and anxiety to them; but have they, in their turn, handled them in the most judicious or in the most really Christian spirit? Anglican bishops, certainly in the past, have only too often been characterized by a quality of spirit which is emphatically unendearing to their younger brethren in the Church. The proud prelacy of Wolsey's day has, in the modern Anglican episcopate, given place to the most extraordinary tendency to impatience and ill-temper that it is possible to conceive.

I myself have known, within the last twenty years or so, four archbishops and at least half a dozen bishops whose ferocity of temper was something little short of satanic. I cannot mention names, nor, indeed, would it be fair that I should do so, but in several cases I have had the testimony of their own children to the truth of what I state, and which I do with a good deal of unwillingness; but I am rather tired of hearing the ordinary parish clergy blamed, almost exclusively, for the failure of the Church to-day, when, as a matter of fact, I know perfectly well that much of that failure has been due to the unpleasing and un-Christlike personalities of their Fathers in God. And so many of them are lacking in kindly sympathy; they do so little to win the love and affection of their clergy.

I remember once, as a very young man, I was summoned once to see the Bishop of my diocese. I had to get up very early in the morning and travel a hundred miles in icy weather, and when I reached the palace the Bishop kept me waiting for an hour and a half beyond the hour he himself had fixed; and when at last I was shown into the august presence, he not only made no apology to me for his gross and unpardonable discourtesy, but he never shook hands with me; he never even asked me to sit down, but he plunged at once into the business we had in hand. When the luncheon-bell rang he marched off without a word to me, much less an invitation to me to join the party, though I had breakfasted at six o'clock that morning and had travelled a weary journey to see him, and had to return that weary distance that very night. That is not the action of a Father in God. And how indignant his utter lack of even the most meagre form of Christian charity and consideration made me!

It is that kind of thing, which could be multiplied a hundred—nay, a thousand—times over, that has helped to do the Church so much harm in the eyes of even her most faithful children.

I could give many more instances of a like nature to that which I have related, but I do not think it is necessary; nor is it pleasant to me to do so. I wish merely to emphasize the fact that the present Bishop of Birmingham is in such matters—and they are far more important than might at first sight be imagined—the direct antithesis to the good and undoubtedly earnest and possibly well-meaning men to whom I have referred, and two of them are still in active harness. As a matter of fact, Wakefield and I have often discussed this very question from this very point of view. "Well," he said to me one day some ten years ago, "if ever I become a bishop, which I doubt, I shall send away no curate hungry and thirsty. They shall have anything they like to eat—even castle-puddings," he added, with sly allusion to one of my own pet predilections.

In Dr. Wakefield the young clergy of the diocese of Birmingham find a wonderfully sympathetic friend, not merely the genial hail-fellow-well-met kind of friend, but the friend who takes the trouble to enter heart and soul into all their difficulties, a friend who is always at the back of them, and who will always see fair play, a friend who will always lead them upward. And it is for these reasons, as many a khaki-clad hero will tell you that the Bishop of Birmingham is one of the most outstanding and best loved figures among the Anglican episcopate to-day.

I hope no one will accuse me of speaking evil of dignitaries; far otherwise is my wish. I regard our Episcopate, as a rule, with the most sincere admiration, for, as a rule again, it consists of the most supremely able and intellectual men that it is possible to conceive. In my own very humble way I revel in a scholarship, in a literary faculty, in a real spirituality and a sincerity of life and vision, of all of which I myself am hopelessly incapable, but which almost invariably form the distinguishing characteristics of these men, who in many respects are the flower of the English race. But unfortunately, in this world it is often the minor virtues which count most in the successful carrying out of a great venture. And what is the mission of the Church but a great, a glorious venture? And so it vexes me when I see the success of that venture imperilled by words or actions or attitudes of life or mind, or certain little undesirable defects of character, all of which might be guarded against or absolutely avoided by watchful care and perpetual self-discipline and self-control.

And, curiously enough, of Mr. R. J. Campbell I would say almost exactly the same thing as I have already said of his bishop. A singularly gentle and amiable nature—far too sweet-natured, if anything—he is a man who, I should imagine, has never made an enemy on this earth. He and his bishop are the most difficult and most irritating people to write about, to delineate in a few strokes, that I have ever had to deal with. One is so tempted to the use of apparently extravagant and exaggerated eulogy, and yet nothing one can say of their natures, so far as mere charm and amiability are concerned, could be too strong.

The main fault I find with Campbell is that he is somewhat lacking in strength of character: he requires a backbone of steel.

I feel in attempting to fashion a portrait of him much as Canova must have felt when he was carving a lion out of a gigantic pat of butter. He must have dreaded lest some fierce heat should have arisen and the lion had dwindled by turns, beneath his very hands, into a bear or seal, a cat or a hare. So with Campbell, even as I write I scarcely feel assured of the lastingness of his religious views, or whether before this book comes out he may not be figuring as the priest of some new and wonderful religion of his own.

For many years I have felt that he would die Cardinal Archbishop of Westminster. And yet, despite the apparent fluidity of his views, one realizes that, under whatever temporary avatar his religious or theological ideal of the moment may endue itself, the foundation of his religion is of the deepest and most vital and most spiritual nature. And that is the saving quality of his life and teaching—deep and earnest and what would be in a sterner nature almost fanatic spirituality.

Campbell knows no life apart from the strictly spiritual, which is not to say, however, that this present world does not also contain a great fascination for him ; but it is his innate spirituality which will ever shield him from the many and frequently fatal allurements of Vanity Fair.

I remember once, a good many years ago, when he was first appointed to the City Temple, I took him into Sir Herbert's Tree's dressing-room, and Mr. Tree, as he then was, was so fascinated with the personality of "the Little Minister," as he at once dubbed him, that he insisted upon his going round with him, after the theatre, to supper at the Garrick Club. There were a number of distinguished men at the table, and it was a gathering at which it would have been difficult for any one person to have had any chance of shining, and yet Campbell, mainly by his utter simplicity and charm of nature, easily outshone his fellow-guests.

And I also remember a well-known editor, a distinguished Oxford don, taking him aside and urging upon him the vital necessity, if he really desired or aimed at becoming a great spiritual force in London, of keeping himself absolutely apart from the world. And that is what I feel, and have felt all along, with regard to Campbell, that his greatest force lies in his marvellous capacity for spirituality ; but it is so subtle and so delicate a spirituality that it can only be preserved, it can only come to its full flower, in the study of the scholar or the lonely hermitage of the anchorite. He is curiously *au courant du jour,* and that is well from one point of view ; but I doubt if it tends to the deepening of his influence as a great spiritual force. And yet even this quality is to the good of the community in general.

His weekly sermons in the *Sunday Herald*, for instance, commended him to thousands who would otherwise never have come beneath his influence at all, and where in the City Temple he preached to a small and fluctuating audience week by week, he preached to at least a million persons Sunday after Sunday through the Press. But I nevertheless hold that such a rare combination of scholarship—or I should better term it aptitude for scholarship—and lofty idealism and deep spirituality would result in a more lasting benefit for the Church, of which he promises to be such an ornament, if he gave himself up entirely to the life of the thinker and the hermit.

Very cool of me, he will say, to outline his career in this fashion ; but it is merely my idea, and it may quite conceivably be absolutely wrong, and that in following what may be his natural bent he is really fulfilling the law of Christ to its utmost intent. The only thing is, we require scholarship in the Church so much to-day and we get so comparatively little of it. The clergy—a great proportion of them, at all events—are not learned even in the alphabet of their profession, and to teach *them* would indeed be a gracious undertaking on the part of my friend Campbell.

I recall the striking, outstanding, and impressive personality of Dr. Forrest Browne, the late Bishop of Bristol, who is still wonderfully hale and hearty, though he must be well over eighty years of age. A tall, almost clean-shaven man, with a fringe of whiskers and a singularly austere face, he nevertheless gave me the impression of a vivid flame of fire burning within a block of ice—and sometimes the flame leaped through ! He was a singularly fine speaker, enchaining the attention of all who heard him, and especially if his audience was composed of working men, as it once was when I heard him in the Bristol Corn Exchange. There sat those vast crowds of hard-headed artisans and mechanics and shopkeepers and clerks, hushed into awed stillness by the fervid and yet curiously remote thought and eloquence of this dominating Anglican prelate. He dealt with a topic of peculiar delicacy, but in so skilled albeit so outspoken a manner that his audience, with splendid sympathy and real good-breeding, never, by movement of face or lip or hand, indicated that they were startled, as certainly they were startled, by his fearless and astonishing outspokenness.

I once got a glimpse into the curiously contradictory personality of the man. He was presiding at the Church Congress about fifteen years ago. One day a clergyman stood up to pass a few remarks upon one of the set speeches of the day. "Come up on the platform," said the Bishop. The clergyman went on speaking from his place in the audience. "Come up on the platform!" cried the Bishop. Still the clergyman went on speaking. The Bishop utterly and entirely lost his temper. "Come up on this platform!" he roared, his face purple with passion. Another clergyman rose in the audience and sternly remarked to the Bishop: "My lord, cannot you see that the speaker is blind?" I never saw such a change in a man. The Bishop hesitated and stuttered and flushed and then pronounced the Blessing and dismissed us. After luncheon, on again taking the chair upon the platform, Dr. Forrest Browne stood up and said—

"I must apologize for what occurred this morning, and for what will be a lifelong grief to me to recollect." And then, with indescribable vehemence, he said: "Sooner than such a thing had occurred I would have cut my throat!"

It was a heartfelt apology, if ever there was one, a veritable *cri de cœur*. The Church of England has few finer men, few nobler characters, in her midst to-day than Dr. Forrest Browne. I like to think that such men exist.

I once stayed with an Anglican bishop who was a perpetual puzzle to me. To this day I hardly know whether I liked him or whether I didn't. He was a colonial bishop, and that, too, of a very minor colony, but he possessed a perfectly inordinately exaggerated idea of his dignity and position. A big, fine, upstanding, clean-shaven man, he had never been anything more than an ordinary country vicar before his appointment as bishop, and he had no pretensions whatever to scholarship or to eloquence, or to any other episcopal qualification. He always gave me the idea that he must have woke up every morning saying to himself: "God, I thank Thee that I am not as other men are; *but why on earth was I ever made a bishop!*"

He would dwell lusciously upon the episcopal office and rank, especially the rank, in his many conversations with me. I remember once he had business occasion to call up a certain English duchess on the telephone, which, from what he said, was at first answered by the butler. Suddenly, as he talked with the man, a seraphic smile overspread his ingenuous and expressive countenance, and, covering the mouthpiece with his hand for a moment, he said to me: "He called me 'my lord'!"

Curiously enough, three months afterwards or so I read in *John Bull* that this very prelate, the Bishop of ——, had incurred a good deal of unpopularity on the voyage back to his far-off diocese, because he had made a formal complaint to the captain of the ship that the unfortunate stewards did not address him by that title to which he felt himself entitled, and which had fallen so graciously and agreeably from the lips of the ducal butler.

He sadly upset me on one occasion, and really placed me in a most awkward position. He gave a lecture in a certain hall in town, and I secured the services of a most charming and distinguished opera-singer, one of the most famous women of the day—a delightful person, married to a distinguished cavalry officer. She sang the National Anthem, and so exquisitely and with such distinction that it was a feature of the whole afternoon. After the meeting was over, a group, composed of the Bishop, with the prima donna seated next to him, and the chairman and one or two others, was taken for the London Press. To my astonishment this group never appeared. Four days later I learned from the Bishop's secretary that late that evening the Bishop had sent round to the papers to say that he did not like the idea of appearing in a group with a public singer! I was absolutely horrified. To accept the kindly, generous services of a woman of spotless reputation, and a woman famed throughout the world for her gifts as a singer, and then to heap upon her so gross and so thoroughly undeserved an insult appeared to me to be an absolutely unpardonable and inexcusable, and, indeed, an entirely inexplicable, piece of snobbishness.

It is such a man as that who really and naturally and inevitably prejudices people against the Anglican Church, for such conduct would be quite impossible amongst clerics or prelates of the Roman Church.

And yet this good bishop was a man of distinctly lofty character, but absolutely lacking in really effective personality.

CHAPTER VII

HAS THE CHURCH FAILED?

BEFORE I quit the ecclesiastical period of my life I will try to deal, as I see it, with the question that is asked so frequently nowadays: Has the Church failed? Personally, it appears a question impossible to answer definitely one way or the other. I think that the war has exposed the Church's main weakness, but it has also elucidated individual qualities which far transcend all her best friends had ever hoped for.

It depends so much upon the personalities of her critics —and their fitness for their self-imposed task. Ben Tillett, for instance, regards the Anglican clergy as a body of slackers and cowards ignobly skulking behind their cassocks. The arm-chair critics in the West End Club who, 'twixt one whisky-and-soda and the next, wax wrathful over the efforts of the missionary agonizing in a far and dangerous field, are equally untrustworthy and unfair, whilst the typical Socialist and atheist is too prejudiced even to wish to find a good word to say of a class of the community whom he detests with a hatred as virulent as it is foolish, ignoble, and uncalled for.

But there are many respects, in my opinion, in which the Church could do much to make herself and her teaching more acceptable to people in general than she does. I have stated quite frankly my reasons, not for abandoning the Church of my fathers—far otherwise indeed has been the case—but for giving up actual office in her service. What, I feel, is so disastrous with the Anglican Church is that she is perpetually stretching out the dead hand from the Middle Ages and laying her icy fingers upon the heated, throbbing pulse of the present moment and chilling the energizing life of to-day.

Well, this is hopeless, and frequently also it is in diametrical opposition to the whole life and teaching of Christ. I can never believe, for instance, that the exclusively Church doctrine which forbids all allowance for or possibility of divorce, under any circumstances whatever, or its stern condemnation of marriage with a deceased wife's sister, were ever inculcated by Jesus Christ. And yet there is nothing upon which the Anglican prelate or priest is more bitter and intolerant to-day than he is upon these two questions. It is positively extraordinary—nay, to me it is almost demoniacal—the fierce fanaticism with which a certain type of Anglican priest will follow up those unfortunate husbands and wives who seek to free themselves from a burden that has become intolerable. I quite realize that divorce should never be resorted to except in the last extremity, but to maintain that all divorce is a sin against God is folly in the last degree.

The stern ecclesiastical opponents of divorce plead always the sanctity and enduring nature of a sacrament, but it appears to me that when that sacrament has been defiled by unfaithfulness, then for the honour of that sacrament it should be abrogated—and the sooner and the more effectually the better. Christ was the essence, the personification, of common sense and of humanity. And it is the Church's frequently unhuman as well as inhuman attitude towards these and similar questions that has greatly helped to alienate the sympathies of the multitude. Because, without a doubt, the Church has failed to secure the masses, and in great part in these latter days she has failed to secure the classes either. But that is not to say she is altogether at fault.

I was discussing this matter with four well-known clergymen the other day, and, without arriving at any definite conclusion either way, their remarks tended to clear certain obstructions from one's outlook on the matter. The clergymen present were—according to their ages—the Rev. H. B. Chapman, Chaplain of the Chapel Royal, Savoy, a keen-visaged, ascetic-looking man with a pungent, caustic mode of expression, a vivid outlook upon humanity, backed by vast experience of the sexes; a man of considerable vision, an eloquent preacher, and one capable of leadership, providing always he chose to put forward his undoubted powers in that and other directions; a man over sixty years of age, but with the heart of youth still urging him on to work that would deter many younger and more powerful men. And then there was that redoubtable figure the Vicar of Gorleston, the Rev. Forbes Phillips, to whom reference has already been made in these pages; a burly, broad-shouldered man with a massive, clean-shaven face, surmounted by a mighty cranium, in itself indicative of remarkable, nay, exceptional, powers of brain, and, indeed, speaking no lie in this particular; for I can imagine no man more capable either in the pulpit, or on the lecture platform, or in the columns of a newspaper, in all three of which capacities he has proved himself capable in the very highest degree. A great ecclesiastical lawyer this man, with a talent for argument backed by keen perceptions, sound common sense, and knowledge wide as it is deep; a fine preacher, and a recklessness of demeanour which endears him to the hearts of men of all classes, and to not a few women also. The Rev. F. H. Gillingham, the Rector of Bermondsey, a fine, manly, upstanding figure, some six feet two inches in height, broad-shouldered and clean-shaven. He, too, is a veritable leader among men, especially when one realizes that he is, in addition to his many qualifications, an almost ideal cricketer, a very useful person in the boxing-ring, and an accomplished athlete all round. Last, but by no means least, and standing well out from the group by reason of a certain charm of youth and boyishness, the eager and enthusiastic figure of the Rev. H. R. L. Sheppard, the lately appointed Vicar of St. Martin's-in-the-Fields, a man full of fervour in the service of his Master; very unprejudiced, and with not a particle of undue clericalism about him; wide-minded to a very unusual extent in so young a man ; and a man who, although he possesses a capacity for vision to an extent very unusual in these latter days, is nevertheless thoroughly practical and common-sense. Mr. Sheppard would never let his heart run away with his head. And it was to these men that I put the question so often asked to-day : Has the Church failed to rise to the great occasion of this war? And if so, in what direction has she failed or what is the reason for her failure?

I may as well say straight away that in the opinion, both individually and collectively, of these clerics the Church has absolutely missed the greatest opportunity ever placed before her or any Church. Confronted by the most real thing the world has ever seen, the Anglican Church has failed to meet it in any way whatsoever.

"Where do you think the Church has been wrong, Chapman?" I asked the chaplain of the Savoy.

"Well," he replied, "it's rather difficult to say straight off ; but, of course, to a great extent it is a matter of personality—the personality of her personnel. Now, I have been wandering about the country a great deal of late, and what I have discovered is that each rectory and vicarage is simply a country house on a small scale : the rector or vicar a good, old-fashioned country squire in miniature. I have discovered dioceses with a thousand clergy or so and only three or four priests—priests, I mean, in the sense of men devoted to the service of God and their Church. Then, again, the Church fears Mrs. Grundy far more than she fears God. Of course she has failed in the presence of the Great Tragedy. She never will face bloody facts—she won't face prostitution, or drink, or venereal diseases. She is too ladylike. The most penal thing about the Church is that she is not out for loss. There is no dash of the gambler in the Church, none of the glory of the Magdalene in her. The Church of England—and, remember, it is of her I speak all the time—is very kind but very unloving, and especially to the found-out. You may break any commandment, so long as you are not found out."

"Yes," rather impatiently cut in Mr. Forbes Phillips, who had been fuming for some time, "but I think you are putting the saddle on the wrong horse. It isn't the rank and file of the clergy who are so much to blame as it is their indolent and do-nothing bishops, who are always sitting on a fence, waiting and seeing. They have long ceased to lead except in some flabby, parochial squabble over the colour, size, shape, and use of a stole. In olden days bishops were chosen for their sanctity. That was good. Then they were chosen for their sanity. That also was good. They are chosen neither for the one nor the other now. If our bishops spent half the time in good works that they spend posing in front of the camera, making poor jests, not always in good taste, and pestering parish priests, who are killing themselves with anxiety, one might hope for a brighter spiritual vision. But, with few exceptions, the bishops compete with actresses for their share of the footlights and the picture space in the cheaper periodicals. Picnics in the trenches, social functions, posturing before the camera, holidays, 'break-downs,' and the like, leave bishops little time for the more serious duties of their office. Wasn't it Sidney Smith who wrote, 'Bishops live in high places with high people and with little people who depend upon them. They walk delicately like Agag. They hear only one sort of conversation, and avoid bold, reckless men, as a lady veils herself from rough breezes.'"

"I think you are a little hard on the bishops, Mr. Phillips," said the Vicar of St. Martin's-in-the-Fields. "Our bishops to-day, without an exception, so far as I can judge, are men of saintly character. They are willing, anxious to do more than is even demanded of them. But they are the victims of a system, and I really don't think they either know or are able to appreciate the exact condition of affairs. You see, like Royalty visiting a hospital, the Church is always dressed up for them. They see everything *en fête,* not as it is on working days. I consider the Church herself and her clergy are to blame even more than the bishops. The

Church is no longer aggressive, and, as we see in this war, a defensive position, however comfortable the dug-out may be, is no good for winning a campaign. It must be offensive. That is just what we are not doing. And also the priest has never had a message unless he himself is stamped with the mark of the Cross. This war is teaching us that age-long truth which has never come home to us yet—every hour of the day the need for daily crucifixion, hourly self-sacrifice. What I should like to see is an intelligent Salvation Army, a really intellectual, thinking, reasoning, and reasonable Salvation Army, started in the Church itself, which should capture all classes."

"Well, Mr. Sheppard," I said, "you have our friend Prebendary Wilson Carlile's Church Army."

At this he smiled.

"Yes," he replied; "but I said an *intellectual* Salvation Army, to appeal to *all* classes. But," he went on, "I still think Mr. Phillips is too hard on the bishops. They don't see the Church in its working garb."

"But that's just my complaint, Mr. Sheppard," replied the Vicar of Gorleston. "They don't know us *as we are* because they don't devote themselves to the grubbier part of their work. The whole system as regards the bishops is wrong. Look at the Bishop of London, who can't get along on ten thousand a year, as he frankly acknowledged the other day. Well, doesn't that speak for itself? A man who can't live on ten thousand a year must be in a bad way, and still more the system which allows or is responsible for it. I often say that if I were a bishop I should pray to be allowed to go about clad only in my cassock, and with no money in my purse, and certainly no palace to live in, and preach and administer the Sacrament to every soul in my diocese. What the bishops want is simplicity of life. Palaces and peerages have utterly and entirely abrogated and nullified the Early Christian idea. St. Paul bowing his head beneath the axe was far nearer the Christ ideal than his Holiness the Pope living in a palace with eleven thousand rooms in it. The Vatican, Lambeth, and Fulham, in the eyes of the man of the world, no matter what class of the community he may be, wage perpetual and unending war against spirituality. They are the embodiment of comfortable materialism. How an archbishop can behold the daily Sacrifice and Sacrament, the Agony and Bloody Sweat of Flanders, and then sit down to his comfortable dinner in his warm, well-lit palace, I cannot imagine. When Samuel Wilberforce was appointed to the bishopric of Oxford, Dean Hook wrote urging that bishops should give up their peerages and palaces and four thousand out of their five thousand a year for the benefit of the poor, and Dr. Wilberforce replied that such ideas were those of revolutionists and would destroy the influence of the bishops ! "

"Well," I said, "you come back to the argument of the clubman and the man of the world—that outside the Sermon on the Mount no Christianity is possible."

"Why, of course I do," replied the Vicar of Gorleston. "It is the only possible course."

"Yes," struck in Mr. Chapman ; "but only possible when you realize that Love is taught by Sacrifice, and is only genuine when it is the outcome of Sacrifice, which is the lesson our men are teaching us in the trenches every hour of the day. You see, the soldiers are living and dying for the truths we only preach, and the sermon in the trenches is far more sublime than any in the pulpit. Have you seen that war film, and do you remember that picture where they all dash out of the trenches to attack the enemy, and one man hesitates at the top of the trench, and you wonder why, and you get almost annoyed with him for not pushing on with the rest, and suddenly he slides down the bank, arms outspread, and you realize he is dead? That was the most solemn sermon of my life ! "

"Well," said the Rector of Bermondsey, "the Church ought to be in the van of civilization ; as a general rule, however, she's in the cart, utterly left in the rear. I think the Church has failed, not so much from lack of heart as from sheer lack of vision and imagination. I don't think she realizes the great facts of life generally as she ought to do. Take the war, for instance. I was out at the Front for a year. One morning the General of our division came in to breakfast with *The Times* in his hand. 'Hullo, Padre!' he cried. 'Does your old Church know there's a war going on at all? I see that Convocation, which is, I suppose, the mouthpiece of the Church, deliberated a whole day as to the propriety of their canonizing Charles the First. Fancy worrying about a question of ecclesiastical etiquette concerning a sovereign dead two hundred and sixty years, while my boys are giving their lives every hour for them, safe and comfortable at home!' It certainly cannot be said that the Church is the Homocea which 'touches the spot,' I fear."

"I feel despondent when I look at the Church," continued the Vicar of Gorleston: "the episcopal apathy, the paltry parochial peddling, the want of a certain note to guide our fighting men, the silence of our leaders on the great religious difficulties that crowd men's minds. What do they offer to the bereaved wife, mother, or child? One fool is giving a series of sermons as to whether a man who dies in battle, fighting for England, goes to heaven! Why, the supreme sacrifice of Calvary, as Mr. Chapman was saying, the gospel of the greater Love, is being demonstrated by our sons serving in the trenches or afloat, and our bishops are so ignorant of the gospel of the Master that they cannot see the heroes' share in the work of redemption, the lifting up of the race. It makes me sick!" angrily concluded the Vicar, as he invited us all down to Gorleston to see his sailors really at work. "They work; they don't gabble, bless their honest hearts. You'll hear some strong language, but I prefer their hot curses to the cold prayers of our latter-day saints. These men have grasped the gospel of self-sacrifice."

"Yes, you are right to a great extent, Mr. Phillips," said Mr. Sheppard. "But where it appears to me the Church has really failed is in the fact that she makes no definite appeal. There is nothing in the

Church that corresponds to the patriotism of the nation. It makes no appeal to the heroic ; it doesn't call for service, much less for sacrifice. Patriotism does. And how can the Church be an appealing force until she reform herself? The Church must become more of a spiritual mission, less of a governmental department. In the hearts of the masses religion, I firmly believe, means far more to-day than it did in the days of the Crimea, let us say."

Well, perhaps they are all right, though I confess I felt, despite Mr. Sheppard's closing words, that the gloom had only been deepened by the deliberations of our little symposium. The truth probably lies in the unsuspected fact that the Church may have done more than we credit her with having done—like our late much-abused Government. The Church much resents, and frequently with reason, the criticism of the man of the world ; but I venture to suggest that frequently that criticism, albeit sometimes it errs on the side of undue severity and undue expectation of and demand for a very rigid standard and ideal of life and practice—practice more than doctrine—is really based on sound foundations. The bishops, for instance, are always indignant at any criticism touching their palaces and their purses—and it is a criticism passed equally by the peer and the peasant, for I have often smiled at the unanimity of their opinions upon that point at all events—but it is a criticism which is easily understandable. You will never find the man of the world in any station of life who can reconcile Lambeth Palace and £15,000 with the life and doctrine lived and taught by the poor, humble followers of Christ whom Dr. Davidson and the Bishop of London succeed to-day. "You never saw St. Paul riding in a carriage and pair," said a man to a former Bishop of London. "So much the worse for St. Paul," coarsely retorted the prelate, short-sighted fool that he was. I prefer the vision of St. Paul, ready and waiting to be offered, welcoming the glitter in the morning sun of the sword with which his head was smitten from his body, to the gaze of the Anglican prelate fixed upon the flesh-pots of Egypt. But prelates of this type grow rarer with the passing years, and the almost invariably high type of the modern bishop gives hope and encouragement for the future.

But there is sore need for revived effort and for revision of existing methods. The Church appears to me utterly to ignore the progress of the ages. She is a vast, glittering crystallization, precipitated like a ball upon this earth, and there she lies, an obstacle in the onward march of civilization, instead of rolling with the times. The people have gone on and left her behind. She no longer leads or even tries to lead. Leadership is committed to the hands of our writers, and even of our dramatists. I mean, they set the pace, and often enough erect and point to the standards. The Church, once the origin and preserver of ideals, is content to stand aside. The Church too much regards her own position, is too timid of doing anything that may imperil that position; never realizing that power is only attained and perpetuated by merit, and that once one ceases to deserve the exercise of power, it automatically falls from his hands. The Church fails to realize the onward rush of the ages. She forgets that religion, not theology, is the mainspring of her existence. Pass twenty thousand years more and how much of Rome or Canterbury will remain upon the earth? Not one stone shall be left upon another, either materially or from an intellectual point of view, whilst spiritually Christianity, in another form probably, may be more paramount and more powerful and all-pervading even than it is to-day. In many respects its teaching and its dogmas call for drastic overhauling. The theories that were conceived in the hermit dens of the Thebaid find but little response in the hearts of the picture-palace frequenter or the scientist of to-day. The Church may well, then, be subjected, in common with all other human institutions, to reform and modification, becoming in course of evolution a society to whom the choicest in the world of thought and action would be called upon to minister.

And that leads to the question of the education of the Anglican clergy. We are sadly in need of really learned men. Some years ago Mr. Forbes Phillips proposed a solution of modern difficulties by the creation of an Anglican Order of Jesuits, a proposition by no means so impossible as might appear at first sight. Few clergy receive so little practical education in their profession, or, indeed, are so unversed in real scholarship as the modern Anglican cleric. I believe that both Presbyterian ministers and Jesuit priests undergo a special course lasting over a period of seven years. That implies men armed at all points, men specialized for a particularly arduous and exigeant career.

We are now, as I write, upon the eve of the National Mission, which will eventuate either as an inspiring impulse or an expiring kick. But, in any case, what the Church requires is waking up.

"Will you let me hold a quiet day in your parish?" once wrote a bishop to the vicar of a lonely parish hidden away among the mountains of Wales. "My lord," was the prompt and unexpected reply, "what this parish wants is not a quiet day but an earthquake."

I am not so foolish as to advocate the abandonment of systematized theology. I only plead that religion shall not be subordinated to and submerged beneath mere theology. Every science, every art, every effort of thought must be subjected to system—organization, canons, dogmas, and doctrines. All I venture to suggest is a theology based on the old dogmas recast in the light of experience and the best thought of the ages—brought up to date, in short. What sticks equally in the gullet of the man of the world in the Mayfair drawing-room or the Pall Mall club, or of the man in the street loafing round the public-house bar is the doubt if the Church really is in passionate earnestness in her mission, if her clergy really believe all they are required to preach. When Charles Peace, the murderer, lay awaiting execution in his Newgate cell, he said to a clergyman one day, "If I believed all you profess to believe I would walk over broken bottles with bare feet from one end of the world to the other to tell my fellow-men what Christ had done for them." I was sitting in the smoking-room of my club the day on which the Bishop of London declared at Tower Hill that he had lost money rather than saved out of his £10,000 a year, adding to a man who had put a question to him on the subject of this same £10,000, "Yes, I know your sort." A cluster of my fellow-members were discussing the incident: an officer in the Gunners, a judge from the Straits Settlements, a commissioner on the West Coast, a well-known barrister—all men of the world, cultured, keen-witted, and each with a distinct bias toward religion and particularly towards the Church, and all of them great admirers of the Bishop of London, as indeed I am myself, but nevertheless the judge appeared to voice the majority when he declared himself as follows.

"Of course," said he, "of course the Bishop knows the sort of man, because he meets him in every class of society, who puts up that query about the enormous salary he receives, and the extraordinary condition of affairs which so arranges matters that a simple-living, teetotal bachelor bishop should in these tremendous days not be able to make both ends meet on £10,000 a year. The truth of the matter is there is no really sound rule of life for the absolutely earnest and consistent follower of Christ but that rule laid down by Him in the Sermon on the Mount. You say that is impossible to-day. Very well, then Christianity is impossible. The only chance for the priest to-day is poverty and passionate self-sacrifice, and any man will follow such a priest to the death. As a very young man," he continued, "I knew Father Lowder at the London Docks, and later I knew Father Dolling, and those men conquered by sheer self-sacrifice. And that is the kind of thing that appeals, because it carries conviction with it. But it wants a fanatic, and a fanatic is out of joint with the times. Unfortunately, no cause is ever won without its fanatic, and the Bishop of London's Church to-day hasn't got one."

And, on the whole, this verdict is pretty accurate. The Anglican Church is regarded by all classes to-day in the light of a conspicuous failure, mainly owing to the fact that it is lacking in spirituality and conviction; it is hampered by its increasing realization of a certain disagreeable sensation of compromise by which it is perpetually fettered and restrained just at the moment of its most earnest impulses. Thousands of the laity realize this to its fullest extent, and certainly hundreds of its clergy do. Indeed, what they themselves frankly acknowledge is the crying necessity for a deeper and a simpler and a more spiritual rule of life—many would gladly welcome the stern discipline of the great Roman Orders, both men and women—a rule of life and doctrine which would leave them no choice in the matter. The half-and-half state of things which is the result of the Anglican compromise between Romanism on the one hand and ice-chilled Protestantism on the other has landed them in a Laodicean No-man's Land which absolutely paralyses them hand and foot. Curiously enough I heard this very matter discussed, upwards of twenty years ago, at a dinner-party at Government House, Bombay, where the whole party was of the laity, and where none spoke with any authority other than that of the intelligence that comes of long-handed-down traditions and vast experience of men and matters.

The then Lady Sandhurst, a sister of Lord Spencer, whose husband, the late Lord Chamberlain, was Governor of Bombay at the time of which I speak, had been telling a small group of us at her end of the table of a conversation she had recently held with Commissioner Booth-Tucker, a distinguished ex-Indian Civil Servant, and a prominent official in the Salvation Army, and she emphasized the effect his conversation had had upon her, and how much she had been impressed by the stress that Mr. Booth-Tucker had laid upon the necessity for absolute poverty and self-denial in missionary work. "It is the secret of any success that the Salvation Army has in India," declared Lady Sandhurst, "and I don't think any missionary work will ever succeed without those qualities."

Among those seated close to Lady Sandhurst were the late Prince Francis of Teck and Prince Henri D'Orleans, a very widely travelled and a singularly thoughtful and charming personality, and they both joined in the conversation that followed Lady Sandhurst's remarks. I remember Prince Francis telling us that the "religionist" who had most impressed, not only the natives in a certain part of India where he had been quartered, but also the English official classes, was a Jesuit priest, a man with the reputation of a saint, and whose deep poverty and extremely rigid and self-denying mode of life and appearance appealed to every single person with whom he came into contact as nothing else could possibly have done.

"Our chaplains out here are good fellows enough," said the Prince, "but you want something more than 'good fellows' in India to convert either the natives or the English, who perhaps want a heap more converting than the natives." And then he added, with an emphasis which rather impressed me: "I don't know much about these matters, but I am quite sure that unless people can see for themselves that parsons really believe their own creed they are no good at the job. And out here in India this is specially true both with the natives and the English. The chaplains, as I say, are downright, good, honest, straight-living sort of chaps, but they don't seem so much in earnest—no, not one half or one quarter so much—as that Jesuit priest."

And Prince Henri D'Orleans, thoroughly agreeing, cast in his vote for Bishop Nicolai, of the Greek Church in Tokyo, who was commonly known as the Apostle of Japan, and who lived a life of consecrated poverty and the most rigid asceticism. And I think there was a general consensus of opinion that until that type of life and man pervaded the Anglican Church any other attempt at reform was hopeless. And this holds truer than ever to-day.

Mediæval conviction, and fanaticism even, combined with a common-sense realization of modern thought and modern necessities—which ought to help to deepen rather than to hamper conviction—is the crying need of the Church to-day.

Of course there are many who will laugh at this and tell us that the days of the monk and the hermit are for ever gone by, with which, of course, as a general proposition, I entirely agree. And yet as a sheer matter of fact the lives lived by the monks of the Thebaid, the thought that issued from those little hermitages hidden beneath the sands of the Libyan desert, were responsible for a capacity for vision and a habit and rule of life which have not, even in these days, altogether lost their influence upon the human race. For had they not lived first, the mediæval saints, the reformers, the apostles of the Italian Renaissance—that tremendous social, religious and political as well as artistic and literary movement which revolutionized the whole of European thought—the homilists and theologians of Elizabeth's and Charles's days, the Quakers, and the Wesleyans and the Tractarians and the Salvationists themselves would probably never have come into existence at all. Religion never had a greater opportunity than it has to-day, nor such hope of universal acceptance, but somehow or another its chosen vessels were rarely so ineffectual and inept—and all for the lack of courage and conviction!

CHAPTER VIII

MY PLUNGE INTO JOURNALISM

A PROLONGED but sadly restricted diet of penny buns was suddenly brought to a welcome conclusion in a manner and by means that were as unexpected as they were unconventional. I shared a cheap bedroom with a brilliant but shiftless artist who was wellnigh as hard up as myself. One night he returned at a comparatively early hour from dining with his cousin, an immensely wealthy peer of the realm. Quite casually he had asked this cousin of his for a small pecuniary loan, and equally casually the duke handed him a bundle of five-pound notes, and my friend passed in a moment from beggary to affluence, and, like the good sort he was, he hurried home, packed me into my dress clothes (which I had been wise enough not to pawn) and then into a hansom, and we drove off to "Jemmy's," one of the few high-class restaurants of that day, and I sat down to the first really square meal I had had for at least six weeks.

Suddenly my friend, who had very thoroughly sampled the ducal vintage, said to me—

"Look here, old chap, you're d——d clever fella; why don'tsh you writesh for papersh?"

"No good," I replied. "I don't even know how to start about it. Besides, I don't know what to say."

"Do interviewsh like American chaps; you get the money and the other fella does the work."

The simplicity of the idea immensely appealed to me. Just at that moment, as though sent by Providence, a little, slight, dark, pleasant-faced man, with a military-looking moustache, passed our table on his way out of the room, and immediately I recognized the famous author of "The Strange Adventures of a Phaeton" and half a score of other delightful romances of the eighties, William Black, one of the most popular novelists of Queen Victoria's reign.

"By Jove! you're right," I said. "I'll start at once."

I went home straightway and wrote a note to Mr. Black, care of his publishers, and in two days I had a most kindly invitation to go down and see him in his Brighton home. Well, here was a way out of the wood. But what was I to do with the interview when I had written it, and what paper was I to represent when I saw Mr. Black? I was shrewd enough to see that it would scarcely do to go entirely on my own, especially when I might have to confess that I had never written a line for the papers in my whole life. However, I lost not a moment in idle thought, but I went straight down to the *Pall Mall Gazette* and asked to see the editor, a certain Mr. W. T. Stead, who had already become notorious, if not indeed actually famous, for an extraordinary series of articles in the *Pall Mall Gazette* entitled "The Maiden Tribute." I sent my name in, which, of course, was quite unknown to any living soul in London, and I was shown up into a small room at the head of a rickety staircase, and after I had waited there for a few moments a shaggy, rough-haired man dashed into the room, and I beheld at once the first editor I had ever set eyes on and the most eccentric individual I had ever met. This was W. T. Stead.

"Well, what do you want?" was his greeting.

A sound measure of common sense, in which I was not altogether lacking, prompted me to reply straight off—

"Will you print an interview with William Black?"

"Can you get it?" asked Mr. Stead.

"Yes," I replied. "I am going down to see him to-morrow."

"Have you ever done an interview before?" asked the editor of the *Pall Mall Gazette*.

"Never," I answered.

"Well, you'll fail, you know."

"I don't think I will," said I. "I know all his books, and I have heaps of questions to ask him."

"All right, try your luck," replied Mr. Stead, "but I hae ma doots!"

So off I went down to Brighton, and sure enough the very first thing the kindly Scotsman said was, "What paper are you writing this for?"

"The *Pall Mall Gazette*," I was thankful to be able to reply.

"Capital," said my host. "Now fire away with your questions."

I forget what they were, nor is it of importance that I should reiterate them here, but at the end of our hour's talk Mr. Black observed—

"Upon my word, I believe you know more about my books than I do myself."

I fled joyously back to town, wrote out the interview, took it down to the *Pall Mall Gazette* that same evening, and the very next afternoon I had the felicity of beholding my article, my very first newspaper article, on the very first page of that famous and historic paper. I had started my career as a writer, and that without any trouble whatever! It seemed too easy and too good to be true, but the cheque that arrived a few days after soon dispersed any fears I may have entertained as to the reality of my good fortune.

And now before I proceed farther with the details of my early experiences in the world of journalism it will be well that I should explain the somewhat peculiar position I have always held in that world. And to do this I shall be perfectly frank, even though such frankness may appear to tell against myself.

To begin with, then, I chose the line of interviewing because it was the line that offered the least resistance. The interview was scarcely known in England at all; I therefore realized that, if it took on at all, it offered me more chances than leading articles, or articles on politics or drumsticks or ladies' bonnets could possibly do. I realized to the full that I was crammed with limitations, and that by interviewing only lay my way out of the *impasse* in which the quittance of my clerical work had landed me. I was perfectly frank with myself, and I knew intuitively that I had neither experience nor knowledge sufficient to admit of my even attempting to write the ordinary newspaper article, but at the same time I was conscious that I possessed certain cheap faculties which would have stood me in equally good stead had I applied for the position of a shop-window dresser. I knew how to put what little goods I did possess attractively in the window. Of course I had always to catch my hare, as Mrs. Glasse has put it for all time, but when I had caught him I had just skill enough to serve him tastily up at table. I have never made any pretensions to being considered a literary man. At the same time, I am not going to run myself down unnecessarily. I have compared my faculty for interviewing with a kind of twin faculty for shop-window dressing. Yes, that's all very well, but you must have *some* goods at your disposal for even the dressing of a shop window. And quite frankly, though I acknowledge that there is no great mental strain involved in, as a thoughtless man once put it to me, asking a lot of silly questions of a busy celebrity, yet it does demand certain qualities which not every one possesses.

To begin with, you must not ask silly questions—that is just the very thing you mustn't do; and to go on, you must know exactly what kind of questions to ask. For instance, I once interviewed Cardinal Manning in the morning, Charles Coborn in the afternoon, and George du Maurier in the evening. I had to discuss the old Tractarian question with the Cardinal; the Ultramontanist view of Catholicism; the curious, delicate, and very subtle spiritual *rapprochement* between Evangelicals such as Henry Venn Elliott and Robert McCheyne and Mediævalists like Thomas à Kempis, Catherine of Siena, and a modern preacher such as Père Agostini. I had also, I remember, to defend the theses of Bishop Gore, Canon Illingworth, and the rest in "Lux Mundi" against the indignation of the Cardinal, who considered them as far worse than anything that had ever appeared in the "Essays and Reviews" of his earlier years. Then I had to rush off to Charles Coborn and discuss with him the authorship and the singing and the popularity and the psychology—if I may so term it—of "Two Lovely Black Eyes," "The Man that Broke the Bank at Monte Carlo," "Come where the Booze is Cheapest," and I had to know something about the songs too—which I did; finishing up with a long and very close and discriminating conversation with the famous *Punch* artist on the curious fads and fashions, phases and crazes of modern society life in London—how he had killed Oscar Wilde's æsthetic vagaries with his clever mordant pencil; how he differentiated between the charming, graceful femininity of the nineties and the prim, dainty reticences of the "young ladies" Trollope so loved to depict in the sixties, and of whom du Maurier himself had given us such charming studies in the historic pages of *Punch*.

Even so humble a *littérateur* as I can pretend to be must possess a certain amount of knowledge combined with tact and discrimination before he can start in to write for the most exigeant of reading publics in the whole world—the London public; and in the special work of interviewing one must be a quick reader and judge of character, while at the same time you must never make your articles too personal or unduly intimate—which is, of course, the curse and disgrace of American newspapers.

No; interviewing is not quite so easy as some people imagine it is, but it certainly does not impose too great a strain upon the ordinary intellect, and therefore I very soon succeeded in making a far better income than I could ever have hoped to do as a curate, or even as a vicar or a rector. As I say, I started in entirely on my own, a course which, while it had its advantages, also had the very great disadvantage that it did not provide me with any of the ordinary journalistic experiences which attend the man who usually steps into the Street of Adventure, as Mr. Philip Gibbs so admirably terms it in his delightful novel dealing with modern life in Fleet Street. As a matter of fact, I hardly ever, from the strictly journalistic and business point of view, put my feet into Fleet Street at all.

Of course circumstances were very different when I started journalism in 1889 from what they are to-day, and no man now could possibly hope to succeed, actually in a moment, as I did. On one Monday I was practically starving; on the following Monday the cheques had begun that delightful flow which they have never altogether ceased ever since. It was as though I had gone into an oil district and at once started a "gusher." It was just as "ridiculous" and "miraculous" and "impossible" as anything you could read of in the pages of the *Family Herald* or see upon the screen of the picture palace to-day. My natural indolence had swiftly and unerringly pointed out to me the line of least resistance, and a certain faculty for luck (touch wood) brought me into touch with the journalistic world just exactly at the right moment. For never again, I suppose, certainly not within the working life of the young people of the present day, will such a golden era, journalistically speaking, present itself as presented itself to me. I reiterate that my success was due, not so much to my own merits, which were feeble enough, as to sheer luck. The moment I started in new papers began to flood the market. In quick succession arrived, and generally flourished too, the *Daily Graphic*, *Strand Magazine*, *Idler*, *Pearson's Magazine*, *Searchlight*, *Black and White*, *Pall Mall Magazine*, *Westminster Gazette*, *Star*, *Morning Leader*, *Answers*, *Windsor Magazine*, and half a dozen more, and almost all of them engaged me to write for them. And then, again, the field was much clearer for new-comers. Where there was one journalist in 1890 I should think I do not over-estimate it when I say there are at least ten to-day.

Let me get back to my work on the *Pall Mall*, from which I have wandered far during this digression. My first interview, as I have said, was with William Black: it was quite a success. So I said to myself, "Well, who else shall it be now?" And suddenly there came into my head the name of my dear old boyish hero—R. M. Ballantyne. No sooner thought of than he was written to, and in two days from the dispatch of my first note I was seated in the Harrow home of the famous writer, discussing with him "How I Write Boys' Stories." I can see him now as I sit here and write: the kindly and extremely handsome face with its silky beard and moustache and Grecian features, and his kindly smile of welcome as one of his sons, who was in the Head-master's House if I remember right, dashed in for a moment to see his father. I remember he told me that before writing "Deep Down—a Tale of the Cornish Mines," he worked and lived for ten weeks as a miner somewhere near Redruth, and when he resolved on his delightful story "Fighting the Flames—a Tale of the London Fire Brigade," he actually enrolled himself under Captain Massey Eyre Shaw, a great personal friend of his, as a regular fireman, and he used to go out to a fire nearly every night. He spent three weeks on a battleship with another friend, Lord Charles Beresford, and then he gave his boys a ripping story of modern naval life. And the same with all his stories.

Then I remember I interviewed Mr. Hall Caine, who has been a dear and valued friend of mine ever since; and in rapid succession to him came Mr. Grant Allen, one of the most delightful men and one of the most charming natures I ever met. Then I unearthed a man whom every one imagined had passed away for ever years before—Martin Tupper. Now there will be lots of people who have never even heard the name of Martin Tupper, and they will say, "Who on earth is he?" The other day I was spending the afternoon with the famous writer W. H. Hudson and the Ranee of Sarawak, one of my oldest and dearest friends, and one of the most artistic and keenly literary women I know. Mr. Hudson happened to allude to Philip James Bailey the poet.

"The author of 'Festus' you mean, do you not?" I asked.

"Yes," he said; "the man of whom Tennyson said he was almost afraid to speak lest he should appear to exaggerate. Have you ever heard of him?"

"Oh yes, I knew him," I replied. "I unearthed him for the *Pall Mall Gazette* years ago, and I remember

I had a most delightful conversation with him, as also I had with Martin Tupper."

"Dear me, that's very interesting," said Mr. Hudson. "Fancy meeting Tupper in the flesh, Ranee!"

"But I never heard of him," replied the Ranee. "Who was he?"

Mr. Hudson and I smiled.

"Well, at one time," said Mr. Hudson, "during the very middle of the last century, Martin Tupper was the most popular writer in England, and that with all classes practically; from Queen Victoria and the Prince Consort down to the cottager Martin Tupper and his famous 'Proverbial Philosophy' were household words. No bride ever went to her new home without a copy of that immortal work in her hands, and I almost doubt if any one could have been buried without it. And so you actually saw him in the flesh, did you, Mr. Blathwayt? That is really interesting. But fancy any one reading him to-day!"

One day, shortly after interviewing Mr. Martin Tupper, the thought suddenly struck me that from interviewing mere individuals it might be well so to enlarge the scope of interviewing as to exploit great systems of thought or of practical work or of social effort and endeavour, and that night I suddenly woke up and found myself saying, "The New Era and the Public Schools." "I've got it!" I said. "That's the thing wherein I'll catch the conscience of the king."

Next morning I dispatched a few letters and then quietly awaited the replies, which came speedily enough. On their arrival I hied me to the office of the *Pall Mall Gazette*, wherein Mr. E. T. Cook reigned in the place of Mr. Stead. I suggested my idea to him.

"Capital," he replied; "but you'll never get them to agree to being interviewed. I am perfectly certain that neither Eton, Harrow, nor Rugby will agree to the idea, though, as Winchester is my own old school, I might perhaps persuade Dr. Fearon to see you."

"But," I said, "Dr. Warre and Dr. Welldon have both consented in the kindliest manner to my proposal, and here are their letters!"

"Well," said Mr. Cook, almost gasping with astonishment, "I simply wouldn't have believed it. However, go ahead now as quickly as possible. Having got those two to start with, we shall probably get all the others," which, I may say, we did, and I interviewed no less than fourteen of the great headmasters of England.

And what magnificent men they were! What a vision of superb scholarship they opened up before me! What a glimpse of real learning and power and of what really constitutes literature in the highest meaning of the word I obtained after my conversation with these wonderful men! How then for the first time I realized what it meant to have the whole future, not only of England but of the whole vast British Empire, entrusted to their hands! It was the experience of my life, I think the most fascinating and the most entrancing, to talk at leisure with Dr. Warre of Eton, Dr. Welldon of Harrow, Mr. Bell of Marlborough, Dr. James of Rugby, Dr. Wilson, the famous Headmaster of Clifton, dear old Dr. Haig Brown of Charterhouse, and Dr. Fearon of Winchester. Taking them as a whole, they were perhaps the very finest Englishmen that I have ever met, and they put the ordinary type of so-called literary men absolutely into the shade. I found them, contrary to my own expectation and possibly even that of Mr. Cook, much more up to date and much less opposed to reforms than I had dared to hope, although I realized with them that our magnificent Public School system is not a thing with which any outsider can ever venture to intermeddle.

"The New Era and the Public Schools" was succeeded by a series of articles in which, with the help of the deans, I endeavoured to prove that the cathedrals might lend themselves to modernization even more effectually than the Public Schools, and Mr. Stead went so far as to suggest that St. Paul's might, on occasion, be well utilized as a Public Bath. Certainly the nave would do admirably for swimming contests, whilst I can imagine the Whispering Gallery would lend itself quite charmingly as a diving spring-off.

And then I started a very amusing and interesting

series of illustrated articles for the *Pall Mall Gazette* entitled "How I do my *Punch* Pictures," in which Harry Furniss, Linley Sambourne, George du Maurier and others took a very prominent part. In all my early efforts for the *Pall Mall* I received the most kindly help and assistance from Mr. E. T. Cook. He was the first editor with whom I really had anything to do, as Mr. Stead left the paper, I believe, the very week after I saw him about William Black, and therefore I studied him with no little interest. Since the day of the great Delane I do not suppose London has ever seen a finer editor than Sir Edward Cook as he now is. Next to sobriety of view and soundness of judgment, I should imagine that vision and discrimination are his outstanding qualifications for a task that calls forth all the mental, and frequently enough in these days too the spiritual, qualities that there may be in a man, and of his possession of all these qualities at their highest and their best E. T. Cook, the late editor of the *Pall Mall*, the *Westminster*, and the *Daily News*, gave ample and convincing demonstration.

I have had but little in the way of adventure during my so-called journalistic career, but of course one or two amusing incidents come to my memory as I write. For instance, many years ago, when I was still quite a young man, I went to interview a certain distinguished person in the neighbourhood of Camberley. Wishing to kill two birds with one stone, I invited myself to luncheon with an old friend, an officer at the Staff College. After luncheon, on a bright, burning summer day, I set out to walk along the tremendously dusty roads to this famous man's house. Can I ever forget that heat, that dust, my own appalling discomfort as I arrived at my destination, dead beat, and as white as a miller from head to foot ; a rather distressing thing in itself for one who always prided himself on his smart attire.

Well, be that as it may, I looked nothing more nor less than the veriest tramp when at long last I rang the bell at the celebrity's house. It was speedily answered by a very charming housemaid.

"You'll catch it ! " she said as she caught sight of me ;

"master *is* in a way. 'E's been expectin' you this last hour and more, and 'e's goin' on like anything!"

And just at that moment the master himself appeared, and he *was* in a way!

"Come in!" he cried; "don't stand there all day. I've been waiting long enough for you, in all conscience, without wasting any more time," and then, in the very midst of that glorious blaze of July sun that poured into the airy and spacious hall, he incontinently proceeded to *light a candle!*

"This poor fellow can't be quite right," I said to myself as I determined to wait developments.

"Just follow me down these stairs," he continued, leading the way down some ancient stone steps into an unbelievably gloomy cellar.

Arrived at the bottom, he walked to a corner of the cellar, held up the candle, and then said—

"Well, what do you think of that?"

"Well," I replied, "I hardly know what to think; at a first glance it gives one the idea that it might be a gas-meter, but then, again, it might be a meat-safe. In any case," I went on, thoroughly entering into the humour of the situation, "don't you think that brilliant scarlet is a little overpowering? A light grey or a delicate terracotta, it appears to me, might meet the occasion better, and would certainly be more in harmony with the mediæval aspect of its surroundings," I added as I gazed round the very monasterial crypt in which we were standing.

My host then took a long and deliberate stare at me, which, I may remark, he had not troubled to do before, and then he said—

"Are you Mr. Blathwayt?"

"Yes," I replied, "I am."

"Oh, well, I took you for the gas-man, and now I shall have all the trouble of coming down here again."

And then we went upstairs and made great friends over a cigar and a cup of tea.

"But don't you dare say a word in your article about that confounded meter, or I shall never hear the last of it."

And this is the very first time I have mentioned it.

You cannot be too thorough in interviewing any more than you can be in any other form of journalism, or, indeed, any kind of work for the matter of that. And in this connection I may relate an amusing incident which was told me many years ago by Lord Charles Beresford. He said that once he was interviewed, on board the Royal Yacht I think it was, which he was then commanding, by young Lord Mountmorres, who was at that time doing admirable and remarkable work on the Harmsworth staff as the then famous and much-talked-of "Mr. Answers." During the course of their conversation, which took place on deck, Lord Charles made some remark concerning the work of his men, especially in going aloft. Lord Mountmorres gazed up at the mast towering far above him, and before his host knew what he was up to he had swarmed up to the dizzy mast-head, and sat there in triumph, waving his cap. I believe the intrepid young interviewer is now a sedate and very popular curate in the Isle of Wight.

As in all other aspects of human life, it is the unexpected that is always happening in interviewing. For instance, when I went to talk to Cardinal Manning on the subtleties of modern and mediæval theology, he was standing at his window gazing down upon some little street gamins playing a game of cricket, and for a long time I couldn't get him off the subject of cricket and his old triumphs when he was captain of the Harrow cricket eleven sixty and more years before. And that very same day when I went to discuss music-hall songs with Mr. Charles Coborn he was discursive on the respective merits of very Low Church Evangelicalism, which he himself preferred and professed, as compared with the High Anglican doctrines and theories as propounded by the Ritualistic Sisterhood of East Grinstead, of which body of admirable and devoted women his own sister was a member.

I wish now I had kept all the innumerable letters I have received from celebrities all over the world in reply to my seductive invitations to come and be killed—interviewed I mean. What an enormously valuable collection they would be by now! Alas! I have retained but few; most of them I either burned or gave away. As an almost invariable rule they were charmingly phrased, even when, as was so often the case—too often for the welfare of my extravagant purse—they were refusals to my request.

I should have been a really rich man had every one to whom I applied for an interview complied with my suggestion. And I may here pause to observe that I never interviewed any one without first writing and asking their permission to do so, and I have made it an invariable rule to send a proof of the interview, before publication, in order that nothing should appear of which they did not fully and entirely approve.

And some of the replies were really interesting as well as kindly. For instance, the late Lord Dufferin, who at the time I wrote to him was our Ambassador in Paris, and who was a personal friend of my own and some of my family, wrote—

> I am afraid I must decline your too, too flattering suggestion, but the deserts of diplomacy are so strewn with the bones of the unwary that I have, alas! no choice in the matter.

I trust I shall not be considered as displaying any very great lack of taste if I quote the extremely kind letter I received from Mr. George Meredith in reply to my request for an interview for the *Pall Mall Gazette*—

> I really regret that the state of my health precludes me from granting you the interview you ask for I have been impressed by the articles you have sent me and I have been delighted by the English in which they are written."

One of the most amusing replies I ever received was from Lord Northcliffe, concerning whom the editor of a certain magazine had asked me to write a character sketch, and to do which the more accurately I felt, as my personal acquaintance with him was of the very slightest,

I ought first to have a special interview. Here is what he said—

DEAR MR. BLATHWAYT,

I am sorry, but I must ask you to excuse me from acceding to your request. I am like the little boy at a school treat who, when the squire's wife came round to him and asked him if he would like some strawberry jam, promptly replied—

No, thank you, marm. I works at the place where they makes it!

When I wrote to James Anthony Froude, the historian, he replied—

Certainly, come by all means. I was deeply interested in your character sketch of my old friend Owen [Sir Richard Owen, the famous biologist]. You have hit him off to the life, and I could almost imagine I was sitting in the room and talking to him.

And now I have said enough, nor would I have dared to say so much but that I think the intrinsic interest of the letters themselves justifies their inclusion in this chapter.

I cannot quit this chapter without a reference to the paper with which I have been continuously connected for nearly thirty years, and which, under the really distinguished and remarkably able editorship of the Rev. Dr. Downes and Mr. J. A. Craig, has fulfilled a great work amongst a certain large class of the more serious-minded portion of the community. I refer to the well-known weekly *Great Thoughts*, a paper more widely read than any other of its special class and kind.

I thus specially single out the names of Dr. Downes and Mr. J. A. Craig for the reason that they are admirable types of present-day Nonconformity, which in many respects has greatly improved on what it was thirty years ago, and to which I have more than once in these pages taken sincere exception. To-day the outlook in that direction is infinitely brighter and more inspiring, and the ministry of the Free Churches, immeasurably broader and more charitable in its vision, is distinguished alike for the deep spirituality and the exceptionally stainless character of its *personnel*.

G. F. WATTS.

CHAPTER IX

SOME PEOPLE I HAVE MET

A LITTLE wind-swept station; Dartmoor stretching wild and gloomy to the rear; a long road gleaming whitely between green hedges, over hill and dale; an ancient coach that is curiously reminiscent of Colonel Cody and the Far Wild West; and lastly, a broad, old-fashioned town, a gleaming piece of water, wooded down to its very edge, across which the evening shadows are falling long and level.

This is Kingsbridge, and here one takes the little steamer that lies in waiting for Salcombe, seven miles down the waterside.

And then the night glooms down upon the lovely little Marine Hotel, from which one catches a glorious glimpse of the great broad sea beyond, and with the roar of the long journey dying down in one's ears and the jolting of the old coach forgotten, with the sweet fresh air blowing in at the window, one sinks to rest in the summer night.

At least, I did that hot July night away back in 1892. The following morning ushered in a perfect day, and by eleven o'clock I was seated with the world-famed historian, James Anthony Froude, in a study that on one side opened into a pretty little conservatory, and on the other on to a lawn and garden that sloped down to the very edge of the sea-beaten cliff, and from the windows of which are obtained glimpses of wonderful beauty.

A very notable figure the historian presented as he sat easily back in his chair. And as I looked at the tall, strong, well-knit figure, clad in an easily fitting suit of summer grey, and noted the sunburnt face and muscular hands, and heard the still youngish voice, I found it almost impossible to realize that I was talking to a man seventy-four years of age. He did not look so much by ten years. To all intents and purposes it was a man in the full vigour and energy of life who sat there talking to me so vividly and brightly of the past, the present, and of that which was yet to come. Mr. Froude had just been made Regius Professor of History at Oxford, and he was extremely happy at the idea of going back to the very place where, many years before, one of his books had been publicly burned in the "quad."

"It is very curious that Lord Salisbury should have chosen me for the post. I went down to Oxford the other day. It is all greatly changed from what it was in my day, and young people are kept much more on the go than ever I was. And yet, curiously enough, the young men at Oxford and Cambridge are much less matured than we were. We were much more men of the world at their age. They have an enormous number of exams. to get through ; indeed, I wonder they can do it at all. But I dislike their light reading—Mark Twain and all that kind of stuff ; far inferior to Bulwer, Scott, and the old heroes."

I ventured an expression of opinion that Mr. Froude himself must have worked very hard in past days.

"Well, I don't know," he replied, with an easy shrug of his shoulders. "I have always been interested in history," he continued, waking up into energy. "I wonder what those people who write and speak against me so fluently and glibly would say if they saw all the old manuscripts and records I have been through. I had studied them all—in Simancas, Paris, Vienna, London. I went through a lot of your family state papers at Dyrham Park when I stayed with old Colonel Blathwayt some years ago—manuscripts that have never seen the light since they were written till I touched them, for I have often brushed off the sand which had been sprinkled on them to dry them."

After luncheon Mr. Froude gave me a cigar, and, lighting a pipe himself, he took me out into the lovely old garden. Pointing to a lonely village which straggled down the side of a neighbouring hill, he said—

"I'll tell you a tale about that village, which dates back to Doomsday Book, and is one of the most ancient in England. Some fifteen years ago the agent wrote to the proprietor to suggest that as the houses were very old, having been last repaired in the days of Edward III, he would suggest that they be burned down and the people sent adrift. This accordingly was done, despite my protestations, and one fine day a hundred people found themselves homeless, while those dear old houses, absolute relics of mediævalism, were burnt to the ground. I must tell you, too, that the village armed and sent out a ship to join Drake's expedition against the Armada. I wrote to a well-known London paper asking that they should expose it all, to which the only reply I received was that his Grace was too useful a member of the Liberal Party for the paper to take notice of his present action, and so risk offending him. Bah!" continued Mr. Froude, with a gesture of disgust, "the cant and humbug of politics sicken me. I always think of what Carlyle used to say to me: 'Dizzy and Gladstone are both charlatans, only Dizzy, at all events, knows he is one.'

"Ah," continued the great historian, "there was a remarkable man, Carlyle, the most remarkable man I have ever known. So intense; none like him. No," continued my host, in reply to a remark as to the peculiarity of his phraseology—"no, he wasn't in the least affected. His style was forged out of his intensity. He had more real faith than almost any one I ever met. I'll tell you the last thing he ever said to me. It was only a short time before he died, and I had gone to say good-bye to him. He whispered very feebly to me, 'Ah, isn't it strange that those People,' meaning," explained Mr. Froude, "the Powers Above—'isn't it strange that those People should have sent so much trouble on the very oldest man in Europe?' which, of course, he wasn't," added Mr. Froude, with a smile of reminiscence at the sad oddity of the scene. And then he continued: "I said to him, 'Well, we don't know Their reasons.' Carlyle at once replied, with all the old canny Scotch caution, 'Ah well, it would be rash to say They have no reason.' It was the last flicker of the old thought. It was very characteristic. He never spoke another word to me. I think his writings hereafter will be of immense value; they will give people something substantial to hold on to. Of all the remarkable people I have known Tennyson and Carlyle in my opinion are the only two who will really live on and on. The people I have known are far more interesting than those of to-day. You will say," he added with a charming smile, "that that is an old man's story, but I think it's true.

"By the by, Blathwayt, did Cardinal Manning ever tell you about our Metaphysical Society? It was started many years ago by Tennyson and James Knowles. Tennyson always wanted to *prove* that there was a future life. That was the origin of it, though he never got it proved beyond the possibility of doubt. There were thirty of us, representing every shade of thought—Manning, Ward, St. George Mivart (the scientific Catholic), Tennyson, Gladstone, Roundell Palmer, Huxley, Tyndall, Ruskin, two or three Anglican bishops, myself, and others. We used to talk of the future life, of conscience, of God. We dined together regularly and then discussed. We lasted two years. We never once quarrelled, though we talked with the utmost frankness and plainness. I remember once we discussed the possibility of miracles. I said there could be no doubt as to their possibility, for there was a living miracle in the fact of such a society as ours existing at all. And at all events, though we could never agree, there was one good result. We had learned not to hate. Curiously enough, neither Manning nor Gladstone impressed us with their power of debating. Manning, of course, was blinded by his superstition. Manning and Martineau, the famous Unitarian and one of our most valued members, presented a curious spectacle sitting together in perfect amity. But then, Manning used to admit"—and as Mr. Froude spoke I recalled how the old Cardinal more than once said the same thing to me—

"that there was great excuse for heresy nowadays; 'for,' said he, 'people have been born into it.'"

There was a gang of men making hay in the next field; this put Mr. Froude in mind of a little story.

"A clergyman came across an immense hay-wagon overturned in the road. A little boy was busily engaged in 'forking' the hay back into the cart. The vicar, taking pity on him, said, 'Come into the vicarage and have a rest.' After a while the boy got restless. 'I must go, sir,' he said. 'Father will be angry with me.' 'Oh, that's all right, my boy. There's no great hurry. Where is your father?' 'Please, sir,' replied the child, '*father's under the 'ay.*'"

An amusing incident in connection with Mr. Froude comes to my mind as I write. A few years ago I accompanied one of Dr. Lunn's great touring parties as special lecturer, and one evening Mr. Connop Perowne announced to the party that I would deliver a lecture on Froude. Rather to the mingled astonishment and amusement of some of us a certain young man, the most unlikely person for anything in the nature of a serious lecture, sprang up from his chair and declared to his companions, "I'll go to that lecture; I wouldn't miss it for worlds." And sure enough he went. After the lecture some one, noticing that he looked rather disconsolate, went up to him and said—

"Well, how did you like the lecture?"

"Oh," he slowly replied, "I suppose it was all right; but I didn't know anything about it, and I didn't understand much of what he said."

"But I thought you were so keen about it when Mr. Perowne gave it out at dinner."

"Yes, I know, but I thought he said '*Food*'!"

Mr. Thomas Hardy had just published his wonderful novel, "Tess of the D'Urbervilles," when I went to stay with him at Max Gate, his residence just outside Dorchester, in the spring of 1892. We had several most interesting talks about the writing of his books, and I was much interested when Mrs. Hardy told me of the immense interest the general public had taken in what they felt was the impending fate of the unfortunate Tess, who, as readers of the story will know, suffered the extreme penalty in the jail at Winchester.

"You cannot imagine," said the lady, "how many letters my husband received begging, and indeed imploring, him to end the story happily. One old gentleman, over eighty years of age, absolutely insisted upon her complete forgiveness and restitution."

"And why didn't you agree to their suggestions?" I asked Mr. Hardy.

"No," he replied, gravely shaking his head; "the optimistic 'living happy ever after' always raises in me a greater horror by its ghastly unreality than the honest sadness that comes of a logical and inevitable tragedy. The murder that Tess commits is the hereditary quality, to which I more than once allude in the book, working out in this impoverished descendant of a once noble family. That is logical. And again, it is but a simple transcription of the obvious that she should make reparation by death for her sin. Many women who have written to me have forgiven Tess because she expiated her offence on the scaffold. You ask why Tess should not have gone off with Clare and 'lived happily ever afterwards.' Don't you see that under *any* circumstances they were doomed to unhappiness? A sensitive man like Angel Clare could never have been happy with her. After the first few months he would inevitably have thrown her failings in her face."

Whilst her husband had been speaking Mrs. Hardy had left the room, and just at this moment she returned with a sketch, done by Mr. H. J. Moule, a brother of the present Bishop of Durham, and who was, indeed, the son of the original of the old clergyman, the Rev. — Clare in the novel, which depicted Woollridge Manor House, one of the seats of the ——, the family to which Tess belonged by right of her descent; and Mr. Hardy placed in my hands an enormous book, containing the pedigree of this family, by which I was able to trace without a break, right back to the Conquest, the records of this stately house.

I asked my host if he had drawn most of his characters from life.

"Oh yes," he replied, "almost all of them. Tess I only saw once in the flesh. I was walking along one evening and a cart came along in which was seated my beautiful heroine, who, I must confess, was urging her steed along with rather unnecessary vehemence of language. She coloured up very much when she saw me, but —as a novelist—I fell in love with her at once and adopted her as my heroine. Old Mr. Clare was a famous Dorsetshire parson whose name is still loved in this neighbourhood. Shepherd Oak in 'Far From the Madding Crowd' I knew well as a boy, while Bathsheba Everdene is a sort of reminiscence of one of my own aunts. Our family, you know, has lived here for centuries. Joseph Poorgrass, Eustacia, and Susan Nonsuch in 'The Return of the Native' were all well-known characters. Girls resembling the three dairymaids in 'Tess' used to get me to write their love-letters for them when I was a little boy. I suppose," he went on, replying to a question, "that unconsciously I absorbed a good deal of their mode of life and speech, and so I have been able to reproduce it in the dairy at Talbothays."

On the following morning, frosty and brilliant, Mr. Hardy took me for a stroll, pointing out as we walked along Egdon Heath, which, bathed in sunshine, lay in the far blue distance.

"Between the heath and us, in that hollow there," said he, "is Talbothays dairy. The road running whitely through the moorland over there leads to the Trumpet-Major's house, near Weymouth. And here," said he, a few moments later, as he pointed to an old red-brick house standing on the outskirts of Dorchester, which, of course, is known to all Mr. Hardy's readers as Casterbridge—"here is where Judge Jeffreys lodged in the Bloody Assize, and upon the spot on which we are now standing, and which to this day is called Gallows Hill, he one morning hanged eighty people."

"By the by," I said, "you must have found it rather painful to condemn poor Tess to death, did you not?"

"Yes," replied my companion. "Such dreams are we made of that I often think of the day when, having decided that she must die, I went purposely to Stonehenge to study the spot. It was a very gloomy, lowering day, and the skies seemed almost to touch the pillars of the great heathen temple."

It will read curiously to the younger generation, this grave and serious conversation and argument about a mere story, about a girl who never really lived and a crime that was never committed; but I can assure those who do not remember the appearance of "Tess" that they cannot possibly imagine the immense sensation the book created and the genuine, heart-aching sorrow that many tender souls endured on her mythical and wholly intangible behalf.

One of the most interesting of my memories is my visit to W. P. Frith, the famous Victorian painter of "The Derby Day," "Ramsgate Sands," "A Race for Wealth," and "The Railway Stations." I don't suppose any paintings were ever more popular or gained for themselves such tremendous fame, or, if I may say so, have so woven themselves into the lives, the intimate home lives, of the English people, and that, of course, quite apart from their artistic merit. Out of sheer mischief I once told Whistler I loved "The Derby Day," and asked him how he liked it. All I can say is—I still live. Dear old Frith lived in a day of sentiment—the homely sentiment of the British fireside and the antimacassar and mahogany tables—and he painted for a public who knew nothing about, and cared not a jot for, style in literature or technique in art, but who were "death" on sentiment and subject. And so, when "The Derby Day" appeared in 1854, small wonder that Queen Victoria and Albert the Good flew, enraptured, to gaze at its simple story, and policemen were specially told off to keep the crowd from crushing one another to death round the wall where it was hung. And sixteen years or so ago I went to see the dear old painter: a charming, very English personality, no long hair or velvet jacket or Chelsea "stunts" about him; a handsome, very national type of face, white whiskers, and a good, sturdy John Bull sort of manner—a man I took to at once, as, indeed, of course every one did who was so fortunate as to be blessed with his acquaintance. Dickens and Mrs. Henry Wood and Spurgeon and Queen Victoria and Sims Reeves and Landseer and A.L.O.E.—these people and the associations and memories connected with their names constituted his milieu, gave Frith his atmosphere, ranged him in his place and period in the Victorian era. And he himself was the very essence of it all. I remember we sat down over a cigar and he pulled out some old diary books, and we settled down for a lengthy talk.

" 'A Race for Wealth,' " he read out of his little diary. "That, you know, was a series on the lines of Hogarth's famous 'Rake's Progress.' Do you remember the trial scene in 'The Race for Wealth'? The barristers there are all portraits, three of them being Serjeant Ballantyne, Poland, and Montagu Williams. I was once engaged, simultaneously as it were, upon the portraits of Lord Chancellor Westbury and the Bishop of Oxford, Samuel Wilberforce, who were always at loggerheads with one another. And one day Lord Westbury caught sight of the portrait of his enemy. 'Ah! Sam of Oxford,' he said. 'I should have thought it impossible to produce a tolerably agreeable face and yet preserve any resemblance to the Bishop of Oxford'; and when the Bishop, on the following day, saw Westbury's portrait, he said, 'Like him, but not wicked enough!' The Derby picture took a lot of doing. Do you remember the little acrobat in the foreground?"

Did I not? Had I not been familiar with that child all my life? I believe it was the first picture of a child-performer I had ever seen. And had I not in later life encountered it in half a hundred dingy London lodgings —generally, curiously enough, in the little narrow entry-hall or passage, behind the front door—say in Jermyn Street bachelor lodgings?

"Oh yes," I replied, "I can see that child now."

"Well," said Mr. Frith, "that little boy used to be the plague of my life. Nothing would convince him that

I didn't want him to turn somersaults. He used to turn them at the most critical and unexpected moments, and one day he turned one bang into me and knocked me flat just as I was painting him. Then that old fellow in the front. Well, he was a pig-dealer, and one day he said to me very confidentially, 'They tell me, sir, you know the Queen.' 'Know the Queen? Of course I do,' I replied. 'Everybody knows the Queen.' 'Ah, but,' said old Bishop—that was his name—'Ah, but to speak to, you know, sir, *comfortable*.' 'Well, I've had the honour of speaking to her Majesty many times. Why do you ask?' 'Well, sir, you see there must be such a lot of pig-wash from Buckingham Palace and Windsor and them sort of places most likely thrown away, and my missus and me thinks if you was just to tip a word or two to the Queen, wich is a reel kind lady, as one and all knows, she would give her orders and I could fetch the wash away every week with my barrer.' "

We began to talk of picture titles.

"It means a lot from the dealer's point of view," said Mr. Frith, "but sometimes they make one squirm. I once painted a pretty young girl handing round wine. The publisher who engraved it titled it 'Sherry, sir?' Lord, how I hated the very word 'sherry' after that! I hated dining out, and always dreaded being asked that question. I went to the publisher and asked him to change the title. 'Lord, Mr. Frith,' he said, 'why, it's the title that sells it! We offered it before it was christened and nobody would look at it. Now it sells like ripe cherries.' "

He turned over a page or two of his diary.

"Ah," said he, "here's an interesting note to me. 'September 14, 1851.—Made pencil drawing of Ramsgate sands. I wonder if I shall make anything of it—who knows?' "

Well, the world knows now. I remember it when I was in the nursery, and it had then been popular for at least ten years.

"I spent the whole of 1861," continued Mr. Frith, "painting 'The Railway Station.' The police officers who are just arresting the forger are painted from two well-known detectives of that day, Haydn and Brett."

And then he went on, with a sudden change of subject—

"Do you know I am the only living man who ever saw Charles I? I will tell you how it was. When I was a boy my father lived in Windsor, and one night in the twenties I was walking home through the cloisters when I caught sight of a procession. First came the sexton of St. George's Chapel with a lantern in his hand, making long shadows as he walked, then two or three canons in their surplices, then the dean, and last of all his Majesty King George IV. I slipped behind a pillar and watched what would happen. They all walked up to a grave which had just been opened, and after a moment or so the dean stooped down and he picked up the head of a man with pointed beard and moustache, and with the eyes and everything complete, and he handed it very reverently to the King, who took it and looked at it, and as he looked it all seemed to crumble into dust and nothingness, and that was the very last of the Martyr King, and I am the only person in the world to-day who ever saw him almost as he was in life."

I was with dear old Sidney Cooper one day when he was painting away for dear life at one of his beloved and famous sheep in his ninety-seventh year. A charming, gentle, grey-bearded old man, who told me he attended his first lecture at the Royal Academy in 1824, when the subject was Michelangelo and the lecturer Fuseli, the famous artist, who was born in 1740—five years before the Battle of Culloden. There's a link for you in the chain of history! and when I saw Mr. Cooper we were in the thick of the Boer War. He told me a story or two about Fuseli. He always carried a red umbrella, and one day a friend met him, a lovely day in June, and he said to him, "What have you got that old umbrella for on a day like this?" and Fuseli replied, "I am just going to call on Constable." "Well, but what has that to do with it?" "Oh," answered the artist, "whenever I go to see him he's painting rain!"

On another occasion Fuseli went with Sir Thomas

Lawrence, P.R.A., to see the latter's picture for that year, "Satan Calling upon his Legions," and Fuseli was furious with the President. "Why, Lawrence," he cried, "you stole that idea from me!" "No," replied Sir Thomas, "from your *person*, not from your works. Do you remember that day on the Pembrokeshire cliffs overlooking the sea and your calling out, 'Grand, grand; oh, it's grand!' I was struck with the attitude into which you had thrown yourself while saying it, and the story of the devil gazing into the abyss from Milton's 'Paradise Lost' came into my mind, and I sketched you then and there. My posture *now* was yours *then*," and as he spoke Sir Thomas took up a sketch-book and showed the identical sketch to Fuseli, who was delighted.

The dear old artist tearfully told me of the hanging of his first picture away back in the twenties. It appeared it had been accepted and then mislaid, and, to make a long story short, the young artist was crowded out when at last it was discovered. But one of the R.A.'s—Vernon—generously removed one of his own pictures, and young Cooper was awarded the vacant space, and that picture, one of sheep, with Canterbury Cathedral gleaming through an April shower in the distance, made his reputation. Sidney Cooper lived into the present century, dying in his hundredth year, and painting to the last, and always painting sheep.

It is a far cry from Frith and Cooper to Florence Barclay and "The Rosary," but we'll risk it. I am not myself what I might venture to term a Rosarian, but I am interested, as most people are, in the personality of an author who at one fell swoop makes a wide appeal to a vast public, and to sell half a million copies of one novel nowadays, as Mrs. Barclay did in the case of "The Rosary," is to accomplish a veritable *tour de force*. High-brows sneer at such popularity; frankly I don't. I am too matter of fact. I envy it, but, with equal frankness, I marvel at it, and sometimes I deplore it. But what would you? Charles Garvice and Florence Barclay and two or three others sell by the thousand where Gissing and —— (it's hardly fair perhaps to name other delightful and inspiring writers) sell miserably by the hundred. Mrs. Barclay may not sell so well to-day as she did five years ago—I don't know—but whilst she lasted very few have ever had the vogue she had. She is a woman in the prime of life, with a ruddy, handsome face, crowned by a splendid head of prematurely grey hair, which only lends value to a pair of dark, flashing eyes, a woman of middle height, strong and capable, who impresses one as being quite unspoiled by all her wonderful success, very unaffected, and I should think kind-hearted and sincerely religious. A woman in a thousand and an immense force for good wherever she may chance to be; a woman quite apart from one's ordinary conception and experience of literary femininity. She is great on addressing Bible-meetings, and I should imagine she would be a vast success in a pulpit; she is, as a matter of fact, the wife of a Hertfordshire vicar, with certain members of whose family, extremely well known in the evangelical banking circles of my far-off youth, my people and I have been more or less acquainted all our lives. She's a brilliant pianist, and she was good enough to play "tuney" things for my special behoof. Unlike Mr. E. F. Benson or Mr. Filson Young, who write so delightfully about music, I am not learned enough in harmonies and double bass and intricate chords and discords and all that kind of thing to appreciate the kind of music I ought to appreciate—and yet please don't write me down as a hopeless Philistine. Mrs. Barclay, the day I saw her, played me the music of "The Miracle" through from start to finish, and she rang it out superbly. I asked her why she called her famous book "The Rosary."

"Oh," she replied, "my reason simply was that when I had half written the book I had to look out for some song for my heroine Jane to sing, and as I had 'The Rosary' among my music I chose that. The whole idea of 'The Rosary' grew out of an allusion to that same Jane in another of my books, 'The Wheels of Time,' in which I speak of her as being plain of feature and face, but that there came a time when the true beauty of her soul was seen in all its perfection."

CHAPTER X

MY SECOND VISIT TO AMERICA

IN 1891 I paid my second visit to America, under very different conditions from those of the seventies; and yet my memories of the earlier visit are infinitely more interesting to me personally, and certainly far more romantic. Nevertheless the second visit was memorable for the glimpses it gave me of people whose names were familiar to me as household words. And particularly interesting to me was my visit to the White House, where, in that year, President Harrison reigned supreme. There are few more beautiful cities on the face of the earth than Washington, and seen as I saw it, from the summit of the Capitol, as it lay bathed in brilliant sunshine far beneath and far around me, stretching for miles on either side, it is a sight that can never be forgotten. The most prominent object in this city of beautiful buildings, of exquisite avenues of unequalled grace—at that time at all events—was perhaps the Washington Memorial, which, some five or six hundred feet in height, towers above the neighbouring buildings and dominates the whole city. You cannot get away from it; it is to be seen for miles and from everywhere. It is the first thing that catches the eye on entering the city by railroad; it is the last object upon which the regretful eye of the traveller rests as he quits the home of the Presidents of the great Republic. "That slim Egyptian shaft uplifts its point to catch the dawn's and sunset's drifts of various gold." In shape it exactly resembles Cleopatra's Needle, but it is even more vastly imposing, as it rears itself from earth to heaven, a superb piece of marble, pure, chaste, virginal. Its pathos, its dignity, its poetry grow into the soul day by day and every day. And beneath it rolls the historic "silver Potomac," the scene of many stirring episodes during the late war. It was my good fortune to be the guest of a lady who was a relative of the great Southern general, General Lee, and I cannot easily forget the pleasure of my visit to this graceful Southern family, in which linger all the best traditions of the Virginian aristocracy. I went one day with them to the beautiful cemetery of Arlington, in which lie some three and twenty thousand soldiers who fell on either side in that vast struggle, of which modern England generally only heard about five years ago for the first time by means of the cinema picture palaces, but in the memory of which is comprised all the pathos and all the romance of so many a home in the great country beyond the seas. And right in the centre of this silent city of the dead stands, ever open to the reverential visitor, the home of the great general himself, and my hostess pointed out to me the rooms in which as a little child she used to play so happily, never dreaming that one day the ground on which she stood would be the scene of all that was so tragic and so sad.

Another day a large water picnic was planned, and some fifty or sixty of us went by steamer down the beautiful river, the Potomac, which divides Maryland from Virginia, passing as we sailed the most deserted and delightfully quaint, quiet, moss-grown city of Alexandria, down whose sun-flecked, shadow-stricken pathways an old-time Virginian squire would now and then slowly and thoughtfully pace up and down, meditating on the glories of the bygone past. And we caught a glimpse of the beautiful amphitheatre of the Chautaqua Society, which nestles among the trees by the water's side, where every summer some twenty thousand people used to assemble for mental improvement and bodily recreation. Arrived at our destination, we seated ourselves beneath the shadow of a fine old fort—a fort that, by reason of its strength, its shape, its moss-covered, ivy-grown walls and deeply-wooded moat, strongly remind one of the ruins of an old Norman castle. I had hardly thought it possible that America could have provided so ancient-looking a building. And here, a large and merry party of Southern ladies and gentlemen—and who are more charming than they?—myself the only Englishman, we seated ourselves in groups. Dinner over and cigars lighted, we watched the fiery sun sink down to rest away in "old Virginny," whilst one by one the stars peeped out and "the pale, sad moon crept out to sit on the lonely hill." Flashing to and fro, and brilliant against the dark green foliage, the fire-flies flew in myriads, whilst the harsh croaking of the bull-frogs, the shrill cry of some Southern bird, the hot, burning air, told me how far away I was from cold, foggy, prosaic old England. And then in the brilliant moonlight we drove from the landing-place through miles and miles of broad, well-laid-out streets, and between avenues of noble trees, which, with the dazzling white State buildings, go towards the making of one of the most beautiful cities I have ever seen, and it seemed impossible to believe that only fifty years previously it had been little better than a swamp, wherein sportsmen shot varied kinds of wild fowl, which were then almost the only inhabitants of what in 1891 had become a crowded and densely populated city.

I spent a day or two at the White House as guest of the President, to whom Cardinal Manning had given me a letter of introduction. It is a pretty house, very modest but very dignified, and I remember the entrance-hall, which was hung round with portraits of previous Presidents. Curiously enough Mr. Cleveland's portrait had been sent in a few days previously, and an ardent supporter of his, who was working might and main to secure his re-election, on seeing it there dryly remarked to me, "Yes, he has sent it on in advance."

The most popular personage in America at the time of which I write was a little child, whom doubtless America herself has forgotten to-day, but who was then celebrated from New York to San Francisco as Baby McKee, the President's favourite grandchild, about whom more stories were told and around whom more political jokes were uttered than has ever been the case with any other child on earth, save perhaps King Alphonso or the Queen of Holland. Baby McKee in those days was historic on both sides of the Atlantic. The President, it was said, ruled the United States, and Baby McKee ruled the President, and for two days also he ruled me. He was a dear little chap, with very light curls and devoted to his white rabbits, which he was always extremely anxious I should help him to feed.

Mrs. Harrison, who died a year or two after my visit, was a plain, homely, very unassuming person, exactly on a par with a Lord Mayor's wife here in London, very kindly, and very wishful to return once again into private life. She used to sit and sew on the veranda overlooking the charming gardens, with its glimpse of the Potomac flowing onward to the sea just beyond, the while the President and I would sit and talk. Just behind us towered a glorious magnolia, which, he told me, was the most northern grown magnolia in America. Now, it so happened he had just returned from his great presidential tour, in the newspaper accounts of which I had been deeply interested. I asked him if it had not been a very splendid and impressive sight, and he commented, as I thought he would do, on the overwhelming impression which was produced on his mind by the constant contemplation of such vast cheering crowds, none of whom he would ever see again.

"It is true," said he, "I often longed to get away by myself, but the sight of those myriads of human beings, assembled with but one object animating them all, and passing before me in endless, stately procession, was grand, and it can never fade from my mind."

As he spoke I recalled to my mind the story which was told of the Shah who had visited England two years previously. One day, as he was passing in procession through the vast crowds of the London streets assembled to do him honour, he observed to his Grand Vizier—

"It is sad to think that one will never see these beautiful people again, and sadder still to think how unknown they are to one another."

And the Grand Vizier replied—

"O Father of the Faithful and King of Kings, do you not remember how our great poet has said—

> 'Full many a soul to lip hath leapt,
> And no man known and no man wept'?"

I asked the President if he had not found it intensely difficult to make, without once repeating himself, the speeches he had made throughout his tour, for in that progression of his he had made no less than one hundred and forty speeches, full of graceful tact and clever allusion to topics of passing or permanent interest, and yet each speech was as fresh and original as its predecessor, and each exactly suited to the locality in which it was spoken. He smiled, and replied that it had become a second nature with him, though often enough it required more thought and study than one would imagine.

"Perhaps," he went on, "the most striking incident of my tour, and one which gave me an artistic suggestion for one of my speeches, was an incident that occurred in one of the seaports I visited. The naval officers had so arranged matters that, when it was night and our steamer came in, the limelight, whilst all around was in pitchy darkness, illuminated and brought out clear and vivid as daylight the national flag, which appeared to hang of itself between sea and sky. It was very lovely, emblematic of the great Republic, sent down by God Himself and illuminated by the light of heaven."

As I sat there a moment longer in silence, surrounded by the deepening gloom, my only companion the ruler of one of the mightiest nations on earth, one realized the beauty of the remark that he had just made, and one felt how thoroughly fitted was such a man to be the leader of his people. The night by now had fully come, and all around was buried in dreamless quietude. Suddenly a vivid flash of lightning sprang from the sky, and there stood revealed to our wondering gaze the lovely memorial, snow white, violet-hued; for one moment it was outlined against the darkening heavens, and yet again and again it flashed for a moment into sight, a solid white flame, as it might be, from earth to heaven.

I was the last Englishman, I believe, to visit Mr. James Russell Lowell at his simple, old-fashioned, quaintly English, and home-like residence at Cambridge, Mass., where I called on him from Boston close by. A maid-servant opened the door and admitted me to the presence of the poet-ambassador himself. At the very first glance I saw how ill he was—the transparency of his complexion, the weak voice, the trembling hand, telling me the sad truth all too plainly. But he would not hear of my calling again.

"On no account, Mr. Blathwayt," said he. "I want to hear the latest about England. You know the English and I are great friends."

I replied very heartily in the affirmative, adding that no ambassador had ever done so much in his own person to establish and maintain an *entente cordiale* between two nations as he. We then discussed, I remember, the duties and office of an ambassador. I cannot forget his smiling remark—

"But, after all, it is a very 'clerky' office nowadays. What with railways and telegraphs and steamboats, all the romance and much of the responsibility of the position of an ambassador has passed away. It may have its good side, it doubtless has; but now that a Minister is in such easy distance of his superiors he never feels his own master; he is at every beck and call from the people at home; he has little or no chance of distinguishing himself; there is nothing now to call forth his dash and energy, no means now by which he can show the world what a nation, in the person of her ambassador, can do. Many a bold stroke of policy is left undone nowadays which in the old times would have electrified the world. It *may* be all for the best," said Mr. Lowell, with a slow, doubtful smile, "but too many cooks, you know, spoil the pudding; and I am quite sure they spoil the ambassadorial temper."

An open volume was lying on the table.

"You see," said he, taking it up, "one gets back to

one's old loves as age creeps on. Scott is always fresh and new to me. I have been dipping into Dickens, too, but I don't like him even as well as I used to do, and he never was a great favourite of mine. His humour always struck me as being forced, and his style was not always as refined as it might have been."

We then fell into a discussion as to the influence of journalism upon literature—literature, that is, pure and simple—which most affected the other, and so on; the respective merits of English and American journalism.

"Your papers," he said, "would be far too stately for us. In one respect you have borrowed from us, and, I may add, improved upon us. Your 'interviews' are vastly superior. It strikes me that an interviewer does take the trouble to know something at least of the life and work of the man he is interviewing. And certainly you are much more discreet. I suffered once myself very severely, and at the hands of the son of a dear old friend. However, that is an old tale."

As I write a mental picture of the whole scene rises before me. He is seated in an armchair with his back to that far-famed "study window" out of which he has so often gazed. He sits there and looks quietly at his visitor, now and again raising a delicate hand to stroke his beard and moustache, or to press down the tobacco ashes in the very small pipe he is smoking, and which he tells me is an old favourite. The room is very untidy; papers lie scattered about; there is a little bust in the corner; a dog lies sleeping on the hearthrug. The great simplicity impresses me forcibly. I can scarcely realize to myself that I am sitting quite alone with one of the most famous of living men. The quaint, homely, farm-like surroundings, scholarly and refined though they be, do not strike me as carrying out the general idea of the surroundings of a poet of world renown, an ambassador of European fame. I recall but dimly the pictures on the wall, though I remember a portrait of Tennyson which he specially valued.

I asked him something about his English friends and the best-known men he had met over here. He spoke very highly of Gordon. "Oh, why did you let him die?" said he. "He was a very Galahad." He was exceedingly enthusiastic of Lord Salisbury as a politician. "He always reminds me of Tennyson's 'still, strong man in a blatant land'; not that I mean," he added, with a smiling bow, "that yours is a blatant land. I never really knew Lord Beaconsfield," he went on, "and I regret it. I met him once shortly before his death. I am always sorry that I was unable to accept the invitation of Lord Cranbrook, who was then Gathorne Hardy, to spend a week at Hemsted Park, where D'Israeli was a guest. It always seemed to me that 'Dizzy' was laughing in his sleeve at everything and every one. He was an Oriental to his finger-tips. He used to give me the idea that he was living a chapter of one of his own novels, a perpetual incarnation of one of his own characters. He might have been an ancient Egyptian or a Roman Augur or even an American, but never an Englishman. Cardinal Manning, again, he is a perpetual puzzle to me. An English gentleman, an Italian Cardinal, a prince and a courtier, a Radical reformer—there is a curious mixture—and yet one of the most winning of men."

He was much interested in my telling him of some conversations I had had myself with the Cardinal. "I asked his Eminence once," I said, "if he was not now and again conscious of the old leaven of Protestantism," and Mr. Lowell was deeply interested when I told him that the Cardinal smiled and laid his hand on my knee and said, "Do you know that is a very home question indeed, but I will gladly acknowledge that my old training has never altogether left me, and I still feel I owe a great deal to it." "I quite believe it," replied Mr. Lowell. "I can distinctly trace Puritan influence here in America in Roman Catholics." He was evidently pleased when I told him that only a few days previously both Cardinal Gibbons of Baltimore and Dr. Corrigan, the Roman Catholic Archbishop of New York, had been regretting to me that the old spirit of Puritanism was dying out in America. "Did they indeed?" said my host; "that is very interesting, and a very noble remark for them to make. But the decay of our Puritanism is only in creed; its influence among all classes is strong and healthy still."

It must be remembered that this conversation took place upwards of five-and-twenty years ago, and that a whole generation has grown up since then, and that things are widely different in America from what they were as Mr. Lowell, who died three months after this conversation, knew them.

Drifting on in a desultory kind of conversation, I happened to make a remark on the respective attitudes of the Southern whites and blacks, and I am afraid I more than half hinted that perhaps both parties were happier and more contented in the old days.

"Oh, but," Mr. Lowell replied, "however that may have been—and I think you are quite wrong—you must not forget the principle involved. Nothing on earth can condone slavery. I never understood the preference of the English aristocracy for the Southerners, although living in England explained much to me that used to be quite incomprehensible. Your social differences, with their exact parallel religious inequalities, Church and Dissent, solved much of the mystery. But nowadays there would be much less of that very wrong sympathy with the South than there was thirty years ago."

I asked him, knowing well his love for England, which country he liked best. "Well, my own land, of course. And yet I have more actual friends on your side than I have here. I can never pass Longfellow's house, which, as you know, is close by here, without a thrill. For years he was my neighbour and dearest friend. Then Emerson has gone too. We are all going, you know—'the old order changeth, giving place to new'—and yet it is all as it should be—all for the best. Oliver Wendell Holmes, gay youth that he is, often comes over to chat with me. He is eighty-two. I am many years his junior. I am seventy-two, but yet I don't feel old. I don't feel my age as I am told by books I ought to feel it."

And indeed it was true. His bright, easy manner, especially his voice, quite untouched by the influence of time—all these things pointed, despite his manifest delicacy, to the very prime and not to the sunset of life.

I rose to take my leave. "Oh, must you really go? I am so glad to have seen you. Try and come again on Friday." As we stood a moment in the sunshine—for he himself came to the door with me—I commented on the very English aspect of his little home. "I am glad you think so, but it is easily explained. We have lived here for some generations. At the back of the kitchen fire range you will find the Royal Arms of England and the monogram 'G.R.' My grandmother, you know, was a loyalist to her death, and whenever Independence Day (July 4th) came round, instead of joining in the general rejoicing she would dress in deep black, fast all day, and loudly lament 'our late unhappy differences with His Most Gracious Majesty.'"

The strains of a distant waltz floated by on the summer breeze. Mr. Lowell smiled. "Dear me, that does remind me of England. I think I heard that last at Lady Kenmare's. How music links the present with the past!"

It was a curious reflection—a reflection that lost none of its interest as I looked at him who had uttered it—the then and now linked by a passing strain of music. As I passed down the little path I turned once again to look at the gentle figure, standing frail and delicate, with fast whitening hair and beard, illumined by the light of the westering sun. An unerring presentiment stole upon me that then he was fast passing to where "beyond these voices there is peace." And three months later, on an August day in the Isle of Wight, came to me the news that James Russell Lowell was no more.

I am conscious that all this must be *vieux jeu* to many of my readers, some of whom were not even born when Mr. Lowell died, but still he was so distinguished a man, and so much loved here in England, that I venture to think this slight memory of him may not be without a certain interest, and I am quite sure most of my readers must know, by name at all events, Oliver Wendell Holmes, the famous and once so popular "Autocrat of the Breakfast Table," with whom I spent several very pleasant afternoons in Boston in 1891. I remember on the first meeting the dear old gentleman took me over to the window.

"There," said he, "over the water is Harvard University, Cambridge, my birthplace. Few people can see at one glance all that I can see—birthplace, college, and the cemetery where so many of my friends and relatives lie buried, and where I hope to lie one day myself."

"Well, sir," I replied, "let us hope that day is still far off. Mr. Russell Lowell called you a gay youth yesterday when I went to see him."

"Yes, my friend, I have worn well; but you cannot cheat old age. I may be able to walk well at eighty-two, which is my age, but you must catch the old man when he is asleep or when he is walking downstairs. It is then that old age tells, then that we feel that we are not what we once were. It is then that the occupation that once was a pleasure becomes a task. I feel that at times now, though not always. I want to be idle now and then. I have just had a very tempting offer to write some articles, but I hesitate about accepting it. No, you cannot cheat old age."

Here the old gentleman fell into a mood of thought, and I glanced round the pretty room, noting the well-known statuette of Thackeray; there, too, in close proximity, were "The Dying Gladiator" and the "Venus de Medici." I crossed the room to look at the bookshelf—books tell so much. The Doctor roused himself.

"I have rather a miscellaneous collection of books," he said. "I tell a good many of my friends that they don't know half of the interesting books that there are in the world. Now, look at that edition of 'The Celebrities of the Century.' That is a wonderful book. I am also very strong in encyclopædias, and I am very fond of those two dictionaries which lie there upon my writing-table, always open. I am fond of shooting a word flying and bringing it down. I criticize words very closely. In all boarding-houses there is a dish called 'hash.' Now, what do you understand by that?"

"Oh," I replied, "in England that is what we understand by resurrected meat."

The Doctor laughed. "Yes, but I don't mean that. Is it minced?"

"No." I thought it was not.

"Exactly," said Dr. Holmes, "you are right; but very few know that. An English lady gave me a written definition of the word, so I know. Look at those red books. 'Old Yorkshire,' by William Smith. I feel I know Yorkshire and the old English life when I have read those works. And there, too, is another book—'The Nation in the Parish.' You never heard of the book, I'll be bound, and yet it is written by a countryman of yours—the rector of Upton-on-Severn. There is genius in that title. It contains the condensed history of Englishmen everywhere."

A question from me as to the books which had influenced him led us into a curious religious and social discussion.

"I really cannot say what books have most influenced me," he replied, "except perhaps the narrowest Calvinistic productions, which early awakened my mind to theological enormities. Look at Scott's 'Commentary'; that is a dreadful monument of bigotry. But the great dykes of the Puritan faith are fast breaking up, although there are men who would rather give up a newly discovered truth than disturb old symbols."

And then came a few memories of and remarks upon his visits to England.

"I was at the Derby in 1834, when Plenipotentiary, whose portrait is on the wall behind you, won the race, and again in Ormonde's year, 1886. I rejoiced much in Salisbury Cathedral. It was the first I had ever seen. Stratford, too—how lovely, how interesting that is! hallowed ground to all Americans. But how many have died since I was in England! I will tell you one thing that struck me very forcibly in London and that was the existence of small quasi-villages in its very midst. Look at Chelsea, for instance, where our good mutual friend Haweis lives. It is a little dimple in a great whirlpool."

I asked Dr. Holmes whom he considered the most interesting and the most pre-eminent people of all those he had known in his long life—and he was born in 1809!

"Ah," said he, "I am indeed surrounded by a great cloud of witnesses. What is it Matthew Arnold says of those three voices that so influenced him in young life—Newman, Carlyle, Emerson? Well, as I go backward I hear many voices, but I have to discriminate. I have to chip the coin a great deal. One man is great in one direction but limited in another; perhaps he is wanting in common sense. Professor Asa Grey—how will he do? He went far beyond his speciality. Then there was that splendid man James Freeman Clarke. But they are all dead. Pretty much all of my friends are dead. Whittier is a man we all revere and respect; but about him there is a certain reticence. I miss Emerson and Longfellow, two of my dearest friends, very much. I used frequently to meet both of them at the Saturday Night Club here in Boston; and that great hearty creature, Agassiz—more life in him than in half a dozen ordinary men, and whose laugh still rings in my ears. And then, of course, there was Thackeray—dear Thackeray. I remember once little Martin Tupper came rushing benignly in to see me. I asked Thackeray if he knew him, and Thackeray cried out, 'Know dear little Tup? Why, of course I do: we *all* do!' However, to answer your question: it is not necessarily the greatest man who lives longest in your memory, or the most learned in *belles lettres*. J. R. Lowell, of course, useful in every way, a valuable man in any community. Emerson too—and his voice! There was a timbre in that you got nowhere else; more like the tone in the voice of some cathedral choir boy. And so delicate, so spiritual, so sweet a man, and yet a man of obvious limitations. He had not much knowledge of or care for science; he was a charming, discursive thinker; a high, stimulating thinker, but not a very deep one. On the whole, to finally answer your question, James Freeman Clarke is the man who, of all others, is the most prominent in the ranks of those whom I have loved and lost."

And then came a long pause, during which the dear old gentleman sat lost in thought. As I looked at him, seated in the dying sunlight streaming through the window, his own beautiful lines rose to my memory—

> Build thee more stately mansions, O my soul
> As the swift seasons roll :
> Leave thy low-vaulted past,
> Let each new temple, nobler than the last,
> Shut thee from heaven with a dome more vast,
> Till thou at length art free,
> Leaving thine outgrown shell by life's unresting sea.

I alluded to them, and he smiled with a quiet pleasure. "Yes, I remember ; those are in the 'Breakfast Table.'" And then he continued : "Did you meet any of the old-fashioned negroes when you were down South? You know there is a regular literature growing up round the blacks in the Southern States. They are people well worth cultivating, extraordinarily individual and interesting. I heard the other day of a negro giving witness in a burglary case against the prisoner. 'Do you call him a thief?' threateningly demanded the counsel for the defence. 'I'm not goin' to say he's a tief, sah, but what I says is dis : If I was a chicken and I saw dat nigger loafin' around I'd roost high—dat's all!' In another case an old darky lay very ill. The minister called to see him. 'Well, Rufus, how are you getting on? Did the new doctor take your temperature?' 'I don't know, sah,' replied the old man ; 'the only thing I've missed so far is my old watch!'

"It is curious how little anecdotes stick in the memory when all else is forgotten," continued Dr. Holmes. "I remember Longfellow told me many years ago that a travelling Englishman 'doing' the United States called on him once. He seemed rather at a loss to explain his intrusion, and at last he said : 'Is this Mr. Longfellow? Well, sir, as you have no ruins in your country, I thought I would call and see *you*!"

"And Dr. Samuel Wilberforce, when he was Bishop of Oxford, told me a thing that immensely delighted me. He had been telling the children at a Sunday School about Jacob's ladder and the angels of God ascending and descending upon it. He was rather startled and put about when suddenly a little boy said to him: 'But angels can fly; a ladder wouldn't be no good to them.' The good Bishop didn't know what to say, but, like all bishops, he had no idea of giving himself away, and so he said: 'Perhaps some other little boy or girl can tell Billy why it was.' A long silence, until at last a little girl piped out: 'Please, sir, p'raps the angels was moultin'.'

"The Bishop told me another good yarn. A vicar had been newly appointed to a parish, and he asked the churchwarden something about his new parishioners. 'Well, vicar, you'll have to go very gently in this parish. Mustn't tread on anybody's toes. Say what you like of the sins and shortcomings of the old patriarchs, Moses and Abraham and Jacob and David, but don't touch on modern failings at all!'

"No," he went on, in reply to a question I put to him —"no, I have no definite opinions as to the respective merits of English and American literature. We have original men: Nathaniel Hawthorne, for instance. Two or three stand entirely apart because they lived apart in a new life: Bret Harte with his Californian experiences; and Mark Twain has told his experiences with the twang upon them and with great freshness. The first and earliest of our national humorists was John Phœnix: he was really funny. As regards my own writing, there was and is no special art about it, merely written from hand to mouth. I began in the *Atlantic Monthly*. I thought I had written myself out, but I waited a little and things came of themselves. I enjoyed writing them, but now, as I said, I don't like to be stirred up to fresh efforts. I am much written to for my autograph, and the one line I often prefix to that autograph is the last line of my 'One-Horse Shay,' 'Logic is logic.' The young ladies at Lowell University," he went on, "have, I am told, got up a society or club called after my latest work, 'The Tea-Cups.' They are going to read and take the characters of the tea-cup circle. I am writing two memoirs at the present moment, one being that of our greatest surgeon. I am a reasonably quick writer, but a slow composer and reader. I write both easily and with difficulty, like Planchette. I am a stupid fellow at times and require the lash ; but when I am stirred up I am impatient, and I don't want to waste time dipping a pen in the ink."

I offered to post his letters for him in the pillar-box at the end of the street as I went by.

"No," he said ; "you are very good, but I have made it a lifelong rule to post my own letters. Then you are pretty sure of them."

A few days after my visit to Dr. Oliver Wendell Holmes I lunched with Mr. Andrew Carnegie at his house just off Fifth Avenue, in New York. Some beautiful fishing-rods stood in a corner. "I am off to Scotland to-morrow," said Mr. Carnegie, "and those beauties go with me." The tributes of his friends were spread in rich profusion about the room. "I count myself happy," said he, as he drew my attention to them, "in remembering my good friends." Herbert Spencer was one of his heroes. "Read what he says," he went on, pointing to some autograph writings on the wall ; "isn't it fine? 'The highest truth a man sees he will fearlessly proclaim.' And Gladstone sent me this : 'But as the British Constitution is the most subtle organism which has proceeded from the womb and the long gestation of progressive history, so the American Constitution is, so far as I can see, the most wonderful work ever struck off at a given time by the brain and purpose of man.'"

Mr. Carnegie was very strong on the payment of Members of Parliament.

"Why don't you hammer away at that in England? I would even tolerate a Royal Family to obtain such a magnificent piece of legislation as that. Great Britain will never be free till she gets that measure passed, which includes all others. It is the very key of the position, but it will be a long time before you will see it in England. It is, and it ought to be, *the* test of a Radical ;

Is he in favour of the payment of Members? If not, away with him."

"But," I suggested, "the poor man might be bribed."

"No—no—no! The poor man is more honest than the rich. More votes are cast in the British Parliament against conviction than are cast here by our homely, homespun representatives. Your men vote for party, ours for principle! Wealth gives no advantages here. It doesn't even elect a President. What struck a number of English gentlemen whom I took over my steel and iron works the other day was, not the improved machinery or the extent of the place, or the evidence of wealth and prosperity, *but the character of the men*. 'We have no corresponding class in England,' said they. The American does not drink; he is regular, he is ambitious to beat the record, he is the hardest-working man in the world. It is merit, not rank, here. The only gauche and awkward men at a great reception I recently attended were the millionaires, poor dears!"

He is quite sincere in his depreciation of mere earthly riches.

"I attribute all my success to my poverty," he told me. "I had no nurse, no tutor. My mother and my father sacrificed themselves for their son; a daily example of proud independence, pure and honest in word and deed. Boys reared as I was always have marched, and they always will, straight to the front and lead the world. *They* are the epoch-makers. The bracing school of poverty is the only school capable of producing the supremely great. And above all other influences I place the influence of a good, a holy, and a pure-minded mother. I cannot tell you what my mother was to me—my good, dear Scotch mother. She died five years ago, and I have never had the courage to look at her portrait since. I am a great believer in Ruskin, and here is a motto of his that I carry about with me." And as he spoke Mr. Carnegie drew with great care from his breast pocket a card, on which was written: "Nor is there anything among other nations to approach the dignity of a true Scotchwoman's face in the tried perfectness of her old age."

I once spent an evening with Julia Ward Howe, who wrote the famous 'Battle Hymn of the Republic,' and she told me how she came to do it

"Late in the autumn of 1861," she said, "shortly after our great Civil War had begun, I visited Washington. One day whilst there I drove out to see a review of the troops. In the carriage with me was my dear pastor, James Freeman Clarke, Oliver Wendell Holmes's great friend. The day was fine, and all promised well, but the enemy suddenly surprised us, and we had to beat a hasty retreat. For a long distance the soldiers nearly filled the road, they were before and behind, and we were obliged to drive very slowly. We presently began to sing some of the well-known songs of the war, and among them—

> John Brown's body lies mouldering in the grave,
> But his soul goes marching on.

This seemed to please the soldiers, who cried, 'Good for you!' and themselves took up the strain. Mr. Clarke told me that I ought to write some new words to the tune. I replied that I had often wished to do so. In spite of the excitement of the day I went to bed and slept as usual, but awoke next morning in the grey of the early dawn, and, to my astonishment, found that the wished-for lines were arranging themselves in my brain. I lay quite still until the last verse had completed itself in my thoughts, then I rose, saying to myself: 'I shall lose this if I don't write it down immediately.' I searched for a sheet of paper and an old stump of a pen, and began to scrawl the lines almost without looking, as I had learned to do by scratching down verses in the darkened room where my little children were sleeping. Having completed this, I lay down again and fell asleep, but not without feeling that something of importance had happened to me. The poem was published some time after in the *Atlantic Monthly*. It first came prominently into notice when Chaplain McCabe, newly released from

Libby Prison, gave a lecture in Washington, and in the course of it told how he and his fellow-prisoners, having become possessed of a copy of the 'Battle Hymn,' sang it with a will in the darkness and loneliness of their prison."

Mrs. Maud Elliott, Mrs. Howe's daughter, then suggested that she and her mother should sing it to me, as I had never heard it set to music. And so, with all the verve and energy of her youth, though she was then in her seventy-third year, and with wonderful brilliancy of execution and delicacy of touch, Mrs. Howe herself struck the opening chords upon the piano. Here is the last verse—

> In the beauty of the lilies Christ was borne across the sea,
> With a glory in His bosom that transfigures you and me;
> As He died to make men holy, let us die to make men free.
> While God is marching on.
> Glory! glory! Hallelujah!
> Glory! glory! Hallelujah!
> Glory! glory! Hallelujah!
> While God is marching on.

As the last long, triumphant chords died away, the poetess rose, and, crossing the room to where I was sitting, she placed in my hands a beautiful copy of these stirring lines of hers, writing beneath them in strong, clear characters—

"Julia Ward Howe offers this copy of her poem to Mr. Raymond Blathwayt."

Among those present that memorable evening was Margaret Deland, the authoress of a once very famous American novel, "John Ward, Preacher," on which a distinguished cleric once preached a very stirring sermon in Westminster Abbey.

"I wrote it as a protest against the appalling bigotry of theological and religious thought in the Middle States," she told me. "I was immensely impressed by the reality of this horrible faith among the best sort of people, and I said to myself, 'Let me find what would be the logical outcome of this belief in a sincere and noble-minded person.' That there never was a John

Ward I felt quite sure, simply because, so far as I knew, there never was a logical Presbyterian—one who would really preach and believe that men and women were doomed for no fault of their own to burn for ever and ever in literal flames of fire. However, since the publication of the book I have heard of a parallel case to the one in my book ; it happened in the Western States. A certain Rev. Mr. Packard, of Illinois, put his wife into an insane asylum because she did not believe in original sin. He said to her : 'It is for your good I am doing this. I want to save your soul. You do not believe in total depravity, and I want to make you right.' The woman then inquired if she had not a right to her own opinion, and her husband replied : 'You have a right to right opinions, but no right to wrong opinions.' She was accordingly placed in a lunatic asylum for three years."

Of course modern readers will not credit this, and yet it took place in the actual lifetime of the millions who are still in their twenties. The bigotry of what is known as the Calvinistic school is unbelievable in its hideous cruelty, its ferocity, and its injustice. And yet I have known splendid people to whom such views were dearer, far dearer, than their own lives. Fifty years ago those views were universal both here and in America ; they are held by thousands upon thousands to-day.

Have you ever read "The Lady and the Tiger"? I once stayed a day or two with Frank R. Stockton, who wrote that book and "Rudder Grange" and "The Casting Away of Mrs. Lecks and Mrs. Aleshine," both of which were immensely popular, at the time of which I write, both in England and America. One day out walking in the woods round his pretty home in New Jersey I told him that some English ladies had told me, if I ever met him in America, I was to be sure to ask him : "Which door did the princess point out to her lover—the one which concealed the lady or the one which hid the tiger?"

"Ah," laughingly replied Mr. Stockton, "tell those ladies as soon as I become a woman I will tell them.

None but a woman could decide that question. That story was not really written for publication at all. I composed it to tell at a literary gathering."

In 1891 W. D. Howells was one of the most popular novelists both in America and in England. Does any one read him to-day, I wonder? To me always one of the most delicate and charming writers of whom I know, and he himself a delightful personality. Rather a dreamer, very much of an academic Socialist; over here he would probably have ranked himself with the Fabian Society. In Boston, the home of culture—ill-fated word—he was in 1891 almost the most distinguished figure in a town which was absolutely stiff with distinction. When I had stated my intention of going to America an English lady said to me: "Now, Mr. Blathwayt, do try and *live* a chapter of Howells. Don't waste your time in the Far West, but find out for yourself and us something of the secret of this lofty cultivation of the Boston society of which we hear so much in England." So when I met Mr. Howells I told him what this lady had said, and how much some of us appreciated the delicate quality of his writing.

"Well, I am very glad to hear it," he replied, smiling rather doubtfully; "but I should have thought you English were far too matter of fact to care for my analysis and dissection of character and motive. It seems to me that the American ideals are as far removed from the English as it is possible to conceive."

"Oh no," I said. "We don't take things so entirely *au pied de la lettre* as you perhaps think we do."

"Well, that's as may be," replied Mr. Howells; "but, ideals or no, it occurred to me that when I began to write fiction I would put away my literary spectacles and look at things from my own eyes. I would take every-day people and speak of every-day events. I remembered what Emerson had written: 'I ask not for the great, the remote, the romantic; I embrace the common. I sit at the feet of the familiar and low. The foolish man wonders at the unusual, but the wise man at the usual. To-day always looks mean to the thoughtless, but to-day is a king in disguise.' And then I realized that the elemental things of life embraced all classes and touched the highest and lowest emotions. Take as an example my book called 'A Modern Instance.' One night, some years ago, I went to see Janauschek play 'Medea.' 'Why,' I said to myself, 'there is an Indiana divorce case.' I determined then and there to write a story on those lines, and take the leading motif of 'Medea.' I would write a story of American life, and see how far at the same time I could keep to the old Greek lines. Then I thought I would do it in dramatic form as a play —'The New Medea.' I would make her a spiritualistic medium instead of a sorceress. Then her father came in. I found I couldn't work it as a play. I gave it up after a while, and wrote instead 'The Lady of the Aroostook.' Then after a while I recurred to 'The Undiscovered Country,' in which the original idea reached its final consummation. I read it to my wife, and when I reached that part which deals with the Shaker village she gave her approval, and bade me go ahead. I wrote several other books, and then recurred to 'The Modern Instance,' which is my best book, and which, in my opinion, is the most artistic book I have ever written. The idea, you see, persisted in being carried out. I could not get away from it."

T. B. Aldrich, the American poet and humorist, was very much to the fore when I stayed a day or two with him in his pretty house at Boston. A short, keen, sturdy, humorous-faced little man, sparkling with wit and brimming over with fun the whole time I was with him. A man everybody loved. And such an amusing letter-writer. Here is a specimen. The letter was in answer to one from his friend Professor Morse, whose writing was almost illegible.

MY DEAR MR. MORSE,

It was very pleasant for me to get a letter from you the other day. Perhaps I should have found it even pleasanter had I been able to decipher it. I don't think, however, that I mastered anything beyond the date (which I knew), and the signature (which I guessed at). There is a singular and perpetual charm in a letter of yours; it never grows old, it never loses its novelty. One can say to oneself every morning: "There's that letter of Morse's. I haven't read it yet. I think I'll take another shy at it to day, and may be I shall be able in the course of a few years to make out what he means by those t's that look like w's, and those i's that have no eyebrows." Other letters are read and thrown away and forgotten, but yours are kept for ever—unread. One of them will last a reasonable man a lifetime.

Admiringly Yours,
T. B. ALDRICH.

I remember that among many things we discussed the methods and sometimes, very rarely, the personalities of different poets of his own period. He showed me the first draft of Longfellow's celebrated poem, "The Wreck of the *Hesperus*," much altered and erased. He told me how the poet had risen in the middle of the night and hastily jotted down the lines—which he elaborated next day—as they came to his mind first in the still, quiet watches of the night.

"I hung outside Tennyson's gate at Freshwater once; but I did not dare go in. How I reverence that man, and how perfect a word-painter he is! What an impressionist! What a veritable master! No obscurity about him. He is as clear as a trout brook, and yet his thought is always fine. I wish I had been able to pluck up courage to go in and see him that day."

We discussed realism in poetry. "I approve of it so long as it possesses that touch of the imagination which lifts it out of the commonplace. The mistake is when a realist, whether an artist, a poet, or a novelist, thinks a thing is fine simply because it is revolting. 'Oh! it is so realistic!' they cry. But, my dear fellow, a rose is as real as an ash-barrel and a great deal sweeter. It is a mere question of taste in the selection."

He hints at this in a verse he showed me he had written a short time previous to my visit.

Romance, beside his unstrung lute,
  Lies stricken mute,
The old-time fire, the antique grace—
  You will not find them anywhere.
To day we breathe a commonplace,
  Polemic, scientific air;

We strip Illusion of her veil;
We vivisect the nightingale
To probe the secret of his note.
The muse in alien ways remote
Goes wandering.

I remember I asked him whence he thought a poet—who is always said to be born one—drew his inspiration primarily.

"Ah! whence indeed, my friend! There are two ancestors of mine in Grantham Churchyard, in Lincolnshire—a Cromwellian, austere and smileless, and his sunny southern wife.

"In me these two have met again,
To each my nature owes a part:
To one the cool and reasoning brain;
To one the quick, unreasoning heart."

And then, passing on to another phase of thought, he said: "I think that had Browning been less of a thinker he would have been more of a poet. His wonderful scholarship, though it gave him vast fluency and power and influence, rather weighed him down. At his best Browning was a great poet, and a most interesting soul."

He wrote me out a little fancy of his, which I reproduce here.

COMEDY.

They parted with clasp of hands,
And kisses and burning tears:
They met in a foreign land,
After some twenty years—

Met as acquaintances meet,
Smilingly, tranquil-eyed—
Not even the least little beat
Of the heart upon either side.

They chatted of this and that,
The nothings that make up life
She in a Gainsborough hat,
And he in black for his wife.

Ah! what a comedy is this!
Neither was hurt, it appears,
Yet once she had leaned to his kiss,
And once he had known her tears.

EPICS AND LYRICS.

I would be the Lyric,
  Ever on the lip,
Rather than the Epic
  Memory lets slip !
I would be the diamond
  At my lady's ear
Rather than the June rose,
  Worn but once a year.

CHAPTER XI

IN MORTIMER MENPES' STUDIO

FOR many years past Mortimer Menpes' studio has been the resort not more of artistic and literary London than it has been one of the favourite rendezvous of Society London, for Mortimer Menpes possesses a personality all his own, which is irresistible and compelling, and which is curiously uncommon. It is the man, to the full as much as it is his supremely fine work either in line or in colour, in each of which he is a master of European fame, that for so many years attracted the extraordinarily varied types of personalities of all classes and professions to his wonderful Japanese house and studio in Cadogan Gardens. Menpes is one of my oldest friends, and I don't suppose any one knows him more intimately than I do. I have made a study of him for the last twenty years, and therefore I claim to speak of him with a certain amount of real intimacy. I remember I met him first at the studio of a very old and valued friend of mine, Mrs. Ernest Maxse, who was then known as Alice Miller, a fine artist herself, and a girl of rare and exceptional charm, both of body and mind ; and to her studio one day while I was there came Mortimer Menpes, bringing with him the famous Jemmy Whistler, who at that moment was in a mad fury with Oscar Wilde, who had just delivered a lecture to the students of the Royal Academy. And then he turned to me.

"Do you know Oscar?" he said. "He is one of my pupils—one of the pupils, one of the disciples of the Master! Do you realize what that means?" he fiercely demanded in his strident American voice. "He goes to

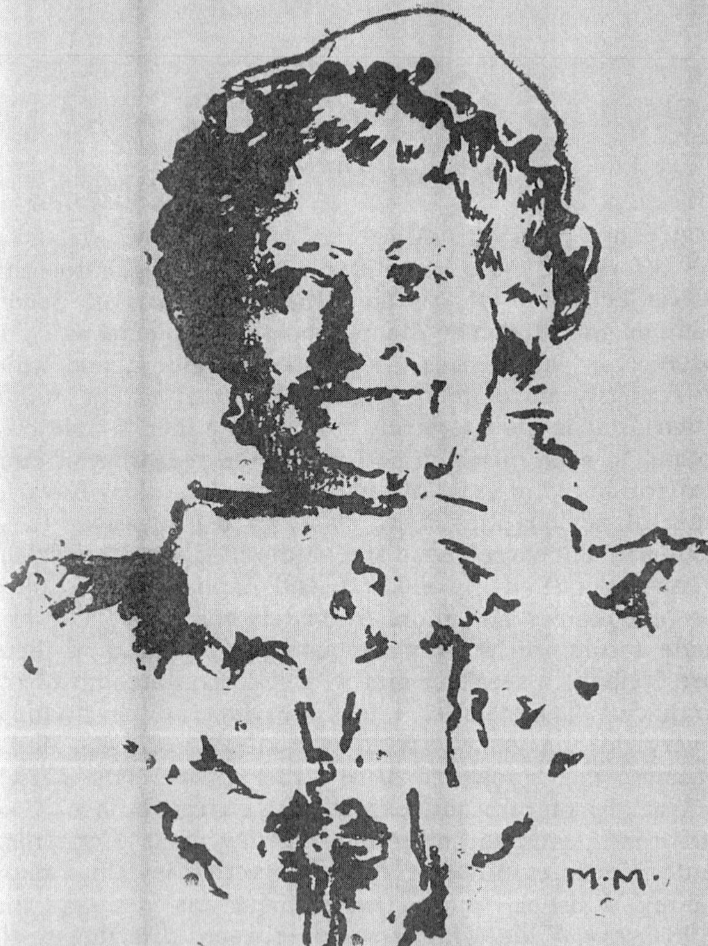

LADY DOROTHY NEVILL.

the Royal Academy with the sweepings of my studio in his hands; he steals the words from my lips—*my* words from *my* lips—and then deals them out to these poor deluded ones as his own: the words of The Master! Think of it! But *are* you thinking of it? Are you listening to me? Think what it means: THE WORDS OF THE MASTER!" Then he turned with added ferocity to Menpes, who was nervously trying to make himself heard above the Master's din: "Memps, you are not to help Oscar with his new house. I won't have you help him; not even with a bucket of distemper, unless it is the wrong kind. Leave him alone in the decoration of this new house of his, and then we shall see the *real* Oscar at last! Leave him in his own piggery, and you'll see what a really suburban chap he is at heart and when alone, deserted by the Master! Heaven grant though," he continued anxiously as a sudden thought struck him, "that he doesn't get hold of Godwin" (a celebrated architect and Ellen Terry's husband), "he might help to keep him straight. Memps, lend me half a crown; I must go and get my hair cut, and you must come with me. What! not got half a crown in your pocket! What excuse have you, then, for having been born and for having lived your early days in the Australian Bush if you haven't got money in your pocket? Now for the hair-cutter! Good-bye, Miss Miller; I am going to carry off Memps and Mr. Blathwayt to help get my hair cut."

Arrived at the haircutter's, we were each of us seated in chairs the most advantageously placed for different points of view.

"It's the feather, Mr. Blathwayt, that is all-important."

"What feather?" I rashly and innocently asked.

"What feather!" he groaned—"what feather! Memps, here is Blathwayt asking 'What feather?'" And then he turned with indescribable energy upon me. "Why, *the* feather, of course; the only feather in the world to-day. This!" he added, with impressive and sepulchral solemnity, as he indicated the far-famed white lock, which flashed out snowy white from his dark curly shock of hair, and of which he was quite inordinately proud.

As the hair-cutter proceeded, with immeasurable care and anxiety, to crop his exuberant foliage, taking special and minute pains with the famous "feather," Whistler launched out into a tirade of abuse against Algernon Swinburne, whom he designated as "the bard living outside the radius," in sarcastic allusion to Swinburne's Putney villa, abuse which was inspired by his indignation that the poet, who had written an article in the *Fortnightly* on Whistler's much-vaunted "Ten O'clock Lecture," had not sufficiently deluged it with praise—had, indeed, been daring and crazy enough to indulge in a very slight and very delicate criticism. Whistler never forgave Swinburne for this, and the unfortunate poet winced beneath his abuse to a quite incredible extent. Some years later Menpes etched a very wonderful portrait of Whistler which he sent to Swinburne, who penned him the following letter of acknowledgment—

> I think the portrait is incomparable, unless it might be compared with Hogarth's Lord Lovat (of which I am so happy as to possess an original subscriber's copy). There is the same marvellous relentless grasp, or grip, of character ; the same unmistakable and penetrative accuracy of rendering ; the same piercing perfection of insight and subtlety and refinement of satirical truth which can hardly, I think, be attributed to Hogarth. All the man is there ; he is henceforth immortal in his own despite. Mr. Watts [Theodore Watts-Dunton] desires me to add that I cannot admire and appreciate your work more than he does.

But my encounter with Whistler took place many years before Menpes built up his wonderful Japanese house in Cadogan Gardens, whither he resorted after his second visit to Japan, his first having resulted in a complete break-off of the long and historic friendship between him and Whistler, who was perfectly furious at Menpes' presumption in going to the Land of the Rising Sun at all.

"It is *my* Japan!" he cried. "How dare that man—Meneps, isn't it?—that robber from the Bush, that kangaroo born with a pocket into which he slips all he can glean from me and my studio—how dare he annex Japan to himself, and then come back to London and try and pass it off as his own!"

And the curious part of it was that his indignation was absolutely genuine and unfeigned. How even Whistler met with the Waterloo that at one time or another almost invariably, in one form or another, awaits the greatest, Menpes tells with vigour and humour. Menpes took the famous little artist with him one day to call on a quaint old lady who had expressed a great wish to see the Master, of whom she had heard so much.

"She was an exceedingly eccentric person," said Menpes in telling me the story, "and I warned Whistler that he would have to be very careful in his dealings with her. 'Oh,' he airily replied, 'when she sees The Master she will be silent! It will be an amazing experience—amazing!' And so indeed it was; not quite, however, in the sense of the word in which he had intended it. We were shown into the drawing-room, and a few minutes afterwards the old lady, accompanied by her maid, with impressive dignity entered the room, balancing upon her head a weathercock with the letters N.S.E.W. and the arrow all complete. She shook hands with me and then she looked at Whistler.

"'Is *this* the Master?' she said, in a voice that made me creep.

"'Yes,' I somewhat quaveringly replied.

"'Oh!' she said, 'there's some mistake here; this surely isn't, it simply *can't* be the Master—the Master of whom I have heard for so many years! *This!* Why, the very idea is preposterous!'

"Whistler was furious. 'Madam!' he screamed.

"'Silence!' thundered the old lady. 'Jane, the wind is in the east.' Jane stepped forward and fixed the arrow in the direction indicated. 'And when the wind's in the east, Mr. Whistler, that means silence.'

"'But, madam, this is simply——'

"But he got no farther. Black with passion, our old hostess screamed out—

"'Jane, the wind's north-east!' Again Jane fixed

the arrow as requested. 'And when the wind's in the north-east, it means the interview is at an end.'

"'This is an outrage, madam, an outrage to the Master,' whimpered the crushed and broken artist.

"'Give me your arm, Jane,' said the old lady, 'and I will go out east by nor'-nor'-east,' she added, as, assisted by the maid and the butler, she made her slow progress from the room, carefully facing E.N.N.E., although her doing so involved an extremely uncomfortable crooked and tortuous and crab-like motion and attitude of body.

"Whistler, too amazed to speak, and indeed too frightened, whispered to me—

"'I suppose we go out east too.'

"The sharp-eared old lady overheard him.

"'You can please yourself, Mr. Whistler; you can go out north or south or east or west or all four together if you wish. I pray you stand not on the order of your going, so long as you go. Ha-ha!' she cried, in the accents of transpontine melodrama. 'Ha-ha! the Master has met with his Waterloo!'

"Whistler said one word only as we found ourselves in the windy street, and one only, 'Amazing!' But to his dying day he never mentioned it, nor did I so long as he lived. She was an exceptional sort of person altogether, apart from her weathercock and the rest. She had made a great name for herself and an enormous fortune—a perfectly enormous fortune—by writing three religious books, books that the whole of England knew as household words at one time. She was deeply religious, but quite—well, peculiar to say the least of it. Every night the servants would file in to prayers, and last of all came the wretched butler, struggling with a huge Muscovy duck clasped in his arms, and which was nightly brought in from the lake to listen to the gospel, 'in order,' as she said, 'that its wild and unruly heart may be tamed.'"

Most of Menpes' most famous work is associated with and came out of that now almost historic house of his in Cadogan Gardens, wherein I have spent some of the pleasantest hours of my life, and where I have met and talked with some of the most remarkable people of the last half-century. I remember once a luncheon at which were present, in addition to Menpes and myself, poor Lady Colin Campbell, then a brilliant and a supremely handsome woman, flashing and eager, an electric and intensely vital personality and a keen and capable critic and discerner of all things human, literary and artistic, an extraordinarily many-sided person ; and Mrs. Brown-Potter, in the hey-day of her fame and beauty—and she was an exceedingly lovely woman at one time of her varied and multitudinous career—two of the most interesting and most alive women one could meet. And also with us was Menpes' and my own old friend, the late Lord Cairns—Herbert, the third earl—who had wandered many a long mile through the fairy-land of Japan in company with the artist and myself—himself one of the most delicately appreciative and artistic and subtlely literary persons I have ever met, in addition to being one of the finest shots and fishermen of his day. Herbert Cairns always remains in my memory as quite one of the most exceptional men of all the remarkable men I have known, a man with a curious faculty for introspection and a capacity for literary and artistic judgment and selection as would have made his fortune had he taken up these matters from a professional and a practical point of view. It was always a puzzle to me when he was really happiest and most in his element : in an artist's studio or with the latest scientific or engineering essay in his hands ; or competing with Lord Walsingham, let us say, at some big country house shoot ; or sitting entranced at Queen's Hall during the sway and rush and turmoil and yet marvellously ordered harmony of one of Sir Henry Wood's great orchestral feats ; or casting a fly on a Norwegian salmon run. I could never be quite certain when he was happiest or most at home, so curiously blended in him was the thinker, the practical engineer, the poet, the musician, the artist, and the sportsman—one of the most all-round men I ever met.

The luncheon was exceedingly good and exceedingly

plain. It consisted entirely of a superb beef-steak, potatoes, and a suet and treacle pudding and a bottle of fervent and glowing burgundy, if I may so describe it. A meal for giants, as I gratefully observed to our host.

"Well," was his astonishing reply, "I am going to paint a portrait of Cecil Rhodes this afternoon."

"But what on earth has that got to do with it, Memps?"—we all called him "Memps"—said Lady Colin.

"Why, surely it is obvious," replied Mr. Menpes, waving a large and singularly capable hand in the air, unfortunately just as he was in the act of carving a piece of the steak for me, thereby delaying my luncheon for at least a quarter of an hour, during which I sat speechless with hunger, impatience, and indignation—"why, surely it is obvious. Here am I going to paint a portrait of this great Empire-builder; this great practical man of affairs; this Napoleon of finance. Why, Lady Colin, you must surely see for yourself that I cannot paint the portrait of such a man on a vegetarian diet, can I? Fancy painting Rhodes or Napoleon, or this new man everybody is talking about—Kitchener—on a cabbage and a milk-pudding, or on a nut and a glass of water! You can't picture to yourself that beautiful creature Constance Collier brought up on cabbage, can you? You get no inspiration, no atmosphere from such nourishment as that. Do you suppose Rembrandt painted his masterpieces on cabbages and caterpillars? An editor the other day headed his article 'Menpes and the Beefy Mind.' Well, why not? I glory in the sneer. Think of it only from the artistic point of view. How infinitely inferior is a nut or a cabbage or a glass of water to this beef-steak! Look at it!" he went on with almost speechless fervour, waving his carving-knife in the air instead of thrusting it into the steak and cutting off a piece for me, as I indignantly reflected—"just look at it on your plate: the rich brown outside of the steak, the juicy crimson interior, how exquisitely it is contrasted against the white plate with the blob of yellow-green mustard on the side, just a little to the right, exactly, balancing the fluffy, floury potato on the left, with the glass of burgundy sparkling in its rich ruby depths in that shaft of sunlight piercing through the lattice-work of the Japanese blind just behind you. How preferable to the pale, indigestible, light green of the vegetarian's badly boiled cabbage, with his dim, misty, indefinite and insanitary and wholly uninviting and uninspiring glass of lemonade-water at its side! Compare a field of cabbages with a meadow full of carvable and appetizing cows! Imagine how immeasurably more inspiring and pulsating and energizing is this burgundy, this wine after Rembrandt's own heart, to—a glass of water! Blathwayt, have some more steak?"

"Thank you very much," I icily replied. "I shall be thankful. I haven't had any at all yet!"

And an hour afterwards the guests, with the exception of myself, having departed, Cecil Rhodes walked into the studio—tramped in rather; a great, big, burly man, with good but very awkwardly fitting clothes on him, badly buttoned up, and no waistcoat.

"Full face, please, Mr. Menpes," he said as he sat down. "So many of these painters want to paint me sideways, or what they call three-quarter. Now, it's shifty to be three-quarter; full face is the only possible way for an honest man to be painted. One of the blighters painted me three-quarter, and I bought the picture and took it home and smashed it up! And then they want to make me out the great Empire-maker; and they all want to put themselves into the picture instead of painting me as a big boy, full of romance, which is all I really am. It's a wrong idea to make me an Imperialist. I don't like politics. I have to do them sometimes, or have a shot at them would be the most correct way of putting it, but really it's romance I'm most keen on. I can't say so to business men; they wouldn't understand me, for one thing; they would think I wasn't to be trusted with finance or politics. They don't seem able to see *inside* things. They don't care for gardens, for instance. I love gardens more than anything else!"

And then Menpes told him a yarn about an old man in Japan he and I had come across in a country district once which immensely fascinated Rhodes. He told him how this old man had got a small garden which he had laid out in such a manner that it exactly harmonized and fitted in with Fuji-Yama, which lay in the rear. He had so adapted his little house and his strip of garden and the paths running through it that they all fell into their due position, in exact relation to the vast and historic mountain rearing its snow pinnacle into the vast Asiatic blue above it ; all the pathways made as though they were disappearing up the mountain-side ; nothing clashed or was out of harmony with Fuji-Yama. And then Menpes told Rhodes how every morning the old gardener would come into his garden and pick one flower, which, with immeasurable care and ceremony, and after long and anxious thought, he would place in a certain position in the room.

Cecil Rhodes pondered for a moment. "By Jove! Menpes," he said, "you've given me an idea for my garden at Groote Schoor. You know Table Mountain there is the one thing in the landscape. I'll keep in mind what you say about that old man and *his* mountain. It's a splendid idea. And I'll have just great blobs of colour. Splash them down in huge beds of blue and crimson and yellows and reds. I'll get all the lines of my garden in sympathy with the lines of Nature outside."

Some years afterwards, Cecil Rhodes lying for ever at rest in his superbly desolate tomb among the Matoppo Hills, I wandered through the gardens at Groote Schoor alone, and as I looked at those vast flower-beds—massive blobs of colour splashed with magnificent and reckless carelessness all over the grounds, with the gorgeous Table Mountain dominating the whole beautiful landscape, with which that garden was in such entire sympathy and harmony—I thought of that conversation that summer afternoon in Mortimer Menpes' studio.

And I remembered how he had tried to picture for us a colossal pergola, two miles long, overshadowed by Italian vines, and in the centre the body of a huge sphinx,

Then he went on to say how he would like to create a vast zoological gardens alongside his own, whereon, from the top of a hill, you would be able to look down and see lions and tigers and elephants and camels and leopards and every other kind of animal all living their own natural life.

Another day I met there George Meredith, who was rarely to be encountered in any London studio, and he was accompanied by his old friend Admiral Maxse, who, as all the world knows, was the hero of his famous novel, "Beauchamp's Career," and who was also the father of two very charming daughters, one of whom subsequently married Lord Salisbury's son, Lord Edward Cecil, the military brother of the famous politicians and theologians, Lords Robert and Hugh Cecil. Admiral Maxse had brought Meredith to see Menpes' portrait of Lady Lytton, who, as Pamela Plowden, with whose father I used sometimes to stay at the Residency in Hyderabad, had made a great name for herself in London Society, and especially in that very select and esoteric section of it known in the nineties as "The Souls."

"There, George!" cried the Admiral, as Menpes placed the beautiful picture in a fitting light—"there, George, isn't that something too perfect for this world at all?"

Mr. Meredith said: "Yes, oh yes; it's a very nice picture of a very charming woman."

"'A very nice picture of a very charming woman!'" groaned the Admiral; "why, you talk as if it wasn't Pamela at all!"

"But, my dear Fred, I think she is beautiful, but you don't seem to think she belongs to this earth at all."

"Well, George, if you had seen her getting out of that cab last night in the amber light of a street lamp, as I saw her, you wouldn't have thought she belonged to this earth either. Now, George, after looking at Menpes' picture of her, I feel sure you must be roused enough to write a nice verse to go with the portrait, and another one afterwards to go with Lady Granby's portrait of her."

George Meredith was evidently smitten with the idea,

and he argued out all the details with the Admiral in that wonderfully resonant voice of his, a voice beside which even Lewis Waller's magnificent organ paled its comparatively ineffectual fires, and with a superb use of the English language, to which it was a real intellectual treat to listen, though not always very easy to follow. And what a picture the old man presented, with his singularly beautiful head and a tie of a certain quality of red, exactly, whether by careful design or sheer haphazard, calculated to emphasize and bring out and contrast with the charming silver hair and beard and the artistic grey of his loose and easy-fitting suit.

I met Lady Dorothy Nevill more than once in that delightful studio of Menpes'; a studio where the afternoon sunlight crept shyly in through the Japanese paper windows, and where the richest and most magnificent effects of colour were produced by a wonderful arrangement of black wood carvings and lavish and yet scientifically contrived and ordered splashings of gold and the most marvellously designed panels of blazing crimson —a wonderful studio, pervaded by an extraordinary sense and atmosphere of peace and silence, and wherein one could almost fancy oneself seated in one of the great Buddhist temples at Nara, beyond which you catch a fleeting glimpse now and again of the gentle ox-eyed deer in the park, and wherein you can just hear the eternal splash and dripping of the fountains playing in the sunlight, or where you are summoned to prayer by the deep tones of a bell that has sent its notes booming and throbbing through the summer and the winter landscape ever since, and indeed long previous to, the coming of William the Conqueror to the shores of Saxon England. It was a delightful studio, and I regret that with all its memories of and associations with the most interesting people of a most interesting period in London's social life it has now ceased to exist. And amongst the most interesting people I met there was that wonderful old lady, Lady Dorothy Nevill, full of memories of a brilliant social past which has long since ceased to exist. For the great Duke himself, the hero of Waterloo, used to write Lady Dorothy the most enthusiastic little letters. When he was in a good temper with her and everything was going well between them he would write them on any little scrap of paper he could get hold of, but when they had had a tiff he would send a formal note on great sheets of heavy creamy paper with a coat of arms on the top of it. Just before he died in 1852 one of the last things she got him to do was to promise to make a magistrate of a special friend of hers, and in a day or two she received, written upon a scrap of paper torn off an edge of *The Times*—

> The deed's done. God help me!
> WELLINGTON.

I remember one day Lady Dorothy, of whom Mr. Menpes has done me an absolutely lifelike portrait, brought out a letter from her pocket, which she handed, with a smile, to the famous artist. It was from King Edward, saying that he had made a note of her request, and would come and see Mr. Menpes' pictures, though he was so busy he hardly knew how to turn; and then he added, with reference to the artist's very unusual name: "What a funny name! Seems to suggest the Egyptian Court in the British Museum."

She was always full of anecdotes, and was immensely pleased sometimes with her own capacity for repartee.

"I had such fun yesterday," she once said. "I was lunching with ——," mentioning some rather exceptionally *nouveaux riches*, "and the lady apologized to me for only three footmen instead of the usual four being present. 'Oh, pray don't apologize,' I said. 'I never eat more than two!'"

And then she told us of some rather extravagant and spendthrift connection of her own whom she was always helping, and who had just applied to her for another urgent loan.

"Well, Memps, I simply couldn't do it, so I said to her—

"'My dear, in order to let you have that last money I lent you I had to go without my carriage.'

"'Oh, my dear,' she said, 'I *am* sorry; if only I had known you should have had mine.'"

I remember one day Menpes said to her: "Lady Dorothy, you ought to write your reminiscences."

"My dear Memps," she replied, "it's rather dangerous that: once you begin your recollections of other people, they start in with their recollections of *you*!"

One morning I walked into the studio, and there I found Menpes busy on a portrait of Sir Henry Irving. The great actor-manager was much pleased with a little anecdote anent himself. Two ladies in the stalls were overheard discussing him.

"Yes, he's splendid," said one of them. "Pity he's got that weakness in his knees."

"Weakness in his knees, my dear! What on earth are you talking about? That's his pathos—his beautiful pathos!"

He was very enthusiastic with regard to the Japanese atmosphere of the studio.

"It always makes me want to produce a Japanese play—a real Japanese play—at the Lyceum," he said to me on this occasion. "What do you say to that, Menpes? I am suggesting to Blathwayt that you should come and help me produce a Japanese play, and I'd like to work this wonderful studio and the drawing-room and that red and gold entrance-hall of yours into the scenes. A room like this seems to write the whole play into my head as it were. Full of drama!"

A lady entered the studio at the moment, a very pretty creature, full of enthusiasm about Nansen, the Arctic explorer, whom she had met at a party over-night.

"Isn't he wonderful, Sir Henry?" she gushingly inquired of Irving, who, more than anything else, absolutely detested anything approaching undue effusiveness, and who rather icily responded—

"*Yes; he stands the cold so well!*"

He had, of course, a strong sense of humour, albeit at times it may have been rather grim and sinister humour.

"I heard a very good story the other day," he said one

morning to Menpes and myself. "A Scotch minister called to inquire after a friend who was dangerously ill.

"'I hope the laird's temperature is not higher to-day!' he said to the old man-servant who opened the door to him.

"'Weel, sir, I was juist wonnering at that mysel'. Ye see, he deed at twal o'clock last nicht.'"

He was also immensely pleased with a yarn Menpes told us. A man had a violent altercation with another man, during which the second man characterized the first as "a dirty hippopotamus." Two years after he sought to bring an action against him for this uncalled-for insult.

"But why on earth have you delayed the matter so long?" said the lawyer he was consulting.

"I never knew what a hippopotamus was like till the circus came here last week!" was the ingenuous reply.

But I think of all the interesting personalities I used to meet at Menpes' studio the most interesting was the late Lord Wemyss, a man of brilliant personality and of the most extraordinarily electric vitality that one could possibly imagine. His very whiskers—the long, far-famed Dundreary whiskers of mid-Victorian fashion—appeared to be alive with electric sparks as it were; his amazing vitality is remarkably indicated in the portrait that Sargent painted of him some ten or twelve years ago.

Now, it so happened that just at the period when Lord Wemyss and myself were daily at the studio, where we would frequently spend the greater part of the day, the carpenters were hard at work putting up the Japanese carvings and decorations all over the house. The day previous to his visit Lord Wemyss had made a very vigorous speech in the House of Lords in connection with a plasterer's strike which was in full blast at the time. Menpes made him and the foreman of the carpenters known to one another, and Lord Wemyss told the carpenter what he thought of trade unions, and the carpenter told Lord Wemyss what he thought of the House of Lords. He didn't begin quite encouragingly either.

"Are you a hearl?" he said—"a real hearl? I mean

wot they calls a belted hearl in the 'istry and poeckry books I was supposed to read at school, and didn't, not me!'"

"Now, then, Longjaw," said his wife, who was acting as charwoman in lieu of any regular servant in the unfurnished and dismantled house, and who was leaning casually up against the unpapered wall, an interested spectator of all that was going on—"now then, Longjaw, not so much lip. Wich 'e's never done talkin', Earl, once 'e begins; wich I don't believe 'e knows 'arf the time wot 'e's talkin' about; wich I don't believe men never does."

"Oh yes, we do, Mrs. Johnson," said Lord Wemyss; "we know a lot more than you give us credit for knowing."

"Wich I said '*men,*' your lordship, beggin' your pardon," replied the lady.

How we all laughed! And then Menpes, to put things right, told both Lord Wemyss and the carpenter how the Japanese workmen who had done all that exquisite work they were handling were in real truth the most accomplished artists and craftsmen he had ever met, and yet so poor and so humble that they could only afford to buy the heads and tails of fishes for their miserable meals, the middles being utterly out of their power to buy. The next day Lord Wemyss, in the light of Mr. Menpes' and the carpenter's revelations, made a fresh speech in the House of Lords, and retailed to a delighted assemblage all that had taken place in the Chelsea studio.

I remember also that at that time Lord Wemyss was very busy modelling a statuette of Venus, and every beautiful woman he met, either in Mayfair or at Menpes' studio—which place fairly swam with them at times—he used to invite to sit to him for this statuette, which, I may add, never appeared to draw near to completion. One lady would sit for the chin, another for an arm, another for the nose, and another for some other part. A sort of composite photograph!

He came into the studio broadly smiling one morning. "I heard such a capital racing story last night," said he. "A very rich woman looking out of her window in Grosvenor Square saw a poor fellow shivering up against the lamp-post. So she wrote on a sheet of note-paper 'Never say die,' wrapped up half a sovereign in it, and sent her butler out with it to the man. That same night, just before dinner, the man was shown in to her, and he handed her £5 10s., saying as he did so: 'Here's your money, lady. Never Say Die won at ten to one, and you were the only one that backed it!'"

When the decoration of Menpes' Japanese house was completed—and it took a whole year in the doing—the artist resolved to give a great dinner and entertainment to the men who had been employed, house-painters and decorators, and Lord Wemyss's friend the carpenter, and a heap more. Lord Wemyss came and took the chair, and Sir Henry Irving and Miss Ellen Terry sat on either side of him, and George Grossmith, senior, and Dan Leno, Lady Dorothy Nevill, Lady Colin Campbell, and many more attended, some to dine, some to wait at table, some to entertain the guests.

Lord Wemyss delivered himself of a characteristically vigorous speech, and as he spoke he frequently emphasized his remarks by banging an empty claret-jug on the table.

"Empty! Of course it's empty," he said. "What were bottles and jugs made for but to be emptied!" And then he told a story of a Scotch minister early one morning on his parochial rounds discovering a parishioner in a ditch, dead drunk. With some difficulty he aroused him. "Donal, man, whaur hae ye been the nicht?" he cried. "Weel, minister," was the hesitating reply, "I dinna richtly ken whether it was a funeral or a wedding, but whichever it was it was a most extraordinar success!"

And then Lord Wemyss enacted a certain butler at a very great public function handing the guests their hats. "Lincoln and Bennett, your grace," with a profound bow and deeply reverential voice; "Scott, my lord," with also great dignity and reverence; "Henry Heath, Sir William," with diminished ceremony, but still with cordial and heartfelt respect. And then comes along a poor bank clerk; "'Ope Brothers," and the most offhand manner. How Johnson the carpenter appreciated it all!

For years that famous studio of Mortimer Menpes was a kind of microcosm of London social life; a mirror of the mighty world of art and politics and literature, science and thinking and acting and energizing humanity generally, and dominating over, or rather it would be more accurate to say permeating and pervading it all, the very modest and unobtrusive, although keenly alert and electric and absolutely vital personality of the artist himself—a man who possesses a wider range of sympathies and interests than almost any one I have ever met. I have not touched upon half the phases of life in which he entwines himself or is involved by the fortuitous concurrence of unexpected or unlooked-for events, nor have I dealt with one-quarter of the famous and distinguished people I have met there: Mr. Winston Churchill, for instance, whom Mr. Menpes sketched for his book on the South African War; or Mr. Balfour, who hurried in one hot August afternoon with Lady Edward Cecil when all his colleagues were out of town and said: "I've got a few minutes to spare, Mr. Menpes, but only very few, as I am at present acting as maid-of-all-work for the whole Cabinet."

And it was there, if I remember rightly, that I last met that wonderfully interesting man, the Rev. E. J. Hardy, Senior Chaplain to the Forces, and author of one of the most amusing and famous books of the last twenty-five years and more, "How to be Happy though Married." And what a lovely story he told me once, and he told it so well too. A very prim and proper and stodgy old-fashioned City man said to his daughter, who was inclined to be a little flighty—a sort of Miss Joy Flapperton, in fact—

"Look here, my dear, I am going to take you in hand. I'll get hold of a staid, sensible, middle-aged man for you as husband—a man of about fifty let us say."

"Well, daddy, if it's all the same to you," replied the impudent minx, "I'd much prefer two—twenty-five years old each!"

Lord Wolseley was often there. One morning Menpes showed him the first set of Baden-Powell's Mafeking stamps, and the great soldier was amazed to see B. P.'s head figuring on the stamp instead of that of his Queen. Menpes then sat down and did a wonderful sketch of Lord Wolseley, and it is a curious fact that only a few days ago Lady Wolseley wrote to him and asked if he had got the original sketch, as it was the finest portrait of her husband that had ever been done.

Sarah Bernhardt and Coquelin always used to pay a visit to Menpes when in London, and I remember one day her declaiming against the habit the English people had of letting themselves go and getting old before their time. "Why," she cried in her beautiful and vehement French, "that beautiful Henry Irving is disappearing beneath his collar, and all because he won't brace himself up!" One day Menpes told her how he and Coquelin and myself had all been down the river and spent the day fishing with bent pins, catching nothing. "It's so like Coquelin!" cried the divine Sarah; "he is so lazy, so lymphatic. Look at him now!" she cried, as she pointed to the famous actor, half-asleep within the depths of a most comfortable arm-chair. "How like a pig he grows! We all resemble animals: Coquelin is a pig and I am a goat. Look at me; you can see it at a glance! Oh! but isn't it dreadful to play with Coquelin! Now, in the play we are doing now I have a violent love scene wherein I have to speak with fervour for ten minutes, and regularly every night, as sure as fate, Coquelin falls fast asleep, and it is very difficult to wake him when his cue comes." And then she turned to and cleverly criticized the technique of some of that marvellous collection of Whistler's etchings—the finest in the world—for which Menpes subsequently received the sum of £10,000.

Sir Edward Burne-Jones came in one morning, I remember, with a couple of pennies in his hand, which Menpes a few days previously had smoothed down and then coated with wax. "There, Menpes!" he cried, "I've done them, and these are the very first etchings I have ever tried my hand at." And, sure enough, there were two wonderful little caricatures of himself—most delightful work they were, too—which Menpes forthwith proceeded to "bite in" with the proper acid.

Mr. Winston Churchill, Menpes told me—for I only arrived at the house after he had left—bounded into the studio, full of life and spirits—this was a good many years ago—and very enthusiastic about art and artists, and talking art really cleverly and knowledgably all the time, and displaying an intimate knowledge of painters and painting. "I wasn't a bit surprised to hear he had been painting this spring himself," said Menpes; "it is only what I should have expected."

One afternoon Menpes and I were sitting thinking when suddenly the late Lady Meux and the very beautiful Lady Essex were shown into the room. "Why, you've got no fire, Memps!" cried Lady Meux, and she plumped down on the floor, and she and I set to work to manufacture one as quickly as possible. Two days later vans with six tons of coal drew up at 25 Cadogan Gardens, "With Lady Meux's love and best wishes to a chilly artist!"

By the by, I quite forgot just now a little incident that Sarah Bernhardt told us one morning. She was acting with Coquelin one day, and he had to say in the play, "Do you object to this cigar?" "No! no! no!" was her answer, which was also his cue to tell her the story of his life. "He looked at me instead," said the actress, "and said, with a glance of extreme disgust at the 'property' cigar, 'Ah! that's because you haven't to smoke it.' Of course there was a roar of laughter all over the theatre, which made him forget his lines altogether, so he calmly took my arm and said: 'Let's go for a walk and I'll tell you the story of my life,' and as he did so he walked me out by one exit and in by another, saying as he entered the stage again, 'Now I've told you the story of my life.'"

Poor Lady Colin Campbell told us a story once which reminded me of some of the old Scotch professors my dear mother used to tell me about in my youth. A very absent-minded bishop couldn't find his ticket one day. "Never mind, my lord," said the ticket-collector, who knew him well; "it'll do at the next station." But at the next station it was the same again, the bishop couldn't find it anywhere. "Never mind, my lord; it's all right any way, whether you find it or not." "Oh no, it isn't, Smith," replied the bishop, in a perfect fever of anxiety, and turning out all his pockets as he spoke—"oh no, it isn't. I *must* find that ticket, for I want to know where I'm going!"

CECIL RHODES.

CHAPTER XII

AMONG THE BOOKS AT HATCHARDS'

AMONG the charming experiences of a much varied life, and chief among the memories of thirty years' residence in London, I would place the many hours I have spent in Hatchards' famous bookshop, wherein for 120 years statesmen, scholars, and society generally have been wont to congregate in ever-increasing numbers; for I suppose at no time in its long and crowded history has Hatchards' been more popular, more thronged and resorted to than it has during the last fifteen years. Books possess an ever-growing fascination for all classes of the community, and more especially for those of the upper classes, who by tradition and habit and long custom handed down and carried on from the days of Lady Jane Grey are trained in the discernment and use of bibliography. And remarkably is this the case, during the latter years, with people whose tastes and inclinations are markedly on the side of sport and games, but who nevertheless appreciate, perhaps all the more keenly and vividly for the contrast, the necessity and charm of books and literature. They see life steadily, these people, and they see it whole, and all the more so that they shoot straight and ride straight to hounds, and they realize its many-sidedness, and therefore you see the stalwart hunting man and the boxing man and the Flying Corps man and the bomb-thrower eagerly and enthusiastically discussing some rare *edition de luxe* or some intricate and highly technical article on Grieg or Tchaikovsky, or tenderly dreaming over Julian Grenfell's or Rupert Brookes' exquisite and haunting stanzas, and you realize the ever-increasing power and fascination and influence of the literary output and accomplishment during this strenuous period of the cannon and the sword.

The upper classes, with, of course, some glaring exceptions, are really among the most intelligent people we have —taking them generally as a class. They have long traditions of culture behind them; they are widely travelled; they are extremely well up in the literature of other countries beside their own; they can institute comparisons therefore, and they have far wider interests and are far more accomplished in varied respects than the ordinary resident in the suburbs or the provinces. They are keenly, vividly, daringly human; they are untied and unbound by the meaningless little conventions which hold the middle classes as in a vice. They possess extraordinary quickness to detect real merit, and many of the most popular authors of the day owe it to the conversation round the dinner-tables of Mayfair and Belgravia that they occupy the position they do in popular opinion. And all this you realize as you stand at Hatchards' counters to-day, the most fascinating bookshop perhaps in the whole world. And with what a delightful history behind it!

In the eighteenth century the great bookshops in London to a very great extent took upon themselves the aspect of social clubs. It was in Tom Davies' bookshop in Russell Street, Covent Garden, that Boswell first met Dr. Johnson, and it was in the rooms of Murray the publisher and bookseller that Walter Scott first encountered Lord Byron and that Gibbon the historian first conversed with Porson the great Greek scholar. It was at Wright's bookshop, almost next door to Hatchards', that Wolcot waited for Gifford, who had lampooned him in the *Anti-Jacobin*, of which he was the Editor—

> Thou canst not think, nor have I power to tell,
> How much I scorn and loathe thee—so farewell—

and that he waited for Gibbon, and seeing him enter, struck him on the head with a stick, in return for which Wolcot was pushed into the gutter.

Hatchards', therefore, in common with shops of the same nature, was the resort and favourite meeting-place of all the well-known people living in London about the time of the French Revolution, and it became even more so in the early days of the nineteenth century, when Thackeray, Macaulay, and the Wilberforces and Hannah More used to forgather and discuss the growth and prospects of Tom Macaulay, the future historian. Queen Charlotte, the wife of George III, patronized Hatchards' from the very day of its opening, for it was at this shop that she purchased "L'Histoire de France" and Baxter's "Dying Thoughts" and many copies of a quaint little tract by Dr. Glasse, the Vicar of Hanwell, entitled "A Statement of Facts," being the story of an eccentric woman of noble birth found near a haystack in Somerset. Queen Charlotte bought liberally, and on one occasion she purchased no less than twelve copies of Smith "On the Prophets," and her purchases here reveal her extraordinary fondness for natural history. George Canning, the great statesman, used to buy most of his books at Hatchards'—pamphlets by Bourke, Franklin's Works, "The Jacobin's Lamentation," and Johnson's Works (twelve vols.).

William Wilberforce used actually to have his letters addressed to Hatchards'. One day he received a communication from the proprietor of the shop that a letter weighing 85 oz. had come to him from Hayti, and that the Post Office demanded a fee of £37 10s. This Wilberforce refused to pay, whereupon the Post Office very handsomely consented to let him have it for 7s.

In addition to all this, Hatchards' was frequently the centre of curious social activities. An amusing society—though unconsciously amusing, for it was serious enough in its objects and intentions—was started at Hatchards', from whence it sent out its propaganda, in 1818—"The Outinian Society," a kind of matrimonial agency, and which met at the bookshop to promote matches between its varied customers, and to determine, as poor Oscar Wilde would have put it, whether they had "pasts" or "futures." Another society hatched at Hatchards' was

"The Social Linen-Box Committee." Later on these absurd associations gave place to really excellent charity organizations and committees, and in one case a first-class governess agency, which societies fulfilled a really fine mission in the growing life and work of the vast metropolis.

Gladstone frequented Hatchards' all his life, though mainly in the thirties of last century, when he used to purchase pamphlets so extensively that he demanded a reduction of 10 per cent., threatening to go elsewhere if his request was not complied with.

Charles Kingsley used to come here regularly with his father, who daily read the paper at Hatchards', and "the old Duke" would walk through to the back room, which still exists in a slightly different form, and there he would state his requirements in a very business-like manner. When his brother's library was sold he instructed Mr. Hatchard to purchase for him a certain shilling pamphlet by A. G. Stapleton with the late owner's notes in pencil. This was put up at 2s. 6d., and ultimately knocked down for £93 to Hatchard, acting for the Duke.

Martin Tupper's queer old-fashioned doggerel, "Proverbial Philosophy," found an enormous sale at this great shop, and the poor old man used to relate with great glee that "when that good old man, Grandfather Hatchard, more than an octogenarian, first saw me he placed his hand on my dark hair and said, with tears in his eyes: 'You will thank God for this book when your hair comes to be as white as mine.'"

Charles and Fanny Kemble and Charles Matthews, Liston, the famous "Paul Pry," of a past day, were all of them frequent visitors at the shop, where, fifty years later I suppose, I myself have seen Henry Irving, Tree, and Alexander all eagerly turning over the pages of the latest novel or review.

I often think if those walls, lined to the ceiling with books of the richest binding, could but speak, how many an interesting conversation they could record of those dead and gone celebrities and favourites of the passing hour. For instance, one Monday morning Charles Mayne

Young, a very popular actor in his day, walked into the shop and inquired the name of the curate who had, on the preceding day, read the lesson at St. James's Church, almost next door. He then requested to have a Bible handed to him, and, in the middle of the shop, he first imitated the sing-song tones of the offending curate, and then, in his fine, trained, sonorous voice, he showed how the Scriptures should be read in church.

Other occasional visitors were the distinguished Canon of St. Paul's—Sydney Smith, "The Church of England and Mrs. Blomfield"—and the famous Countess of Blessington, Count D'Orsay's wife, and a beauty distinguished for her wit and for her own not inconsiderable literary gifts, which made her a conspicuous personage in the thirties and forties of last century.

And it is as a social and a literary resort that it exists to-day almost as much as ever it did in the past, whilst from a business point of view it is more prominent and influential than ever. I don't suppose that anywhere else in London can you measure and estimate, with almost barometrical exactitude, the worth and popularity of a writer and his works as you can at Hatchards' to-day. In a sense in which it can be said of almost no other library in the world, Hatchards' is a great determining factor in the success or failure of the new novel, the new biography, or the new book of poems.

The proprietors, who carry on the shop under the old and now really historic name, are Mr. A. L. Humphreys and Mr. Edwin Shepperd, two men of widely differing qualities, who are nevertheless admirably met in this special connection. Mr. Shepperd, many years Mr. Humphreys' senior, though the two have worked together for not less than thirty years in these very premises, where they each started as assistants to the last of the Hatchard family, controls the strictly business portion of the concern; while Mr. Humphreys, who is the son of a well-known Somersetshire clergyman, supervises it from the literary point of view. He is himself a man of rare taste and fine literary accomplishment. He is therefore a reliable authority, and he knows more of what is likely to suit the men and women of this vast conglomeration that we term London than any other living man. His knowledge of books is quite astonishing, and many a time have I sat talking to Mr. Humphreys at his table in the centre of the great room at Hatchards' while the best-known people of the day have flitted in and out of the shop, and their chauffeurs and footmen have rested on the very self-same benches, outside the shop, whereon the flunkeys of the great-grandparents of the smart folk inside used to sit and wait for their masters and mistresses a hundred years ago, so curiously does history, even in the smallest details, repeat itself amidst all the rush and turmoil of modern London life.

And here I have seen Mr. Churchill, who is interested in everything in the way of books, especially those dealing with Napoleon, come in and graze and ruminate among the well-filled shelves with that ease and discrimination which always indicates the really cultivated and scholarly mind. There, too, I have seen that handsome and stately woman, one of the most beautiful of her day, Lady Ripon, who, like Mr. Churchill, is interested in all good art and literature, and especially in books on music or a newly published volume of Arthur Rackham's exquisite designs.

Here, too, comes Mr. George Leveson-Gower, once Gladstone's secretary, getting a little elderly perhaps, with a host of interesting recollections of his own, one of our really fine classical scholars, and yet vivid and up to date and thoroughly *au courant* with all the literature of the day. Austen Chamberlain, much more of a *littérateur* than ever his father was, widely interested in history, and indeed in the best of any form of literature, is a frequent visitor to Hatchards', as also is Viscount Grey of Fallodon. One of the most discriminating readers at these delightful book counters is the Dowager Lady Londonderry, one of the few modern women who prefer really solid books as compared with mere novels, in this way resembling another frequent customer at the shop, Lady Rothschild, who is never led aside by the craze of the moment; very level-headed, possessed of the universal mind, and yet of a mind that is singularly discriminating in its choice of the really good in literature. I have seen Mr. Birrell, too, a reader also of the solid book, and with a great knowledge of books, though he never allows himself to be weighed down by that knowledge, never the mere bookworm, far too keen a sense of humour for that. Lord Knollys comes here often enough, also with a wide sense and knowledge of books and affairs, and with what memories of the greatest of his day! Can you imagine the run on Hatchards' if such a man perpetrated a really candid revelation of what he has seen and known of the world during the last fifty years. Hatchards' could scarcely contain the books to supply the demand nor the Bank of England a sum sufficient to induce him to write it. Mr. Lewis Harcourt, as one would expect in the son of one of the wittiest and readiest men of his day, is a great book lover in addition to being the collector of all those wonderful books relating to Eton which he recently presented to his old school. Mr. Lloyd George doesn't often trouble Hatchards', and when he does it is generally to ask for some book dealing with his beloved Wales.

I have been greatly interested during my visits to Hatchards' the last few months to note the books that are most asked for during these days of stress and turmoil. As a rule they have been mainly novels and books dealing with the war, though Lord Redesdale's Memoirs were wonderfully popular. There is now a new class of readers, most of whom are on their backs—I refer, of course, to our wounded soldiers, officers and men alike. Well, if you really want to get them books they will appreciate you cannot do better than get them such a book as Nesta Webster's "Chevalier de Boufflers," which gives one a great amount of new material concerning the French Revolution. Then, of course, Patrick McGill's books and Ian Hay's hold the field among all the newcomers, whilst Philip Gibbs' "Soul of the War" and F. S. Oliver's "Ordeal by Battle" are quite extraordinarily popular, as also are all of Boyd Cable's books. You will be safe, too, in buying your wounded friend a really good detective story, or anything you can get hold of bearing the signature of O. Henry, the American writer.

This is merely in passing. The fascination for me of such a shop as Hatchards' lies as much as anything in the books themselves. I am not in the very remotest sense of the word what you call a bookworm, but there is a subtle and indefinable lure in a bookshop which defies mere words. The binding, the smell of a book, its own inner associations, the thought of the myriads who have once perused its pages with what feelings one can but faintly imagine, but who have now for ever passed away ; the glimpses it gives into a world which you have never even imagined ; its intimacy with people who are but as shadows to you ; its delicate mirroring forth of an existence of which you had not, before you turned its pages, but the very faintest idea, all these things spell endless fascination for the real book-lover. What a veritable revelation of humanity is even the humblest book, and it is a revelation such as only can come to you in Hatchards' or the Bodleian or the British Museum or one of the great libraries on the Continent, or at an auction-room such as Sotheby's. You buy a book there not always or solely on account of its original contents or intrinsic merit, or even because of its quaint or beautiful binding. As the years roll on the value of a book is often gauged by its associations, by its own individual history, by some special fact of interest connected with its owners, and, most especially of all, by any autographic value which those owners may have attached to it. There are books to-day which, by reason of pencilled margins or autographed presentations, possess a hundred times their original value, or the value they would otherwise have possessed, and your true book collector is well aware of this. For instance, with regard to the extrinsic value of autographed books, Mr. W. C. Hazlitt tells us of Henry VIII's Prayer Book, in which the royal memoranda were of signal interest and curiosity. On the back of the title, under the royal arms, the King himself writes : " Remember thys wryghter wen you doo pray for he ys yours noon can saye naye. Henry R." At the passage " I have not done penance for my malice " the same hand inserts in the margin, "Trewe repentance is the best penance" ; and farther on he makes a second marginal note on the sentence, "Thou hast promised forgiveness"—"repentance beste penance." This evidently was a sort of family commonplace book. Inside the cover Prince Edward (afterwards Edward VI) writes : "I will yf you will." The volume, which contains other matter of great historical value, appears to have been given by Henry VIII, shortly before his death, to his daughter Mary, for on a small piece of vellum inside the cover he has written : "Myne owne good daughter, I pray you remember me most hartely when you in your prayere do shew for grace to be attayned assuredly to yr lovyng fader Henry R." The Princess subsequently gave it to her stepmother, Catherine Parr, and it has a motto and signature of that lady's second husband, Lord Seymour of Sudeley, the admiral. Now, how is it possible to estimate the value of such a book as that?

Charles I borrowed a volume of tracts from Thomason the stationer, and clumsily let them fall in the mud, whereby their then value was considerably depreciated. To-day the British Museum regards those stains as outweighing by far the intrinsic value of the quaint old verbosities they so sadly dim !

And if you ask for them Hatchards' will bring you books of surprising interest, great beauty, and even greater rarity, which will fascinate you by the extraordinary interest of their contents. There is a set of books there of which I had never even heard, entitled "Portraits, Memoirs, and Characters of Remarkable Persons," from the revolution in 1688 right up to George IV's reign, books that give you an interesting glimpse into an England of which we have but little idea in the present day, and of people of whom only their names survive for the general public, but of whom you can read here a vast number of really interesting details. Take, for instance, that book on which Grantley Berkeley and the men of his day were practically brought up, and which was dedicated to George IV. in 1821, Pierce Egan's "Life in London, or the Day and Night Scenes of Jerry

Hawthorn, Esq., and his elegant friend Corinthian Tom, accompanied by Bob Logic the Oxonian in their Rambles and Sprees through the Metropolis." Look at the admirable coloured plates: what a glimpse they afford us into a London that was far more joyous and amusing and adventurous than any we have ever known! Here we see Tom and Jerry in the coffee-shop—the restaurant of the period—or in the saloon at Covent Garden, or "sporting their bits of blood among the Pinks in Rotten Row." Then another richly coloured print by George Cruikshank depicts them in a cockpit backing Tommy the Sweep. One of the most suggestive pictures in the whole book, and one which more almost than anything else reveals the vast difference between the London of my grandfather's day and the London as I know it, is the one which shows them at a match which had been arranged at Cribbs' Parlour—Cribbs being a champion heavy-weight boxer of that day—between the Italian monkey Jacco Maccacco and a dog of 20 lb. weight. The monkey not only smashed up this dog, but he so mishandled several others that were pitted against him that they subsequently died of their injuries.

Another intensely fascinating work (in four volumes) to all who are interested in racing is that which was compiled many years ago by Henry Taunton, M.A., splendidly illustrated, and which gives every winner of the Derby, the Oaks, and the St. Leger right away from 1702 to 1870. The series opens with a portrait of Tregonwell Frampton, Esq., the Father of the Turf, "Keeper of ye Running Horses at Newmarket to King William III, Queen Anne, George I, and George II."

And then one of Hatchards' most treasured volumes, though it probably will not remain long in their possession, is a wonderful edition of Bartolozzi's Holbein's portraits. A huge monster of a book this, containing full-page portraits of hundreds of famous people in the days of Henry VIII. I might mention that most of the originals of these portraits are in the possession of King George. Strikingly beautiful and wonderfully revealing in their humanity are these portraits of the men and women in the upper classes of sixteenth-century English society: Sir Thomas More and his father, the judge; Lord Chancellor Rich; Riskemeer, a Cornish gentleman; Sir Nicholas Poines, Knight, a very handsome fellow; a delightful portrait of Sir Thomas More's son, quite unusually and unexpectedly modern and good-looking for that day; the Lady Mentas, Lady Ratclif, the Lady Montegle. As likely as not this book will eventually find its way to New York or Boston. The Americans to-day buy most of our best books and our most valued pictures.

It is an interesting fact, and one worthy of note to-day, that an increasing number of people find a great fascination in the exploitation of the mystic. Not in the mysticism of the vulgar spiritualistic charlatan from Kansas or San Francisco, but rather in the delicate and cultured mediæval mysticism of Catherine of Siena or St. Thomas à Kempis, of whose famous "Imitation" Hatchards' probably sell more copies than any other shop in London. The Society woman, however frivolous she may appear to be, seeks frequently enough to satisfy her soul's longings, the craving for "other worldism," which in these days is never very far from the woman's heart, with Fielding Hall's "Inward Light" or Maeterlinck or Francis Stopford or Richard and Isabella Ingalese's books on the history and power of the mind, and whose treatises dealing so vigorously and with so much insight with occultism and cosmogony and evolution are somewhat by way of taking the place of George Bernard George as the Society girl's priests and prophets.

And, of course, all books dealing with sport are always popular. Sponge's "Sporting Tour" and Jorrocks stand first. Mr. Humphreys told me once, I remember, that on one occasion a splendid healthy sportsman rushed into their shop, proudly introducing his eldest son. He was overjoyed, he said, because his boy had reached an age when he could read and appreciate "Handley Cross." "I have never read any other book in my life," he proudly declared, "and I never want to. An Englishman cannot possibly ask or want more"!

It is a curious fact that somehow, though the modern sporting writer does not possess Surtees' wonderfully breezy style, yet the writers on sport are far more frequent than they were in his day, when not one man in a hundred could have written a book to save his life. And of course Nat Gould, with his seven million readers, is by far the most popular novelist in the world, and he is a purely sporting writer.

One of the most interesting incidents that ever occurred in the history of Hatchards' was intimately connected with the late Cecil Rhodes, and of which Mr. Humphreys gave me a most exact account. About twenty-three years ago Mr. Rhodes, accompanied by Mr. Rochfort Maguire, called on Mr. Humphreys and told him that he had recently re-read Gibbon's "Decline and Fall," and he had been so much impressed by the book that he thought of forming a library which was to consist of all original authorities used by Gibbon in writing his history. Mr. Rhodes emphasized two things from the start "First," said Mr. Humphreys, "whatever I sent him should be in English, and whatever authors required re-translation, they should be sent absolutely unabridged ; and secondly, he stipulated that as he fully realized the magnitude of the work, I was not to limit myself in any respect. I was to get together a body of men who would be glad to co-operate in such a work, and whoever was employed he wished to be well paid. He took out his cheque-book before he left and gave me a handsome cheque as a preliminary payment. I soon got together a body of scholars, and appointed one who was to be a general editor of the whole series of volumes. The large series of classics issued by Didot, by Lemaire, Panconcke, Teubner, Valpy and Nisard, and many others were all supplied to him, with the idea that the translations which had been undertaken would be used with them. After some hundreds of volumes had been sent out to Africa of these translated texts and others, I proposed to Mr. Rhodes that he should supplement the undertaking by getting together all the information that I could from the best biographers in all languages who had written books relating to the Roman emperors and blend the best of them together. This plan Mr. Rhodes fully approved, and a supplementary series of volumes was prepared, which resulted in the most extensive collection of biographies of the Roman emperors and empresses. I had to scour the Continent for these, getting hold of scholars who had gone into the minutiæ of the periods dealt with—such, for instance, as the madness of Caligula. At one time I had as many as twenty scholars engaged to do this work, in addition to indexers, typists, and binders. All these books, illustrated with drawings from rare coins, etc., were bound up in morocco in volumes of a handsome square size. Besides his great interest in Roman history, Mr. Rhodes was taken up at one time with the cults and creeds of the Phœnicians, Greeks, and Romans. He was also very interested in the ruins of Zimbabye, and any facts that I could get together relating to the early history of that part he greedily read."

I have dealt with Hatchards' mainly from the Society point of view for the simple reason that more than most Society is interested in books to-day. They may not have time for very deep scholarship or patience either with the quiet, simple life of the student ; but all that is sincere, that is open air, that is not written with the object of grinding some particular axe, that comes with real conviction, never fails in its appeals to these, the Athenians of modern England, these spinsters and knitters in the sun, and to-day these gladiators in the most bloody arena the world has ever known.

CHAPTER XIII

THE ROMANCE OF A LONG DEAD DAY

I SAT one sweet spring morning with an ancient, yellow-hued letter in my hand; it bore the date of the year 1679, and it was written by the Duke of Albemarle to the Right Hon. William Blathwayt, who was a Secretary of State in those far-off days; and I had just disinterred it from among a vast pile of state papers and letters, which had either been written to or by him, and which bore the signatures of some of the most famous men in the reigns of Charles II and James, his most unpopular brother. Among the papers was a great quantity of letters from Cardinal Mazarin, and one lengthy document was the contract of marriage between Charles and Katherine of Braganza, the preliminary arrangements of which, so the legend goes, were placed in the hands of my ancestor.

For two hundred years and more those documents had lain in Dyrham Park, the old family seat of the Blathwayts, so unknown and so undisturbed that the gold-dust with which they were dried, long summer days ago, fell from them in a glittering shower when I shook them apart that spring morning in 1910. And now, severed for ever from their old home and their long connection with the one family, they are scattered remorselessly to the four quarters of the earth, having been sold for a record sum at Messrs. Sotheby, Wilkinson, and Hodge's famous and historic auction-rooms. And in these letters themselves—apart from all their share in Empire—what story, what romance, what long associations! Here, for instance, in this letter from the Duke

THE PICTURE GALLERY, DYRHAM PARK.

of Albemarle, who was then Governor of Jamaica and who was formerly the famous General Monck, with its old-fashioned conclusion, "your affectionate friend to serve you," faded and discoloured now, and one imagines the burning tropic morning it was written in the charming old-time Spanish town, which I know so well, with the beautiful red cathedral over the way; and its hurried dispatch to where some old-fashioned caravel lay swinging on the Caribbean tide; its long passage into English waters; its arrival at the Plantation, or, as we call it, the Colonial Office, in Whitehall, and where William Blathwayt, as Secretary of Plantations, literally held sway over the whole British Empire as it was then—Whitehall which must surely then have been a lovely highway, with just a glimpse of the grey old Abbey at the vista's end. And then, years after, its removal through country lanes and across the Wiltshire wind-swept, sun-flecked, shadow-stricken Downs to the Secretary's sweet old home, where, undisturbed, it lay for two long centuries with its own little story of the Empire hidden within its carefully folded sheets, for each faded, time-scented document is a link, however small, in the long history of the English nation.

It may be as well, before dealing more in detail with these documents, that I should endeavour as briefly as possible to depict somewhat of the personality of my ancestor and his life and character and surroundings as they have scantily filtered down through many generations to the present time.

William Blathwayt, whose father was a lawyer in the days of Shakespeare and Ben Jonson and who was descended from a very ancient North Country family, was born in the reign of the first Charles. In very early life he entered the diplomatic profession, and served his political apprenticeship under Sir William Temple, whom he accompanied to The Hague. For some years he acted as Colonial Secretary to the second Charles, though it was as Secretary at War that he accompanied the ill-fated James II to Salisbury. Him, however, he appears to have deserted at almost the last moment in favour of the new monarch, William III, who, without doubt, was, as his two royal predecessors had been, greatly attached to him. He was Secretary of State to William during the long campaign in Flanders. But it was as one of the Lords Commissioners for Trade and Secretary for the Plantations and Clerk of the Privy Council that he became the recipient of an enormous number of semi-official communications from Government and other officials in North America and the West Indies. And it is these West Indian papers which supply almost invaluable material to the historian of these important islands. Even to this day, in the Government buildings and record offices in Jamaica and Barbados, you will find dispatches and letters, all bearing orders from and all signed by William Blathwayt. In these papers, in short, which also include documents of great importance from the North American colonies, as they then were termed, and from India and Africa, we behold, as it were, an Empire in the making, and in singularly vivid fashion is revealed to us the manner in which the early Imperialists wove new patterns into the flag of Empire. And foremost amongst these was Mr. Secretary Blathwayt. William Blathwayt in those days controlled and helped to rule an Empire which was scarcely less wide in extent than it is to-day. For to his charge was committed the care and supervision of the colonies and dependencies of India, South Africa, West Africa, then known as "Guiny," the West Indies, and, most important of all, what are now known as the United States of America. Australia, it is true, so far as the Empire is concerned, was non-existent, but Massachusetts and Virginia and Pennsylvania, New England, and New Jersey most amply replaced her. It will be readily understood, therefore, that the charge of these great colonies, or plantations as they were then universally described, involved an amount of detail, an anxious supervision, an exercise of tact, discrimination, and common sense, a knowledge of affairs, and a capacity for statesmanship such as the most pre-eminent of our rulers to-day would not deem insufficient for the carrying on of the whole of the twentieth-century Empire. And Blathwayt was exactly the man for the job. He was in certain respects a curious and a complex character. As revealed in the diaries of Samuel Pepys, whose funeral he attended in an official capacity, and of John Evelyn, both of whom admired and respected him, and indeed, as depicted on canvas by Sir Peter Lely and Sir Godfrey Kneller, he appears to have been a somewhat chilly, aloof, and distant personality; very prim and, I should imagine, a little inclined to severity in his judgments of his fellow-men. And yet I discovered many expressions in that vast correspondence expressive of real fondness for the man, who was probably much more human and approachable than his ordinary official exterior may have promised. Of one thing I am certain—and one gets a hint of it in Macaulay's history—and that is that he was always and obviously a worshipper of the rising sun; and the extraordinary manner in which he gained and retained the liking and attachment of the gay and debonair Charles, of the morose and gloomy James, of the silent Prince of Orange, and of the stout and stodgy Anne displays him, not only as a very human person but also as a very master in the devious methods of the wily and time-serving courtier. But that he was a pre-eminently kindly man at heart, though one quite obviously given to Court scandal and chatter, is amply revealed in many a little sentence and paragraph in his otherwise stiff official dispatches to the innumerable Governors and Commissioners of Colonies and Plantations in the Western world, who one and all regarded him as friend and confidant no less than as the official go-between 'twixt them and their royal master.

It was in the golden days of the Merry Monarch that my ancestor met and wooed a certain lady named Mary Wynter, and with her he used to roam round the old estate of Dyrham, in Gloucestershire, which was then in the possession of the Wynters, having passed into their hands from the Russells. Mary Wynter, who had no brothers, brought it as her dowry into the possession of the Blathwayts, in whose hands it has remained ever since, for he who lives there to-day is Mr. Robert Wynter Blathwayt, a man devoted to country sports and who is appropriately enough married to a Chandos-Pole-Gell, which is one of the most sporting families in England. I like to think of my ancestress taking her lover into the old church at Dyrham and showing him the tombs of her forefathers, one of whom was Admiral Sir William Wynter, who sailed with Drake to the Spanish Main, and who it was who finally demolished the Spanish Armada by sending his fireships into the midst of proud Philip's fleet, whilst his nephews, in the following reign, expiated their share in the Gunpowder Plot on the same block from which the head of Guy Fawkes was severed from its shoulders. And it was in Dyrham Park, in the great dining-room of which you can still see the two portraits by Sir Peter Lely of Charles and Katherine of Braganza which the King presented to Blathwayt, as also Lely's portraits of William and Mary, and upon the walls of which still hangs some of the old stamped Spanish leather with which they were decorated in Charles's reign, that William Blathwayt brought his long and busy life to a close. For there is little doubt but that it must have been a life often overburdened with work and responsibility, though fraught with variety and interest of a quite exceptional description. In many respects the duties of a Colonial Secretary at this date were immeasurably more complex and complicated than they are to-day. Blathwayt, for instance, had to deal with Bombay, Goa, Siam, and Tunis, no less than he had to supervise the fisheries of Newfoundland, restrain the witch-burners in New England, and control and organize the capture and execution of Captain Kidd and his notorious crew of "pyrates" and freebooters. He was in his own laborious personality Colonial Secretary, Secretary for India, and Foreign Secretary all in one; and at the same time he often appears to have controlled the movements of the Army as well—certainly as regards its colonial disposition. One of the documents that appealed to me very specially was that in which the Earl of Bellomont,

Governor of Massachusetts, reports to Mr. Blathwayt the capture of the historic and storied "pyrate" Captain Kidd, whom he pungently describes as "the greatest lyer and thief in the world."

In an enormously lengthy letter, at the end of which he querulously complains that "he has writ himself almost dead," the Earl, under date of Boston, July 8, 1699, says: "It will not be unwelcome news to tell you that I secured Captain Kidd last Thursday in the goal [sic] of this town with four or five of his men." He then goes on to relate how that Kidd, who had been hovering on the coast towards New York for over a fortnight, at last sent on shore a certain Mr. Emot, "a cunning Jacobite, a fast friend of ——, and my avowed enemy." Emot assured Lord Bellomont of Kidd's innocence, but, adds the writer, "he conveyed three or four small jewels to my Wife which I was to know nothing of, but she came quickly and discovered them to mee and asked mee whether she was to keep them. On the following day the Governor had noticed that he [Kidd] designed my Wife a thousand pounds in gold-dust and ingots, but I spoyled his compliments by ordering him to be arrested and committed that day." And then Bellomont described how that Kidd acknowledged he had left his big Moorish ship hidden in a little creek in a West Indian island, of which only he knew the name, with a cargo of £30,000 on board, while the sloop in which he was captured contained no less than £10,000. Lord Bellomont then goes on to say: "I am forc'd to allow the Sheriff 40/- per week for keeping Kidd safe, otherwise I should be in some doubt about him; he has, without doubt, a great deal of gold, which is apt to tempt men that have not principalls of Honour. I have, therefore, to try the power of dull iron against gold, put him in irons that weigh 16 pound weight. I thought it was moderate enough, for I remember poor Dr. Oates had 100 weight on him when he was a prisoner in the last Reign"—referring obviously to Oates the poisoner. I might mention that in this, his last voyage, which was in a Genoese ship of some 400 tons, with eighty sailors on board, there was a terrible mutiny in the ship, in which Kidd and his officers slew no less than thirty men : a cinematographic glimpse of horror and tragedy which cannot easily be surpassed.

And then I picked up another letter which was perhaps one of the most tangible relics of romance that I had ever come across, for it was a letter in his own handwriting from the notorious freebooter and buccaneer Sir Henry Morgan, who had been made Lieutenant-Governor of Jamaica—presumably on the principle of setting a thief to catch a thief—and in this letter the sinner turned saint relates to Blathwayt his capture of a "pyrate" vessel in the neighbourhood of Port Royal. The letter, which came to England "per the *Golden Fleece*, Capt. Bannister, Commander," is as follows: "Last Saturday about 9 at night I had notice of one Capt. Jacob Everson, a noted privateer, being at anchor with a brigantine he had lately taken from the Spaniards in Cow Bay, some four leagues to windward of this port, upon which I secured all the wherrys and presently man'd a sloop with 24 souldiers and 36 seamen and their respective officers and sailed thence about 12 at night. Sunday at noone we came up with them, boarding the sloop we lett fly the King's Jack against which they fired 3 muskets wounding only one slightly; in returne we gave them a full vollie and killed two and wounded some others. So entering carryed the sloop with 26 stout men, the others with the Captain jumping overboard when some of them with him, its thought, were killed in the water as they were swimming to the shoare." In his reply to this letter Blathwayt, dropping, as he often did, into scandal and gossip, in a letter, dated November 7, 1680, tells his "deare friend, Sir Henry Morgan," that "one Turberville has made a further discovery of the Plott declaring that My Lord Stafford and my Lord and Lady Powis would have engaged him to kill the King and this day he is to attend the House of Commons to be examined by them." In one of his letters Sir Henry Morgan invites Colonel Blathwayt, of the Royal Horse Guards—the Secretary's son—to visit him in Port Royal, from which glittering and infamous place, indeed, most of his ingenuous epistles are indicted.

But I fancy that Colonel Blathwayt, rigid military disciplinarian and master of Court etiquette that he was, and as pictures of the period depict him to have been, a great dandy also, must have felt himself out of place in the company of the wild and hoary-headed old ruffian who, by some means or other, had persuaded Mr. Blathwayt to make him Lieutenant-Governor of the island of St. Iago de la Vega, as Jamaica was more generally known in those days. I can picture Colonel Blathwayt's amazement at the spectacle presented to his wondering gaze of the Spanish sailors and British buccaneers as they reeled through the streets of what was then known as the most wicked city in the world, with thick gold earrings glittering on their sunburnt necks and every man-jack of them pirates and murderers. And what a scene of riot and lust and waste and plunder and opulence unbelievable, and brilliant colouring and gold and jewelled cups, and exquisite fruit and foliage and lovely half-caste women must have presented itself to his gaze as he wandered through the streets of Port Royal, reeking with sin and the scent of wine and the memories of uncounted tragedies and unnumbered murders and long-forgotten revels and old-remembered vices! And through this welter of gorgeous glory and unnameable vices, through the splendour and the turmoil of it all, wandering in and out would be seen the stately figure of the Governor himself, the Duke of Albemarle, who was a great friend of the Blathwayts and who must occasionally, one would think, have suffered severe qualms of conscience concerning his more than dubious Assistant-Governor. Or stout old Admiral Benbow, beside whose tomb in the parish church of Kingston, Jamaica, I was standing but the other day, as it seems to me, and more than one of whose lengthy letters concerning the famous Gulf of Darien expedition I encountered among the Blathwayt papers, would stroll down to spend an evening with the old buccaneer and the son of his official chief at Whitehall.

One day in 1681 King Charles was playing idly with his world-famed spaniels when suddenly there appeared Mr. Secretary Blathwayt, ushering in the famous Quaker William Penn, who craved his Majesty's permission to name his new province in America "Carolina" in the King's honour. Blathwayt, however, rigid High and dry Churchman that he was, stepped hastily forward in protest. "No, your Majesty," said he, "let the Quaker name it after himself." The King, with an amused glance at his usually imperturbable Minister, smiled humorously. "Very well, Mr. Blathwayt," said he, "let it be called Pennsylvania." Penn must have been of a forgiving spirit, though, for he bore my ancestor no grudge, and subsequently wrote more than once to "my much valued friend, William Blathwayt." In one letter, which throughout was extremely vigorous, he begs to recommend his kinsman, Captain Markham, to the Secretary. "I have dispatcht him my Agent to attend the Court for the Compleatment of my business: perform thy usual kindness and no Province ever rise faster to a condition of being grateful than this will doe. As yet, the care and expence have been myn eminently and I may putt in my eye ye remainder of my Profitt by ye sale of ye land of this Province."

On another occasion, in October 1681, a very pretty ceremony occurred when Blathwayt took down to Windsor Castle a party of North American Indians, carrying with them their annual tribute of beavers' skins from the tribes of the Chickahominies, the Rappahannacks, the Appamatox, the Wyanokes, and others, Mr. Blathwayt bearing with him also a letter for the King's perusal written by Lord Culpeper, the Governor of Virginia, in which he begs Blathwayt's consideration for the colony in granting a new patent, "we being the first that broke the ice and underwent the brunt, at our own charge, for the enlargement of his Maj[ties] Dominions in this heretofore most howling wilderness amidst wild men and wild beasts." It must have been a picturesque scene this, and one wonders what the impassive Indian chiefs in all their glory of feathers and warpaint must have thought of Windsor Forest and their first glimpse of the grey pile of Windsor Castle. And how curiously Charles must have gazed upon them in return! We can be certain he would win their hearts by his kindly reception of them as they were severally presented to him by Mr. Secretary Blathwayt.

I picked up another letter, a veritable voice out of the past and which vividly recalled the days and scenes of Nathaniel Hawthorne's "Scarlet Letter." It was written to Blathwayt by Sir William Phips, the Governor of Massachusetts, under date Boston, 1692. "On my arrival here," says Sir William, "I found the prisons full of people committed upon suspicion of witchcraft. Continual complaints were made to me that many persons were grievously tormented by witches, and they cryed out upon several persons by name as the cause of their torments." However, Sir William Phips, in the middle of the "tryall" of these poor wretches, had to leave "to command the Army at the Eastern part of the Province against the French and Indians, who had made an attaque upon some of our frontier towns." When he returned he found these people had been tried, and twenty of them executed, "many thought to be innocent." He therefore dissolved the Court of Justice, and goes on to assure Blathwayt that the Reverend Increase Mather and several other divines "did give it in their judgment that ye Devil might afflict in the shape of an innocent person, and that the look and touch of a suspected person was not proof against them."

Among his other North American duties Blathwayt, who was largely responsible for the founding and early conduct of Harvard University, controlled the Newfoundland fisheries, and, incidentally, we learn from his papers that in 1698 "the King's Shippes carried away 293,469 cod fish from the country, that number, however, being only half that which the Fishermen had secured the year before."

In one of his letters to a certain colonial Governor,

Blathwayt, dropping the strictly official, relates how he had that morning met the Duke of Monmouth at the Court, where, apparently, the Duke was courteously received by King James, and "where many of the Parliament men did call upon him." In another of his official letters to the Earl of Carlisle, Governor of Jamaica in 1681, he gives us a fleeting glimpse into the fading Court of Charles II in a morsel of gossip which creeps into a postscript at the end of a long, dry official document. "The Duchess of Portsmouth," he says, "has been very ill of late and is therefore beginning a journey to-morrow into France where she intends to remain about three months to drink the Bourbon waters. The Duke and Duchess of York are in Scotland, but shee being with child will return speedily to London."

In reply to this epistle the Earl of Carlisle, whose name is still remembered in Jamaica and whose monument, if I remember rightly, I saw in the old cathedral church at Spanish Town in 1909, writes: "I pray your continuing that care and kindness to mee at so great a distance who will not be wanting to any opportunity that may give you further testimony of my respect for you." As an instance of the very literal difficulty of carrying on the work of a great Empire in those days, one constantly comes across reference in this voluminous correspondence to the delay caused by wind or weather, or even by great calms, on either side of the water; or now and then a Governor in the West Indies would send a messenger laden with official documents down to the harbour only to find that the captain, tired of waiting, had sailed half an hour previously.

But Blathwayt's concern in matters colonial did not stop at high politics; his microscopic vision embraced the animalculæ of the infinitely insignificant. For instance, Sir William Stapleton, the first Governor of the Leeward Isles, in 1679 wrote to the Secretary the following amusing and significant epistle—a letter abounding in quaint knowledge of human nature and the foibles and frailties of those high in office: "Mrs. Witmore being so unhappy by your displeasure to loose her license to trade has been persuaded by her friends at Court (of which some are persons of quality) to petition His Majesty to have restored unto her, but as she rather trust to your goodness than offend you by any complaint I am obliged by the intervention of her friends to intreat your favour towards her. I doubt not but you will the more readily grant this request as she has waved all other means of obtaining her desires than by an entire submission to you." And then he goes on to make a drastic proposal with regard to a much more important matter: "I cannot omit offering to your Honor's prudent consideration the destruction of the Caribean Indians, who have been in the last french warr, and will bee in the next a greater plague and terrour to English planters than any Xtian enemy."

I could write on and write on till it's dark, as Kingsley once said in a very different connection, for there was scarcely an end to the variety and quantity of these wonderful letters and state documents, of which Froude the historian used to speak with enthusiasm, but I have said enough to give my readers a sort of glimpse at the office and duties and countless responsibilities of an old-time Secretary of State. It was a romantic and picturesque Empire, that over which the English monarchs held their sway in those far-off days. No passion for reform ever seized upon the gentleman adventurers of Charles's sunny reign, and no telegraph-wire ever hindered the progress of Empire in the days when the grim old Sir Henry Morgan held high revel upon the Caribbean Seas. A man had to rely on his own strong right arm, his own courageous and daring brain.

It was then the man and the moment; and under the simple, honest sway of Blathwayt, and the heroes controlling British destinies far away from the seat of government, the Empire, as well as the world, went very well then. But with the advent of the telegraph-wire, as Mr. James Russell Lowell observed to me five and twenty years ago, the romance of the Ambassador's life had passed away, and frequently, too, his opportunity.

Most of this chapter has been written from the notes I made for my own article upon the Blathwayt papers which appeared in the September number of the *Fortnightly Review,* 1910, to the proprietors and Editor of which my best thanks are due.

CHAPTER XIV

HOW SETON-KARR DISCOVERED THE GARDEN OF EDEN

I AM on my way to India. We are far down the Red Sea and it is getting very hot. It is a bright and charming morning, with a sweet, soft wind blowing all the happy hours through. Walt Whitman's "splendid silent sun" blazes down upon the ship. The band is playing, the sea sparkling, and every one seems brimming over with buoyancy of spirit and pure light-heartedness. The scene is picturesque to a degree: the long lines of perspective, the great tossing world of waters, the notes of music heard only by those few hundreds of people on board and then flying away to be lost in far-off space, the sun-flecked, shadow-stricken deck—all go to the making up of a most curious and picturesque *tout ensemble*. I say curious, because life on board a great P. and O. liner is such a veritable microcosm of social life at home, and people arrive at a peculiar intimacy, and a singularly vivid conception of one another such as would scarcely be possible under ordinary circumstances on shore, and within the limits of a very circumscribed space you encounter a more varied, and frequently an immeasurably more interesting, set of people than you may be accustomed to do in the every-day life you lead in London, or wherever your home may be. Let us look at that group underneath the awning right away aft. I can see it almost as vividly as I saw it that February or March morning fully twenty years ago. That man, nearest to us, with the clean, well-cut features, and the gaze of the visionary no less than the clear, definite outlook of the practical man, artist, and *littérateur*, as well as soldier and man of affairs—that is Ian Hamilton, who was then acting as military secretary to Sir George White, the Commander-in-Chief in India ; next to him is his beautiful wife, looking very much like that wonderful white-gowned portrait which Sargent painted of her somewhere about the middle of the nineties—two of the most charming people you could wish to meet, and he always delightfully interesting to talk to, especially on art or books, on each of which subjects he spoke with more than ordinary insight and perception. Next to them that gallant, kindly soldier, Sir William Gatacre, returning to his Bombay command, with his exceedingly clever wife, Lord Davey's daughter ; then come a small party, consisting of Lord and Lady Ruthen ; Lord Cairns, a very old friend of mine ; Mrs. Murray Guthrie, one of the most popular people on board ship ; Charlie Yorke, sportsman and tea-planter, returning to Ceylon, and his cousin, David Mitford, who is now Lord Redesdale ; and last, but by no means least, Captain Heywood Walter Seton-Karr, the famous explorer, sportsman, writer, and author, who is vigorously discussing with his brother explorer and my own very dear friend, Harry de Windt, the best method of keeping warm in a snow-covered hut with the thermometer 60 degrees below zero.

The contrast between the two men makes some of us smile, though one realizes their many points of contact. Only Harry is so vivid, so humorous, so absolutely vital and effervescing with life ; small, wiry, like whipcord or a Toledo blade, and wonderfully smart in appearance and with such a collection of good stories and such an inimitable way of telling them. And de Windt is the most popular man I know.

Seton-Karr, tall and thin and burnt red with the sun, very sandy and very Scotch to look at, though not the least so to talk to. He always is crammed with reminiscences, which is not surprising when one reflects that he never rests in one part of the world hardly for more than a month or so at a time. He is off to India, but last year he was in Somaliland ; next year he meditates a trip to Alaska. And so it goes on year after year; so it will go on to the end; for no man was ever more seized, save and except perhaps myself, with the passion, the restless, unsatisfied longing, the absolute hunger for travel, as are he and Harry de Windt.

"What was that you were saying last night about having discovered the Garden of Eden?" said de Windt.

Seton-Karr looked very miserable at being thus ruthlessly dragged into the limelight. He is always delightfully modest, almost painfully shy, but, nevertheless, once he does begin to talk he is quite extraordinarily interesting to listen to. So there was a general clamour that he should tell us "all about it," though most people were under the impression that Harry de Windt was only pulling his leg—and ours too, perhaps. But no; there really was a story behind his joking words, and right well did Seton-Karr tell it to us.

"Oh well," he began, a little awkwardly, for he was always very loath to speak of his many adventures and accomplishments in the world of sport, "it's rather a long story, and the Garden of Eden is only one little bit of it. You'll have to hear the whole just to get that part. You see, I was following up a lion that had carried away a sheep from our zareeba the night before. I was going along following up his spoor, with my eyes fixed on the ground, when I caught sight of a stone digging implement. I at once saw that it was a palæolithic instrument, and a perfect type of the well-known implements that have been discovered frequently in Europe and Asia, but never, so far at all events, in Africa. This, however, supplied the missing link, and afforded me a perfect instance of the continuity of the human race. I might as well say here, before I forget it, that I took it home and showed it to the great authority on prehistoric instruments, Sir John Evans, and he agreed with me as to its value in demonstrating the theory most of us know in other connections, that the course of human civilization, if not, indeed, the human race, is invariably towards the West. So the discovery aided in bridging over the interval between palæolithic man in Britain and in India.

He thought it added a link to the chain of evidence regarding the original cradle of the human race, and that it tended to prove the unity of race between the inhabitants of Asia, Africa, and Europe in palæolithic times. Well," continued Karr, "that instrument lost me my lion, much to the disgust of my Somali boys. I felt I had indeed discovered the missing palæolithic link. I looked round and took careful bearings. The country in which I stood was a rolling upland, an immense plain about three thousand feet above the sea. I knew, therefore, that if I was to find more of these implements I must look for them upon a hill, where the settlement must have been in those far-off days. Carefully surveying the district, I caught a glimpse of a long, low hill some fifteen miles from where I stood. 'That is where they lived,' said I; and so on the following morning I struck my camp and we started off for this district. After a march of eight hours or so we arrived at the hill. Here I discovered that there were four rivers converging there, three of which surrounded the hill, the fourth joining at the foot of the hill from the north. On the east was an immense basaltic plateau, perpendicular cliffs enclosing the north and east sides; through this the four streams united force their way by a narrow and very precipitous sort of gorge. This exactly resembled the Garden of Eden as described in the Bible. This hill was covered with an exquisite forest of mimosa and other trees; there was also a beautiful variety of aloe plants, flowers of the most wonderful tints, grasses of every description; there were heaps of sheep and some of the most beautiful goats in the world, all eating as though they had to catch a train and not much time to do it in, while they were looked after by some very jolly little Somali children.

"'Yes,' I said to myself as I looked round, feeling quite certain of my ground, as, indeed, no one could help doing who knows his Bible ever so little—'yes, there is the gorge in which the Angel of the Lord stood with his flaming sword.' I see you are laughing, de Windt, but I mean it, though I am quite willing to grant it may be explained on natural grounds if you take it that the Cherubim with the flaming sword was in reality the volcano which threw up this barrier of once molten lava, in which case Adam would have been driven westward into the middle of Africa. In any case, I was pretty well convinced by then that I was actually standing in the Garden of Eden. I camped down by the biggest river for the sake of the water, and from there I made daily visits to the hill and searched the ground thoroughly for palæolithic instruments, which I found in a quantity far greater than had been discovered in any part of the world, and of the most perfect description as well as of the earliest period. They were every bit as fine as those I discovered in the flint mines of Egypt which had been manufactured thousands of years before the pyramid of Sakkarah was built, and that is about seven thousand years old. Nothing could have been more satisfactory than this find. For all I know I may have discovered the very spade with which Adam delved. There were, of course, no remains of dwellings. They were pastoral people, who dwelt then, exactly as they do now, in skin tents. When I speak of 'Adam' I speak of him in the sense of prehistoric man. Amongst the instruments I discovered were small stone axes, stone hammers, grinding-stones for pulverizing seeds made of quartzite, and small flakes of flint with sharp edges to be used as knives. There were disc-shaped scrapers for dressing hides, kite-shaped and spoon-shaped. I looked about for evidence of fire and I found iron pyrites, which were evidently used by Adam to strike a light. Then there were other borers for sewing skins together with sinews. 'Adam and Eve made breeches for themselves,' as the very old-fashioned Bibles had it, although of course at first they used fig-leaves, and, sure enough, I saw a number of fig-trees all over the place. There were heavy javelin heads of stone which he lashed on to handles, and which he probably needed very badly, for the place must have been infested with lions in those days. I myself have seen six or seven of a morning walking together before breakfast. Sling stones lay everywhere about the place. A good many people, I honestly believe, think that Adam and his sons used spades made in Birmingham. Well, he didn't. To begin with, Birmingham itself wasn't made then. He used a very heavy, pointed, stone digging implement, of which I discovered great numbers, all piled together. Of course Adam returned to Eden as soon as the Tree of Life had been removed, and it is quite certain that the place became largely populated in later days, as we are distinctly told that 'Eden traded with Tyre.' We must take it that Africa was, according to Huxley and Darwin, the country of Eden and the home of man. 'And the Lord God planted a garden *eastward* in Eden.' As Dr. Cunningham Geikie says: 'Eden, a name derived from the old Arcadian word for a "country plain," not, as has been supposed, from the Hebrew word for delight, has been sought for in every part of the world'; but I have good reason, judging from its physical conformations, for my own theory that the Garden lies in Somaliland. As Darwin says: 'It is more probable that our early progenitors lived on the African continent than elsewhere.'"

Here Harry de Windt struck in. "Speaking of Darwin reminds me——"

"But it wasn't *you* who were speaking of Darwin, Mr. de Windt," said an interested and much amused and very charming lady who was sitting next to him.

"Never mind," replied the undaunted Harry. "I am going to speak of him now whilst Karr gets his wind again for another lap. Speaking of Darwin reminds me that Mrs. Darwin once, hearing a fearful row in the kitchen, went down to see what it was all about, and the cook said: 'Well, mum, you see, it's like this; wich Mr. Briggs [the butler] 'e wants to prove as 'ow we are *all* descended from Darwin, and some of us 'as our doubts!'"

As soon as we had finished laughing there was a universal shout to Seton-Karr to go on with his story.

"And don't interrupt again, Mr. de Windt," said his pretty companion.

"Well," said Karr, "where was I? Oh yes, I remember—stone implements. Primal man certainly used only stone, for Tubal Cain, who invented metal instruments, was only born when Adam lay a-dying. Scripture and science are both agreed here. The great difficulty has been to reconcile the four rivers—Gihon, Pihon, Hiddekel, and Euphrates—with any known rivers. Two at least of these were over a mile wide, and quite unsuitable for irrigating a garden. Now, these texts are capable of a double interpretation, and we may take it that, whilst there were four rivers in miniature for purposes of irrigation and domestic use, the larger interpretation signified the four continents as known to-day. Darwin has proved that the Red Sea was dry and that Adam had free communication with Asia by land. The Red Sea, with its coral reefs, was once dry land. Then I remember that Sir Charles Lyell tells us that Darwin has proved that there is a slow and continuous sinking of all land on which there are reefs of coral resting. I think it may prove that the biblical statement that Havilah was a river with gold was actually true, as a traveller only last year stated that he extracted gold from the sand at the rate of 500 oz. to the ton, and that in his opinion there was enough gold to discount the Klondyke output for twenty years. And I myself have seen deserted gold-mines, now unworkable for want of water, in the western desert, on the borders of Abyssinia. I should like, and, indeed, I propose, to take out a party of theologians and scientists, that they may study the birthplace of the human race on the spot."

"Didn't you discover the lost emerald-mines of Egypt last year?" I asked.

"Yes," replied Seton-Karr. "When I discovered the lost flint-mines of prehistoric Egypt, and when I was exhibiting the Pharaohnic implements I found there in London, Mr. Streeter, the famous Bond Street dealer in gems, came to me and said: 'You must go and find the lost emerald-mines now.' So off I went to Cairo. I got my first information from Mr. Floyer, the Director of Egyptian Telegraphs, with whom I purposely travelled in the same ship, as I knew that he had a thorough knowledge of the whole country. From him I obtained information as to the best part of the desert to search for these mines. Mr. Floyer had scoured the whole of the eastern desert of Egypt in search of the ruins of the Roman stations where the bullocks were kept that served the caravans that plied between the Nile and the Red Sea, northwards from the famous Berenice, the ancient Marseilles of Africa. Mr. Floyer told me that he found that the ancient tourists had, as the modern Cook's trippers would, if they were allowed, scribbled their names on the rock-cut temples. But the names included those of Darius, Cambyses, and Xerxes."

"Well," said I, "I came across an old temple in the desert, near Thebes I think it was, and there I saw a whole lot of men, some of whom I know myself—well-known British generals and others—had cut their names in the temple stones."

"Name! name!" cried some of the party.

"No, I won't give any names," I replied; "but you would all know them. I beg your pardon, Karr; please go on."

"Well," continued Karr, "I set off from Assouan with nine camels and twelve men, the very scum of the bazaar, as no decent man would so tempt Providence. We all walked, as the camels were too heavily laden to carry us. For the first five days, eighty miles' march, we had to carry our water in iron drums. Following the directions of Mr. Floyer, I struck due east. The first hundred miles were sandy plateau rising to the watershed, and after that a descent by a sea of mountains to the Red Sea. I found the mines one day by seeing the ancient watch towers from which the Roman soldiers shot arrows at the convicts and prisoners of war working in the mines when they tried to escape. Underneath the towers were the openings of the shafts, with a stream of grey talus full of mica-schist coming from these openings. Here I camped for many days and descended every shaft, working underground, lighted by candles, in an atmosphere like a Turkish bath, and fearing that every blow of the

Sheffield tools would bring the whole ancient roof down upon us, when we would have been buried for ever, as all hands were below and there would have been none to rescue us. There were three or four distinct periods of working, the earliest being the mere tortuous badger-holes made by prehistoric Troglodytes, down to the square, straight shafts of the Ptolemies and the Roman emperors. Many of these shafts and the whole district swarmed with the deadly cerastes, or horned snake, the bite of which is fatal. Professor Sayce is the only man who is known to have been bitten and to have survived. Fortunately he was struck on the ankle-bone. His cook, close by, happened by marvellous chance to have an iron heated red-hot in the fire, with which the Professor at once burnt himself to the bone, and even then he was ill for a month with a swollen leg. I found one cerastes under the floorcloth of the tent. The snake had followed a little desert rat which had come for food. The Roman shafts were at least five hundred feet deep, and you may imagine what dangerous work it was descending them, knowing that a slight blow might bring the whole mass down upon one's head. I found a sufficient number of gems to warrant us in at once proceeding to take out a concession from the Egyptian Government for their further working and development. Though I searched all my men at the point of the revolver in the centre of the desert, and found no gems concealed upon them, I was told that on the very day I left Assouan for the north emeralds were offered for sale in the bazaar by three different sets of merchants."

And here the explorer ceased his deeply interesting story. Far away in the dim distance we could catch a glimpse of the very land—Somaliland—of which he had been talking. At least, I suppose it was Somaliland, and then I remember, as though it were yesterday, I went down to my cabin to make a few rough notes of all that had been said. I glanced out of my porthole. What a rush of life and motion, and how inspiriting and irresistible it all is ! and ever "the sound of many waters" in my ears. A bright rainbow flashes now and again in the sun as the rays of light fall upon the dancing spray. Now and again a great green transparent wave lifts its crested head almost to the very porthole, and one sees it a moment poised in mid-air, a mass of light and shadow, ere it tumbles over with a subdued roar. But the stately ship, unheeding, cleaves its onward path, leaving ever behind it a glittering, snow-white track. The clouds chase each other through the blue wind-swept vault of heaven, and we are glad at heart.

CHAPTER XV

COSTUME AND CELEBRITIES

THIS, I fear, is going to be a very trivial chapter. But it is written of set purpose in a period of great national stress and after hours of anxious work on behalf of war charities, etc. I personally find it a relief to turn from time to time to the absolutely trivial and unimportant, and I believe many of my readers will think the same. And in a way the subject of dress is always interesting. After all, it is more by dress, by costume, than by anything else that we differentiate the nations and the ages. Nothing denotes the passing of the years so much and so definitely as dress. A glance at a costume determines half a century, almost to the day, and variety, which is the salt of the earth, is the one thing that adds joy to travel. It is the costume of the country which gives colour to the landscape almost as much as do sunshine, foliage, and flowers. Nor is costume so unscientific a subject as some people would have us imagine. Like every other human study, it lends itself especially to the skill and brain of the expert, and it demands all his care and knowledge and pains too. You would find this out in a moment if you talked with Mr. Percy Macquoid or Mr. Percy Anderson or Mr. Hugo Rumbold on the dressing and costuming of a great play, or if you interviewed one of the leading cinema film photographers. Although, at the same time, what fearful mistakes some of these good men make out of sheer ignorance or sheer carelessness! Some time ago I saw a long cinema play on "Edwin Drood." Now, the period of "Edwin

Drood" was in the late sixties. They dressed it generally as though it were a Count D'Orsay period of 1840; and had they kept to that well and good, but, unfortunately, they introduced an old family lawyer in the costume of 1780 and wound up with a yacht's crew bearing all over them the date of 1916.

The same with a film depicting "John Brown's School Days," period 1830-40, in which they contrived to display a hunting squire in the costume of Dick Turpin. This is immensely to be deprecated in the sacred cause of art and verisimilitude, though, of course, in itself I frankly own it isn't a matter of vital importance.

Costume is frequently as indicative of character as it is of centuries or countries; it is invariably interesting to note the costume of the people one meets, especially when they are people who have won a prominent position for themselves in literature, art, or politics. Unfortunately, the Quartier Latin is fast becoming a mere memory, though attempts are being made to revive it in Chelsea and the Café Royal. I regret the passing of distinctive costume, because to a certain extent it is to deprive the world of picturesque variety. The Quartier Latin of George Du Maurier's student days in the fifties and sixties of the last century and that quarter of Paris so picturesquely hinted at for our behoof by Henri Murger, Dumas, Guy de Maupassant, and Balzac is passing into the limbo of forgotten things, and yet how reckless and delightful it must all have been, as well as how distinctive and with what a charm and fascination all its own! I am quite prejudiced enough in favour of entire smartness and up-to-dateness of costume to appreciate to its fullest extent all the diatribes so freely launched against the typical Bohemian's lengthy locks and the artist's beard and the fearful hats and still more appalling ties which constituted the main trademarks, as it were, of the ultra-unconventional and of the almost pedantically ferocious opponents of ordinary up-to-date civilization. I have shared that prejudice myself just as, at times, I have taken sides with the "strafing" of the hopelessly unbending votary of fashion who has nothing but abuse for any one who dares to step aside from the beaten paths of conventionalism.

I understand and sympathize with both sides. I am, in my own person, unyielding in my devotion to the most absolutely correct costume, although at the same time I can shudder at its inartistic and unæsthetic terrors! The rack could confer no worse tortures upon me than would overtake me if I were forced to walk down Bond Street in a frock-coat and a billy-cock hat and brown boots on a June afternoon. One of the proudest moments of my life was that moment when two men passing me in Piccadilly five or six years ago glanced at me, and one of them—Max Beerbohm—said to me: "Hullo, Blathwayt! It's you, is it? I had just said to my friend here, 'I wonder where that man gets his coat from. I wish I could find out.'" And then, in the regular Beerbohm-cum-Tree fashion, he indicated its lines and curves with a graceful, sketchy movement of his hands in the air. To the present-day young man that means little, because "Max" has for some years now ceased to live in England; ten years ago he was, in such matters, more than Petronius Arbiter himself! It only remained for Sir George Alexander to compliment me upon the crease in my trousers. I have a good mind to run round to the theatre and ask him to do so now. Perhaps he will if he ever reads this! I merely mention these trivialities as an assurance that there is nothing of the Quartier Latin—whose disappearing glories I bewail from a purely æsthetic point of view—about me. At the same time, at my age, I am no "dude," no "Knut," nothing at all of the masher, I trust. But why the years should bring slovenliness in their train I never could imagine. To-day, however, you find the artist with short hair and woefully particular about the crease in his trousers and the author with the smartest dinner-jacket that heart could desire, both looking very clean and trim and West Endy and hopelessly unromantic and unpicturesque.

I heard the other day that a well-known literary man had protested against the idea of a certain really brilliant man of genius being able to write well on the score that he dressed too well. "You can't do both," he said. As a matter of fact *Knuts* are frequently quite exceptionally intellectual, or else they are very clever with their hands. Hugo Rumbold, for instance, the Guardsman, paints brilliantly ; Caryll Craven, a brother-in-law of the Duke of Richmond, was a particularly smart person twenty years ago or so, but what an artist he was, and probably is, in the decoration of a house, and what a cook ! I remember he and Alaricus Delmard, another tremendous masher in his day, between them dished me up a dinner that would have delighted the heart of Lucullus himself. And Delmard was equally an artist with his brush, and as a pianist he won the approval of such a brilliant amateur and *executante* as Lady Charles Beresford herself in the old days five and twenty years ago. And you are never too old to learn how to dress. Take my old friend Hall Caine, for instance. The most prejudiced will not deny him the possession of brains, at all events. When I first knew Hall Caine, some five and twenty years ago, he was openly and unashamedly the worst dressed man I ever met. Always scrupulously clean and with snow-white linen—always. But his ideas of costume were positively startling. It is on record, I believe, that he once went to a very smart garden-party in a soft Alpine hat, a low-cut collar, frock-coat, brown knickerbockers, plaid stockings, and brown boots ! And I quite believe it. To-day, and for many years past, he is absolutely one of the best-dressed men I know. He still wears his long hair, which, as he demonstrated to me once beyond all argument, is the best thing he could do, and which certainly suits him as it would not suit me, but his attire is beyond the cavil of the strictest dandy. Nothing neater, nothing more unassuming, nothing in better taste, nothing that would suit him so perfectly could possibly be devised than the dark grey, extremely well-cut, suit that he habitually wears to-day, with the admirably built trousers exactly "shaped" over his well-shod feet ; a full Ascot tie, with a very unostentatious pearl pin exactly in the right place, and there you have Hall Caine, one of the best-dressed men of my acquaintance. To his old friends it came as a revelation of something quite unexpected in his character, because it was nothing less than a revolution from all to which he had, for years, habituated us!

Grant Allen, with no pretensions to smart apparel, was, nevertheless, always a pleasure to look at. Tall and slight, in an admirably cut loose grey suit, with snowy collars and cuffs and very neat walking shoes, he might have been an ordinary country squire for all he displayed of the typical untidiness of the traditional literary man.

James Anthony Froude the historian was very similar; nothing whatever remarkable about his dress save its exceptional good taste, added to which a very considerable distinction of character and appearance gave one the impression of perfect artistic completeness and satisfaction. Have you ever realized how distinctive a feature of their personality and individuality is the costume of certain well-known men about London? What absolute landmarks they are about the town! For years, of course, "Charlie Buller's" short-cropped, curly locks and very smart jacket were as familiar in Pall Mall as the Guards' Monument; and the last time I saw him he was wheeling a perambulator along the front at Worthing—and even then the halo of a great London dandy faintly floated over his head. And for how long a period was the handsome and distinguished personality of General Brocklehurst, now Lord Ranksborough, a despair to the youthful Guardsman, who, lacking his distinction of appearance, would vainly endeavour to emulate his lofty ideal. But all this is very *vieux jeu* to the present generation, though, by the by, I am just as much of the present day as a young man of twenty. The fact, however, remains that you hardly ever see a real typical dandy to-day—and this without any reference whatever to the war, for I wrote these very words almost a year or so before the tragedy of August 1914—though Colonel Brabazon, Sir Robert Hermon-

Hodge, Lord Spencer, and Lord Chesterfield, among the men in the very latest prime of life, still testify to the fact that good dressing is not altogether a thing of the past among us who recall a period when London was the smartest city in the world so far as men's dress was concerned. Now I am not certain that New York is not taking its place. One of the very smartest-looking and best-dressed men I ever saw was, of course, the King's elder brother, the late Duke of Clarence. With his tall, singularly graceful figure and handsome, delicate features and absolutely perfect taste in dress, he was, one summer morning, nearly thirty years ago, the last time I saw him, easily the most distinguished-looking person in the whole of the West End. Any one would have turned to have looked at him, even had they not known who he was. Then, of course, the Marquis de Soveral is as *soigné* and well-turned-out a figure as one would wish to see, although the Duke of Rutland and his brother, Lord Cecil Manners, by reason of their height and fine distinction, can give him points and a beating. And we all knew and smiled at the late Sir Oswald Mosley's "John Bull" hat, just as we know and recognize Mr. H. B. Irving by his somewhat old-fashioned and very distinctive "topper," or Sir Squire Bancroft, with his hat very much on one side—like the late Lord Redesdale—and his single black-rimmed glass in his eye. These figures are all as characteristic and as much part of London and of town life as are famous buildings—Westminster Abbey or St. Paul's or the Tower. The only thing is, man passes, but his works remain, and Dr. Johnson gives place to the old Duke, and Count d'Orsay is succeeded by Disraeli, and in place of the great Victorian statesman we catch a fleeting glimpse of Mr. Lloyd George and "Megan" laughing at the ducks in St. James's Park. And so the world fulfils itself in many ways and with many people; but London still goes on, and goes on in very much the same way as it always did. It is wonderfully what it was when I was young, though, naturally enough, I suppose, it doesn't appear to me to be quite so varied and interesting and romantic as it used to be when Temple Bar so picturesquely and abruptly severed the street of adventure from the Strand, and a whole Alsatia, a wonderful rabbit-warren of ancient houses, redolent of Charles's golden days and reminiscent even of Tudor times, used to cover the spot where Aldwych and the Law Courts now stand, or when a stone lion "wagged" its tail, according to Theodore Hook, over the gateway of Northumberland House, now replaced by the Grand Hotel, or the old Duke on horseback topped the arches at Hyde Park Corner. But London is always changing, and where it will end who shall say? My grandfather, I believe, shot snipe in Kensington, where St. Mary Abbotts now stands; but then, you must remember, he actually saw Johnson and "Bozzy" walking down Fleet Street together, so he is very old game indeed. In the National Gallery there is an extremely interesting painting depicting Regent's Park about 1800; it is a wild and picturesque scene with which the artist has presented us, with a herd of cattle in the foreground, as though, indeed, they were in the Highlands of Scotland.

Piccadilly is thronged with the memories and the ghosts of a dead and splendid day, and even I, with my own comparatively brief record, am now and again confronted with the shadows of the past. The last time I ever saw and spoke to that stately old lady, one of the most picturesque and typical Victorian figures, Maria, Marchioness of Aylesbury—"Lady A," as she was universally known—was at a crossing in Piccadilly, when she seized hold of my arm. "My dear Mr. Blathwayt, for goodness' sake take me over to the other side! It's horrible the crush nowadays." And then, almost in the same breath, she added: "What's become of your cousin Glynne Turquand? Haven't seen the man for ages." What a picture she was of a daintier and a more fragile day than anything we moderns ever see in Piccadilly to-day, with her iron-grey curls and her smart frocks—a Dresden china shepherdess to look at, but with marvellous vitality and vivacity and a singularly pungent tongue, though with a heart of gold behind it. And she could tell a good story, too, and, by the by, one she told me cast rather a lurid light upon a certain phase of London society. I believe, if I remember rightly, she was actually present on the occasion, which took place, I think, in the Diamond Jubilee. One of the Indian princes was showing a party of his London friends the beautiful presents and jewellery he had received from various potentates, and he had just laid down a handsome gold watch which had been presented to him by the Czar when the electric light unexpectedly flickered out; when it blazed up a moment after the watch was gone! "Ladies and gentlemen," calmly cried the Maharajah, "the electric light will be turned out, and the guest who has just taken up the watch to look at it can then put it back on the table!" And the light was turned out for a moment or so. The clink of some metal object was heard on the surface of the table and the light went up again, when it was found that not only was there no watch, but in addition a magnificent gold cigarette-case, studded with diamonds, which had been presented to the Prince by Queen Victoria, had also disappeared! Talking of "Lady A" reminds me of her nephew—or was it her son?—who was extremely well known in London and sporting circles generally twenty or thirty years ago. He was a queer fellow, and though we hadn't much in common, yet I couldn't help being amused at times by his pranks and his conversation. I remember once going into a club of which both he and I were members, and as I entered the smoking-room he cried out—

"Here's the blighter will tell us which of us is right! He's the sort of chap who knows all about these history Johnnies! Look here, old son," he continued, "who was it got 'outed' at Waterloo—Nelson or Wellington?"

"Neither," I replied. "It was Napoleon Bonaparte."

"There! I told you so!" he cried as he vehemently smacked the knee of a well-known sportsman as simple and ignorant as himself—if that were possible—"I told you so! I knew it began with an N!"

What a curious man that was! Most of my elderly

readers will have guessed to whom it is I refer. A good-hearted fellow, if ever there was one, but a sadly wasted life was his and a great position terribly abused.

The very last time I saw Mr. Gladstone was in Piccadilly. He was walking down the street in the full blaze of a gorgeous summer evening in evening dress, with a light overcoat on and the famous stick-up collar and, if I remember rightly, a red rose in his button-hole, and with his marvellously carved face, looking like old ivory, and flashing eyes and irresistible personality, with all the memories and almost the traditions of a splendid life behind him, he riveted all eyes upon himself. He was in vigorous conversation with one of those unfortunate women with whom Piccadilly and the Haymarket actually reeked in those days, at least, five and twenty years ago. At last he stopped, and as I passed I heard him say distinctly as he gave the woman a card, on which he had pencilled a few words, "Ask for Mrs. Gladstone, and be sure you come." I learned afterwards that for years he and his wife, among their other many energies, had devoted themselves to rescue work in the streets of London. It was a passing but an interesting glimpse into a great personage's inner life.

I think, however, that the most remarkable figure I ever saw in Piccadilly was a perfectly beautiful old man, clad in the Quaker costume of Charles II's day—not the Quaker costume of the early part of the last century, but in the exact costume that William Penn must have worn on that day my ancestor presented him to the Merry Monarch. And this old gentleman's face was cut to match his costume: very delicate features, face clean-shaven and framed in long hair which fell about his shoulders. How quaint and how unbelievably artistic and picturesque he looked threading his way through the very modern crowd of only four or five years ago, the wide knickerbockers, the dove-coloured stockings, the dainty ruffles at his wrists, the wide collar falling over his shoulders, exactly as though he had stepped out of the portrait-gallery at Hampton Court.

As a matter of fact I believe he was a medical man, who sometimes lived in Kensington and sometimes in Somersetshire, and for all I know he may be alive to read these words and this description of himself to-day. I saw him in Piccadilly twice, and once I travelled with him in the Tube—actually in the Tube!—so that it will show you it is not so very ancient a memory, after all; and yet the vision of him in the roar and turmoil of twentieth-century Piccadilly rolled away, not years only but absolutely centuries, and one got a breath of a sweeter and a lovelier England than anything of which we have ever known or dreamed. Well, you can imagine no greater contrast than he and Basil Hallam would present; but, as a matter of fact, I was actually talking to that charming and ill-fated person on my last occasion of seeing this old Quaker. "Isn't he wonderful?" said Hallam. "I wish Sir Herbert was here. Wouldn't he revel in him?" And curiously enough the selfsame idea had occurred to me. By the by, the mention of poor Basil Hallam, one of the best-dressed men I ever saw, and whom I knew but very slightly, of course, for there yawned between us the cavern of almost countless years, reminds me of a funny story of the Lincoln Handicap he once told me. A wire from the course was handed in at the office of a certain newspaper, which ran as follows—

Lincoln. Ob. Dean Swift. Roseate Dawn.

The sporting editor had gone home, and the sub-editor, who wasn't up in racing, couldn't at first make head or tail of it, until suddenly it struck him, "Why, of course, 'ob.' means *obiit*." So he swiftly penned the following paragraph for the latest edition of his paper: "We deeply regret to record the death of the famous Dean Swift, author of that popular hymn, 'The Roseate Hues of Early Dawn.'"

Mr. Augustine Birrell, with his glasses and rather lengthy hair and not too well-fitting overcoat, but with always a pleasant smile upon his genial face, is a frequent figure in Piccadilly. I never see him but what I think of the droll story he tells against himself. He got into a third-class carriage in the North one day and sat down. A little girl sitting opposite appeared to be very uneasy, and he realized he was sitting on her paper, so he handed it to her, and although he noticed she didn't even then appear satisfied, he opened a book and began to read. Suddenly the train drew up at a wayside station, and the little girl got up and said to him, "If you please, sir, may I have my fried fish?" It had been wrapped up in that sheet of paper! One of Mr. Birrell's specially personal stories always delights me. He was anxious about certain disquieting physical symptoms which he was experiencing, and he flew off to a famous specialist. He arrived at the great man's house terribly overheated, as it was a burning day in June and he had walked far and fast. Shown into the waiting-room, where he was told he would have to wait some time, he took up a medical work of reference and he actually turned up the very disease from which he suspected himself to be suffering. The first words he read were, "A notable feature of this disease is that the patient is incapable of perspiring." Mr. Birrell passed his handkerchief over his damp and heated forehead, took up his hat, and walked light-heartedly into the street.

One of the most notable and distinctive personalities connected with Piccadilly is, of course, Admiral Lord Beresford, known and admired for at least two generations as "Lord Charles" or "Charlie Beresford" pure and simple, one of the most genial and popular persons it would be possible to meet. The very first time I ever saw him was nearly forty years ago. He was riding slowly down Piccadilly with the late King Edward, then Prince of Wales, and Mrs. Langtry, the newest of all the beauties in the town that year, and very lovely she looked too. Years afterwards I used to spend many week-ends at his charming house on the outskirts of Richmond Park. Lady Charles in those days was a very pretty woman, with a very strong personality; very cynical, almost too much so at times, but with the kindliest manner and a wonderful sense of humour; well read and *au courant du jour* to an almost uncanny degree, a brilliant musician and yet also with a great habit, as Whistler would have expressed it, of the needle and thread. She always struck me as being remarkably accomplished in that direction, if one so ignorant of such matters may venture to express an opinion. I have referred to her cynicism. It was really the natural outlook of an exceedingly clever and a very outspoken woman who absolutely detested anything approaching snobbery or anything that savoured of affectation. No woman ever knew her world better than she did, and no one ever possessed a keener vision for the almost inevitable foibles of humanity. One always met a most interesting crowd during those summer week-end parties of hers, when she would spend the long, hot days mostly in a huge Cairene tent or Shamiana on the lawn. The old Countess of Shrewsbury would often be there—"Theresa, Countess," as they used to speak of her—a charming personality, full of anecdotes of the great ones of a past day, and full of stories, too, of Malta, where she had spent a good deal of her time. And another guest was that very dainty and graceful person Lady Constance Leslie; and there, too, was the present Duchess of Leeds, then Lady Carmarthen, a pretty, interesting woman, who always appeared to me to have read every book ever written. I remember one night at dinner the talk turned on political elections, and I asked her if a certain story I was told of her husband, Lord Carmarthen, was a fact. It ran as follows: Somewhere in the very late eighties or the very early nineties he had successfully contested Brixton as Parliamentary candidate, and he won it mainly owing to a very smart retort he fired off in reply to a question shouted at him from the back of the hall—

"Does your mother know you are out?"

"Yes, she does," promptly replied Lord Carmarthen, "and next Tuesday she'll know I am in!"

"It's perfectly true," said Lady Carmarthen, "because we sent one of the footmen with instructions to call out that very question. But it absolutely won my husband the seat."

I don't suppose the Duchess will mind my telling this story after so many years. It is too good to be left untold.

Of course Lord Charles himself was always, and is to-day, full of the most delightful yarns. Here are two of them, anyway. One of them, indeed, he told the same night Lady Carmarthen told hers. He was addressing a political meeting in Ireland one night, and a man kept interrupting him so much that at last Lord Charles told him he must come up on the platform and state outright what was his grievance. So the man clambered on to the platform, and when Lord Charles asked him what was the matter he said, "Lord Charles, ye're no man!" (Fancy saying that to a Beresford of all people in the world!)

"What the —— do you mean?" said Lord Charles.

"Well, I remember the last time one of your family stood for Waterford I was up to my knees in blood and whisky for a month, and at this election, begob! I tell ye, divil a drop of either have I seen!"

On another occasion I was staying with the Beresfords at their house in Chatham when he was in command of the Steam Reserve there. We were turning out some letters out of an old box late one night when these two gems appeared, written to him by a ship's stoker—

MY LORD,

Last night my wife had twins, and we want to ask your Lordship if we may call the little boy after you, and if you will ask the Princess of Wales if we may call the little girl after her?

The second letter, written a few months later, ran as follows—

MY LORD,

I am happy to inform you Lord Charles Beresford Brown is well and hearty, and Princess of Wales Brown died at 4 o'clock this morning.

I remember in connection with Lord Charles Beresford an instance of honour amongst journalists which would have been almost impossible among a certain type of reporter in America. Lord Charles was lying off Great Yarmouth with his fleet some years ago, and I took the Vicar of Gorleston on board the flagship to have luncheon with the Admiral. During the course of the meal Lord Charles said to the vicar: "Oh, Mr. Phillips, I wonder if you can do me a favour. Something occurred this morning that I rather want to 'scratch out.' It was a piece of pure thoughtlessness on my part. The Mayor and Corporation came off to give us an official welcome, and I took them all up on deck and waved my hand at my ships lying all round and I said, 'There, gentlemen, there's something to make German Billy keep his hands off us.' Well, I heard afterwards there were a number of reporters with the party. If that careless remark of mine gets into the papers, there'll be the very devil to pay at the Admiralty."

So the vicar said, "I'll put that all right for you, sir, as soon as I get ashore."

An hour afterwards he and I went and routed those young men out. But there was no occasion for us to have done so. Lord Charles would have been perfectly safe in their hands. "We guessed he didn't know there were any reporters on board, and we had all agreed to leave that remark out, because it was obviously not meant for the Press."

And all this quite unaffectedly, without the slightest idea that they were doing anything out of the way, so unconsciously high was their standard of personal and professional honour. I can hardly imagine the journalists of any other country in the world being willing to forgo what they would regard, in the language of the profession, as so decided and acceptable a "scoop."

It is curious how a great thoroughfare, famous throughout the world, links us with the past. The other day—last Alexandra Day, June 1916—I stopped outside that delightful old print shop in York Street, just behind St. James's Church, and I was much interested in an old-fashioned print representing Queen Alexandra driving through London on her wedding-day in March 1863, with all that quaintly clad crowd of that now far-off day cheering the lovely Danish princess like mad. A moment afterwards I turned into Piccadilly, and just as I did so the same lovely lady drove by once again through the streets of London, and the famous thoroughfare re-echoed once again to the shouts and cheers of the people of London as the children and grandchildren—aye, and the great-grandchildren—of the people whom I had seen cheering in that quaint old-coloured print in York Street gave vent to their joy at seeing once again the selfsame person, and looking just as beautiful as she had done more than half a century previously and very nearly as youthful.

I met Alfred Capper in Piccadilly the other day, a refreshing, stimulating, and delightful personality. He at once buttonholed me.

"My dear fellow," he began, "we've been having a most fearful time since I saw you last, and I am seriously afraid I shall have to send Mrs. Capper and Margaret and Randolph to the seaside or they will all break down hopelessly."

"I am very sorry," I replied; "but what on earth is the matter?"

"Well, my dear fellow, that's the mystery of it. As a matter of fact it has been solved at last, but the ill-effect on all my household is perfectly deplorable to think about."

"Well, but what is it?" I said, for I could see by a certain tell-tale twinkle in his eye that the story was not wholly one of tragedy.

"Well," he said, "about a fortnight ago the children came rushing into our room at midnight to say that they couldn't get a wink of sleep as some man in the next house snored so frightfully that he literally shook the house. 'Come and hear him for yourself,' they said. So my wife and I went upstairs to the other side of the house, and sure enough there was some one snoring so frightfully that I began to wonder if it mightn't be some wild animal: perhaps an explorer from South Africa lived next door and had brought home a gorilla or a hippopotamus with him, and knowing what queer creatures people do keep in their bedrooms sometimes, I thought it just possible that this might be the explanation of the affair ; for the noise was so appalling that it was impossible to believe that an ordinary man could make it, and yet there was something absolutely human in the sound, and I came to the conclusion that it must be a man in a very serious state of health. And this noise went on till 3.30, after which peace reigned supreme and we were all able to get a little much-needed rest and sleep. We anxiously awaited the next night. At eleven o'clock Randolph, who is only eight years old, rushed into our room. 'Oh, mummy, it's perfectly frightful! That horrible old man has begun snoring again, far worse than last night. Come and hear him.' So we went and heard, and true enough the snoring was twice as bad as it had been the night before. In addition to its uncannily human quality there was about it something of the trombone, as though the trombone-player in a band had fallen asleep and snored through the pipes of his instrument. It was perfectly appalling. 'Well, my dear,' I said to my wife, 'we must rig up a bed downstairs on the other side of the house for the children. It is impossible for them to sleep up here or to think of attempting it, and it will affect their health to lose two nights' rest running.' So we went downstairs and we rigged them up a bed for the night, and after a while they got off to sleep. The next night it was just as bad as ever, and the next night and the next, and we all began to be worn out, and Randolph—you know how fearfully delicate he is—looks like a shadow. So I thought: 'Well, it's no good going on like this. I'll write a letter to the people next door. After all, we can't be expunged from off the face of the earth ; calmly and quietly wiped out of existence, without making some kind of protest, and, besides, it may really end the evil.' So I sat down and wrote this letter." And as he spoke Alfred, who had never ceased gesticulating, with enormous vivacity, and underlining every other word, and who had been declaiming all this to me with the utmost vivacity, took a letter out of his pocket and read it vigorously at the top of his voice as we stood at the corner of the street, every one who passed us looking amusedly at the great big fellow, so earnest and so vivid and so actual—

"'DEAR MADAM [so the letter ran],

"'I trust you will pardon the liberty that I, an absolute stranger, take in addressing this letter to you, but I am compelled to do so in the interests of the health and happiness, both of body and spirit, of my wife, myself, my step-children, and my servants. It is a somewhat delicate matter upon which I venture to approach you, but it is a matter that cannot be left in a state of quiescence, which, by the bye, is a ludicrously inappropriate word to use under the circumstances, for that is exactly the state in which it does *not* leave us. For days past, or rather I should say nights, my whole household has been disturbed, and our health has been wrecked and our whole lives, physically and mentally, have been rendered an absolute purgatory by reason of an extraordinary, an incredible, and an entirely unprecedented faculty and capacity for snoring which has been exhibited and put nightly into practice by a member of your household. A certain touch of homely familiarity in the sound, horribly exaggerated though it be, leads me to the almost certain conviction that it is a human being who thus disturbs the waking hours of the night, although at times a certain quality of the trumpet, and that most assuredly not at its most musical, which runs like a diapason note through the main current of the noise, and which more resembles a trombone than anything else, has engendered, the last two nights especially, a suspicion in my mind that it might possibly be caused by a wild animal, possibly a gorilla, very improbably an extremely youthful hippopotamus, though this latter suspicion faded from my mind when I reflected that an amphibious animal of that description would naturally be consigned to the bathroom, which of course I knew lay on the other side of the house. But I put away this idea altogether, as being too wildly farcical, though truth to tell it is not one half, no, nor one quarter, so farcical, so far removed from the realm of actuality, as is the appalling and unbelievable disturbance to which I and my unhappy family are nightly subjected. Unless it ceases, Madam, we shall be forced to abandon our home, forfeit our lease, and seek shelter in some retired nook, far from the haunts of men and the snores of the ultra-wearied, in the West of England. We have come to the conclusion it must be some male member of your household. I beseech you to move him to the cellar, or the garret or the next street. If he stays, Madam, we go. We have no alternative. I am, Madam,

"'Very faithfully yours,

"'ALFRED CAPPER.

"'P.S. My wife, whose heart is very sympathetic and whose hearing is curiously keen and subtle and sensitive, has just told me that she fancied that she had detected a certain asthmatic quality in last night's snores, and therefore she would venture to recommend that your uneasy and noisy sleeper, if human, partook of a cup of strong black coffee immediately before retiring to rest.'

Well, I sent the letter in by hand, and went out for a walk last night. When I returned I found a charming, delicate little lady and her daughter standing on the steps waiting for the door to be opened.

"'Are you Mr. Capper?' said the elderly lady.

"'I am,' I replied.

"'Oh, Mr. Capper,' she said, 'I am so glad to see you. I got your letter this afternoon, and curiously enough I was just about to sit down and write a similar complaint to you and ask you if you could not move your bedroom to the other side of the house—as you are the only man in your house I came to the conclusion that you were the culprit—for we also could never get a wink of sleep for this same snoring.'

"'How perfectly extraordinary!' I said. 'What on earth can it be? And there it is again,' I continued. 'May I go with you into your house and we will try and find out?' I must add that the lady had told me that the only people in her house were herself and her daughter and two youthful maids. So it couldn't possibly have been them. Nor was it. We went all over the house, and at last, in the bathroom, discovered it was one of the pipes which had gone wrong. However, all's well that ends well, and, anyway, it has given my wife and the children an excuse for going to the seaside, and so they are off to-morrow."

Just at this moment Miss Ellen Terry passed us, looking wonderfully well and youthful as she waved her hand from her car to her old friend "Alfred."

"Marvellous woman; she never gets a day older," said Capper. "Did I ever tell you of the time when I introduced her to the Vicar of Gorleston? I happened to be staying at Gorleston, giving my entertainment, the very week that Miss Ellen Terry was playing at the Yarmouth theatre, two miles away. So, knowing I was in the place, she wrote to me—

"'I can't get to your entertainment and you can't get to mine, so do come and see me at 10.30 at the Queen's to-morrow.'

"I replied I would be delighted to do so, and might

I bring the Vicar of Gorleston, who was very anxious to meet her?

"Next morning, punctually at 10.30, we arrived at the Queen's Hotel, and were shown up to Miss Terry's room and we knocked at the door. 'You can't come in!' she screamed. 'You can't come in! I'm not dressed yet! Oh, is the vicar there? Oh, well, he's so used to sick-rooms and mothers' meetings and ladies in distress or even in *déshabille* that perhaps he won't mind seeing me as I am!' And out she came from her bedroom into the sitting-room, looking perfectly entrancing in a long white, mysterious, lacy robe, with fascinating pink and blue ribbons here and there and her beautiful hair down her back. She never looked more charming as Ophelia or even as Juliet. 'Oh, Mr. Phillips, I am so glad to meet you!' she cried as she nearly hit him in the eye with some weighty tome she was carrying in her hand. 'I have heard so much about you. I *beg* your pardon. I hope I didn't hurt you. This is Mrs. Beeton. She has been my companion for thirty years or more, and I never go anywhere without her. Help me choose my dinner for to-night, Mr. Phillips, and come and help me eat it, too, if you can. I am always pleased to meet clergymen. I think, if I remember rightly, one of my husbands' fathers was a clergyman, and indeed it was he who gave me this very book on our wedding. Now, which one was it?' she dreamily added as she knitted her brows together for a moment in puzzled thought. 'Oh, well, I can't fix his name at the moment. However, it doesn't matter; whichever one it was, he gave me this book, and he also gave me this little crochet-needle, and I was just about to make some new frillies for this comfortable, but, I suppose, somewhat unconventional, garment I am wearing now.' Oh, she was delightful! But how charmingly stage-managed it all was!"

And one of the handsomest figures in Piccadilly to-day is, as it has been now for many years, Margaret, Ranee of Sarawak, one of my oldest woman friends. I first met Lady Brooke, as she was more generally known in those days, somewhere in the eighties, with her cousin, old Lady Londonderry, a very stately and remarkable personage throughout many years of Queen Victoria's reign. The Ranee to-day is a prominent figure in the social life of London, and she is specially to the fore in any great work of charity; a very handsome personage and a singularly fine pianist, as well as being extremely well read, though I am bound to add in a most desultory fashion, she is as delightful a conversationist as she is swift in proceeding from subject to subject, with no regard whatever to their natural sequence: in the most inconsequent manner she switches you on to one subject and then off again, just as you are beginning to get interested in it, and all the time she is possessed of a sense of humour which keeps you perpetually smiling, a precious quality which she shares in equal quantity and quality with her brother, Harry de Windt, also a friend of mine of vast antiquity, he himself being of the most youthful, and her son, Harry Brooke, whom not even Hugh Benson could have surpassed in his almost uncanny faculty for extracting humour from the most unlikely subjects and people and in the most unexpected quarters, frequently at the most inappropriate moments, which only adds to the priceless value of the humour. Down at Ascot, where she mainly lives, the Ranee is the centre of a circle of distinguished friends, who all love her, who fly to her in the hour of trouble; and she is the much loved mother of three married sons, whose wives are nearly as charming as their famous mother-in-law. I hope to goodness they won't mind my saying this; one of them, a beautiful creature, will pardon it if only on account of the fact that I knew her mother and her aunt years before she knew them herself, for Gladys Brooke was born a long time after my sister and I stayed with her mother and her grandparents in the early eighties, when Jean Craig had not become Lady Palmer and long before she introduced Kubelik to the London musical public. And as to Sylvia Brooke, the Ranee Muda, I met her father before even he had met her mother, so far as I know. The present

Lord Esher was then acting as Marshal to his splendid, handsome old father, Sir Baliol Brett, as he then was, the judge with one of the most magnificent voices I ever heard, who was holding the Spring Assizes at Dunchester in the spring of 1876. I was then at the Theological College, and having annexed one of the most charming girls in the city, I took her off to hear the cases at the court. Sir Baliol Brett spied us from his seat on high, and sent Mr. Reginald Brett round to the back of the court with a message that he would like us to come and sit next to him on the Bench. So up we went, this charmingly pretty girl and I, in cap and gown, and sat beside the judge, who thus greeted my fair companion: "Now, this is very good of you; this is one of the consolations of being a judge. Will you have some sweets?" And as he spoke he handed Nellie Washbourn (if she's alive to-day, she'll remember it well) a box of sweets; and that was my only meeting with the famous Sir Baliol Brett, a splendid figure of a man, of a type which, alas! we only meet too rarely to-day. He was infinitely more the kind of man one reads about than one is ever likely to meet in real life. He was a great advocate as well as being a great judge, and there is a story told of him which amusingly demonstrates his quality. He was once defending a man in a murder case, and he got hold of the man's children and dressed them up in black and pointed them out to the jury as they sat and howled with grief in the court. In consequence the prisoner got off. At the conclusion of the trial a farmer, who came from the accused man's village, came up and said to the defending counsel—

"You made a very touching speech, Mr. Brett."

"I did my best," replied the barrister.

"Ah," said the farmer; "but I wonder if you would have been so eloquent had you seen those children as I saw them only yesterday afternoon; those children who were crying their eyes out to-day here in court were playing in their backyard as I drove past, and they had a poor, wretched cat with a string tied round its neck, and they were swinging it backwards and forwards, singing—

> "'This is the way poor daddy will go!
> This is the way poor daddy will go!'"

"Well, never mind," replied Mr. Baliol Brett; "anyway, it got the verdict!"

I've wandered far from the Ranee and Piccadilly. But that is the one merit of a book like this: you can be as desultory as you please and one thing leads on to another. The grand old judge's granddaughter married the eldest son of the Ranee, and one day will reign supreme in that gorgeously lovely island, and her brother, his grandson, married pretty Zena Dare, a girl than whom I have rarely met one more delightful, and so the generations extend themselves and the world grows wider every year. And the Ranee still remains the best of a very charming group of people.

CHAPTER XVI

BEHIND THE SCENES

THE world behind the scenes possesses and maintains a fascination for a large section of the community quite out of proportion to its place and importance in the body politic. It is a great factor in the life of the nation, how great few people realize in any degree whatever, while at the same time quite a considerable portion of the community altogether neglects, or affects to neglect, the existence of the stage at all. And yet with it all there is a decided tendency to overdo the popular enthusiasm regarding the stage, and especially the individual players, which is calculated to harm the cause in the end rather than to further it. The actor is not sacrosanct, nor is it desirable either for himself or his art that he should be perched up on a pedestal, as he so frequently is, through no fault of his own. One makes one's little protest against a condition of things which is as distasteful to the best type of actor as it is to the thinking portion of the public in general. I have for many years dwelt half in and half out of that wonderful and undoubtedly fascinating world behind the curtain; and I have found, with few exceptions, that theatrical people, especially those of the newer school, are amongst the most interesting and charming people of the day, and as a rule, in these modern times and with the modern type, immeasurably better and far more generally intelligent than they are popularly credited with being, the simple truth of the matter being that they come from a totally different class from what they almost universally came fifty years ago and for long generations before the Victorian era, and

M.M.

therefore they possess advantages denied to their predecessors. All this is so obvious that it is waste of time to insist upon it. Whether they are better actors or not is quite another question, though without a doubt the new class of actor is far better suited to play his part in the Society dramas of Pinero, Jones, Sutro, and half a score of others of the dramatists of the day than were the clean-shaven, blue-chinned, throaty-voiced men of the old school, who as a rule were entirely incapable, through sheer ignorance and many another disqualification, of playing even a thinking part in the life of a modern drawing-room in Mayfair—or even Brixton, for the matter of that. And so with the new school has sprung up a new angle of vision altogether, a fresh and invigorating point of view, a totally different type of individual, a woman whom one is charmed to encounter in any society and under any circumstances; a man of the world, fresh from the Public Schools or the 'Varsity or the messroom or the Guards Club, with a taste in art and a faculty for literary discrimination which is scarcely surpassed by the most distinguished writers themselves.

I am not proposing to fashion these pages into a kind of critical column of the performances upon the actual stage of my many theatrical friends and acquaintances. I shall not do more than, in a few cases, hint at their delightful personalities—personalities which, as much as anything else, get them well over the footlights, to use an expressive professional phrase, and which, indeed, help to endear them to the public, who enshrine them in their hearts and fuss over them to an extent that would have absolutely startled our staid forefathers in the days of Trafalgar and Waterloo. In fact, as I say, we are all a little inclined to overdo it, as modern England, indeed, is inclined to overdo almost everything. However, that's another story.

My most intimate friend on the stage, and one of my oldest friends in the world, is Sir Herbert Tree, who may be regarded, I suppose, as one of the pioneers of this new school of actors of which I have been speaking. I have known him now for hard upon thirty years, and yet there is always something new, something fresh, something unexpected in the man. An extraordinarily subtle and delicate personality, possessed of a keen and singularly practical vision, cleverly concealed behind an apparently dreamy and absent-minded appearance, Herbert Tree is immeasurably more perceptive than the casual stranger would imagine. Nothing ever escapes him—no little action, no expression, no slip of the tongue on the part of his visitor ; he takes it all in as he sits and "dreams along," as it were, in the most desultory of conversations. He is very impatient of stupidity—wherein I confess I sympathize with him with all my heart ; he is, of course, quite intolerant of anything approaching under-breeding ; he is as little of a snob as I suppose it is possible for a British subject to be, far less of a snob, for instance, than I regretfully confess myself to be, or than most of the people in any class of the community one meets to-day ; he is extraordinarily wide in his interests and his sympathies, and he is one of the best business men I have ever met. This, perhaps, is partly owing to the fact that his naturally extravagant and delightfully generous disposition is kept within the bounds of reason, as far as is possible with such a nature, by his general manager, Mr. Henry Dana, one of the most exceptional characters I have ever met in any walk of life. Henry Dana, the son of Mr. McCullough Torrens, a well-known Member of Parliament for many years in the heyday of Mr. Gladstone's tempestuous career, has for twenty years guided the fortunes of His Majesty's Theatre as very few men in London could have guided and controlled them.

But, when all is said and done, Tree is still the ruling spirit at His Majesty's. It is not, however, only as a theatrical manager that he shines pre-eminent. He would have succeeded in any career. To what a lofty position, for instance, he would have ascended had he gone into the Church or embarked upon the career of a soldier or a sailor. In any case, he would always have been at the top of the tree. And—which is so rare—he is witty as well as he is possessed of the keenest and most irrepressible sense of humour. His one great failing, indeed, is that he cannot see life save through the concave crystal of wit, and therefore, at times, his is apt to be a somewhat distorted vision. In penning an article, for instance —and he is one of the most really literary writers I know—he would gladly murder a convention, however precious to the heart of the British public, for the sake of an epigram. Brilliant as his articles and lectures often are, they are at times a little too epigrammatic. He is apt to sacrifice too much to mere wit. This really is inartistic. A Christmas plum-pudding, for instance, cannot be all plums, there must be a sufficiency of good plain and stodgy suet also ; but with Tree you frequently cannot see the suet for the plums. Into every life some porridge must fall, it cannot be all *marrons glacés*. At the same time, Tree possesses a mind of a remarkably fine order, and one that is capable of covering a wide range of thought. Neither a scientist nor a theologian, for instance, I have more than once heard him sustaining a vigorous conversation with men such as Sir Oliver Lodge on the one hand, and a skilled ecclesiastical dialectician on the other, and Tree has, in each instance, put forward suggestions that displayed him not only in the light of a keenly intelligent man, but of one who possesses vision, imagination, and a capacity for applying each faculty so that it shall be of practical value in discussion and execution. He, as are so many others of his craft to-day, is a standing contradiction to the assertion, once well justified, that the actor neither learns nor thinks or wishes to do either. The great national work that he has done with regard to the great national dramatist is the outcome not more of an artist than it is of a thinker. I have frequently been associated with Sir Herbert in the production of one of Shakespeare's dramas, and I can testify from my own knowledge to the enormous pains that he takes to verify every "statement," if I may so express myself, that he makes upon the stage. He and the leading Shakespearean students of the day have frequently spent weeks in the British Museum and in the Bodleian Library verifying the smallest details in each play, so that the production is a marvel of historical accuracy as well as being a veritable picture of the times. And men like Louis Parker and Percy McQuoid and Percy Anderson, the famous dramatist, and painters and costume artists will testify to the truth of what I say. No outsider can imagine the vast amount of research that goes on for weeks before the production of a Shakespeare play at His Majesty's Theatre.

This, however, is too obvious to bear re-telling. The great essential quality in Tree's acting is his own individuality, which is constantly altering upon the stage. Isidore Izard in "Business is Business," Fagin the Jew, Svengali, Colonel Newcome, Falstaff, Mark Antony, Caliban, and Malvolio—surely these, individually and collectively, give the lie to the oft-repeated statement that Tree is always Tree. I know of no actor who is so little a slave to his own extraordinarily vivid and vital personality as Herbert Tree. He is pretty much always himself in private life, and always full of the kindliest consideration, and with a sense of humour that never fails. He was at a big semi-public dinner one night when Mr. Birrell hurried in, very late and rather breathless, and as he took his seat next to Tree he whispered in his ear: "I've been so busy I hardly know how I managed to get here at all." A little later Tree rose to make his speech. With a humorous glance at his companion, he said: "Mr. Birrell has just told me he doesn't know how on earth he got here. Well, ladies and gentlemen, he hasn't had anything"—and then he leaned over Mr. Birrell's shoulder and anxiously peered into his glasses—"had any more since he came, and, any way, I'm sure some of us will see he gets home safely." No one enjoyed this more than Mr. Birrell.

And nothing amuses Tree more than a joke at his profession. I forget whether he tells this little yarn of himself or of Mr. George Grossmith, as one of them was paying a cabby: "Ah! I thought I wasn't mistaken. It's Mr. Tree. I thought so. My wife used to be in the 'profesh.' She used to swim in the tank at the Aquarium with the Beckwiths." And the boastful old-time "pro.":

"Ah! my boy, when I played Hamlet the audience took fifteen minutes leaving the theatre." "*Was he lame?*" And Mark Twain's admirable story of an incident that occurred to him in Australia, which he visited during the height of the great gold rush, and of which he told Tree on his last visit to England. Landing at the quay one day, he asked a loafer to carry his bag for him to the hotel, and he would give him a shilling. The man smiled, put his hand into his pocket, pulled out a handful of sovereigns, threw them into the sea, and walked off without a single word!

As is common with people in all classes of the community, the music-hall has entered very considerably into the practical politics of my humble life, and I have watched its progress with considerable interest, though my personal connection with it has been confined mainly to the writing of a few fugitive articles here and there. From my earliest childhood I have almost unconsciously dated the passing years by the popular song of the moment; and the very first which I can remember my nursemaids singing far back in the sixties is "Champagne Charlie." That was a song every one sang in those delightfully degenerate days, and I think it was first precipitated upon the town by a famous person known as the great Vance, whom I myself heard in later life at some music-hall in the provinces, and who had a vast reputation for many years, not only in the strictly music-hall world, of which, of course, I knew nothing myself, but also in the great world of the streets and even of the West End drawing-rooms, a reputation he shared with his contemporaries Macdermott, Leybourne, and others, whose very names I really forget at the present moment. The music-hall of those days scarcely existed as a music-hall at all; it was more like a glorified tavern, where the chairman of the evening's concert or entertainment sat enthroned on a seat at the head of a long table, accepting drinks and cigars from, and exchanging badinage of the freest and easiest description with, all classes of the community—young fellows in the Guards, famous pugilists, boys up from the 'Varsity or Sandhurst or "the Shop," bank-clerks, drapers' assistants, it didn't much matter who they were so long as they had the money to pay for the great man's drinks and smokes and the cheek to address so high and mighty a personage. The songs were very primitive, very elemental, and sometimes extraordinarily and extremely coarse and vulgar, though frequently witty and rather amusing. As I say, I can date years and recall periods as much by the names of the popular songs of the day as I can by any other method. I wonder if any of my contemporaries remember a song that was popular in our schooldays, in the early seventies, "Can any one tell me where Nancy's gone?" and have they as clear a memory as I have of the two great and possibly the most famous ditties ever sung in the streets of London in 1878, "Tommy, Make Room for your Uncle" and "We don't want to Fight, but by Jingo if we do," a song that very nearly launched us into war with Russia, and that immortal ditty about the same time, "Woa, Emma!" Then, of course, in the early eighties came "Wait till the Clouds Roll By, Jennie," and "Grandfather's Clock," which "stopped short, never to go again, when the old man died." At that period also we all sang—

"Oh, George, tell them to stop!"
That was the cry of Maria;
But when she said "Oh!"
He let the thing go,
And the swing went a little bit higher.

The first Jubilee year was made almost more famous and memorable than even the great Royal Procession had made it by the singing by Charles Coborn of "Two Lovely Black Eyes," which was sung to a really sweetly pretty tune that captivated the whole town. But I suppose no song in the whole history of popular street and music-hall songs ever made so gigantic a sensation or had so enormously wide a vogue, or enchained the fascinated attention of such vastly differing sections of society as did the memorable and absolutely unforgettable song which Lottie Collins launched upon a deliriously enchanted community, "Ta-ra-ra-boom-de-ay." You heard that song all over the world, sung by the most unexpected people—I myself heard two little *mousmés* humming it as they wandered by the shores of Lake Biwa in the Land of the Rising Sun.

And so we come down to the present day. The music-hall of the twentieth century promises to be, in one way and another, an even more all-pervading influence in the life of the community than it has ever been. And with the passage of the years comes a vastly more artistic and scientific method of handling the whole question! Such men as Oswald Stoll, Alfred Butt, C. B. Cochran, and others are artists, financiers, one might almost say statesmen even, men of affairs to their finger-tips, and they bring to bear upon their work, not only the vision and imagination of the poet, the dramatist, and the artist, but also the culture and the point of view of a really thoughtful and educated man, together with a wonderfully keen appreciation of what the public really demand and what they really appreciate.

To them is practically committed the guidance of a people's tastes, and to their hands is entrusted to a great extent the moral welfare of our young men and young women. And this is where their chief difficulty comes in, and wherein their course is rendered really arduous and dangerous. However, the majority of them steer fairly clear of the hidden rocks, and as a rule they rarely come to grief. What they have to remember is that the music-hall is but one of the many avatars by which and in which the community of to-day seeks to express its passing emotions.

I can never forget a conversation I once heard at the captain's table on board a big P. and O. liner voyaging to India, between a very high Anglican canon and a rather bigoted and prejudiced little dissenting minister. As a matter of fact, the canon and I a day or two previously had had a rather vigorous discussion on a certain theological matter upon which we held diametrically opposite opinions, and, as with Paul and Barnabas, the contention had been so sharp between us that a considerable constraint existed between us; so I was rather amused and a good deal pleased to find that the very bitter and narrow-minded religionist, as I had somewhat hastily set him down to be, could be in reality, and with regard to certain aspects of human life, quite broad and human and generous.

The topic of conversation between these two divines centred around, of all people in the world, Maud Allan and her then famous and much-talked of dances at the Palace Theatre. The dissenting minister, who, I may state, frankly declared he had never seen her dances, nevertheless denounced them in the most ferocious manner possible: "horrible, degrading, suggestive, indecent: a scandal to the community, a stain upon the moral life of London!" and a lot more to the same effect, and all in the most perfect sincerity and good faith. I will give him credit for that. And suddenly the canon, the bigot of my contest, the hopelessly tyrannical ecclesiastic, struck fiercely in: "You say you haven't seen Miss Maud Allan dancing, and yet you dare to condemn her in that ridiculous and extravagant manner! Well, I tell you you are absolutely in the wrong. I have seen her fourteen times. I went to every one of her special *matinées* at the Palace, and I think that her spring song dance, her realization of Botticelli's marvellous 'Primavera' and her translation into movement of Mendelssohn's and Chopin's and Beethoven's music are not only the most exquisitely artistic things I ever saw, but they also provided me with some of the most intellectual moments of my life. I say it deliberately. Those quiet afternoons in that beautifully darkened theatre, with that wonderful music and that solitary figure flitting in and out of the shadow and the sunshine of that brilliant stage, gave me more occasion for thought and real intellectual enjoyment than I have ever experienced outside the quiet reading of one of the Greek plays. It brought all the life of joyous and happy Greece into action once again. And you can sit there and speak of it as vulgar and gross and indecent! Why, it's unbelievable! The mind that can discern immorality in those dances must indeed be in a deplorable condition."

Now, curiously enough, at this time I myself had never seen Maud Allan, and therefore I could not, even mentally, take sides in the discussion. As a matter of fact, I thought each antagonist had indulged in wild extremes of language, and I am even more convinced of it to-day than I was then. At the same time, I am bound to own that when I did see her dances I was enormously impressed by the extreme charm and fascination and the curiously subtle allure of the whole entertainment. I felt, right across the footlights, as Maud Allan danced in and out of the shadows and the sunlight of the stage, as my friend the canon had expressed it, that here was no mere dancing girl, no mere flickering, jibing spirit of mockery, the pastime of a frivolous and a jeering crowd, but here indeed was a woman to whom appealed, as once it might have appealed to George Herbert in the rectory garden beneath the Wiltshire Downs or to Lady Jane Grey patiently pacing beneath the grey walls of her prison tower, all the wonderful romance and poetry of life, with a vivid consciousness of the great ocean of light in which this little life of ours floats as a cloudlet above the far horizon.

And so I got an introduction to her and went and spent a long summer morning with her while she told me the pretty romance of her varied life. In and out of the flickering light and shadow of an old English garden, heavy with the perfume of an English summer day, Maud Allan and I paced the wide-stretching lawns and talked of her curiously fascinating art. "My dancing," she said, "is not based on any modern conventions at all. It is really, as it were, a continuation from where the ancient Greeks left off, and by combining our modern music with their movements I attempt to infuse into the rhythm of the dance something of the thought of to-day. You see, my dances are entirely dependent upon the music; and just as the arches and the columns of a great temple vibrate to the chords of the organ or the peal of the trumpet, so does my soul vibrate to the music of my dance. I know nothing of the technique of dancing, and the arts of the ordinary coryphée mean nothing to me. I have sought all my attitudes and movements in the art galleries of Europe, on Etruscan vases and Assyrian tablets, and I have modelled my attitudes and motions on their crude perspectives. Salome was probably as untaught as I, and she must frequently have stopped to look at the very self-same old Assyrian tablets I looked at, and unconsciously, I expect, she incorporated them into her famous dance before Herod. I regard dancing as a wonderful mode of expression: all savage tribes, the world over, express their emotions—joy, fear, triumph in victory, grief at the loss of their warriors—in their dances. Dancing is an expression of life, as the pirouettings of a ballerina on one toe can never pretend to be. And yet," she went on, with a reminiscent smile, "the most exciting dance of my life was not on a stage at all—it wasn't even meant to be a dance. I was dancing along a desert track in California when suddenly I heard a loud hissing, and a huge rattlesnake sprang at me. To my horror I discovered I was actually standing on its mate. And then a lot of snakes sprang at me. I had wandered into a regular colony of them. I dodged here and dodged there, and sprang to one side and then to the other, and then I shaped my course for home and ran for my very life, pursued the whole time by these fearful creatures. At last I came to a mountain stream, plunged into it and dashed across, and I was safe. It was the most horrible and shuddering experience of my life, but oh, what a *motif* for a dance!"

Curiously enough, some of the finest acting I have ever seen has been that of absolutely non-professional amateurs, and frequently enough amateurs who had never even acted in amateur theatricals. I refer to the pageanteers of half a dozen years ago or so. Some of the acting at those pageants absolutely surpassed the very best acting I have seen upon the English, French, or American stage; nor can I imagine upon the finest stage the possibility even of such gorgeous *spectacle*, which was such an outstanding and characteristic feature of those pageants. In superb fashion the history of England presented itself in glittering lines of purple and silver and green and gold, and in great splashes of colour it demonstrated all its romance, and with sound of trumpets and the clash and clatter of arms and armour it conveyed in wonderful degree all the might, majesty, dominion, and power of the English nation. Pageant-makers like Louis N. Parker, who really invented them, George Hawtrey, Lascelles, Hugh Moss, and others, easily and absolutely surpassed the finest efforts of the greatest masters of scenic drama, for the simple reason that they were granted wide and open spaces, vast crowds of people, and they possessed advantages of Nature the like or possibility of which had never even been dreamed of by the actor-manager "cribb'd, cabin'd, and confined" within the limits of a small and restricted theatre stage. I saw a very great deal of this pageant-making while it was in full blast, so to speak, and one of the things that impressed me much at the time was the curious and almost incredible swiftness with which a mere amateurism was, by the very nature of things, forced into an absolute and highly expert trade or profession—I mean so far as the maker of the pageant was concerned. It very soon became a great business, almost like a department of state government. The way in which the whole thing was organized on almost scientific lines, and the speed and promptitude with which it was realized and acted upon that such scientific organization was essential, was a veritable lesson in the whole art of human life. And of course it was necessary when you reflect that as many as five thousand people took part in the Pageant of the English Church and the same number in the Pageant of Chester; that each person required not only a special costume, but to be initiated into his part; that in many cases they had to be catered for; that the mere issuing of tickets and the sending out of prospectuses involved a large staff of clerks; and that really vast building operations had frequently to be undertaken. A pageant in the first decade of the twentieth century, though a totally new and untried departure in the amusement of the people, was by no means an enterprise lightly or thoughtlessly to be undertaken. Think of the authors and the authorities to be consulted, the employment of the artists, the choice of material, the determining upon costumes, and the verifying of their period and their accuracy. And then the actual handling of vast armies of men and women—especially women! Imagine what it is to arrange for the entry at the exact and psychological moment of an army of three thousand men, the placing of a park of artillery, the disposal of half a dozen troops of cavalry, the calling out of a body of a thousand infantry! I remember the wonderful and ingenious mechanical and electric contrivances by which George Hawtrey was surrounded when he was directing the pageant at Chester. Many a summer evening did he and Mrs. Hawtrey and Lady Arthur Grosvenor and myself sit, perched up far above the heads of the mediæval multitude surging at our feet, in a roomy sort of crow's nest, and he would touch a button here or a button there, with neither fuss nor anxiety, and a quarter of a mile away you would see, a vast army of Cavaliers or of Norman soldiers, as the period demanded, dash out from the thicket or the tents wherein they were hidden, and in a moment, as it were, the whole air resounded with the clash of battle, the neighing of horses, the shrilling of the trumpets, the cries of the wounded, and the shouts of them that triumph. A wonderful and an inspiring scene! And what gorgeous effects of colour! what magnificent realizations of the charm and beauty of a dead and gone England! I can never forget those superb processions of priests and monks and nuns of every description, and the brilliant costumes of kings and queens and gallant cavaliers and lovely women, and the glittering of armour in the dying sunlight, and the exquisite chanting of some old Latin hymn, and, above all, the perfect naturalness of the actors and the acting. There was no *mauvaise honte*, no *gaucherie*, no awkwardness. I used to be astonished at the entire air of "the manner born" in which the good citizens of Chester, both male and female, went about the work, which was not work to them at all, but real pleasure and entertainment. And of course the acting came as an absolute revelation. On no stage have I ever seen anything to surpass the scene between James I on his entry into Chester and his reception by the Mayor. The King was in reality, and most appropriately, a Scotsman, and incidentally a chemist, and the Mayor was one who had actually himself been Mayor of Chester. Those two men simply didn't act. They *were* the King and the Mayor. Not a single actor in London could have surpassed them; very few, indeed, could have come within measurable distance of their performance. I had noticed the same thing the previous year at the Church Pageant, where Canon Dalton, the King's old tutor, gave the most marvellous rendering of Latimer preaching before Edward VI that could possibly be imagined.

And that was a very beautiful pageant which Mr. Forbes Phillips presented in his parish by the North Sea, and of which he once gave me a very amusing account.

"I am getting up a pageant at Gorleston," he said one day, "and I can assure you it is the stiffest job I have ever encountered in my life, mainly for the reason that my people are such literalists, so tremendously in earnest that I find it more difficult to restrain their enthusiasm than I find it to urge them on; and they are born actors, though, as I say, sometimes a little too literal. The other day, for instance, my schoolmaster, an admirable person, who plays Julius Cæsar in Britain, sought an interview with Boadicea, a magnificent personage, well over six feet high, and he wandered among my dwarf gooseberry bushes, looking carefully under each one, crying out: 'Boadicea, Boadicea, come forth! Where art thou hidden?' And the other day I met one of my greatest friends, an old North Sea smacksman, and I said to him—

"'Going to help me with the pageant, Sam?'

"'Ah! Vicar,' he replied, 'a pageant's all very well when you've got a light 'eart to go in and worry yourself 'arf dead about it, but we've got the biggest mess aboard our smack as ever you 'eard on, and afore the skipper and me goes out together dressed up as Norman knights or like them Charles's Cavaliers as you wos tellin' us about the other night, 'im and me 'as to 'ave it out. I feel a doosid sight more like bein' Oliver Cromwell and cuttin' orf 'is silly old 'ead for 'im!'

"'Why, Sam,' I said, 'what's the matter, old chap?'

"'I'll just tell you, Vicar, wot's 'appened,' he answered. 'Last November the skipper and the mate and me and the two men *and* the boy, we clubs together to buy a concertina, and on Christmas Eve the skipper and the mate they goes ashore, and they goes up to the "Three Jolly Dogs" to make a night o't, and the skipper 'e goes an' busts the blarsted thing a-playin' "'Erald Angels," and now 'e says we—*we*, if yer please—'ave got to pay for it. I'll pageant him!' he viciously continued as he hitched his trousers up and indignantly took himself off."

But in no direction has the dramatic art so developed as it has in the world of the cinema. Many of us are even beginning to prefer the cinema to the legitimate stage or the music-hall, mainly for the reason that, whilst the human voice is absent, it nevertheless has enormously enlarged and widened the whole scope of the theatre, and has enabled us to realize of what the drama may be capable. For in a certain subtle way the art of the theatre—the art of actual acting—not only does not deteriorate, but its possibilities are considerably increased. Facial expression, where there is no voice to help forward the *motif* or the story, gains new importance upon the screen, and this is widely being recognized by the best players, and also the fact that the despised assets of the legitimate stage count for much in the moving picture theatre. The other day at luncheon I found myself seated next to a very charming young woman, and I said to her—

"I know you so well by sight, but I can't think where we've met; and I seem to know your voice too."

"Do you ever go to the cinema?" she said.

"I know!" I suddenly cried—"I know, 'The Isle of Man and John Storm,' of course," I continued; "and then you were a nurse in a London hospital and you went to a fancy dress ball and you played John some shameful tricks. I expect you led my dear old friend Hall Caine an awful dance?"

"Oh, he's a dear!" said Miss Elizabeth Risdon, one

of the very prettiest and certainly one of the most charming cinema actresses of the day, either here or in America, and one of those women who go far to prove the truth of what I have always maintained, that personal charm is more than half the secret of the picture palace, a truth which America has realized from the first, but which is only just beginning to dawn upon the British film producer. "And so you saw me in 'The Christian.' I like acting to the camera better on the whole than the ordinary acting, of which I've had a lot. It's fresher and more vital. And then, of course, you get so much more experience on the cinema than on the ordinary stage—I worked out the proportion the other day, and it actually came out as six hundred parts to one."

"And does the quality or kind of part vary as much?"

"Every bit as much. Of course just at first to the ordinary actor it's very new and strange and rather difficult. It is a tremendous thing to have to cut out the effect of the voice, and you have to make up for that cutting out. You see, we always rehearse with words, and one is apt to forget that the words will never be heard, only the movement of the lips is seen. What one has to remember all the time is facial expression and gesture. I never read the story I am acting. I often don't know even what the subject of it is. I simply trust the producer, who tells me exactly what has gone before my scene and what will follow it, and in that way I get a kind of hint how to play my own special scene."

"And do you think the regular old stage hand is best for film work?"

"Yes, I do, most decidedly, because we are naturally much more flexible, and also much more disciplined. What we have to do, and it is the most difficult thing of all, is to discover the new technique of the screen and the camera. It is amusing the tremendous number of friends one makes upon the screen. Do you know I have autographed more than thirty thousand of my portraits for the Y.M.C.A. military huts this year alone, and I get hundreds of letters asking me about my adventures and how much people have felt the pathetic parts of the play, for that is what appeals most to them. I often think what dear people there are in the world, and I feel sorry I can never meet them; and the cinema, far more than the ordinary theatre, seems to put you in touch with so many."

I think I may tell here of my first actual contact with the people of the stage. It was at Dunchester, more than forty years ago. One lovely October afternoon as I was wandering listlessly down to the cathedral, being obliged to "keep" the early chapel I had failed to keep that morning, I encountered a lady I knew. "Oh, Mr. Blathwayt," she said, "are you going to the service? Will you take my friend Miss Bury?"—I thought she said —"I must go into the town. She is very anxious to see the cathedral," and she hastily and inaudibly introduced us to one another. So of course, as the little lady was charmingly pretty and evidently of my own age, I was delighted, and we soon found ourselves in the magnificent Norman nave looking at an old Crusader's tomb, and I said: "He looks rather dead, doesn't he?" and she replied: "Oh, he looks deader than dead." Just at that moment I caught the sound of that "last grand Amen" of the choir, and immediately afterwards the organ began to peal, and I said: "Well, if you like we'll go into the service; anyway I *have* to." So in we both marched into the chancel, and immediately after us came the choir and clergy. I can see them as I write after the passage of two generations: Thomas the photographer, a tall, handsome man with a big beard—I dare say he's alive now—who sang bass, and then my tailor, old Hargreaves, who was tenor, and all the rest of them. And then came Minor Canon Loxley, a tall, singularly good-looking, highly bred man, with black whiskers, and a single glass perpetually in his right eye, an extraordinarily fine and picturesque specimen of mid-Victorian Anglicanism. I might note in passing that his son, Captain Loxley, R.N., went down with his dog at his side when his ship was sunk early in the war. And then there was Minor Canon Edgar Sheppard, a man also with a very attractive presence, and one of the most beautiful voices I have ever heard. He is now Sub-Dean of the Chapels Royal, father of H. R. L. Sheppard, Vicar of St. Martin's-in-the-Fields, and a well known and very popular figure at Court. But I really think the gem of them all was that beautiful old Canon Harvey, Rector of Hornsey, a very tall, thin old man, with a splendidly cut head, enshrined in white hair, very delicate features, and such a "presence" and such distinction as it is almost impossible to see nowadays. There are thousands to-day who, if they ever chance to read these words, will recall that gracious apparition slowly pacing to the lectern, with a beautiful cambric handkerchief in his hand, which he constantly raised to his lips, and his noble and dignified reading of the lessons of the day. I mention all this because it was so typical of those days—days over which floated a golden halo of which we know nothing now. And how marvellous the frame within which the picture had its setting: the arching roof far away above our heads and hidden in a kind of eternal mist, through which the organ chords pulsed and throbbed like the emotions of a human soul, and the sun filtering in through the magnificent windows and painting the tesselated pavement with the most glowing tints of green and red and purple and silver and gold, and the fugitive rays lit up the columns of the nave for a moment or so and then sank down and faded away and all was gloom again. I could see my charming companion was immensely impressed.

After the service we were wandering through the nave when, just as we passed the cloister gateway, the Dean came along with a little frail old clergyman, and as he unlocked the gate he caught a glimpse of us.

"Come along, young people," he said, "if you want to see the cathedral. Why, it's Raymond Blathwayt," he continued, catching closer sight of my face. "Well, my boy, how's your father?"

And then we all went through into a part of the cathedral railed off from the rest, and the Dean told us the wonderful story of the great church and its historic tombs and memories.

"You and your friend must come into the Deanery and

have tea with us. Just wait a moment; I want to take Dean Stanley into the Library to see some MSS.

"That's the famous Dean Stanley," I said.

"I never heard of him," was the innocent reply of my fair companion.

"What! never heard of the Dean of Westminster?" I said. "Why, he was Arthur in 'Tom Brown's School-days.'"

"I never read boys' books," she replied; and then: "I say, if we are going to tea at the Deanery it will look better if we know each other's names, won't it? I didn't catch your name, and I don't think you caught mine."

I agreed it would and I gave her my card, and then she said—

"My name's Florence Terry. I expect you know my sister Ellen by name."

"Ellen Terry," I said, in a puzzled sort of way. "Yes, I think I've heard of her. She's an actress, isn't she?"

"Yes, so am I, and our company came here last night for the week. You must come and see me."

At that moment the two old deans, who must have been nearly fifty years older than us two, each of whom was in the 'teens, came out of the Library, and we all set off for the Deanery, which actually joined the cathedral. We had tea in the drawing-room—the *Aula Regia*, built in 1115—and the Dean drew our attention to the beautiful panelling of the spacious room, "because," he said, "you ought to notice it, for it was put in by Archbishop Laud when he was Dean here." And then he took us into his study. "There, my dear," he said to Miss Terry, "this room is eight hundred years old, and some of the Parliaments of England have been held in it." And then he took us upstairs and showed us the bedroom in which William Rufus, lying sick and ill, thrust the mitre into the hands of the trembling monk Stigand, and thus made him Archbishop of Canterbury much against his will; and as the Dean talked the wild red sunset flamed in at the window, and then, as the light died down and the darkness crept on apace, I realized to the fullest extent the romance of our surroundings. Now and again there would be a lull in the wind, and we would hear, borne upon the breeze, the splendid deep tones of the organ as it thundered down those long-drawn aisles. And it grew darker and darker, and we could scarcely discern the window-panes, against which was once driven the smoke and flame of the fire that burned poor Bishop Hooper to death. And the Dean pictured to us Henry VIII wandering about the Deanery, where he spent part of his honeymoon with Anne Boleyn; and he told us about poor Edward who was murdered so horribly at Berkeley Castle, and whose body was buried hard by in the cathedral.

Whilst the Dean of Dunchester was showing Miss Terry some of the old portraits in the hall, Dean Stanley and I had a talk—if conversation between a stately old ecclesiastic and a very youthful student can be so designated—and I was very pleased when he said: "Are you a son of the clergyman who started lectures for the convicts at ——? I remember hearing about them from Canon Kingsley and Mr. Frederic Denison Maurice, and I was immensely interested in your father's work." I told him I was.

And then I saw little Flo Terry safe to the theatre, and I brought a large party of young Militia officers in the evening to give her a hearty welcome, which they did, when she appeared on the stage. I may say that I saw a lot of her that week. A charming, lovely nature, whom, quite obviously, everybody loved.

CHAPTER XVII

OVER THE HILLS AND FAR AWAY

To over-top the blue hills far away, to sink beneath the distant horizon, that is ever the dearest wish of the boy, always a wanderer and an adventurer at heart. For me, though I knew it not till the other day, the spirit of Jack London's charming little poem has always been, as it were, the guiding inspiration of my wandering life.

Follow the Romany pateran
West to the sinking sun,
Till the junk sails thro' the homeless drift
And the East and West are one.
Back to the road again, again
Out of a clear sea-track,
Follow the cross of the gipsy trail
Over the world and back.
The wild hawk to the wind-swept sky,
The deer to the wholesome wold,
And the heart of a man to the heart of a maid,
As it was in the days of old.
The heart of a man to the heart of a maid,
Light of my tents be fleet,
Morning waits at the end of the world,
And the world is all at our feet!

And morning always waited for me over the hills and far away, and beyond the sun sinking into its golden glory in the West lay always the land of romance for me; and it is not a bit less so to-day.

Those very words, "over the hills and far away," always conveyed to me, and they do still, a sensation of romance and adventure with which all my happiest days are associated. The long, white road winding away in the distance, glimmering through the summer dusk, and finally losing itself in the over-top of the hills, the King's highway, so reminiscent of other days, re-echoing once again to the heavy tramp of the Roman soldiers, resounding with the clash and clatter of William of Normandy's armies and with the songs and oaths of Charles's gallant Cavaliers, and reminiscent of the good old days of Claude du Duval and Dick Turpin. And the grey and ancient Norman towers of the little churches hidden away behind the trees just off that fascinating highway; the sails of the old-fashioned mill turning and creaking in the autumn breeze; the waddling of the ducks and geese across the wind-swept common to the village pond; the metallic cry of the wildfowl flying home, far above one's head, in two long lines, meeting like an arrow's point in the far-advanced front; and the road goes winding on, ever leading the fascinated wanderer into the heart of the mystic and the unexplored—in a word, the unknown! And all the time the great white clouds clamber over the top of the swelling downs and the shadows chase each other in never-ending succession over the great greenswards which rise from the valleys into the azure blue of the summer sky. But always the open road, the lovely, historic roads of old England and the memories of those who have walked along them: old roads and old bridges, almost equally fascinating. The old bridge over the swift-flowing stream, in the dark shadows of which, if you look keenly enough, you can just discern the waving tail of some crafty, cunning old fellow that half the village has angled for for years and angled in vain, and the long, lovely, old red-brick wall, with grey lichen on it and green mosses exquisitely contrasting themselves against the rose-red of the wall itself, above and beyond which you catch a glimpse of the graceful Tudor chimney-stacks of the old manor-house.

And thus I start my wanderings through the Empire and round the world, ever impregnated with the romance of that Empire which was literally initiated amid the fond, familiar scenes I have just outlined. For the long, white road led to the hills, and far away one came at last to the open sea, and beyond those ever recurring, ever receding horizons the gentlemen adventurers of Elizabeth's splendid days, and Nelson's sailors, and Jellicoe's blue-jackets, roved and roamed ere they came to the glowing East or the sunset West, and in those lands wherein it is always afternoon, no less than amid the placid meadows and quiet rectories of the homeland, the story of Empire has been written in letters of blood and gold and fire.

And of all the world's romances the British Empire's is supreme and best. From the latest joined subaltern, up through a scale of ever-increasing magnificence to the King-Emperor upon his throne, the British Empire is the greatest and, without question, the most sublime fact in human affairs that the world has ever known. Nothing can equal it in history, and its accomplishment is no less full of poetry and romance than was its far-off conception in the days of Alfred the Great. And yet, though as a stern fact it has existed for centuries in the knowledge of our great soldiers and sailors and statesmen, it has comparatively only recently come into being for the majority of English people, and the Canadians and the Anzacs have done more to advertise and make known to us the British Empire as a substantial fact than all the writings of Froude and Kipling, Professor Seely, Lord Macaulay, and all of them put together. At the same time, it is undeniable that it is to the literary man that the Imperial idea of to-day is mainly due, although it is owing to the soldier and sailor that the Empire itself first came into existence and has become the greatest fact of modern history ; yet few there be who realize exactly what it is that constitutes the British Empire, and who and what are those the pillars upon which it rests secure. For the main characteristic of our Empire is that it is built upon and it exists supreme in the individual character of the individual Englishman scattered far and wide throughout its domains. Here a little and there a little, line upon line, precept upon precept, the sterling character of the Sixth Form boy at Eton or Harrow, the unconquerable spirit of the British Tommy and the British blue-jacket, the patience and justice and fair-mindedness of the Civil servant in India or the Commissioner upon the deadly coast of West Africa, the political insight and the keen vision of the colonial Premier—these are the qualities which, beneath the glitter and the poetry, the pathos and the romance of Empire, as the literary man sees it, have raised it to, and maintain it at, the lofty level upon which it rests to-day.

What has always struck me more than anything else in my wanderings through the Empire is the individual nature of its government, the manner in which a handful of white people sway and hold in control the overwhelming masses of black people whom they have succeeded, not only in conquering, but in most cases in reconciling to its rule, so that in India, for instance, seventy-five thousand British hold dominion over three hundred million Easterns of varied nationality and even more varied characteristics. And yet, as a white wave flashes now and again out of the purple of a vast and surging ocean, so do the English people carry aloft this white plume of all that is best in their ancient nationality far above the heads of those myriads surging around and beneath them, whom, making all allowance for the overwhelming magnitude of their task, they rule so wisely and so well. And it is all individuality and personality, the character of the man himself. I cannot run through a great gorge on the Indian railway and see the white engineer surrounded by his myriad native artisans and mechanics, building one of those magnificent bridges which have helped to make India what it is, without a realization coming upon me that there, indeed, stands a veritable pillar of Empire. Or it is a Forest Officer, far away from almost every comfort of civilization, cut off from friends, and almost bereft of human sympathy, exposed to the onrush of wild beasts and subject to every kind of fever and sickness, who daily carries his life in his hands, uncomplaining and unconquerable, working with but small hope of reward and pursuing only justice and seeking only the "glory of going on," as Tennyson so well terms it: such is the man into whose faithful hands is committed the welfare and the honour and the upholding of the integrity of the British Empire. And how great is the responsibility which is placed upon his shoulders!

I remember once being with the Governor of a great colony in which the blacks outnumbered the handful of whites as ten to one. Less than thirty miles away great battles with terrible slaughter were taking place every day, and the very town in which I was then living was laagered and under strict martial rule. And on the Governor's wise handling of the situation depended the lives of all the white people in the place. And I cannot forget the speechless dismay and indignation which used to fill his soul when a long wire in cypher would come in from some official seated in a safe and comfortable arm-chair in Downing Street, bidding him undo all he had just been doing with such infinite care and knowledge and the wisdom that can only come to the man on the spot.

Looking right away over the Indian Ocean, which glittered in the brilliant sunshine upon our left, he said to me one day: "Shakespeare said it was conscience that makes cowards of us all, and I say conscience be d——d! It's that beastly telegraph wire! We could settle all this in a week if it wasn't for those fluffy bits of paper." And as I looked at the brave and kindly face, drawn with anxiety, I realized, as in a flash, the terrible, individual responsibility of Empire. One knows, of course, that certain Members of Parliament exist mainly for the restraint of prancing pro-consuls, but none know, save those who have seen it for themselves, the whirl and fever and tempest of passionate indignation that overwhelms the colonist of the Empire at the interference of those who, so far as practical experience is concerned, are absolutely ignorant, and dangerously ignorant, of the actual condition of affairs in which, with all the goodwill in the world, they are so rashly interesting themselves.

However, it is time I came down to the tangible and the concrete, and before I have finished, this very irregular and haphazard record of travel will have landed us in almost every part of the British Empire. And I begin with a brief account of a visit I paid eight years ago or so to the exquisitely beautiful island of Jamaica. Through the sleet and bitter cold of a December morning the great liner slowly forged her way down the Bristol Channel, and as I sat in the delightfully heated music saloon, listening to the haunting strains of the "Merry Widow" Waltz played by the ship's band, and gazed through the windows at the slanting, driving lines of mingled snow and rain, I smiled with joy as one of the stewards remarked to a comrade: "Thank goodness, we shall be in white jackets again before we know where we are."

And true enough were the words he spoke, for five days afterwards we had slid into summer seas, and white awnings kept the sun's rays from our heads, and light flannels and grape fruit were the order of the day. The Azores lay like a green *parure* of emeralds to our rear, and we were hourly nearing the magic region of the Southern Cross. And one brilliant, burning January morning, only thirteen days after the sleet and snow of Avonmouth, we passed along a low-lying coast, girt with waving palm-trees, washed by a glittering surf and backed by the magnificent Blue Mountain range—and this was Jamaica! And then Port Royal, with all its romantic memories of pirates and buccaneers, where Captain Kidd once reigned and raged supreme, and Drake and Frobisher, in still earlier days, used to fight the Spanish galleons, and where, long after, Nelson and Rodney brought in their magnificent battleships, with their white canvas towering like spires to the azure sky. Port Royal, thick-grown with foliage and quiet and almost deserted, pushes a long stretch of sand into the Caribbean Sea, and behind Port Royal lies lovely Kingston, and our voyage is at an end at last.

Despite the heat, a delicious breeze is blowing off the waters, and we realize we are really in the tropics, which is in itself worth the whole delightful voyage—the seeing the tropics for the first time; though I, who know the tropics east and west, can assure my readers that it is a sensation that never quite leaves one. The tropics are altogether different from anything that one has ever known. Sights and sounds and scents are all new to the traveller fresh from the wind-swept streets or snow-clad fields of England. Almost before you realize it you are transported from the depth of winter to the height of such a summer as you have never dreamed of in your wildest imagination. Take only this first tram ride over the six miles that spread themselves between Kingston and Constant Spring Hotel and gaze on either side of you upon the magnificent trees and foliage that line the long white road, flecked with purple shadows bathed in overpowering sunlight, and what a revelation of colouring it all is! Look at that superb cotton-tree, from which Tom Cringle and his fellow-middy surveyed the country round him a century ago; study its exquisite old trunk, grey and silver, with its immense buttresses jutting out into the roadway. What a contrast it presents to that grove of graceful palms bending beneath the morning breeze! How that hedge of crimson bougainvillæa blazes in the golden light! How delicious is the heavy scent of the hydrangea! Look at that exquisite white and purple convolvulus, with the humming-bird hovering over its magic petals and darting like lightning in and out its wonderful chalices. And there is a garden full of orange-trees, heavy with the golden fruit. Could anything be more beautiful than that plot of banana-trees, with the great green leaves, three feet long at least, outlined against the pure blue of the sky that overarches all this lovely land—unless, indeed, it is the crimson flower of the cactus which so securely hedges it all round, and that clump of feathery bamboos with dainty maidenhair ferns thick upon the grass all round?

In that brief forty minutes that lies between Kingston and Constant Spring I saw more colour and more exquisite foliage than I had imagined was possible, and more wonderful trees and flowers than I was able to count or bear in mind. And the road itself was a mass of colour, a moving parterre of human flowers, for the native women crowding to and from the local markets were almost as brilliant and varied in their attire as were the flowers themselves, and as they paraded the streets or crammed themselves into the electric car they were always chattering, always laughing, always good-natured. They know nothing of cold or misery or real want, for they always have enough for their simple requirements, and so they are quite happy and content.

Apart from the natural beauties of a tropical land which press in upon one on every side, a winter such as I spent in Jamaica affords one a glimpse into Empire-building generally and the governance of an ancient and important Crown colony—a veritable lesson in Imperialism. For here, as it were, is the British Empire in a microcosm—here, reflected as in a mirror, one catches a faint far-away resemblance to the mighty world around and beyond. It is England and the Empire repeated here, as throughout the whole world it is so often repeated, in miniature and in detail. The man-of-war lying upon the sunlit waters of that magnificent harbour ; the British "Tommy," whether white or black, swinging through the crowded streets ; the stately old archbishop driving along the country lanes on the way to some village Confirmation ; the Governor of the island attending some great social or official function : these, and such spectacles as these, all of them gathered together within the compass of a few miles, and witnessed within the brief space of a brilliant Jamaican midwinter morning, speak to the visitor of a grandeur and a fullness of life of which he only, as a rule, obtains detached and far-away glimpses, at long intervals, at home. Here he is brought into actual personal contact with the builders and upholders of Empire ; here he can see for himself the wheels of the great clock of the British Government slowly grinding out their daily meed of work.

For many reasons Jamaica, with its glowing history of the past behind it, is one of the most vivid and interesting of all our colonies. And yet it is pathetically though very beautifully running to seed. That was its main charm for me. It was not nearly so intensely modernized and up to date as some of the other islands—Trinidad, for instance. Though much nearer home, it appears, despite its yearly annual invasion by America, to be far more old-time than any other spot I know of in the whole Empire. Crumbling literally and beautifully into decay, its ancient capital, Spanish Town, is a materialization, as it were, of the whole decadent spirit of the lovely island. And who would wish it otherwise? though I am bound to own I write of it as I knew it eight years ago or so. Things may have altered, though I rather doubt it. And pre-eminent among the white population was the stately and yet simple and homely figure of the erstwhile North Country Wesleyan minister who then bore ecclesiastical rule in our West Indian Empire as his Grace the Archbishop of the West Indies. Dr. Enos Nuttall was a man of whom any community in any part of the world might well be proud. A splendid Elizabethan figure, he always reminded me of Burleigh: a fine ecclesiastic, astute, autocratic, and yet wonderfully sympathetic, and a man of genuine and unaffected piety, he was an even finer statesman. The Archbishop of the West Indies was one of the greatest Imperialists and one of the most outstanding personalities I have ever met, and in him the late King Edward always recognized one of the most sagacious personalities in his realm. The West Indies were intensely proud of him. I rejoice to think he was one of the most valued friends I ever possessed. And a man of apostolic simplicity of life: he was living when I knew him in a stable-yard, his own house having been demolished by the terrible earthquake that laid Kingston in ruins in 1907.

Another equally remarkable man, in a very different manner, was the Governor, Sir Sydney Olivier, K.C.M.G., of whom I saw a great deal during my two visits to the islands in two consecutive years, and a man whom it is difficult, if not impossible, to summarize in a paragraph. However much I may have differed from him, as most people did, in his social and political opinions, I was vastly impressed by his absolute sincerity, his remarkable kindliness of nature, and, above all, by his possession at all times and in all places and in the presence of all sorts and conditions of men, of the courage of his own convictions. Slightly cynical, a little pessimistic perhaps, he was, nevertheless, the man of all others to whom a real discerner of character would appeal for help and sympathy in the hour of need or distress. But where, perhaps,

Sydney Olivier was apt to fail was in his comprehension of the average point of view, though, as a matter of fact, I don't suppose he ever seriously endeavoured to arrive at any comprehension of that point of view, much less to adopt it. When you reflect that he was a Fabian of the Fabians, a man of a curiously subtle, frequently exceedingly caustic temperament, it is scarcely to be wondered at that he should find himself hopelessly out of touch with a community composed almost entirely, on the one hand, of Colonials of old-fashioned views and of many years' descent in the island, bristling with a hundred prejudices, stiff with ancient traditions ; and on the other of English naval and army officers, hopelessly Tory and sporting in their somewhat frivolous and thoughtless outlook upon life. What else could you expect, and what blame could you possibly attach to either side? The community was always demanding in hopeless accents and with uplifted hands, "What next?" And I fancy the Governor rarely failed to disappoint them, vastly "intriguing" them all the time, however.

I had a very interesting taste of his quality myself once. I had delivered a lecture on the Empire at which the Archbishop presided and the Governor moved a vote of thanks to me, which, to my intense amusement, assumed the form and aspect rather of a vote of censure. It was a vastly interesting occasion, for a more remarkably diversified gathering could hardly be imagined. There stood the Governor, keen, subtle Fabian Socialist ; close beside him the stern, rugged, and stalwart figure of the Archbishop, who, with his Archdeacon, was whole-heartedly on my side ; in front of him the leaders of the island life in every grade ; the gay Society throng of uniformed officers and pretty, frivolous women ; and behind them again the keen, intellectual faces of some of the leading politicians and of that admirable band of men by whom the law and justice of the colony was administered ; and behind them yet again the wistful, emotional faces of the black and coloured population. And in the presence of this heterogeneous and multi-minded, multi-coloured audience, his Excellency announced his differences of opinion from the lecturer, who was, nevertheless, in some respects the one of all others most in sympathy with himself.

Sir Sydney Olivier began by courageously declaring his belief that Dr. Clifford, to whom I had not very sympathetically alluded in my lecture, was his dear friend, and that so far from regarding him as an enemy of Empire, he, for his part, would gladly see him pilgrimaging round that same Empire and laying a restraining hand upon those prancing pro-consuls who did the British Empire so much real harm. He then passed to an exposition of his own remarkable views on the greatest of all our Imperial problems, viz. the relations between whites and blacks, and how far fusion between the races was possible or desirable. To one like myself, and like all the white people present that night, and in common with every single white man or woman, almost without exception, who has had actual experience of the black man in the mass, such a doctrine is horrible to the last degree.

And yet vigorously as I differed from almost every word he said, I was delighted with the simple loyalty to his own views, however unpopular they might be, and to his own friends, and I was charmed with the honest, outspoken courage of the man. In certain respects Sidney Olivier is one of the most interesting men I have known, but how far he was a suitable person to rule over an old-fashioned British colony, with the restricted outlook and very much the identical point of view of a Tory squire and his vassals in a retired English village, I am not prepared to say.

With reference to what I said of Dr. Clifford to which the Governor took such exception the facts were simply these. I referred to and heartily denounced his regrettable speech at the City Temple, in which he spoke of the Anglican Church and its close alliance to the beer-barrel, a remark from which Mr. R. J. Campbell, the chairman, then and there vigorously dissociated himself.

On my return to England I wrote to Dr. Clifford and quite frankly told him what had occurred. When he retired from active work at Westbourne Park, realizing what a fine work it was, after all, that the grand old minister had consistently carried on on behalf of the community during his long period of service in London, I wrote and expressed to him my regret that he was about to quit finally the scene of so many well-won triumphs and such self-devotion and self-sacrifice on his part. And here I reproduce his kindly reply—

18, WALDECK ROAD, WEST EALING, W.
October 1, 1915.

DEAR MR. BLATHWAYT,

Will you forgive my long delay in acknowledging your most kind and gracious letter on the intimation of my retirement from the pastorate of Westbourne Park.

It has now taken place, and I wish to express my sincere thanks for your congratulations and good wishes. I appreciate both thoroughly, and shall cherish them as a very refreshing souvenir in the autumn of my life.

With kind regards,
I am truly yours,
JOHN CLIFFORD.

Somewhere in the middle nineties I found myself in Warri, Southern Nigeria, where two or three Englishmen were engaged in carving out of the dim and misty and terror-haunted forests of West Africa a new territory for the British Empire. To-day there are no less than eight hundred officials, to say nothing of hundreds of native clerks and thousands of Housa soldiers, engaged in establishing, consolidating, and rendering waterproof for the next five hundred years an Empire which is second in importance only to that of India itself. But when I saw it Southern Nigeria was only just creeping out of its stone age and the horrors of Benin City were but faintly conjectured even by the British officials themselves. It was one of the most fascinating episodes of my life; it was interesting beyond all imagination to behold this marvellous work in its initial stages and to watch the slow building up of a new Constitution, much as one might watch the erection of a vast bridge spanning one of the great rivers in India. It was a specimen of statecraft engineering which it would be scarcely possible to witness to-day, for the simple reason that that kind of work is almost completed over the entire Empire.

I was staying with the Acting Vice-Consul, Dr. Felix Norman-Roth, one of the most remarkable men I know —an engineer, a skilled operating surgeon, a statesman, a builder of Empire, such as you read of in Cutcliffe Hynes' books or such as Kipling's famous Anglo-Indian heroes ; a man of charming character, immensely popular with his contemporaries, and quite idolized by the simple and childlike natives of the West Coast, who, for all their childlike disposition, could be very devils to Englishmen or Germans who ill-treated them as, to confess the truth, was only too frequent in the days of "the palm-oil ruffians," as the early traders were commonly known some twenty years or so ago ; for previously to the nineties and the arrival of the Government officials Warri and that part of Southern Nigeria formed a part of the Oil Rivers Protectorate and was run almost entirely by these hard-shelled old traders—fine fellows many of them, fearing neither God, man, nor devil, but devastated body, mind, and spirit by the demon of drink, which, to speak the truth, is almost irresistible in that appalling climate and among those swarming hordes of ants, beetles, mosquitoes, and innumerable pests of every description.

It was a queer land at the best, and ever at the back of it, like an appalling thundercloud that might burst at any moment, a vast army of savages, hidden in the primeval forests and given over to the most ghastly rites and superstitions ; terror and disease and death lurked at every corner.

The Vice-Consul's house, situated just above a great crocodile-haunted river, twice the width of the Thames at Westminster, was built on columns, twenty feet high, to allow of free currents of air beneath, where was also situated the court in which English and native trials were held ; in the upper story were the officers' messroom and bedrooms, while a fifteen-foot deep veranda ran round the whole building, and here I would sit and watch the primeval life of the natives all round me, for they were practically in exactly the same condition as they were five thousand years ago and more. Any amount of snakes lurked in the bush, wherein very rarely one caught a glimpse of the bush deer. Groups of palm-trees of every conceivable variety, and some of them very beautiful, reared their stately stems and waved their exquisite plumage beneath that brazen sky, and ancient cotton-trees gave a kind of supreme distinction to the landscape, whilst the neighbourhood revelled in orchid parasites, either upon the trees or growing in rich profusion upon the ground; butterflies of every description and gorgeous in black and crimson and gold fluttered in the dazzling sunshine, whilst here and there a grey paroquet clave its way from tree to tree upon wings whose irridescent plumage glittered in the golden rays. But, as usual, it was the human element, entirely negroid, that really provided me with the greatest matter for thought and that most appealed to the ethnological student, and I would sit and watch the English trading with the natives for palm-oil and palm-kernels, borne in upon their heads by trains of natives from the far interior, in exchange for Manchester cottons, gaily coloured shawls, scissors, and knives, and especially for coral; those were the articles that most appealed to the native mind. One morning a large number of men and women came and seated themselves hand in hand round the flagpole, from which floated out upon the gentle breeze the dear old familiar folds of the Union Jack. And just at that moment Roth came out on to the veranda and seated himself at my side.

"What are they all doing there?" I said.

"Oh," he replied, "that's rather interesting: they are all slaves who have run away, and seated beneath the British flag they know they are free for the time being and cannot be snatched into servitude again. In an hour or so they'll have to appear before me in the court, and I shall have to decide whether they are to be freed or to be sent back again to slavery."

I may here remark that very shortly after this

conversation, owing to some questions which had been asked in Parliament, an order came out from the Foreign Office, as it was in those days, that on no account were slaves, once escaped, to be redelivered into slavery. But the wonderful romance of it all! Remember, we were living in the heart of savagery, in the very infancy of the world, as it were, among a people devils at one moment, babies the next.

One blazing hot morning a native was brought in so terribly mangled in one of his legs that Roth determined he must amputate the limb; so he and "Charles," of whom I will speak later, having summoned certain chief men of the district to be present, administered chloroform to the man and the operation was safely performed. As the poor fellow recovered consciousness he asked Roth, through "Charles" (Roth's native servant), when he was going to cut off the leg. "Oh," his friends shouted in reply, "the dotty [doctor] kill that man, cut leg off, and then bring him for life!" And they wouldn't believe Roth when he assured them that the man had only been unconscious, and next morning they actually turned up with three dead and rather smelly bodies which they had exhumed from a local burying-place and which they desired Roth to bring to life once again. I can never forget the scene nor the dismay when Roth told them it was impossible. "No," said Roth, "that no be my palaver; it be palaver for God that lives for top," he continued, pointing reverently to the brazen heavens above him. By the by, it was very curious to watch that group of men as they stood round Roth as he sawed away at the injured limb. They were one and all seized with such nervousness that it assumed all the characteristics of hysteria, and simultaneously they imitated the motions of a man sawing, hissing loudly as they did so in imitation of the hissing sound of the saw.

After that operation and one or two other incidents Roth became in their eyes a great Fetish doctor, whom they feared more than any one else on earth, and yet whom they also loved more than any one, white or black.

Charles was a marvellous personage, a real character, and a great hero. On the great Benin River Expedition one day a rocket fired by the British from a trough, by some accident, fell among the English officers, knocking some of them over. At once the savages rushed in, and several of them attacked Roth, who was in command. Charles flew at them, and killed two straight off. Felix Roth said to him afterwards—

"Charles, weren't you afraid?"

"No, sah," was the plucky fellow's reply. "I no fear, but my belly live for go round," which was a wonderfully vivid mode of describing that uncomfortable sensation that the bravest man is subject to in the moment of supreme danger.

When I was out there the whole place was savage; there were no roads, only little bicycle paths, more like tunnels than anything else, cut through that cruel bush, which was otherwise impassable and full of unspeakable danger, and to-day there are great railways and wonderful motor roads and hundreds of miles of telegraph-wires. All supplies came by steamer up the river, and we had no fresh food, only those splendid tinned foods from the Army and Navy Stores, not one tin of which, Roth told me, had ever been known to be bad.

Roth had planted a number of roses he had brought out from England, and they, he told me, bloomed all the year round; they never ceased to scent that desert air; and he also had brought out with him four pairs of carrier-pigeons, which were the progenitors of the thousands upon thousands that fluttered round the building from sunrise to sunset. One day Roth and I, seated on the veranda, saw a great crowd of natives coming up from the river, which was crowded with their canoes. They seemed greatly excited, and very soon we discerned that a girl was walking in the midst of them, screaming and shrieking, and they holding her by the hands and trying to prevent her from doing herself an injury. Charles went out to receive them and speedily returned. "Them people from them village bring them girl got them devil." Roth and I went downstairs and out into the courtyard. Roth turned to me: "That girl's got hysteria," he said. "This is very interesting, for I had always thought it was a purely civilized complaint, and, of course, these are savages. Now," he said to the head men of the village, "take off her silk and leave only her loincloth on her, and make her lie down on the gravel on her belly, and hold back her arms so that she can't do anything, and I take them devil away." And he took out his watch, and deciding that ten minutes would suffice for his purpose, he said, pointing to the dial of his watch, "When them thing go for there, devil leave her and them girl be all right." So they flung the girl face downwards on the gravel. Now, these natives, black as coal, possess skin, exquisitely soft like velvet, of which they are abnormally proud and which they keep always scrupulously clean. The girl kept her forehead held stiff above the gravel and her naked chest too, so that no dirt could approach it. The exertion of this, combined with her native horror of the possibility of earth polluting her much prized and tenderly cared for skin, soon restored her to a normal condition, and ere ten minutes had passed she was as right as rain. I need scarcely add that thenceforward Roth was regarded with even deeper superstitious awe and reverence than before, and to this day "dem devil doctor" is regarded by them as little less than a deity —and a high-class one at that.

Sometimes that delightful fellow, whose funeral *cortège* I suddenly encountered in Piccadilly one summer day some twelve years later, Sir Ralph Moore, the Consul-General, would dash in to see how his subordinate was getting on. And I specially remember one of his visits, for it was coincident with one of the most touching and most poignant memories of my whole life.

One morning there was a great excitement in our little colony, and, running out on to the veranda, I saw a big steamer alongside the wharf and a small crowd of natives, grinning and chattering, as a prisoner was conveyed by the native police from the canoe to the court-house beneath. Sir Ralph Moore and Roth suggested I should accompany them and hear the trial of the famous river pirate, a man who was responsible for many murders and for the loss of much valuable merchandise from the interior, and who had just been caught and brought in, as I had seen for myself.

A curious scene: the blaze of sunshine outside the court-house, the groups of natives lying upon the grass chattering and gesticulating about the yard, inside a deep hush, a kind of green subdued light filtering through the lattices and falling equally upon the handsome faces of the judges and the poor wretch between his guards, and a group of natives in the background. The man was splendidly plucky and never turned a hair. Of course he hadn't a dog's chance from the moment he was captured, and he was sentenced to death forthwith. He was informed of his fate and that the sentence would be carried out at dawn the following morning. He merely shrugged his shoulders. "It was *ju-ju*—finished!" Sir Ralph Moore, as Consul-General, signed the sentence of death, and then the poor wretch was taken out into the courtyard beneath our veranda and chained to a pillar to await the last hour.

I was foolish perhaps, but somehow or another I was immensely sorry for that man; he was so plucky, so unconsciously debonair, so unconcerned; he didn't appear to worry over his fate in the least, certainly not one-half, not one-quarter so much as I did. He would look up to the veranda and gaily smile at me, and I would feebly and faintly smile back; I hadn't the heart to do more. And then the shades of night came down. He was just the same, though the leaden hours were stealing by. We had dinner, and a couple of planters joined us and got merry with wine and made great fun of the poor wretch outside. To me it was all so horrible, so revoltingly cowardly: we so comfortable and well fed, he so lonely and defenceless.

"Well," I said, "anyway, he's the best-plucked un I ever met anywhere or in any part of the world."

"Oh," they jeered, "he's only a b—— nigger!"

"He's a *man*. I wish I could say that of every one," I replied, utterly careless as to what they might think or say or do.

"Meaning us?" said they.

"If you like," I replied.

That night I could not sleep much, though I fancy the poor wretch, chained to his post beneath my bedroom, rested well enough. I could hear his breathing in the deep, mysterious stillness of the tropic night and the clanking of the chain as he would restlessly shift his position, a faint cry now and again from the forest, and the sound of the river flowing by and lapping against the wharf. And then I must surely have dozed off, for I was roused to full consciousness by a gentle shake and Charles's voice in my ear. "Sah, you live for get up. Nigger man he live for die," he chuckled as he put my coffee and biscuits at my side. A slight noise in the compound, and with indescribably heavy heart and with a certain indefinable hesitancy I glanced out of the open window. Yes, his last hour indeed had come, for, as I looked, a small company of Yoruba soldiers marched up, the poor fellow struggled to his feet, and the sergeant in charge unchained him and he "fell in" in front of the firing party.

Roth's voice sounded softly in the doorway. "Come on, Blathwayt," he said; "it's time we were off."

I never took my eyes off that wonderful man as we marched up to the place of execution, in and out through the early sunlight and the shadows of the night, which even then had scarcely fled away. Half-way up he complained of his ankle, which had been sadly galled by the iron band by which he had been chained to the pillar. We saw it was indeed bleeding, so Roth gave orders the band was to be taken off. Arrived at the execution-ground, a little natural clearing in the bush, the firing-party formed up on one side, whilst the prisoner took his seat opposite on the trunk of a fallen tree, sitting down in quite an easy and unconcerned posture. Roth stepped forward and very gently asked him in his own language if he had anything to say why he should not be shot.

"No," he calmly replied. "If you no kill me, other people do same as I have done; if you kill me, the other people not do it and keep good."

Roth then said, "Bandage his eyes," and the orderly stepped forward to do his bidding. The prisoner put out his hand in protest.

"I no fear. I want to die like black man."

Then the orderly said to him—

"White man has bandage when he shot."

At once the prisoner's face changed, and, putting his hand to his heart, he replied—

"I like them white man; he got proper heart. Put that bandage on. I die like white man."

He was bandaged, and then Roth, stepping forward with a piece of chalk in his hand, drew a glaring white circle upon the poor fellow's naked breast right round his heart. To my unspeakable horror the Yorubas burst into a fit of laughter. It was an immense joke to them, for they are absolutely heartless, absolutely devoid of imagination, no bowels of compassion, no sense of gratitude or kindly feeling whatever. The orderly, at a sign from Roth, gave the word of command, the Yorubas levelled their rifles, a sudden crash, the man fell backwards, kicking up his legs as he did so, and all was over.

"Throw his body into the bush!" said Roth.

"Oh, but why not give him decent burial?" I asked.

"To teach these people a lesson," replied the Acting Vice-Consul. "They will see his dead body treated like carrion and it will never be forgotten."

"Carrion!" I replied. "Carrion! God send my last end may be as splendid as his! That's the bravest man I ever saw." And even as I spoke his body was cast, unhousell'd and unsepulchred, to the horrors of the West African bush.

And that's just a glimpse, as it were, into the romance and mystery of Empire-building. There is a small sequel which also affords another glimpse. A few days afterwards Sir Ralph Moore turned up with a rather serious face.

"I say, Roth," said he, "do you know all this time we have been passing sentences of death and we had no right to do so! Don't do any more, there's a good fellow."

Charles I saw once again, coming out of Oxford and Cambridge Mansions, clad in a silk hat and a smart frock-coat, with, I am disgusted to add, a smart, good-looking servant-girl on his arm, whom he was taking off to a music-hall. He grinned all over as soon as he saw me.

"How did you get to know that girl?" I asked him.

"Them lady," he replied, casually indicating her with his thumb—"them lady live for top; go carry them coal up; I go help her."

And thus whilst Roth and his like are Empire-building in the forest primeval the Cockney servant-girl, more shame to her! is doing her best, in her vulgar and criminal ignorance, to undermine the Empire here at home. I could dilate upon this aspect of Imperialism, or rather un-Imperialism, for hours, but to what purpose? It is the one impassable gulf between the travelled and the untravelled Englishman, between the man who knows and the man who doesn't. But you may take this as gospel, that the main crux, the most difficult and disturbing problem of Empire, is not whether the nigger is a man and a brother, but whether we can permit him to be a brother-*in-law!*

I wonder when the romance of our West African Empire will be written and who will write it. I think the West African officials are about the finest Englishmen we have in our midst to-day—men redolent of the best traditions of Good Queen Bess's days; men like Mr. F. S. James, "Long James," as that handsome and genial giant is affectionately known to his host of friends (he is now Colonial Secretary at Singapore), James who some years ago built a magnificent Residency in place of the old Vice-Consulate at Warri, which the Nigerian officials with delicate humour at once designated "St. James's Palace," Major Armitage, Major Porter, Captain Condon, and half a hundred more congenial spirits who are the leading lights of the West African group one encounters in all its glory in the smoking-room at the Sports Club. Of these men it is impossible to write too highly, nor indeed would they wish it. But they are the men of whom the Empire may well be proud, of whom indeed frequently, judging by the way it treats them, it is not worthy, but men who have done more for the prestige of the Englishman and the proud tradition of the flag than any men have ever done, not even excepting the heroes of Drake's and Nelson's and Wellington's deathless days. And that's that! But more I cannot, less I will not say.

I have related one tragic incident in my very sketchy account of Empire-building on the deadly West Coast in the early days. Let me give you now a glimpse, equally true and actual, into the lighter and more humorous side of that wonderful life of the Englishman right away, all by himself, on his own, and absolutely free and independent of the conventions and traditions of ordinary British civilization. One day I was sitting talking to Roth on the veranda at the Warri Vice-Consulate when a native chief was ushered in.

"Hullo, Sir Richard!" said Roth; "and how are you getting on?"

"Ho," replied the darky, with a broad grin illuminating his ingenuous countenance at the sight of one of the most popular white men in West Africa in that day—"ho, I lib for come see them white man in big palaver-house."

After he had gone I asked Felix Roth why it was he had always addressed the man as "Sir Richard."

The Acting Vice-Consul laughed heartily. "Ah! there's a story to that, and I'll tell it to you now. Some time ago H.M.S. *Alecto* came up the river. One day Commander Jack Dash, who was in charge of her, said to me: 'That chief of yours is a d——d good sort. He's sent me a most beautiful harem. I'll have the chap on board and knight him.' Well, sure enough, despite all I could say, Dash had the ship decorated from stem to stern, flags flying everywhere and flags on the wharf, and a devil of a stir all over the place. At midday he sent a guard of honour on shore, who lined up on the quay, and then the chief came down, passed on board, and was received in great state by the Commander and his officers. After a while Dash bade him kneel down, and then, drawing his sword, he caught the negro a fearful whack on the shoulders with the flat of it and cried out, 'Rise, Sir Richard Ogeebee!' and 'Sir Richard' did rise, and 'Sir Richard' he has been ever since. There was rather a dust-up about it at home, I believe; but I know when King Edward heard of it he sent for Commander Dash and made him tell the whole story, which immensely amused him."

I think these little glimpses into the building of Empire impart a kind of humanity into the more serious side of politics which is not without its value. The type of men we send out upon this work is of the very best, and it is extraordinarily interesting to note how they carry out their task entirely on lines and methods of their own. The principles of the copy-book and very often the stiff, undeviating canons of the Catechism are ignored for a rough-and-ready rule of thumb which frequently corresponds far more to the humanity that lurks in the breast of every man, whatever the colour of his skin, than all the lofty, high-toned principles and maxims of Christianized civilization. The gentleman adventurers of Elizabeth's and Charles's days still exist, and indeed they are, when all is said and done, by far the best people either for the task of colonization or Empire-building or for subduing and educating and winning over the native races. It is a marvellously difficult task, and it can only be properly carried out by such men as those of whom I have been writing. The victors of Nigeria and the West Coast generally are the descendants of Drake and Raleigh and Frobisher and all that wonderful crew, and you cannot beat them.

I am proud I know some of them. They are the finest men we grow to-day.

I have tried to give you a little picture of the Empire in the making and the part that each man plays; for even "palm-oil ruffians" had a share in the preliminary building of the Empire, though 'twixt their hideous ruthlessness—for no words of mine can even begin to give you an idea of the severities and the actual brutalities of these men at their worst—and the splendid restrained but relentless justice of the Imperial officials there was a wide gulf fixed, although the methods of these latter form the golden mean between the cruel brutality of the old-fashioned traders and the ridiculous sentimentalities of the Labour leaders or Dissenting ministers here at home. I can picture an Empire established on the lines of and run and vigorously maintained by the palm-oil ruffians, but God save me from an Empire founded and conducted by certain of the milk-and-water school with whose bleatings in Parliament and on the public platform we are only too familiar to-day.

Empire is and can be maintained only by the perpetual, unfailing maintenance of the supremacy of the white man over the black. Whether we are right or wrong in invading his territory and annexing it to the British Empire is another question altogether; but having done it, we can only maintain our position by a vigorous assertion and upholding of our absolute supremacy. Now, this truth is realized to its fullest extent by the white man all over the Empire. It is not realized nearly as much as it ought to be by the stay-at-home Englishman, and especially the stay-at-home Englishwoman, and this is gradually but surely spelling disaster to our Imperial prestige. And, as I have already hinted, miscegenation between white and black is at the root of the trouble. As a matter of fact it ought to be made a penal offence for a white woman to marry a black man. If an Englishwoman knew she would get five years' penal servitude for marrying a negro, it would make her think twice before she committed such an outrage on all the primal decencies. Some of you will think this is exaggerated language. Well, ask seventy million Americans and all the white people in South Africa what they think of my suggestion, and their reply will astound you.

But putting aside this question of intermarriage between the races, which ought never even to be discussed, the question of our rule and governance of the native races, East and West, is one that may well be committed to the hands of boys brought up at Eton and Harrow, Winchester and Rugby on the one hand, and to Sergeant What's-his-name on the other. It is men of their type who more than any other in the whole world have solved the problem of Empire-building and of commending the British Raj to the native mind, whether in India, South Africa, or North America. It is an immensely difficult question, and can as a rule only be solved by the man on the spot ; but that man must be an Englishman of a high type. I maintain this for many reasons. What I mean is this : The settler, the colonist, long out from home and unrestrained by the public opinion of the Mother Country, is apt to "go very wide," to regard matters too exclusively from his own point of view, which frequently enough is the point of view of the jungle. Some years ago I was visiting a certain far colony, and an appalling rebellion broke out among the natives, which the colonists undertook to quell themselves. And they did quell it, but only by the exercise of the most drastic measures. Of course the defence of the colonists was a very strong one. I quite realized that. It ran as follows : "We are a handful of whites, as one to ten. If they beat us, they will murder every woman and child in the land and put them first to the torture. We must exterminate the b—— brutes if necessary." My friends and I felt that and realized the validity of their defence, and yet, Tories though we all were, as opposed to the sentimental Radicals at home, we were greatly distressed and perturbed at the inevitable slaughter we knew was going on in that dim, dark forest not fifty miles from where we were all living.

It is a delicate and a difficult matter to decide either way, though I think that, as a rule, the ordinary British official in India or on the West Coast of Africa has contrived to solve it in the most practical and the most satisfactory manner possible. At all events, no other nation on earth possesses the same intangible and yet absolutely definite method of handling the natives East and West as our British soldiers and civilians have handled them for the past two hundred years or so, Mr. Outhwaite and Mr. Ramsay Macdonald notwithstanding.

CHAPTER XVIII

OVER THE HILLS AND FAR AWAY (*continued*)

"FIXED light right ahead, sir."

The words floated in through the open doorway of my deck-cabin as the "chief" made his report to "the old man" on the bridge. I slipped out into the chilly dawn, and as I did so the telegraph-bell tinkled once, then again, and then suddenly and startlingly there was a dead stillness; the engines ceased to throb for the first time since we had left Madeira and the ship had stopped dead short, and right ahead of me I was conscious of an immense mountain towering out of the sea, and in a moment I realized that it was Table Mountain and we were in South Africa at last. I need scarcely say that I am not about to indulge in a long dissertation on Africa. I propose merely to give the most fleeting impression of a short visit I paid to this, one of the most fascinating countries in the world, some ten years ago. Indeed, my travel impressions are so slight and trivial as to be hardly worth setting down; but as a matter of fact I am hampered by exigencies of space and the consciousness that, so far as my wanderings are concerned, mine is a thrice-told tale and a tale that has been told a hundred times better by a hundred different people. One thread of thought seems to link these varied impressions together, and that is the crimson thread of the Imperial idea. To me the British Empire is the most superb materialization of the most beautiful dream that the world has ever known, and, wander where I may, this ideal of Empire is ever presenting itself to me in gorgeous and fascinating fashion. My memories of Cape Town are of an exceedingly picturesque city, over which hangs the great mountain, from the wonderful, all-pervading and all-pervasive influence of which no department of the life of the community is ever wholly free ; nor, indeed, would any one ever desire to be freed from its gracious influence.

There is scarcely anything in the whole story of landscape throughout the world which is so extraordinarily penetrating and powerful as the dominating nature of Table Mountain. It is one of those irresistible and inescapable influences which exercise a real bearing on human life and without which a landscape would lose all its character, and the human element of the community would lose something which, unconsciously perhaps, has gone far more to the constitution of its character than it is in any certain degree aware. There is nothing so soothing in South African life as the influence and atmosphere of the great mountain that broods in eternal silence over that vast metropolis, and nothing so menacing, so almost terrifying. It depends so much upon individual character or atmospheric conditions. In any case, it is a supremely beautiful influence, and he who has once passed beneath it must ever long to pass that way once again before death overtakes him. To see that white tablecloth of morning mist unrolling itself from off the mountain-top as the darkness of the dawn gives place to the brilliance of the rising sun, whilst far out at sea white-sailed vessels pass in and out of the historic bay, is to experience an artistic joy that is beyond all words.

To many people, of course, Cape Town is a dull place enough, and I quite grant you that bereft of its mountain it would be provincial and prosaic to the last degree ; but as it is it constitutes one of my most charming memories. I liked almost everything about it, and especially its wonderfully pretty suburbs—Stellenbosch, Wynberg, Rondebosch, Muzenberg, and Simon's Bay on the one side, and Green Point and Houts Bay on the other, where the Indian Ocean rolls in its magnificent green breakers that burst in foam upon a noble beach.

It was at a little hotel on the beach at Sea Point, couched beneath the great mountain, that I spent some of my pleasantest days in South Africa. This is a part of Cape Town that is comparatively little known to the ordinary English visitor to the colony, but it is so charming and so restful, and it provides one with so many delightful memories for after-life, that I cannot refrain from dwelling upon its nameless fascination. Curiously enough the only time I have ever seen it really described from the pictorial point of view is in a novel, "The Unconscious Bigamist," wherein the author enlarges upon the wonderful charm of the district. I cannot do better than quote her verbatim. She is describing the experiences of her heroine, who was stopping at the very hotel I stayed in some years later—

"Each moment, as she rode, the surrounding scenery increased in beauty. To the right the vast ocean stretched away to be lost in the far distance where the blue of sea and sky meet in one interminable embrace. The faint waves, sparkling in the sun, were broken every now and then by the sudden waterspout of some sportive whale, while close to the rocky shore the sea-birds wheeled in tireless flight, or floated, silvery specks, like a fleet of fairy vessels on the rippling blue. To the left rose the great grim range of mountains known as the Twelve Apostles, their jagged sides seamed and cut by deep fissures of sparkling quartz. A narrow footway leading up the precipitous sides of the mountain became visible. From the great altitude the view was even more impressive than it had been below. Far beneath her sparkled the sea, a bewildering expanse of blue, the only sign of habitation on the rockbound coast a small wooden hut or shanty, looking a mere speck in the distance, surrounded by the vivid green of the barely ripened field of mealy cols—the one cultivated spot, an oasis midst the vast masses of rocks and boulders, Nature's playthings hurled in wanton, riotous confusion, one upon another. Above and beyond stretched the jagged points of the mountains. In the distance one could detect a hillside clothed, as it were, in a silvery mantle of pale, shimmering green, which, on closer inspection, proved to be groves of eucalyptus-trees, the pearly tints of their silver leaves making a soft break in the stern, naked majesty of the rearing height beyond, glowing purple and orange in the clear translucence of the morning sun."

This fairly accurately describes one of the loveliest scenes upon which my eyes have ever been fortunate enough to dwell, and the memory of the week or so that I spent at Sea Point is one of the pleasantest memories I retain of my visit to South Africa—South Africa wherein I think one always leaves a portion at least of one's heart.

I suppose that the interest of travel oscillates as a rule between the influences of human companionship and that of landscape and of Nature generally, and with some people, notably in my own case, the influence of Nature is always more powerful and infinitely more all-pervading than that of human companionship, for which, as a rule, I do not, except in rare cases, very particularly care. But scenery always makes for me an absolutely irresistible appeal. I think that was why I enjoyed Durban so much. The really exquisite beauty of the suburban district known as the Berea, a comparatively lofty eminence, which splendidly dominates the town, and from which one obtains a magnificent view of the Indian Ocean spread half round the horizon, and which is bordered, almost instantaneously, as it were, by the primeval bush, in which the foot of man, so I was told, had never trod, fascinated me by its quality of unusualness. For here, it appeared to me, civilization and the primal wild met and touched in a way quite incomprehensible to the ordinary untravelled Englishman. The prosaic tramcar, crowded with exactly the ordinary business man one sees here in London, daily oscillating 'twixt Brixton and the Bank and the Bank back again to Brixton, and with the same type of suburban woman one meets in Oxford Street any day in the week, and school-children hurrying home from school just for all the world as they do in Putney and

Clapham, passes on one side rows of charming little villas, with their pretty gardens, from whence is borne the sweet, cloying perfume of mimosa and bougainvillæa, and on the other the wild, savage, untrodden, impenetrable, primeval bush and forest of undeveloped Africa; and down below the river, only a few years ago haunted by crocodile and hippopotami, and to-day the resort of the bank clerk and the shop girl of, in certain respects, hyper-civilized Durban. But the sensation of the wild and the savage is always there, far too much so for safety and comfort the Natalians will tell you. For they are ever conscious of that tremendous black and menacing thundercloud, as it were, which always broods over the distant horizon, the menace of the native population, which outnumbers that of the whites as ten to one. It is that, of course, which helps to give its touch of romance to life in South Africa, and it is that which, more than anything else, so immensely differentiates the South African's view of the great colour question from that of the hopelessly, stupidly ignorant untravelled Englishman. The one knows what he is talking about and the other doesn't, and no one who has not actually lived with the black man in the mass is in any way qualified to express an opinion upon the subject. At the same time, I wish that one could arrive at a golden mean upon a question which is usually disfigured by bitter, almost unreasoning prejudice upon the one hand and by ludicrously, pathetically childish ignorance upon the other.

When I was in Natal the situation between whites and blacks had long passed the straining-point, for war had actually been declared and terrible battles had been fought only twenty-five miles or so away from Durban itself—Durban which indeed was partly laagered and under martial law. And scarcely less strained were the relations between the English and the colonists from the interior, the one set of people regarding the actions of the other, in trampling out the native rebellion, as characterized by almost unnecessarily drastic action. I don't want to touch upon this subject more than I can help; but I am bound to say that many of the colonial methods of carrying on the war met with the most outspoken disapproval on the part of the English, many of whom were military men and all of whom were bigoted Tories and quite untainted by any suspicion of what is commonly regarded as Radical or Labour sentimentality and undue feeling on behalf of the natives. I recall one evening in particular, in one of the Durban hotels, when a most unpleasant scene occurred between three Tory cavalry officers and three colonial officers, during which they almost came to blows in the vigour of their discussion concerning the proper treatment of the natives, the colonials warmly defending their methods as opposed to what they termed the suicidal sentimentalism of the English.

But immediately afterwards I went outside, and there I saw a low-class Englishwoman, just arrived by the mailboat, familiarly chaffing and joking with the Zulu 'rickshaw man, to the intense disgust of a group of Natal farmers who were standing close by, one of whom broke out, "That woman" (only he didn't call her "woman" exactly) "ought to get the 'cat' and *then* twenty-five years' penal servitude!"

I went up to her and told her just what had been said, and at the same time ordered the man back to his stand.

One finds it difficult to establish the golden mean method of dealing with a question upon which the whole of our Imperial supremacy is founded. On the whole these matters are better left to the man upon the spot. The best-intentioned untravelled English official in Whitehall only makes a mess of things by his ignorant interference and the hopelessly unintelligent and uninstructed orders which he sends out to madden and stultify the man on the spot. I talked with a Salvation Army captain on the subject one day in Durban. "Well," he said, "when I was in England all my sympathies were with the Labour Party; to-day I realize that they would wreck an Empire."

And that night at Government House the party round

the dinner-table only emphasized what the Salvationist had said. It's all pretty crude this, and no one is more conscious of its crudeness than I am; but it is absolutely true. What the man of action does one day on the spot the man of amiable theory undoes the next day five thousand miles away in Whitehall. And South Africa knows this, just as India knows it; just, indeed, as Canada and Australia knew it; but they have contrived somehow or another by sheer determination and pluck and resolution to shake off from their shoulders the dead hand of officialism stretching out from an ignorant and sentimental Home authority and endeavouring to paralyse all their action and all their efforts, and always—and that is the pathos of it—with the best will in the world. A few days later I sat with a small picnic-party beneath the shadow of Majuba Hill, and my host, pointing to that tragic scene of ineptitude, said to me, "There's an undying memorial to England's national crime of procrastination and official timidity."

It is always interesting to me to watch the curious manner in which each portion of the Empire faithfully reflects the Motherland, how in its institutions and in its forms of government especially it is, as it were, a microcosm of the vast united whole of which it is itself but a small part. And especially is this true in respect to ceremonial, than which nothing perhaps exists more complete as a link with the past or a connecting link in the great chain of Empire, nothing so helps to preserve and carry on tradition, nothing is so redolent of a splendid and a stately past, and therefore nothing which plays a more authoritative or definite part in the life of a great community. I was greatly impressed by this truth when I one day paid my visit to the Houses of Parliament in Cape Town, where by the courtesy of Sir Walter Hely-Hutchinson I was allowed to sit in what is known as the "Governor's Bay," and whence I had a full view and good hearing of the Speaker and the whole proceedings. It was interesting to observe exactly the same etiquette, the same ceremonies which prevail in the

Mother of Parliaments in Westminster, and to realize that the traditions born and cherished for centuries upon the banks of the Thames are faithfully observed and reproduced wherever the Union Jack floats upon the breeze, never mind how far away from the great central seat of government. The Speaker in his full-bottomed wig, the Sergeant-at-Arms, with his sword, his cocked hat, and his knee-breeches and silk stockings, the chaplain in cap and gown, the barristers in their bob-wigs, the ushers in their characteristic uniform, and innumerable other little reminiscent touches and points of etiquette and stately ceremonial, all remind you that whether you are in Cape Town or in Melbourne or in Ottawa, or in the Legislative Chamber in a little West Indian island in the Caribbean Sea, or raising your hat to the Viceregal procession in Simla, you are still and always in an outpost of the great British Empire.

And you are confronted by the unfailing characteristics of the British people, at their noblest and their best and at their most dignified, when you are in the presence of or listening to the debates of the colonial statesmen, for somehow or another the capacity for statesmanship is a quality of character which is singularly distinctive of the man born and bred in a British colony or who has lived much of his life in the Colonies. Why this should be so it is difficult to say, but somehow or another the bush, the prairie, and the veld have been, and still are, prolific in the production of the capacity for statesmanship at its highest and its best. Whether it is the influence of an outdoor life, the curious constraining and formative character of a life devoted to sport, of a life wherein a man, thrown back on primeval and elemental conditions, is thereby stiffened and hardened and rendered of steel-like quality, armed and ready at all points for any and every emergency, it is difficult to say; but the fact remains that, as a rule, the colonial statesman possesses qualities which frequently place him on an absolute equality with the Englishman brought up at an English Public School, with all the long traditions of breeding and literature and education behind him.

When I was in South Africa, John Xavier Merriman was one of the outstanding personalities in the life of the colony. I lunched with him one day, and in some curious fashion he reminded me the whole time partly of Froude the historian, partly of Professor Goldwin Smith, at whose house I had been a guest some years previously in Toronto. In all three men there was a definite, caustic capacity for speech, and in each man the same pungent and unusual outlook upon the world and upon human affairs in general. A tall, slight man, with a vivid face and a certain distinction of character and appearance, he was a man whom it was impossible for even the casual passer-by to overlook. He was an extremely clever man and, like his father, the late Bishop of Grahamstown, a widely read one. I think that in Cape Colony, generally speaking, he is feared rather than he is popular. He is one of those men whom, instinctively, one regards as being beyond and above his fellows, and concerning whom one is prepared to hear that he is not on all fours with the usual hail-fellow-well-met type of man who is universally accepted as a popular favourite. Like John Inglesant, Mr. Xavier Merriman stands somewhat aloof from his fellows, and is apt to be misunderstood accordingly; but I am bound to own that to me he was a delightful personality, and the hour or two I spent in his company are numbered amongst the pleasantest memories of my South African tour. And most assuredly his was the most distinguished figure in the Parliament House the day I visited it. Mr. Merriman is, however, scarcely a typical colonial statesman, as I believe he was educated at a Public School and either Oxford or Cambridge.

And of course there is always the changeless, or perhaps it would be better to describe it as the ever-changing, glory of the veld. I have witnessed the coming of the dawn in the Australian bush, when the gum-trees loomed thin and ghostly in the dim twilight; I have watched the shadows chasing one another in never-ending ripples over the widespreading Canadian prairies;

I have lain awake beneath the myriad starlight upon the desert of the Sahara ; I have sweated beneath the burning midday sun as it has drawn up to itself the delicious perfumes of trees and flowers and grasses in the wilderness of Judæa ; and I have experienced the unforgettable lightness of heart that is his who wanders over the Campagna on a Roman holiday ; and yet none of these surpass, though in different respects perhaps they all equal, the exquisite beauty of a crimson sunset upon the South African veld. And indeed nothing more beautiful can be imagined, nothing more appealing to all the senses can be desired. The manner, for instance, in which the distant range of hills outside Volksrust, in the Transvaal, cut themselves out of cardboard, as it were, against that azure sky, and then stand out dazzling and brilliant above the horizon, clear as crystal, in that translucent atmosphere, the whole range soaked the while in the crimson rays of the setting sun, is perhaps one of the most marvellous, as it is also one of the most beautiful, things in all this beautiful world, and ever the silence and aloofness that haunt and give their chief charm and their distinctive character to the great Lonelinesses of the world, as I have seen and known and loved them and have here feebly endeavoured to describe.

And yet they bore some people stiff !

And what an opportunity they provide, not only for the artist but for the architect. I was in Pretoria when the great Government palaces—for they were nothing less—were being designed and built upon the edge of the Transvaal veld. How that wonderful landscape lent itself to the designing of magnificent gardens, and how superbly the Italianate palaces and pillars and pergolas outlined themselves against those immeasurable immensities of distance that you see only in their highest perfection and that are saturated with their maximum of mystery only in South Africa !

One of the most saddening and depressing features of modern travel, especially in the East, is the hideous and devastating influence of Western civilization, for which in large degree British Imperialism and American enterprise and German irrepressibility are responsible. The charm of Palestine hitherto has been the fact that, being under Turkish rule, it has not been seized with that passion for progress and reform which so disfigures and disgraces Anglo-Saxon civilization. And have you ever paused to realize how hideous that same civilization almost invariably is? Personally, I frankly confess I am no bigot for reform, and progress, as a rule, I simply detest, and so perhaps I speak from a singularly prejudiced point of view; but as I wander Eastwards through this lovely world and watch the devastating track of the progress-monger and the reforming fanatic my heart sinks within me and there is no spirit left in me at all. Think to yourself for a moment of that exquisite rose-red wall which Suleiman the Magnificent flung so recklessly and with such artistic prodigality round the holy places confined within that little rocky grey city of Jerusalem, and picture to yourself the modern builder knocking it down in order to make room for a penny tramcar line from the Jaffa Gate to the Mount of Olives! And yet this horror has actually been suggested; whilst it is a ghastly fact that you can take the electric tramcar all the way from the Cairo of mediaevalism to the Pyramids of the Pharaohs, instead of jaunting there quietly and artistically by yourself upon that sunny roadway beneath the grateful shadow of the palm-trees and the lebbek-trees, that charming road which leads you straight from streets wherein Richard's Crusaders wonderingly wandered to the very edge of the lonely and mysterious Libyan desert! And think of British tourists, in smart evening coats and carefully cut white waistcoats, stiffly and uncomfortably and oh! so unromantically and inharmoniously sitting in the African moonlight round the mystery and the mysticism of the inscrutable and immemorial Sphinx!

And even worse: you must remember, if you are British of the upper classes, that it is, on the whole, rather bad form for the British resident in Rome or Athens or Cairo to display the slightest interest in the ruins and memorials of that gorgeous and glorious past which have endowed those cities with their deathless and indescribable charm and fascination. Such it is to be "hagged" down by Western civilization.

Cairo twenty years ago and more was the most divine place on earth; although it dates only from the tenth century, it nevertheless comes straight down, in its associations and memories, from the Pharaohs of the Bible; the mother of Jesus and her husband and Child are held by tradition to have passed one night at least within its walls; its association with the heroes of the "Arabian Nights" is undoubted; its streets rang to the martial tramp of the hosts of the Crusaders; up to yesterday almost it was the most exclusively mediaeval city in the world; but to-day those wonderful mushrubiyeh lattices, which gave all their character and distinction, and conferred an indescribable sense of charm upon the ancient streets of Cairo, and which I saw in all their glory undisturbed in 1893, have passed away for ever from the Sharia Gamamis, the Bab-el-Wazir, and the Sugarieh, whilst those lovely old wooden-roofed shops which hung so gracefully over, and which provided the ancient streets with such an artistic skyline in varied parts of old Cairo, have been razed to the ground to make room for the plate-glassed monstrosities of Maple and Shoolbred. In fact, I always say that, with inconceivable rapidity, Cairo and Palestine and India and the Far East are taking to themselves all the attributes and much of the hideous appearance of Tottenham Court Road on a Saturday afternoon, and mainly owing, I fear, to British Imperialism and British fever for progress and reform.

And to think of those marvellous Cairene bazaars—those dim mediaeval caverns, if I may so express myself, wherein now and again a shaft of sunlight pierces athwart the misty shadows of many dead centuries and just picks out, and for a moment gorgeously illuminates, some wonderful carpet from Damascus or some delicately hued rug from Bagdad or a shimmering, glancing length of silk from far Cashmere, and for a background the impenetrable gloom and mystery of a building that gives you somehow the impression that it was hewn out of the virgin rock when the world was young.

But they are giving place to nice little English shops nowadays, such as you can see by the thousand in all their dingy squalor or ghastly pretentiousness in the Fulham Road or the Bon Marché beyond the railway arch in Brixton!

Never mind! Our Western civilization is marching, or had I not better say trampling, ruthlessly on!

But I, foolish and fond, cling to the Cairo I have dreamed of all my life and that I was happy and fortunate enough to see in all its pristine splendour. I always think of what the writer in "The Thousand and One Nights" says of this thrice-blessed city—

"He who hath not seen Cairo hath not seen the world. Its soil is gold; its Nile is a wonder; its women are like the black-eyed virgins of Paradise; its houses are palaces; and its air is soft—its odours surpassing that of aloes-wood, and cheering the heart: and how can Cairo be otherwise when it is the Mother of the World?"

But to see Cairo at its best you must climb the Citadel and watch the sunset over the desert from that proud eminence. Here you have the city spread far beneath you in all its incredible magnificence; a hundred red minarets cut the skyline, a myriad houses of every conceivable type and architecture lend infinite variety to the wondrous scene; you can trace the streets stretching far and wide in every direction; you can even discern the individualities of the multitudinous and multi-coloured crowds that are thronging those Oriental highways; and far away you realize with a thrill, if you are beholding them for the first time, the triangular forms of the ancient Pyramids, betwixt you and which flow the historic waters of the Nile, glistening in the sweet evening light. And the desert, immense and impalpable, and a wonderful purple; not yellow or tawny—you are too far away to discern its actual colour—but a deep and a beautiful and a mysterious purple, lies all around you. And, with startling suddenness, the sun disappears beneath the horizon-line, and in an instant, without warning and when you least expect it, a cannon crashes out the sunset hour on the parapet immediately under your feet. And at once an indescribable babel fills the air; the sound of many voices assails the rock on which you stand, and cutting right across them, and clear distinguished from them, and rising far above the earthly tumult of a wearied world, there floats upon the air the wailing cry of the Muezzin calling the Faithful to the sunset prayer. And the sun is set and you think it is all over, and you draw a long sigh and you say, "Let us go now"; and yet all the magic and all the marvel and all the undying wonder of it has yet to come. For almost ere you begin to retrace your footsteps an unearthly radiance fills the sky and laps the world in its soft embrace, and suddenly a thousand window-panes flame back the deathless glory of this unspeakable splendour. It is the *crepuscule*, that far-famed, oft-told light which the poets tell us was never on sea or land, and upon which Moses must have gazed awe-stricken a hundred times over, and the miracle which for millions of years has nightly fulfilled itself upon the banks of the Nile.

And then you hurry back to your hotel to a French menu and the "turkey-trot" or the "bunny hug."

But then, you see, you are civilized!

And yet it is those selfsame wondrous people who criticize and bewail the French menu and who "turkey-trot" round and about the Sphinx, as I have seen them do myself, and who are saturated through and through and revel in and are proud of their civilization, who hold Egypt to-day as the gateway to India and the key to the whole British Empire!

What a marvellous people they are, of a surety the most marvellous, because the most unexpected and the most contradictory and the most complex, that the world has ever seen! The Englishman at the foot of the Sphinx, who has watched and watched like a Providence, as Kinglake once wrote, with the same earnest eyes and the same tranquil mien. "And we,"—Kinglake in splendid prose goes on to say—"we shall die, and Islam will wither away; and the Englishman, straining for ever to hold his loved India, will plant a firm foot on the banks of the Nile, and sit in the seats of the faithful, and still that sleepless rock will lie watching and watching the works of the new busy race with those same sad, earnest eyes, and the same tranquil mien everlasting. You dare not mock at the Sphinx!"

* * * * *

"Wake up, Blathwayt, wake up!" And a hand gently laid upon my shoulder brought me back from the land of dreams to this prosaic earth once again, and, looking up, I encountered the gaze of poor Herbert Cairns. "Wake up! We've got to be off to India now! The ship is coming through the Canal and we have only just time to get on board!" It was about four o'clock on a February morning in the little waterside hotel at Ismailia, where Lord Cairns and I had spent an uneasy and uncomfortable night upon the two sofas the deserted dining-room afforded. And so once more I started in pursuit of that sun and the land upon which that sun never sets—the British Empire. Cairns, like myself, was an enthusiast for the splendour of the past—he was far too much of an artist and a poet not to have been so—but the elements alike of the sportsman and the man of affairs that helped to compose his somewhat multiple personality induced in him an extraordinary interest in the story of our occupation and conquest of the ancient East—in the story, in short, of the British Empire; and I cannot easily forget the keenly actual and vivid view he took of a problem which is of undying interest to the political historian. I remember one day, as we were passing down the Red Sea, how interested he was in the question as to who had really most helped to develop the Imperial idea—the statesman, the soldier, or the literary man.

"Well," he said, "on the whole I should be inclined to plump for the literary man. Had it not been for

Froude and Kinglake and Seely, and then, of course, markedly from the very popular point of view, Rudyard Kipling, I don't think the average Englishman would ever even have known there was a British Empire at all, and I am quite sure he wouldn't have cared a damn about it ; I don't believe he does now, as a matter of fact."

I am speaking of the middle nineties.

"But," he continued, "I think we owe more to our great merchants and business men, and, of course, to our great engineers and contractors than we are apt to imagine. I call the chairman of this very line we are now travelling by, the P. & O., one of the greatest Empire-builders we have ; old Sutherland has done wonders for the Empire with the P. & O., and the men who are building the C.P.R. are doing just as much in the West. And don't forget the work the engineer has done for the Empire. I realized that when I was up in Newcastle working at Armstrong's ; and I realize it more and more whenever I see what engineering is accomplishing in India. Still, I think that their work would be apt to be lost sight of if it weren't for the literary man, and that applies, of course, to the work of all men who are actively engaged in the service of the Empire."

Of my stay in India what can I say in so brief a space as this but what is as a hundred times told tale?

I recall, however, one gorgeous memory, bathed in the silvery light of an Eastern moon. I gave a lime-light lecture one night in the palace at Gwalior, where I was a guest of Sir Donald Robertson, the Resident there, and the Maharajah Scindia himself worked the lantern. He was a very young man in those days and devoted to everything connected with engineering and driving railway trains and anything of a mechanical interest. I could no more have worked the lantern than I could have flown, but he was an absolute master at it and never made a single mistake. It was a wondrous scene. I paused once in the midst of my discourse, partly to give my audience a rest, but mainly that I might imprint the whole occasion on the tablets of my memory. Outside, the most gorgeous moon, sailing in the most purple sky I had ever seen, illuminated that huge snow-white marble palace, giving it more the semblance of a wonderful piece of architecture soaring into the blue heavens of a fairy-story or an endless dream, and the many pillars of the palace cast wonderful, clean-cut shadows upon the ground, that at first sight gave the impression of a vast snowfield upon the summit of Mont Blanc, so dazzlingly white was that all-pervading light. And grouped round me was the young Prince, in the Mahratta dress and turban, with his Prime Minister and the princes and nobles of the Court, scintillating with diamonds and with some of the most marvellous jewellery I ever saw pinned about their garments ; and on the other side the British Resident and his A.D.C.'s, gorgeous in their crimson and golden uniforms, and a few English ladies in ordinary ball or dinner frocks—and, of course, no native women present. The whole scene had much the effect and suggestion, greatly heightened by the marble seats and tables, of a magnificent painting by Alma Tadema. And in connection with the Maharajah of Gwalior I recall how, a day or two later, I accompanied him and his Court and the British Resident on a lengthy railway journey through his dominions—he himself indeed driving the engine part of the day and getting as black as a sweep in consequence. Late in the evening we arrived at a huge wayside station, where a strange incident occurred.

A number of Sepoys were drawn up as a guard of honour for the Prince ; a vast assemblage of native gentlemen and local zemindars and merchants and money-lenders and ryots were gathered together, who all prostrated themselves on his appearance, gorgeously clad in native costume, upon the platform. And then an English engineer was brought up under guard and charged before the Prince and the Resident with an offence of which I did not ascertain the details. What struck me very forcibly in the whole unpleasant affair, and in marked contrast to the surly and defiant behaviour of the culprit, was the dignity, the sincerity, and the genuine kindliness and fair-mindedness of the young Prince, who certainly was not more than eighteen years of age at the time, but who throughout displayed a marvellous amount of tact, good breeding, fine common sense, and a real desire to act with absolute justice.

And that, too, was a glimpse into the hidden workings of Empire, and one realized on that wide station platform, open to all the winds of heaven that blow and crowded with a gorgeously clad and brilliantly hued assemblage, that the spirit of Imperialism is doing as much as anything else to link the peoples of the East in harmony and sympathy with the peoples of the West.

It is the loneliness of the Canadian prairies which constitutes their chief charm to me. There is something in the awe-inspiring silences and the purple distances of the Canadian prairies and the wonderful flashes of sunlight over the windswept cornfields that appeals to me as nothing else on earth has ever done ; and even the uncultivated prairie, where the foot of man has never trod, possesses a fascination that is without compare. And think of the exquisite charm of an autumn day in Canada, a golden day in October when the fall has really begun. I remember one evening in a railway journey from Toronto, I think it was, to Ottawa, we passed through a forest at sunset, and the spectacle was such as to fill one's soul with awe and one's eyes with joy, it was so overwhelmingly lovely and magnificent. I can remember many years ago the late Dean Farrar showing me a water-colour of a Canadian forest in October, and saying, "I can never get an Englishman to believe it is unexaggerated and a real depiction of what one actually sees." And as that picture, so was the spectacle of that never-to-be-forgotten evening. It would be well worth any one's while to run over to Canada just to spend a few sunny days in the woods, and to see for oneself the gorgeous hues of the autumnal foliage—red, green, glowing yellow, and brilliant blue. The brilliance of the scene baffles all human description ;

no artist's palette can provide the colours necessary to depict it, and not even Tennyson's nor Swinburne's verse could adequately describe that wonderful sunset, as I saw it, a few years ago. One felt as though one had been suddenly ushered into the glittering golden presence of God Himself.

Like most great open spaces, the prairies provide you with the most extraordinary optical delusions or illusions. On the desert you encounter the mirage, but what I recall most pungently of the prairie is the marvellous semblance it presents at the sunset hours to the waters of the ocean. I have stood in the midst of an untouched and unreclaimed prairie in Manitoba and I have gazed for half an hour at a stretch at the far horizon, and have even then been almost unable to persuade myself that I was not standing upon the seashore watching the waves rolling on to the beach. The semblance was so exact that there was no detail left untouched, there was absolutely nothing to mar the firm conviction that you were standing upon the seashore gazing over miles of rolling waters.

And it was in the middle of a great Manitoban prairie that I once obtained a peep into another phase of Empire. I was being driven to one of the C.P.R.'s depots by a dear little woman, the wife of a farmer who was too busy to get away himself, and who therefore sent me in by his weekly cart, which she invariably drove, to the local town, forty miles away from his homestead, to fetch the family groceries. During the course of our drive that sunny Canadian morning we had occasion to pass through a new little township which was being carved out, as it were, of the wide and desolate prairie.

"Did ye iver see the like o' that now?" said my companion. "It's a city it'll be before we know where we are. Two months ago there wasn't stick or stone in the place. It reminds one of a story I heard the other day at the depot we are going to now. An Irishman was on the train, and he and another man fell to talking, and the Irishman said, 'Where is ut you live?' and the Canuck said, 'I come from Boosterville.'

"'Boosterville, is ut?' said the Paddy. 'Why, I was there myself three weeks ago.'

"'Three weeks ago?' said the Canuck. 'Gee, you oughter seen it this morning!'"

We off-spanned for a couple of hours in the noonday heat. We sat and ate our simple little luncheon beneath the shade of some trees, whereunder our gallant steeds were also enjoying their welcome rest and feed, at the edge of a noble bluff, wherefrom we obtained a superb view of a whole world of distances, and away beneath us glimmered and glittered in that gorgeous sunshine a swift flowing river, rather a rare sight just in that part of Manitoba. And after our meal we sat and talked, and that conversation is just one of the things I shall remember to my dying day. She was just a simple little Irishwoman, and very homesick at that, with a charming brogue and a quaintly pretty phraseology which I shall not attempt to reproduce, with here and there flashes of wit and wonderful insight and evidently much of that ultra-melancholy of temperament by which her race is more characterized than any other; and yet she talked so interestingly and so openly and she developed so charming and unusual a point of view that as I travelled in the railway-carriage that night I transcribed our conversation almost word for word into my notebook.

I had told her that I had come so far West to try and get a bit of an idea of the manner in which they were carrying out and building up their bit of Empire on the lonely prairie. And she replied rather caustically—

"Empire-building, is ut? And it's you that don't know the loneliness of ut and what we women have to go through. I take no stock in the Empire, and I don't think any one about here ever gives it a second thought. Faith, I don't believe they know about it at all, at all; you can't worry about things like that when you've got all you can do to live. And it's the women, annyway, it bears hardest upon. Oh! the loneliness of ut all, the cruel, crushing loneliness. And my husband doesn't understand. He's Canadian born and thinks there's no place like Canada, and they're a hard people, annyway. I mind me when my little Jack was coming to me—God rest his soul!—I was alone in that farm-house of ours, and never a woman to give me a helping hand, and the baby came, and I nearly died. We haven't time to think of Empire, and, annyway, if we did, what's the Empire to us poor Irish when you English treat us as you do and drive us out here to live a life I'd rather be dead than live? You English think you're everybody; but see how ye're hated. It's not only we Irish hate you, but, faith, the people out here hate you worse—far worse. And it's your own fault. Just ask anny Canuck that comes along what he thinks of your old Empire—built up, as you call it, out of the tears of women like me! A lot your Government would ever think of what we Irish go through and what we put up with from you!"

"Well," I said, "don't tar us all with the same brush. There's some of us would astonish you if you knew how at heart we sympathize with you, though we don't go all the way with you. Yet we feel that we English don't even begin to understand the Irish character any more than the people here understand us."

"And whose fault is ut," she said, "that ye're not understood over here? Have you ever seen an Englishman getting out at the depot here—any sort of Englishman, a remittance-man as we call him—with all his swagger and his affectations and his silly, useless hands, or a little Cockney, with his nasty voice and his nasty mind and his pig-headed idea that he knows a thing or two more than any one here knows ut, and him born in a slum and bred in a workhouse and out here a bare week?"

I thought it was time to change the conversation, so I said—

"Are you fond of reading?"

"What's the good of being fond of reading without the time to read?" asked my little Irishwoman. And then suddenly and eagerly she said to me: "Did you ever hear tell of Dora Sigerson? Perhaps you know her?"

"Well," I replied, "I believe I passed her the mustard once, but I can't say I know her."

"Fancy that, now!" she exclaimed. "The luck of some people, and me that would give anything to tell her how happy she's made me. Do you know her poetry?"

"Yes, I do," I replied, thankful at being able to give her a definite and a satisfactory reply at last—"yes, I do, and it was a very great writer, Mr. George Meredith, who told me to be sure and read her poems. I remember he said, 'They're rough and harsh, sometimes, but they have the soul of things in them.'"

"'Rough and harsh,' is ut? Well, they've not been rough and harsh to me. Listen, and I'll try and say one; it's my favourite of them all; it breaks my heart, and yet I seem to love ut." And then with her sweet Irish voice and quite without any awkwardness or pose or shyness she softly repeated those tender lines, "A Meadow Tragedy"—

"'Here's a meadow full of sunshine,
  Ripe grasses lush and high;
There's a reaper on the roadway,
  And a lark hangs in the sky.

There's a nest of love enclosing
  Three little beaks that cry;
The reaper's in the meadow
  And a lark hangs in the sky.

Here's a mead all full of summer,
  And a tragedy goes by,
With a knife amongst the grasses,
  And a song up in the sky.'"

And then, to my dismay, the sweet voice faltered, and with a sudden flinging of herself upon the grass she burst into a passion of tears.

"It's my little Jack," she sobbed out at last—"it's my little Jack; he was killed in a meadow, and the birds were singing then, and those lines seem to tell ut me all over again, and yet I love them; but Jack was all

I had, and he nearly had my life when he was born, and he was all to me ; he was everything ; he was my life, and the horse ran away and kicked him on the head in the corn and he never spoke again."

And she too was silent for a while. And that was *her* meadow tragedy.

"But oh, don't say the woman who can write what that woman writes," she went on a moment or two later, "is rough and harsh ! Think what she's written about dear Ireland ! "

I tried to explain what Mr. Meredith had meant by his expression, but I don't think she really grasped my words.

"It's always the ould country with me," she said ; "it's laughin' at me my husband is because I'm always wearyin' for Ireland. Do you mind what Dora Sigerson says about it, about lavin' Ireland, I mean?

"'I have left you behind
In the path of the past,
With the white breath of flowers,
With the best of God's hours,
I have left you at last.'

But, then, ye're English ; ye'll not be after understandin' me at all, at all."

"Do you know," I said, "that you do the English a great injustice? In some ways I honestly believe they are not only as sensitive and understanding as you Irish, but even more so—at times, I mean—only you don't or won't take the trouble to understand *us*. A great soldier once told me that the Sikhs and the Highlanders and the Irish never run away, but he said the Cockneys, who are very nearly the bravest and pluckiest soldiers in the world, sometimes do—and they run, not because they are cowards but because they are, in a way, the most sensitive and the most imaginative people in the world. They imagine something and they're off in a second ; but they are quickly rallied, and then they are the devil. You spoke just now of the Cockney's 'nasty mind,' but I don't think that's quite fair. I belonged to a society once called the Gordon League which used to provide very grand Sunday evening concerts for the very, very London poor. And we used to give a flower to each person on the sacred condition that it wasn't to be taken into a public-house that night. And do you know no one ever refused the flower and no one ever took it into the bar? The flower meant more to them than anything—even drink. Well, that doesn't look much like a nasty mind. I have a great liking for Irish priests, but sometimes I have thought them anything but sympathetic and understanding. You rather laugh at my enthusiasm about the Empire, but I think that, whilst no one would fight for it more fiercely than the Irish soldier, no one would administer it better than the Englishman. And just because he is, what you say he is not, really understanding. All over the world and with all sorts of people he has proved himself to be the most understanding person in the world."

"But you said a while back you didn't understand the Irish a bit."

"Yes, and I say so again, but I am bound to add you don't give us a chance to do so and you never try to understand us at all. But that's touching on very delicate political ground, and I hold that the Empire is above all politics. Let's go back to the poetry. Can you remember any more of her lines?"

"I'll just say ye my favourite lines of all and then we must be goin'," she hastily added as she pointed to the lengthening tree shadows, across which the prairie chickens and the merry little gophers—the prairie apology for our squirrels—were flitting gaily to and fro. "I must tell ye I always say these lines to myself when anything goes extra crooked or my man is cross with me more than ordinary. They are so big; they seem to take me right out of meself: I forget everything and nothing seems to matter.

"'The seas that shake and thunder will close our mouths one day,
The storms that shriek and whistle will blow our breaths away.
The dust that flies and whitens will mark not where we trod.
What matters then our judging? We are face to face with God!'"

Six weeks later and my little Irishwoman was found floating upon the lonely creek. She was at rest at last—and with Jack.

Some of my readers will think this is very sentimental; perhaps it is because it is a page out of real life. I have never forgotten that sweet autumn day upon the Canadian prairie, for it taught me a lesson and it gave me one more tiny glimpse into the mystery of Empire, one more fragile vision of the mighty task that Britain has undertaken these many hundreds of years.

It is the marvellously comprehensive grasp of Empire that possesses such a fascination for those who have wandered the world over and seen it actually in the making. It is the most marvellously comprehensive thing in the world. Look at that savage down by the riverside there in the heart of Central Africa—a man with no language and scarcely understanding the most elementary signs, a man who is even now, at this very moment, only just beginning to emerge from his stone age; and yet it is perfectly on the cards that that man's son may one day be a Premier in the service of the British Empire. We gather them all up and fashion and fuse and melt and mould them into one marvellous, homogeneous piece of work, as it were, a great and supreme accomplishment of art. Like a glittering mosaic, they are all subdued into one great harmony—a harmony of colour in which there are no blemishes, a harmony of sound in which there are no discords at all. You can see the pomp and majesty and glory of Empire when the King passes in stately procession down Pall Mall with all his princes and his premiers and his prelates, his soldiers and his sailors, his horses and his carriages, and his great-hearted people cheering him to the skies, or when his Fleet is thundering him a superb salute off Spithead, or in the midst of the glittering splendour of the Delhi Durbar. But for me I think my most penetrating vision of Empire comes to me when I bend over the little drummer-boy fast asleep in the clanging, echoing Indian station, or sitting in the midst of that lonely Canadian prairie with my little Irishwoman, or talking quietly to some colonial Premier.

However much it may mean to you or however little, it is nevertheless an inescapable fact that the British Empire is not only the greatest political fact the world has ever known, but even more, it is the most supreme work that has ever been accomplished by the human race. And it is all due to one thing—

"You rule your Empire by character."

That is what Prince Ito said to me in Japan twenty years ago.

CHAPTER XIX

CHOTA-HAZRI ROUND THE WORLD

CHOTA-HAZRI—the early tea of Anglo-India—has established itself right round the world as one of the most grateful, popular, and sociable or delightfully solitary little meals that one can possibly imagine or desire, and the *chota-hazris* of which I have partaken in my journeyings through life and round the world form some of the most pleasant memories of a singularly happy, and to me, at all events, romantic and memorable career. All kinds of associations crowd the mind when I pass *chota-hazri* in review down the long corridors of memory, and some of these innocent little festivities stand out before all others, pregnant with the vision of some quite unforgettable moment of my life.

The solemn chanting of the monks in a Franciscan monastery just outside the splendid rose-red wall of Suleiman the Magnificent, which gives such exquisite colour and character to the city of Jerusalem, broke the stillness of a half-awakened dawn, and I lay for a few minutes listening to the sonorous Latin chorale throbbing through the corridors of the great stone building, until the door quietly opened and a monk appeared carrying my early tea in his hand and with a classic greeting upon his lips. He threw the window open, and the tinkling of the sheep-bells greeted my ear, and I could distinguish the pattering of myriads of tiny hoofs as the shaggy little Eastern sheep scrambled down the stony pathway on their way to the lonely hillsides and mountains round about Jerusalem, and even as I lay there I caught a glimpse of the great Russian monastery that so splendidly tops the Mount of Olives, glittering in the early morning sunshine. And in that early cup of tea I seemed to myself to sum up and to harmonize all the wonderful, the unparalleled history and traditions and associations of the sacred place wherein I sat that peaceful spring morning twenty years ago. Away in the distance I caught a glimpse of the little ancient stone bridge that carries you over the brook Kedron, and on the current of that stream my mind floated down the long ages that had elapsed since Abraham had offered his first sacrifice in that very spot to the night when Christ so wearily crossed it for the last time on His blood-stained pathway to the judgment-hall; and my memories visioned for me the horrors of the great siege, and the tramp of the Roman legionaries gradually gave way to the triumphant shouts of Richard and his Crusaders, and all the mediaeval glories of the Eastern city spread themselves out in grey and silver and delicate reds, and the most daintily graceful architecture that has ever beautified and ameliorated the unspeakable desolation of one of the wildest and most forbidding landscapes that one can see upon the face of the earth, though in that peaceful morning light it contained infinite fascination and charm for the artistic eye and the poetic mind.

I think it is Mr. Edmund Gosse who has strikingly remarked that Jerusalem is a city that has turned reddish with the concentrated dust of centuries. Under this coating of dust there lurk fragments of all the civilizations which have swept over it one after the other, one in the steps of the other, which is wherein appears its irresistible fascination, that and the extraordinary charm of its sacrosanct remoteness. As I drank my tea that morning perched high up in the dormitory tower of that Franciscan monastery, I realized with a thrill of delight one's absolute aloofness from the nineteenth century, from civilization, and from all that spelled the modern world. Jerusalem lay beneath and around me, and Manchester and Piccadilly were as though they had never sickened my heart with all their horrible stupidities and vulgar banalities.

One brilliant chilly morning, very early, camping out near Memphis, I was lying, wrapped up in a long cloak, fast asleep at the foot of the famous step Pyramid of Sakkarat, when suddenly I felt a sharp dig in my ribs, and a clear feminine voice said: "Wake up, Arab, and make us a fire." I looked sleepily up at a very pretty Englishwoman, and I fear I was a disgusting and a horrible object, unshaven, unbathed for days, and burned black with the wind and sun of the Libyan desert. However, I obediently shuffled along and speedily helped them to kindle a fire.

"Will you have some tea, Arab?" said the lady, whereat her equally pretty companion scornfully said—

"Fancy asking an Arab to have tea! He wouldn't know the difference between tea or coffee, I'll be bound."

I bowed profoundly and sat me down cross-legged upon the ground, the while my fair hostess poured out three cups of tea, discoursing vigorously and with fluent ignorance upon the magnificent memorial of the past beneath which we were so placidly seated.

"How stupid you are, Maude!" said the other lady. "He doesn't understand a word you say, and if he did every one knows these Arabs are absolutely uninterested in their own country and its tombs and monuments."

Just at that moment I took up their little travelling tea-caddy and absent-mindedly stuck my eyeglass into my eye to inspect it the more carefully.

"Why," cried "Maude," in startled horror, "you are not an Arab after all!"

"I never said I was," I replied, with a nervous grin; "but as you took it so absolutely for granted I felt I couldn't do anything else but try and play up to the part as well as I could."

In marked contrast to the foregoing little episode I recall an early cup of tea on the terrace of an old English country house, whence one commanded a far-stretching view of a singularly placid champaign, wherein old Norman churches reared themselves above great masses of foliage, and wide-spreading moorlands spread themselves beneath a sky of rare delicacy, and where the glitter of an historic stream, unwinding itself like a blue riband amid the wealth of verdure through which for ages it had cut out its unhindered course, was the only dazzling thing in all that restrained and harmonious English landscape—just that pleasant land of England which Shakespeare has so endeared to us, her loving children, and which, from many points of view, has no parallel upon this earth. And even the very house wherein I sat was redolent of a splendid and a colourful past, with its magnificent kitchens, like the crypt of some great cathedral church, which were actually built in 1175, and wherein, my host told me, a fire had been lit daily and unceasingly for something like seven hundred years, and without failing once—even that house summed up within its stately architecture, which so splendidly dominated the whole widespread scene, the story and the long, long traditions of a race and a nation that had gone forth conquering and to conquer the wide world over.

And this, again, was widely different from a *chota-hazri* at Government House, South Australia, where my hosts were the Acting Governor and the then Premier of the State, and where, most unusual thing in that part of the world, we sat over a fire and drank our tea as comfortably as one would do it by a kitchen fire at home—always, in my experience, the most comfortable place for tea and hot buttered toast in the world, because only in the kitchen can you obtain it in perfection. And Sir Samuel Way, one of the most notable persons I have ever met, a little short Methodist with a grey stubbly beard, and a perfectly delightful sense of humour and the kindliest heart and the most genial nature in the wide world, Chief Justice of his colony and a keenly discriminating lawyer, statesman, and *littérateur*, unfolded his mind on many matters Imperial, and in the doing so he gave me a glimpse into a future which is only to-day being realized.

"Did you warm the teapot before you made the tea, George?" he asked his faithful factotum; "because that is what so few people ever remember to do. I am sure you never do, Kingston," he observed to the Premier, Mr. Charles Cameron Kingston, also a remarkable man, a tall, fine fellow, with a light beard and moustache and a fist to fell an ox, a great friend of mine, a splendidly typical Antipodean statesman, keen, far-sighted, and full of vision and imagination, a man who I think was never as much appreciated as he ought to have been. Mr. Kingston shook his head.

"I am not a great tea-drinker, your Excellency, but I know I shall enjoy that cup."

"Well, Mr. Blathwayt," continued his Excellency, "what do you think of the aborigines?"

"Well, sir," I replied, "it's not so much what I think as what you think that really matters."

"Well," he replied, with startling suddenness and emphasis, "I'll tell you what I have been thinking about in the night, and that is the necessity for a much more frequent and intimate interchange of thought and opinion between ourselves and the Mother Country. I want to see a regular Imperial Council, at which all the Colonies or Dominions, or whatever you call them, may be fully represented, and where they can take their share in the rule and governance of the Empire. We cannot put up for many more years with the present condition of things, nor will the outside world let us. We are bound to have a say in international politics, if only for the safety and welfare of the Empire. We have two great bugbears down here in Australia [this was in 1895] of which you at home have little or no knowledge—Germany's activities in the Southern Seas and Japan's almost inevitable aggressiveness. And, besides, we are growing up; we are passing out of the stage when we speak of missionaries and apostles of Empire, and we are beginning to realize that to effect any real and lasting good we must become active statesmen of Empire, in touch with the very heart and soul of Empire, in intimate, frequent, personal touch. The Empire can no longer isolate itself as a mere conglomeration of colonies; it is now a nation, and must take its place in the comity of nations, and have its share in the rule of the world. I quite own that we can't do without you, but I am almost more certain that you can't do without us. We are not even a Commonwealth yet here in Australia, but I trust that is definitely on the way; but what is still more essential is that a great Imperial Council shall embrace the whole Empire, and give meaning and authority and definite object to all that is meant by the word Empire. I am convinced it will come one day, though I may never live to see it."

And the memory of that *chota-hazri* conversation came to my mind the other day, when I read that this Conference or Council or Imperial Cabinet was at last on the very verge of materialization.

A flying-fish, glittering in the morning sun, splashed itself down at our feet upon the deck of a P. and O. just as a China Inland Missionary and I were settling ourselves down to *chota-hazri* one burning hot morning in the Indian Ocean on our way up to Hong-Kong. He picked it up and flung it back tenderly into the sea, rather to my sorrow, as a flying-fish is one of the rarest dainties one can meet with in the tropics, east or west—and I, who have eaten them in Barbados, know what I am talking about. And then I sat down to eat my toast and study my companion, whom I intuitively realized was a singularly remarkable person. Tall, thin, rather cadaverous, utterly and entirely removed from the world, and trying hard to cultivate an austerity of demeanour which was in vigorous antagonism to a very simple, genial, childlike nature, he nevertheless gave me the idea of being one of the saddest men I had ever met. And later on I realized why this was so. He was a member of that extraordinary society, the China Inland Mission, which, though it does not appear to be theologically connected or knitted up with any special religious body, is nevertheless hostile to the point of insanity towards anything of the Catholic type of mind or practice, whether Roman or Anglican. It visions life generally and the life religious from an almost incredibly narrow point of view, and yet it is devoted and self-sacrificing to a degree that has not been surpassed even by the Jesuits themselves. In a way it has a certain curious affinity, and especially the female portion of the Mission, with some of the rigidly "enclosed" Orders of Catholicism, though wholly without the humanness and the broad-mindedness and the worldly knowledge and sympathies of the Catholic Orders. Its women are apt to be forbiddingly austere, and where the tender aloofness of the Catholic nun is imposed on her by tradition long handed down and the inescapable discipline of the founder, the unpleasing austerity and stern remoteness and condemning demeanour of the female China Inland Missioner is the spontaneous outcome of a very rigid, uncompromising, and frequently, I fear, a naturally unloving heart, prompted, I honestly believe, by vigorous conviction and the comfortable assurance that all without their own narrow circle are hopelessly damned to all eternity. But the men are different, though men and women alike are devoted and self-sacrificing to a point such as has not been surpassed since Christianity was first preached upon this earth.

I had a very interesting conversation with my missionary friend that morning, although I was painfully conscious that his wife and sister, who joined us later on, regarded me, as they regarded every one else on board that vast liner, as lost beyond all hope of redemption. And yet one admired them intensely, in spite of their quite exceptional acerbity of manner and their sublime lack of the really inner and loving spirit of the highest form of Christianity. One admired them because they were so obviously sincere, and one realized that they would face torture, and even death itself, as indeed they had done, a hundred times over sooner than they would prove traitors to their Christ and their creed. They had realized the beauty and the necessity for an ideal; they lived in a world of which the majority of us upon the ship knew and cared nothing whatever. This world and the things of this world meant nothing to them; and often as the careless waltz upon the ship's deck those hot nights in the Indian Ocean swayed the majority of the passengers to and fro beneath that splendid Eastern moon, and the glittering Eastern stars gazed sadly down upon the restless scene, and I caught their rapt gaze penetrating the velvety darkness of the Oriental night, a hesitation used to cross my soul, and the question from unknown depths would arise within me: "Have they not indeed chosen that better part which shall not be taken away from them?"

And as the distant mountains of China sprang up out of the horizon one hot morning I overheard my friend, two of whose relatives lay murdered martyrs in the land we were so fast approaching, say in the words, as he told me afterwards, of Valignani, great Francis Xavier's successor, as he gazed upon the self-same mountains: "O mighty fortress! when shall these impenetrable brazen gates of thine be broken through!"

I was seated one burning morning at sunrise at *chota-hazri* with Norman-Roth, of whom I told you in Chapter XVII, in his bungalow in West Africa, and I put to him the question so many Englishmen ask as to when the natives would be able to have a definite share in the government of their own country; asking the question, however, more for the benefit of the untravelled Englishman, well knowing and approving beforehand in my own mind of what his answer would be. He looked at me and smiled.

"Hullo!" he said, "you've not turned Exeter Hall surely?"

I laughingly shook my head. "Not I," I replied. "I know my savage world better than that."

"I should think you did indeed," he replied; "though I quite appreciate the good heart, and to a certain extent the sound common sense, which prompts the question. But here, even more than in India, it is either white man rule or chaos, though, where we can, we not only recognize native traditions and native custom and native law and ordinances, but we avail ourselves of the advice and services of certain headmen and tried and approved natives. Here, as you can see, we are absolutely in the rough; the natives here are only just slowly creeping out of their stone age. They are where the ancient Britons were three thousand years ago. In Sierra Leone and other parts of the coast which have been long inhabited and governed by ourselves or the Portuguese or the Germans they are much more civilized, as we call it, and many natives take a very definite share in the governance of their own country. But even with them the savage dies hard. I'll give you an instance. There was a certain Queen's Counsel who had actually been knighted by Queen Victoria. Well, one night at a great Government dinner, after he had made a splendid speech, got up in full-dress rig, evening tie and swallow-tails, and with his order glittering on his stiff shirt front, he turned rather wearily as he sat down beside a friend of mine, whilst the whole gathering were loudly applauding his speech, and he said to him: 'I feel that some day I shall take all this off,' pointing to his Western finery and the blue riband of his Order across his chest, 'and put on the old loincloth and fly back to the forest to join my ancestors.' And do you know, that is what he actually did a year or two later. And don't you remember Grant Allen's wonderful little story where the young African Oxford graduate—the Rev. John Creedy—'went fantee,' and abandoned civilization and Christianity and the whole thing? And I myself was on an expedition up-country once, where we had to put down a rebellion, and I came across a stark naked native howling and yelling, with the arms and legs of a native he had killed in battle hung round his neck, as they do in those parts, and I recognized him as a man who had taken classical honours at one of our great universities! It's no good, my dear fellow; the 'man and brother' theory is all very well at a missionary meeting or in the Independent Labour Party, smug and safe in conventional, innocent old London, but out here it is simply suicidal even to think of it. The whole theory of our Empire is based on the superiority of the white man over the black—and don't you forget it!"

As Roth sat there, talking so quietly in the vast stillness of the tropic dawn, I could not but reflect upon the fine type of men to whom we entrust the building up and the maintenance of our Empire. They are a type of whom, thank goodness, I have met many specimens, and they are just the men I most admire and whom I can best understand. You can see any amount of them at a certain West End club any day of the week. There they sit, in vast bunches from various quarters of the world, each representing the Empire in its most interesting and fascinating phases. Men from the Malay Presidency, men from the West Coast or the Gold Coast or Northern Nigeria, men who have spent their lives carving the Empire out of the wilderness of Rhodesia or Nairobi, men from the lonely forests of the Himalayas and soldiers from Secunderabad or Potchefstroom—you scarcely know where they come from. They are very slangy sometimes, and they are apt to be perhaps a little unnecessarily curt in their remarks, and they are learned in many kinds of cocktails, and they talk very little, but when they do you would do well to listen. For these lean, silent, sunburned men, hard as nails, and with abundance of relentless ruthlessness behind their calm exterior, are just the most interesting men you have ever met, and they are just the men it most interests me to meet. They cannot talk half as beautifully and grammatically as did the talking Sanhedrin I used admiringly to listen to in a famous London literary club of which I was once, for two years, a timid and an absolutely speechless member, well realizing my own exceeding unworthiness, but every word they say carves out a cameo from a background of wonderful and actual and vital happenings and experiences. For these men are the builders of that wonderful cosmos that we know as the British Empire ; they are the lineal descendants and successors of the gentleman adventurers of Elizabeth's spacious days and the glorious old buccaneers of Charles's golden reign. I hope they won't catch me a clip over the head for saying all this, but, at all events, they will know that one amongst them at least realizes how worthy they are of all appreciation.

And my talk with Norman-Roth reminds me of another similar chat at *chota-hazri* I once had with the late Sir Trevor Plowden, Lady Lytton's father, when I was staying with him at the Residency at Hyderabad. We were discussing the same question, but under what extraordinarily different conditions and surroundings, as I had discussed with Roth a year or two previously. But in lieu of the forest primeval and of the stone age of that wild and desolate African district, I was surrounded by the magnificent predominance of a civilization thousands of years older than that of Britain herself. Beneath the walls of that splendid Residency, which, indeed, is said to be the finest private house in our Indian Empire, passed in never-ending procession the varied humanities that go to the formation of one of the most fascinating, interesting, and cosmopolitan districts in India. The stately Brahmin, with his long-descended caste marks outlined white and clear upon his forehead, or the crimson-bearded and perchance green-turbaned Mohammedan, or possibly the clever, wily Bengali Baboo, graduate of some famous English university, a haughty Sikh cavalryman, or one of the Nizam's negro soldiers of fortune: they are all there in gorgeous and colourful profusion, and all forming part of the British Empire, just as Norman-Roth's poor African savages had done, and therefore all of them claiming the attention of any one seriously interested in the study of the solution of those innumerable problems which Imperialism is always presenting to us for our puzzlement. And Sir Trevor and I were again discussing the question of the possibility or advisability of native rule.

"It is all," said he, "so much a matter of national tradition and personal ideals. However lofty these people may be at their best, in practice they are apt to fall far short of their own teachings. For instance, to mention only one detail, you will find it difficult, sometimes impossible almost, to get judges or magistrates to sit at a case beyond the usual hour of closing court. They will rise to the minute, even though another hour might mean the release of the accused. But no, they will send him back to his miserable cell sooner than subject themselves to any inconvenience, however slight, which they are not legally compelled to undergo. And in a hundred ways this disregard of other people's rights or other people's sufferings proves to us beyond any shadow of doubt that it would be impossible to entrust them with too great a measure of self-government. And that is what you cannot get the English Radical Member of Parliament to understand, and yet it is just one of the things, one of the main points, upon which the whole of our Indian Empire really depends."

And just at that moment the Vikar-el-Umra, the Nizam's Grand Vizier, came driving up the great sunny and shadowy roadway, with his magnificent cavalry escort clattering behind him, and being a Mohammedan, and therefore independent of the rules of caste, he was able to join us in our early morning meal. The whole scene was so typical of the gorgeous East, and it was such a veritable cameo of Empire, that it has never faded from my memory—a scene, as it were, cut clean out of the Book of Esther or lifted wholesale from the "Arabian Nights," unbelievably rich in history and romance, and full to brimming over with colour and poetry and all the fascination of those stories of Sir Walter Scott's wherein my childhood was so plenteously saturated.

Nearly forty years ago I was seated at *chota-hazri* with a sugar-planter in the hill districts of Trinidad, when suddenly a loud scream rent the air, and immediately afterwards a pistol-shot rang out clear and sharp from a little negro shack in a clearing in the forest. We rushed off to the house, and arrived just in time to see an unfortunate negro girl gasping out her last breath, shot through the heart by her paramour, who had immediately escaped into the almost impenetrable jungle. My friend, who was also a magistrate, got together a posse of fellow-planters and started in pursuit of the murderer, whilst I arranged to take the poor girl's funeral that evening at sunset. Just after my return from the sad ceremony my host re-entered the house.

"Well," I said, "did you catch him?"

"Oh yes, and we've buried him, too," was his startling reply.

"Well, that was appallingly quick work," I said. "But surely you ought to have brought him back for proper trial?"

"So we would have done, of course, had we had the chance," answered my friend, "but he was too quick for us. We chased him for hours, sometimes on his track, sometimes losing it altogether, but about three o'clock we suddenly came across him, quite unexpectedly, in a little clearing, ten or twelve miles away. As soon as he caught sight of us he sat down, put his rifle barrel into his mouth, and shot his head clean away, and we buried him 'all standing,' as they say, just where we had found him. It's rather dreadful to think of those two lovers well and happy together at six o'clock this morning and this evening each of them dead and buried!"

I was leaving New York for England next day, and a wealthy American friend of mine, thinking I was making some stay in that gorgeous metropolis of the West, sent me a card of honorary membership for the Metropolitan Club, commonly known as "the Millionaires' Club." As all my worldly possessions at the moment consisted of my travelling gear, my steamer ticket, and £12 11s. 6d., the idea "tickled me to death," as they say in the Western States, and I flew off very early next morning and ordered myself the most elaborately gorgeous *chota-hazri* that I could think of, determined to live up, as far as it was compatible with my humble means, to my idea of what an American millionaire would be likely to do. I am bound to add I felt myself a most frightful fraud, for I was well convinced that there was not a bell-boy in that dazzling establishment, let alone a waiter, a butler, or a hall porter who was anywhere near as close to the workhouse as I was. How I chuckled!

I recall an exquisite breaking of the dawn upon the veranda of the Galle Face Hotel in Colombo, with the great waves of the Indian Ocean breaking in snowy surf almost at our feet, and the spray dashing in upon our faces with a marvellous sense of refreshment that burning tropic morning, and the palm-trees bending in the splendid breeze, and the metallic cry of a kite, circling magnificently in the far-off blue, thrilling down through the glittering atmosphere, and the impudent grey crows stealing the bread-crumbs from the table, round which were seated Harry de Windt, the explorer, gallant old Sir Alexander Buller, in command of the China Squadron, and myself. And I recall Harry's relation of an amusing incident in which he had once taken part.

"When I was A.D.C. in 1879 to my brother-in-law the Rajah of Sarawak, I travelled inland with him and my sister, the Ranee, to one of the forts in a Dyak country of what was in those days very savage tribes. One evening at the fort there was a war-dance in honour of the Rajah, in which about a dozen Dyaks in full war paint took part. I used to dance this Dyak war-dance very well, as my sister will tell you, so I joined the band of Dyak dancers, without saying anything, stripped myself naked, put on the feather loin covering, then bounded in and danced with the rest—danced like mad! The Rajah and my sister were seated, in great state, on a kind of throne in the large hall where we were dancing, and which was only dimly lit with a few oil lamps, so that you could not distinguish a face at any distance. But the Rajah spotted my light skin against the copper ones of the Dyaks, and he rose from his seat in a towering rage. 'How has that d——d Chinaman got in!' he yelled. 'Throw him out of the fort at once!' I don't think my sister was ever so frightened in her life, though she laughed heartily afterwards."

Just at that moment the sound of a ship's bell striking eight bells floated in across the heaving waters, and immediately afterwards came to us, exquisitely softened and harmonized, the beautiful strains of the Russian National Anthem as played by the band of a Russian man-of-war. And then, after a minute's silence, came across the waves that wonderful morning of Southern splendour, the moving, stately strains of our own National Anthem. The old Admiral sprang to his feet, and we, of course, followed suit, as that unparalleled hymn of Empire, the most stirring and the most memory-haunting and memory-reviving harmony in the world, recalled to us once more the meaning and intention and the all-paramountcy of the English people.

CHAPTER XX

WITH HUGH BENSON IN JERUSALEM

A BURNING Eastern sun poured its rays pitilessly down upon the little village of Bethany, where we lay, Hugh Benson and I, just outside the tomb of Lazarus, too weary to move.

A voice broke the lazy silence.

"Look, my gentlemans, this the house of Simon the Leper ; but Simon very poor man, not live in castle. So most likely this castle built by crusaders."

"But, Joseph ! " I cried in horrified accents ; "this is rank unbelief ! How dare you cast doubt on these old traditions ? "

"Well, my gentleman, what shall I do ? I have to get my bread ; I poor dragoman. I have to tell you these things of old tradition, and then I tell you what I think myself. You can believe what you like, and Mr. Benson, the son of the lord of Canterbury, he believe what *he* like. For me, I only believe in the hills and the mountains ; they cannot tell lies. But come, my gentleman, the sun is going down and we must get back to Jerusalem."

Joseph was a picturesque figure as he stood in his Syrian garb, with clear-cut, handsome features outlined against that cloudless sky : keen and vigorous, witty and humorous, with a flow of anecdote and a power of vivid description and a caustic capacity for characterization which would have enraptured a smart London dinner-party. And always a gentleman, this Arab boy of the unspeakable slums of modern Jerusalem. And yet with a pathos and sense of romance which you might search for in vain in a London boy of the same class, condition, and bringing up. Not the most delicate *nuance* ever passed him by. And a sense of humour such as I have never seen equalled, not even by Hugh Benson himself, who, of all people, was the most supremely gifted in that direction of any one I have ever met. He used to stand open-mouthed as Joseph would meander on, turning to me now and again to stutter out, "G-g-g-gorgeous! perfectly g-g-gorgeous!"

Yes, Joseph was one of the most complete and remarkable characters I have ever known: fearless, outspoken, proud, and independent in every particular.

"To-night," he volunteered, "I go to see my lady. To-night her brother will not be there, so I go. I marry her next month. So, please, my gentlemans, be very quick!"

As we wandered round the Mount of Olives, bathed in the crimson sunset, wherefrom musically tinkled down the monastic call for evensong into the lonely valley, wearied with the heat of the day, I put my lips to a flask of whisky.

"Ah, my gentleman, that very bad for you—you should drink only water," said Joseph, with serious sadness in his wonderful liquid eyes.

But the next day, as we halted for a few minutes by a wayside caravanserai on the long military road to Hebron, Joseph groaned aloud with pain, and I said to him—

"Joseph, you are very much off colour to-day; what is the matter?"

"Too much whisky last night, my gentleman. I very drunk; not possible more drunk!"

"But, Joseph!" remonstrated Hugh Benson, "you, the teetotal lecturer of yesterday afternoon! Impossible!"

"Ah, yes, my gentleman, but that very different. I can speak to other peoples—oh yes! But never can I say 'no' for myself. Always I getting drunk when peoples ask me to have whisky."

An hour or two later, Joseph, feeling much better and with a twist of humour on his flexible lips and a twinkle of merriment in his handsome eyes, volunteered some personal recollections of those whom, for the past few years, he had personally conducted through Palestine and Egypt.

"Once an English lord come to the hotel and engage me for dragoman. Next day I go to the hotel and he standing there and I say, 'Good morning, my lord,' and he look at me and say nothing. So I say again in loud voice, 'Good morning, my lord.' And again he say nothing. Then I say, 'My lord, I 'ave wish you "good morning" twice and you say nothing. You too grand for poor Joseph, you must 'ave a lord for your dragoman. To-day I telegraph to Lord Cromer—I know Lord Cromer [as, indeed, he did]—and Lord Cromer speak Arabic and all language well, and I say to him, "You come and be dragoman for this lord, for I will not."' " And though the peer wellnigh descended to his knees to Joseph, Joseph would no more of him.

"Another gentleman he come and he take me for dragoman, and he say: 'Joseph, we will not spend much money.' So he send me into villages for onions. Always he buy onions and a little bread, never meat or wine or good food, and always I very ill. At last I say one day: 'My gentleman, always I have stomach-ache. Onions very bad for me,' and I leave him alone by the Dead Sea. Two months ago he write me from London: 'Joseph, I coming to Jerusalem again and I want you for dragoman again.' And I write, 'Sir, I going away to America next week.' Well, my gentleman, last month I go down one day to the hotel and I see this gentleman and I afraid to speak, and he say to me, 'Joseph, you said you were going to America!' I say, 'Sir, are you going to stay in Jerusalem?' and he say, 'Yes; three months, Joseph,' and I say, 'Well, sir, I go to America to-morrow.'"

Joseph and our Syrian driver—a huge person, an exact type of the Syrian porter class, many of whom I have seen carrying as much as six huge, heavily laden trunks on their shoulders at once, and one of whom my friend Mr. Connop-Perowne, who knows Palestine as few people know it, declared he once saw clambering up the steps of an hotel in Jaffa with a grand piano on his shoulders—Joseph and our driver laughed much during our drive to

Hebron, and as we sat by the roadside resting, in the midst of the lovely flower-scented wilderness of Judæa, I said to him—

"You and the driver are old friends, Joseph?" To which he promptly replied—

"This driver very bad man. My old grandfather kill his grandfather because he speak very badly to my grandmother. Now one day this driver kill me—only I kill him first. Never shall I forget to kill him." And as he spoke he handed his cigarette-case to the huge, smiling, and utterly unconscious Syrian, who, of course, did not understand what we were saying.

"Are you fond of travelling, Joseph?" asked Benson.

"Always I travel," he replied, "but always I come back to this poor little village," pointing to where Jerusalem lay silver-grey against the blue of the mountains of Moab. "Once you have lived in Jerusalem, always you want to come back to it, and always I think of poor little Jerusalem."

But Joseph could be rather terrible; most Orientals of that type can be. Amongst other things he was a great matchmaker, and he gave us a painful exhibition of his prowess in that direction. The day after our Hebron expedition, Benson and I joined a small party of ladies and gentlemen staying at the hotel on an expedition to the Jordan. I was riding on a few yards ahead of Benson and Joseph, when I overheard the latter say—

"Your friend very old, eh?"

"No," laughed Mr. Benson, "he is just forty."

"Oh no!" replied Joseph, quite seriously. "He forty forty year ago. He eighty. He married?"

"I don't think he is," replied Mr. Benson.

"Well; old girl here; he like marry? She like marry very much. I ask," and he galloped swiftly forward to an old maid who was my special *bête noire*.

"Hi! my lady!" he called out at the top of his voice. "You want marry my gentleman, eh? He old, but very strong husband!"

I caught him up at the moment and *vi et armis* stifled further revelations, which was well; for Joseph, in common with the rest of his race and kind, indulged at times in a kind of humour and in dissertations that would have put Rabelais or the Court of Elizabeth to the burning blush ; as it was it was with flaming cheeks that the poor lady pressed on her steed down the rocky paths that lead to the rapid-flowing Jordan.

At the period of which I speak Mr. Benson was curate of Kemsing in Kent. Even then, though he had not entered upon the literary career, he was an extraordinarily interesting person, full of humour, crammed with original ideas, fearless, independent, and very unconventional. His angle of vision was not the least that from which the typical Anglican curate timidly glimpses that vast welter which we call human life. Hugh Benson was an immensely sincere soul, and yet he was almost visibly willing to allow his vision, where matters spiritual at all events were concerned, to be obscured by the most impossible doctrines and traditions that were quite obviously the outcome of the basest forms of superstition. And this was more obviously in evidence in Jerusalem, perhaps, than it could possibly have been elsewhere. He would accept as gospel what to my mind was absolutely impossible, and he repeatedly failed to realize that certain sacred shrines and sites at which the strictly orthodox were invited to bow their heads, with unquestioning faith, literally lay invisible, as they had done for centuries, thirty feet below the surface of the ground. I can never forget the awe and reverence and the passion of adoration, for instance, with which he entered the "upper chamber" wherein the Last Supper is fabled to have taken place, whereas it was quite palpable that the room had not come into existence for centuries after that most sacred scene in the history of the world had been enacted, on that spot very possibly, but amid totally different surroundings and in a building that had for untold centuries been hidden from human eye.

There is so much that one can believe in in Jerusalem, so much that is obviously genuine, so much that literally jumps to the seeing eye and that appeals to the understanding heart, that it used to argue to me a lack of discernment or power of discrimination, remarkable in so delicately sensitive and susceptible a brain as Benson's obviously was, when he would accept, almost as a necessary doctrine of salvation, utterly false and palpably absurd relics and shrines and traditions that wearied and depressed and disheartened a person like myself by their folly and childishness. Such things cheapened the whole wonder and charm and mystery and beauty of the most wonderful and sacred city in the whole world. For, like Pierre Loti, though I may not believe in much of what I saw, nevertheless the pathos and romance and undying sanctity of Jerusalem pierced my very heart. I remember one day as Benson and I quitted the Garden of Gethsemane, which with the brook Kedron, hard by, is one of the sacred sites concerning which no man with a reasoning head upon his shoulders can have any possible doubt whatever, we were hideously jarred and pained by a number of Cockney tourists who were riding alongside of the holy walls of the garden, screaming out at the top of their raucous voices, "And 'er golden 'air was 'angin' down 'er back," and I turned to Hugh, "Aren't they absolutely indescribable? Do you remember what Pierre Loti says in his exquisite book on Jerusalem when he flies out against '*ces bruyants touristes*'?"

And then we fell into a dissertation as to whether such people possessed either brains to think or souls to feel—coming at last to the perfectly fair and reasonable conclusion that, given the opportunity, every one of those braying trippers would probably, if not almost certainly, prove themselves worthy of the divinity that was so carefully hidden away out of sight within them. It is pure thoughtlessness and ignorance, scarcely more, I sincerely trust, but it jars hideously nevertheless.

> At Pompeii I saw a woman bend
> Above this dead, pronounce an epitaph,
> The mother of a child it may have been.
> Oh, horrible! I heard a woman laugh.

And then, passing the Damascus gate, and leaving the Valley of Jehoshaphat far behind in the rear, we climbed the hill to where the great Franciscan monastery now stands, and lying down beneath the exquisite rose-red wall which Suleiman the Magnificent threw round the sacred city six hundred years ago, we surveyed the beautiful scene. Far in the dim, blue distance the mountains of Moab lay bathed in the sunlight, a flock of sheep outlined itself against the brilliant sky, and the voice of the shepherd calling to his sheep by name came across the long centuries to our ears, and Hugh said, "Isn't that wonderful? 'He calleth His sheep by name, and His sheep hear His voice.'" "Yes, I said, "it so reminds me of what Canon Farrar said to me when I asked him what guide-book he would recommend me for the Holy Land. 'Guide-book?' he said. 'My dear fellow, there is only one guide-book for Jerusalem, and that is the Bible. You will find it is exactly like walking through the pages of the Bible.' And so it is." And then I went on, pointing to "a green hill far away," "Surely that must be Calvary itself?"

"No," he replied, rather regretfully, "I am afraid it isn't. It is inside the Church of the Holy Sepulchre, you know. You haven't been there yet, have you?"

"No," I replied, "I haven't. But what a pity! That is so exactly 'the green hill far away, without a city wall.' And there *is* the city wall; it is exactly outside the Damascus Gate. One could picture the whole procession pouring out of the city and the weary Saviour, after that long walk, fainting just outside the gate."

"Yes, I know," replied Benson, "but tradition is all against it, and Queen Helena is more likely to have known the real site than either General Gordon—after whom this particular hill has been named—or ourselves. Come, let us go down to the Church of the Holy Sepulchre." And so we once again re-entered the Holy City and pushed our way through the pressing crowd—a marvellous Eastern crowd that thronged those wonderfully picturesque bazaars; long, dark tunnels as it were, incredibly ancient-looking, with the sunlight creeping in, here and there, with the effect of piercing golden arrows, illuminating hidden corners of silence and of mystery, and throwing splashes of dazzling brilliance upon the exquisite damasks and carpets, that came from Damascus, and that one encountered in all directions, whilst outside, all the time, in those long, gloomy streets, which mainly consist of slimy, slippery stairways, came pouring down the gorgeously apparelled Oriental crowd: Jews in their gabardines and with the long ceremonial curls hanging down on each cheek, exactly as they did in the days of John and Richard Cœur-de-Lion, and Bedouin Arabs, come in for marketing from Hebron or the hill-country of Judæa, and shepherds and Turkish soldiers, and charming little white Syrian donkeys, or sulky, groaning, grunting camels. And then, oh, wonder of wonders! the sound of the most exquisite, the most unbelievably magnificent singing fell upon our enchanted hearing, and suddenly there burst into view a great crowd of Russian pilgrims, heralded and preceded by their priests, those poor, humble people the Russian moujiks, clad in the peasant costume with which the pictures have made us so familiar, the long hair, the bearded faces, the women, many of them, bent and broken with age and years of suffering and the tears streaming down their cheeks as they caught the first glimpse of that wonderful Church of the Sepulchre of which they had heard and thought and dreamed all their lives long, and to see which they had travelled so many, many weary miles, and starved and saved and agonized so many, many years. One poor old woman fell, almost at my very feet, in a dead faint. And then once more upon the evening breeze there floated out that magnificent chant from the Greek Liturgy, the Kontakion, "Give rest, O Christ," and they pressed wonderingly and yet reverently beneath the dim portals of the most sacred and historic shrine in the world. After a while Hugh Benson and I too entered the church, and he took me at once to the sacred tomb, where, bending down, he kissed the marble stone upon which tradition has it they laid the body of our Lord. I am bound to say nothing on earth appeared less likely or credible to me; for so far as I can recall it, it has no appearance of a tomb rough-hewn out of the hillside, rather it reminds one of a more or less elaborately built-up sarcophagus in an Anglican cathedral. Now, the so-called "Gordon's" site exactly fulfils and realizes one's expectation and imagination. At the same time, I am bound to add that scientific exploration and excavation have demonstrated fairly clearly that the Church of the Holy Sepulchre actually stood just outside the walls of the Holy City, and remains of that wall have been found within recent years just within the precincts of the sacred building. In Benson's mind there was no doubt whatever. Whilst I would wander through the city with to the full as much of the spirit reverential as he possessed, yet it was also with a wistful kind of incredulity or scepticism. He believed, or appeared to believe, everything he was told: my reason, my common sense, bade me doubt almost every particle of tradition as utterly worthless that was forced beneath my notice, either by professional guides or else by Anglican or Roman clergy, who frequently throng the place in large numbers. And I think, as a rule, the High Anglicans would believe anything—in Jerusalem, at all events. They appear to abandon reason and common sense and the evidence of facts absolutely and entirely. Still, that is almost preferable to an action such as that of which one well-known minister was guilty when he deliberately stretched himself at full length, boots and all, in the alleged tomb of our Lord in the Church of the Holy Sepulchre. That was nothing more nor less than an outrage!

It is a curious study in psychology, that which is presented by nations or individuals as to their capacity for reverence and their attitude to what is most sacred in human life. To the ordinary English mind outward reverence in the presence of those things which concern the hidden side of existence is almost impossible. At four o'clock in the afternoon I had seen British Yahoos singing ribald songs outside the Garden of Gethsemane; at six o'clock I had knelt with a crowd of wearied but ecstatic and exquisitely singing Russian pilgrims within the Shrine of the Holy Sepulchre. I have seen British tourists standing jeering and laughing at Mohammedan soldiers prostrating themselves at their evening prayers on the edge of the desert, and I have compared the bearing and attitude of my countrymen with the superb dignity and supreme proud indifference of the Oriental, and marvelled to realize that in each dwells the soul of divinity and that, only too frequently and in many notable respects, even with the lowest of them, the Britisher's soul really is the finest in the end. And again one asks oneself, What is it that constitutes reverence and the jealous care for sacred things? A few years ago I went to the Queen's Hall to see a private view of that magnificent film "From Manger to Cross," which, by the by, was actually taken in Jerusalem itself, and I sat next to Mr. G. R. Sims.

Now, Mr. Sims is nothing if he is not a thorough man of the world, and his paper is nothing if it is not the paper *par excellence* of an absolute man of the world. And yet I will venture to say that there is no paper in England which, though it makes no religious professions whatever, would nevertheless guard more fiercely and more jealously the sacred things and the long-handed-down traditions of the Christian faith than would the *Referee*, or for the matter of that most if not every single one of the great London dailies. At the conclusion of this performance I turned to Mr. Sims and said—

"Well, that was very beautiful, wasn't it?"

"Yes," he replied, "it was beautiful, undoubtedly, but I don't like it. There are some things too sacred for public demonstration, and this is one of them."

I confess I was rather pleased to hear what he had to say on the matter.

Next day warm expressions of approval of the film from such people as the Bishop of London, F. B. Meyer, I think the Dean of St. Paul's, and a host more of the London clergy appeared in the papers, which, however, many of the papers themselves condemned on exactly the same grounds as those upon which Mr. Sims had condemned it. The appeal that Jerusalem makes to the individual man or woman depends upon the individual soul.

Hall Caine once wandered through the Holy City bewailing to me all its hideous squalor and the dirt, disease, and poverty of its population; he loathed its superstition, he hated the silly fables and traditions by which its most sacred spots are desecrated and overladen. He could see no good nor charm in it at all. And yet he who could deny Hall Caine the possession of the most absolutely religious and reverential type of soul, though as absolutely unorthodox, simply doesn't even begin to know the man at all. I often wonder, though, why certain people ever do go to Jerusalem, or, indeed, to any place of the kind. The bars are very inferior, and I don't know of a single billiard saloon in the whole place, whilst it would be wellnigh impossible to get the Starting Prices within the shadow of the Jaffa Gate. But yet they do go, and sometimes they are such absolute fish out of water that they compel one's sense of humour almost to the point of hilarity. Hall Caine was out of place there, undoubtedly, but that was owing to excessive refinement of soul. All that he saw of poverty and misery went to his very heart and rendered him perfectly wretched. But Hugh and I happened across a certain young man who was so gorgeously inappropriate to the occasion that one could only look on and wonder what would happen next. It happened on this wise. Benson and I had driven out to Bethlehem, and half-way along the road we stopped at Rachel's Tomb to survey the magnificent scene, spread far and wide around us. There beneath our feet lay those selfsame fields wherein was once enacted the pretty and deathless love story of Ruth and Boaz and where, centuries later, "shepherds watched their flocks by night, and glory shone around." The day had been rather dark and stormy and great purple clouds rolled up from distant Carmel, but just as we halted for our rest the sun burst brilliantly through and the whole landscape was bathed in splendour. In the far distance one discerned Jerusalem, like a city carved in ivory, outlined against the dark blue hills and presenting exactly that wonderfully cameo-like appearance with which we are all so familiar in the dainty little paintings that so exquisitely characterize a mediæval Florentine missal. Beside us was the tomb, standing over the very place where Jacob buried Rachel, amid the long, loud lamentations of the Children of Israel four thousand years ago, and ahead of us lay the ancient and sacred city of Bethlehem—a moment and a scene one would imagine sufficient to call forth the loftiest sentiments in any one possessing, even in the remotest degree, a heart or a soul. And at that moment the silence was broken with, "I beg your pardon, but could you oblige me with a light?" and, turning, I beheld the most typical Society Englishman that you could possibly imagine. I had some matches with me, but no box, so, calmly walking aside, our friend coolly and casually struck a match against Rachel's Tomb, lit his cigarette, and then observed—

"Jerusalem's a stiff old hole to stay in for long—don't you think so? And we've no billiard-table at the hotel, which makes it ten times worse."

I looked at him and I said: "Well, don't you take any interest in all these—well, buildings and traditions and tombs and everything, you know?" I concluded very lamely, for I was paralysed by such superb unconsciousness, the more so that Hugh Benson was quivering with laughter in my rear.

"Well, sir," he said, "I've no use for that kind of thing whatever! It all bores me as stiff as the lady who they tell me is buried here." And he flung himself wearily down at my feet.

He turned out to be the son of a very well known Cabinet Minister and a thorough good fellow, who never got annoyed even when, having been mourning the Criterion bar, I told him he had better get back there as speedily as possible.

"But I'm going on to Japan," said he.

"So am I," I replied.

"We'll go together," he answered.

And we did. We went through India together; but I don't think he ever troubled even to get up to see the Taj. The whole of his time he spent in billiard-rooms and drinking-bars, and I well remember one day, months after the scene at Rachel's Tomb, he and I were travelling together from Tokyo to Kioto and all one wonderful afternoon we ran round that magnificent mountain Fuji-Yama till at sunset there was such a glory of crimson, such an unearthly glow upon the eternal snow that enshrouds that marvellous summit, that I saw the tears rise unbidden to the eyes of more than one of the English onlookers travelling in the train that day. My friend was deep in bridge, as he had been all day, with a party of men as thoughtless and as apparently soulless and as hopelessly inartistic and unimaginative as himself.

"Come and look at this, Jack," said I, in the faint hope that the unspeakable glory of the heavens would appeal to him.

"Bother you!" he said. "You'll put me off altogether. I hate your old sunsets!"

It is hopeless, quite hopeless, trying to reach the souls of some people, and yet this fellow was delightful from many points of view—a wonderful sense of quite unconscious humour and good-hearted and generous to the point of folly. I got to love him, the more especially that he kept me laughing the whole time I was with him, which was for many months, as we travelled together all through India and Japan and Ceylon. Benson even in the few days that they were together in Jerusalem learned to love him. I can never forget one night going suddenly into the little hotel dining-room just within the Jaffa Gate and beholding an astonishing spectacle. There was Hugh Benson and this young man seated, one on each side of the table where we all three had our meals together, hacking one another under the table for all they were worth.

"Hullo!" I said. "What on earth are you two fellows up to?"

"Oh," said Hugh, "don't you remember how fond the little chaps at school were of hacking a boy who took the last piece of bread and butter at tea? I was showing Jack how solemn and intense and earnest they always used to be. No hurry, no excitement; simply b-b-breathless intentness!"

That was Hugh Benson all over! In some respects I don't think I ever met a more charming character than Hugh's. Father Martindale's "Life" gives a marvellously true picture of him. As I read it I could often fancy I heard Hugh talking. I could hear his delighted chuckle when anything appealed to his sense of humour, and that was certainly every quarter of an hour. But I think Father Martindale has a little missed or lost sight of his wonderful tenderness of heart and soul; perhaps he lost that quality as he grew older, though I must confess I never thought so myself, and I kept up my friendship with him almost to the last days of his life.

He was so kind-hearted and helpful too. I was very unwell whilst in Jerusalem, and I was also greatly disabled by a broken right arm. He acted as my amanuensis the whole time; no light matter, as I had many letters to write and several articles, which he would insist on taking down at my dictation. One day I complained of the cold, and he went down and returned with a huge scuttle laden with coal and wood and very soon had a brilliant fire burning in the little stove. In the middle of his labours some new visitors entered the room, a handsome elderly white-bearded man—"like one of the Apostles," whispered Hugh to me—and three or four rather pretty and very charming girls, the eldest of whom at once set to work to help Hugh light the fire, and the two had great fun over it. In the course of conversation it turned out that the old gentleman was Mr. Richard Cadbury, and the girl who helped with the fire was the very girl who subsequently married Mr. Alexander, the missioner who became so famous under the designation of Torrey and Alexander. But I think the most amusing episode in connection with Hugh Benson in Jerusalem occurred at Bishop Blyth's. One day Hugh came home and said, "The Bishop has asked us both to dinner to-morrow night." So upon the following evening at the appointed hour we walked down to the episcopal residence and were shown into the drawing-room, where we found the Bishop and his family gathered together. And more delightful people than Bishop Blyth and his family it would be difficult to meet. Every one loved them. Rather to our surprise they appeared obviously surprised to see us, but they welcomed us most kindly, and we started a difficult and laboured conversation, all the more laboured that it was quite evident something had gone wrong. And then the dinner-gong sounded, and Mrs. Blyth and her daughters had a whispered conference, although no one, much to my puzzlement, made a move for the dining-room. At last Mrs. Blyth said—

"We were just going in to dinner, Mr. Blathwayt. I hope you and Mr. Benson will be able to join us, though I fear you must be satisfied with pot-luck."

I replied: "Thank you very much. Mr. Benson asked me to dinner here to-night. Didn't you, Benson?"

Mr. Benson, who was busily discussing the ritual of the Greek Church with the good Bishop, turned round and said: "I beg your pardon; I didn't quite catch what you said."

"Well," I replied, "you asked me to dine here to-night."

"Oh, I see," said Mrs. Blyth; "but it was to-morrow night we were expecting you."

Benson struck hastily and anxiously in: "May we come again to-morrow night, Mrs. B-B-Blyth?"

We all laughed, and both our host and hostess replied—

"Come every night. We shall be only too pleased."

A silly, simple little incident, but it amused both Hugh and the Blyths and myself immensely, the more so that he was so delightfully unconcerned.

Hugh Benson was characterized always by an entire absence of gaucherie or self-consciousness; never was a man less of a snob in all this world and never was a man blessed with so manifest a sense of all that is well-bred and everything that implies real refinement and good taste than he; he never made one feel awkward, he never annoyed one, and though in a way very eager and dashing and impulsive, he never got on one's nerves. As I have frequently remarked, he had a perfectly gorgeous sense of humour, to use his own favourite phrase, and he was always a keen and delighted onlooker at the drama or the comedy of human life. He loved "characters"; he could even find a quiet satisfaction in the study of stupidity, if it was stupid enough. He could enjoy a joke all to himself. On one occasion he was shifting the piano in his rooms at Cambridge. Suddenly a singularly dense and stupid friend of his dashed into the room. He stopped short when he saw Hugh struggling with the heavy piano.

"What are you doing?" he bleated.

"Oh," replied Benson, "I am taking it down the town to be tuned."

"Wouldn't it be better to ask the tuner to come up here?" was the idiot's superb comment.

I recall with great amusement the unutterable dismay with which Hugh and I one day confronted a Latin priest in the Via Dolorosa who, speaking neither English nor French, solved, or rather attempted to solve, the difficulty by resort to the tongue of Virgil and Julius Cæsar. Apart from the fact that his pronunciation of Latin was very naturally and most properly that of the Continent, as opposed to the bald simplicity of the Anglican Latin of Hugh Benson and myself, neither of us could put half a dozen words together that bore any relation either to sense or syntax. "How p-p-p-perfectly d-d-d-dreadful!" stuttered my delightful friend. "I wouldn't have come to P-P-P-Palestine had I known this was waiting for me!" And we shook dismayed heads at the puzzled and good-natured priest, who was really anxious to help us and to answer our questions, and incontinently fled.

"I always hated study and scholarship—*exact* scholarship, anyway," said Benson; "but I confess a little more Latin would have been useful with that good man."

I remember on another and a totally different occasion I was caught out in a very similar manner. I had landed at the Piræus with a very dear old friend of mine and a contemporary of my father's at Cambridge—the late Archdeacon Emery, the father of the Church Congress—his daughter, and a brilliant young rector, who also was of the party. An Athenian newspaper boy handed us that morning's paper. I grieve to say that the Archdeacon, the rector, and I were all stumped by it, bowled middle wicket; we stood speechless and dismayed in its reproachful presence until Miss Emery took it from our hands and read it out, translating as she went as easily as though it had been the *Daily Mail* or the *Daily Telegraph!* I only mention these two incidents by way of illustrating my contention that "exact" scholarship is but rarely found even in what are sometimes humorously termed "the learned professions." The Archdeacon was, I believe, a High Wrangler, but neither Benson nor the young rector nor myself possessed the slightest pretensions to anything approaching really first-class classical attainments. It was a subject Benson discussed with me more than once and over which he often grew quite amusingly indignant and impatient.

A few months after his passing over to Rome I was talking over the matter with Hugh Benson, and I asked him what his general feelings and experiences were like. "Well," he replied, "it's just like coming out of a very still, quiet, foggy little sitting-room, with all the windows close shut and a big fire burning and a cat lying on the hearthrug and an old lady fast asleep in an arm-chair, with her glasses slipping down over her nose, and a stillness so deep that you can hear the coal-dust dropping in the grate, and then going right out on to the top of a hill with the winds blowing from every quarter all at once and you have to shout out at the very top of your voice to make yourself heard at all, and there is nothing but a rush of life and hope and energy and inspiration. And, besides, it is all so human; it's an epitome of humanity; there is nothing timid and conventional and respectable and middle-class about it. It's for the Neapolitan beggar at the cathedral gate and for the king on his throne. Catholicism knows no distinction of persons and Anglicanism thinks of nothing else."

It is a curious fact that at the time of our visit to Jerusalem Hugh Benson was much more attracted by the ritual of the Greek Church than he was by the Latin service. Why, I don't know. The Greek appeared to me to be infinitely more overladen with the most impossible superstitions and the priests to be socially and intellectually and from the very practical view of personal cleanliness far inferior to the Latin priests ; to pass, as we did in the Church of the Holy Nativity, straight from the gorgeous and overpowering incense-laden ceremonial of the Greek service to the quiet, modest, restful office of the Latins was like passing from High Mass at St. Alban's on an Easter Day to the Quaker meeting-house in the Sabbath stillness of Bishopsgate on the first day of the week. Why Benson liked it so much I never could understand. We often discussed these and sundry matters as we lay, as we were fond of doing, upon the side of the Mount of Olives and gazed down upon the Holy City, spread gloriously out before us.

How exquisite that scene—the most famous and classic in the long history of humanity ! There was the rose-red wall of Suleiman, wonderfully broken up here and there, marvellously artistic in the harmony of its outline and its wonderful colouring, with its superb mediaeval gateways ; and there, too, the Mosque of Omar, perhaps the most perfect piece of architecture in the world, and hidden away in the background the Jews' wailing-place, wherein their sorrowing and lamentation, though ceremonially ordained, is nevertheless so genuine that I have seen the tears raining down their poor, thin, worn cheeks ; and you catch a glimpse of the Tomb of Absalom, whereon to this day the passing Jew casts a stone in token of his horror of his unfilial conduct ; and far beneath us lay the little Garden of Gethsemane, with its grey and ancient olive-trees, beneath one of which it is just possible our Lord passed His night of agony. We used to lie and drink all this in : the wonder of it and the beauty, the majesty, and the deathless romance of it.

It appeared as a very epitome of the history of the world! And we would discuss the story that is most wrapped up in it and for how long that story would continue to be told. And I remember one day our conversation fell upon that curious evolution of Christianity the modern Anglican bishop. Between us I think we knew every bishop on the Bench, and we discussed them at length. I was quite frank with him. I said—

"I remember seeing your father once drive away in a very grand carriage from a garden-party at Marlborough House, and I couldn't but smile as I thought of our Lord and John the Baptist, with his rough wooden cross and little coverlet of sheep's wool, going to a smart London party in the height of the season."

And Benson laughed heartily and said, "How St. John Baptist would have hated it! though I doubt if he would have been admitted." And then he went on: "But, of course, I see your point. As a matter of fact, you know, people run down the Archbishop with his £15,000 a year and his palace and his carriage and all that, but really he is often more hard up than otherwise. I assure you the position takes so much keeping up that £15,000 a year, though I own it appears enormous, is barely enough. Often enough my father had to meet extra expenses out of his own private money."

Hugh Benson and I parted the day following this conversation, but I never lost sight of him. I used to go and stay with him in Kemsing, and I frequently met him when he was living with Bishop Gore in Westminster Abbey. We were friends to the last, and when the Editor of *Everyman* asked him to name a personal friend who might write a character sketch of him for his paper he wrote me as follows—

"Will you do it? There is not one of my friends who knows my views better than you do or would do it with greater sympathy."

And so I wrote it, only eighteen months or so before his lamented death. He was a rare and beautiful soul. I have never met one quite like him, and I do not suppose I ever shall. Though he was my junior by some fifteen years or so, and though he possessed the gift of faith to a far greater extent than it has been granted to me, we were in more complete concord than almost any two people I have ever met, and I sorrow to this day over the untimely death of one of the purest and bravest souls I have ever known.

MR. H. B. IRVING

CHAPTER XXI

MYSTICISM, MATERIALISM, AND MESMERISM

I FORGET how the conversation first began at luncheon that day, but I rather fancy it was started by Mrs. Alfred Curzon telling us some interesting happenings or coincidences in connection with crystal-gazing, of which a friend of her's had recently had a close personal experience. It appeared she had encountered a certain crystal-gazer who had informed her that what he saw in the crystal at the moment of conversation were some hideous and terrible leonine heads, fierce rows of teeth, and a crown. Well, so far all right ; but a week or so later this lady paid a visit to —— Palace, and, seated in one of the great staterooms, she happened to raise her eyes, when she was immediately confronted by the lions' heads *and* the teeth *and* the crown. She mentioned this to Lady ——, and a crystal was produced, and looking into it, the lady, after a while, dimly discerned a long hospital ward, white beds, white-capped nurses, and all.

"That is curious," observed Lady ——, "for I was just thinking of my nephew, who is in hospital at this very moment."

"Now," said Mrs. Curzon, "what I want to know is, how was her thought conveyed to my friend's mind without a single word being spoken?"

"Well," ventured Mr. Algernon Blackwood, who was seated at the table, "that opens up such a big question that it is hopeless to attempt to settle it at a luncheon party. Still, we may speculate on it to a certain extent. You know how wonderfully news, which is, after all, but a tangible expression of thought, travels in Africa or in India, where the bazaars know everything that is happening thousands of miles away before even the official circles hear of it. Don't you think that in time we may reduce all this to a scientific method of communication? I will try and explain exactly what is in my mind. Thought appears to me to be dynamic; that is, with every thought an actual force leaves the brain, and all force acts via wave vibrations. Now, as you know, the one teaching common to all forms of new belief to-day —the new mysticism, in short—is that thought is dynamic, and more important even than acts, since an act is merely the result of a thought."

"It seems to me," said a clergyman who was present, "that must surely, in the long run, lead to the belief that prayer is actually scientific, which is what I have been trying to teach for years."

"I think so," replied Mr. Blackwood; "and if once this action got into the pulpits and churches as a living reality you would find that the effect would be revolutionary. It is what we want to-day, an idea like that, which would do more good, because it probes deeper, and is really more scientific, than a whole succession of National Missions on the very conservative and rigid lines on which this National Mission is being held. The truth of the matter is, ordinary religious forms are crumbling, and if the Churches want to get up to date, if they are really to keep in touch with the needs and hopes of everyday people, they will have to strike out on new lines altogether."

"Don't you think we are getting a little bit away from the idea we started with?" said our hostess, one of the cleverest and most thoughtful women of the day. "I do want to follow up that idea of thought transference, as I suppose it is called. I think, with Novalis, that man began in instinct and he will end with instinct. Which is why, perhaps, animals are more sensitive to the supernatural, or even to the actual, whilst yet it is a great way off, than any human beings can ever be. Look at horses, how they tremble passing through a road said to be haunted, or in the African bush when not even a leaf is stirring. And how often we have heard of late of animals being very uneasy hours before a Zeppelin raid has actually taken place, or 'materialized' one had better say in the present connection."

"Quite right," said Mr. Blackwood. "That is why I would always hold that as we grow wiser, or the more we 'cast back' to primitive conditions, the more we will discover the true place of intuition in the whole theory of life. In a book I once wrote I chose to embody some of my chief characters in the form of centaurs, because their animal bodies, symbolical of instinct, were combined with the brain of the human being. And all are moving towards Deity—that is, towards the highest. I wish we could recover our lost powers, such as we undoubtedly possessed in the days when the world was very young and we were close to Nature; and yet I don't want to lose reason, which is the outcome of our later civilization. Of course I am thinking now in whole æons of time. This is a truth which we can see actually illustrated in children to-day, who, quite unconsciously of course, are far nearer the big things than we are. My heart sinks at every new invention. We had strange knowledge in the primitive days of the woods and the hills and the streams which we have altogether lost through sheer reason. Now, I want to reconstruct all that. I feel like Walt Whitman felt when he spoke of 'the friendly and flowing savage.' Who is he? Is he waiting for civilization, or is he past it and mastering it?"

"That's the whole crux of the matter," said Mr. H. B. Irving, who had been listening with the keenest attention. "Some one says that civilization is a disease, and that no nation ever gets past it—it simply dies of it; and some one else has said that no nation ever has overcome civilization, for it has always succumbed to it. I often think that the more we are civilized and the more we trust to mere reason the farther we get from the simple thing called truth, and which is yet the most complex and sometimes, I honestly think, the most difficult thing to attain, to understand, and to master that there is in the whole of life."

"Exactly," said Blackwood; "I feel that too. I always think of man as a little speck in the midst of enormous things; but I can't help thinking that there is a new power, a new teaching coming into this world, and that this dreadful war is, as it were, the birth throes of a new attitude. Quite deep down in me, almost beyond the place where I can find words, I have a profound conviction that this war has to do with the birth of a new age altogether, and at present the only sign of that new age is the very great and remarkable increase of human sympathy. And this will give us an absolutely new vision of life, another outlook altogether from anything we have ever even dreamed of before. Every one to-day is forced out of himself and is compelled to look over the hedge to see what is going on elsewhere, and in this way we may arrive at truth."

"Yes," replied Irving; "but I didn't quite mean that. I wasn't regarding truth in so far away and so exalted and so abstract a fashion as that. I meant that it is almost impossible to get at the truth in ordinary everyday life. It is difficult to think it, to speak it, to expect it in other people. I suppose it is convention, our habitual conventions, our whole conceptions of existence. We don't live true lives. We display one side to one person and another to another and a third we never show to any one but to the reflection in the looking-glass, and he's so dreadful sometimes that we don't even like to look him full in the face. Well, where's the truth in ourselves when we are so confoundedly multiple?"

"Why, Mr. Irving," said our hostess, "you must be thinking of that dreadful play of yours, 'Dr. Jekyll and Mr. Hyde.' It always made me creep with horror."

"Precisely," replied the famous actor-manager; "but that play embodied a far greater truth and a far commoner truth than most people realize. Nearly everything in that play was true—if we regard it from the psychological point of view and from the point of view of the very upper-class scientist or physician who has carefully studied the question of human psychology. Do you remember that in Stevenson's book, from which, of course, my play was constructed, he speaks of Hyde stamping in rage upon the quivering body of a child in his path? Lots of people said that was simply rot, the outcome of a diseased and morbid imagination. Well, all I can tell you is this. I once knew a brilliant writer, to the world a charming personality, and, curiously and contradictorily enough as it turned out, he was also a great philanthropist. And once, in the dead of night, that man confessed to me that he dare not be left alone with a baby, because he always had an inexpressible longing to crush the life out of its body. The truth of the matter is Hyde lurks in a number of Jekylls. Canon —— declared from the pulpit many years ago, when Stevenson first published his book, that 'every man is a Jekyll and Hyde.' As a matter of fact it was absolutely true of himself."

A clever young physician, who had borne no part in the conversation hitherto, but who is frequently consulted by authors and dramatists upon questions of this nature, here struck in with the remark—

"Well, what you all seem to regard as purely spiritual and psychic I should be inclined to attribute rather to actual physical and material causes. What I mean is this: human character has an actual physical basis. It actually depends upon the physical conformation of the cortex of the brain whether we live the life of a sinner or a saint."

"Well," I ventured to remark, for I am the poorest and most inept of all the conversationists I ever met, "with many of us our whole life is one vigorous struggle to keep out of prison, the workhouse, or the grave."

"That's rather a grim rendering of my theory," replied the doctor; "but I don't know that it's so very far from the truth—which is generally unpleasant. But what I feel is the enormous importance of the apparently insignificant. An East End mother, for instance, feeds her three months old baby on gin and bacon, and a half-developed brain with a death on the gallows is frequently the inevitable end. The conformation of some people's brains is such that they cannot do anything else but commit the crime it impels them to commit."

"Yes," said Mr. Irving, "and often for such a terribly, pitiably trivial a cause. I once saw a man who had murdered a young couple with their infant in order that he might possess himself of a little shop in a London slum."

And then our hostess made us all laugh.

"I think I had better get my crystal out and try to see something a little bright and hopeful in it. You are all getting dreadfully morbid in your search for the truth."

"Ah!" said the clergyman, "I don't know that even an optimistic crystal leads us nearer to truth; I am quite sure it often lands us far short of happiness. At all events, I know Planchette does. I'll tell you of an experience I once had," he continued, as he helped himself to a glass of port and leaned confidentially forward, as he who has a good tale to tell. "I once invested my humble earnings in a wonderful and a very artistic concern, and a really genuine one, too, for the matter of that, which was being converted into a big company. I went to see the promoter one day, and we had a long talk—a very learned talk—on art and the Stock Exchange and the price of shares and the condition of the market and Consols and everything financial you could think of. And at last I said to my business friend—

"'So you think it all promises well?'

"'Promises well!' he cried. 'Look here, my boy. Do you believe in these clairvoyantes? You don't? Well I do, and so do thousands of men on the Stock Exchange.' (And so they do," remarked the parson parenthetically.) "And then my friend went on: 'I sent one of my old gloves to a wonderful person in Bond Street, and two days later she sent me a letter.

"'"You are interested in a great scheme," she wrote. "I can't quite make out whether it's art or business or Stock Exchange shares or what it is, but anyway it will turn out beyond your fondest hopes. You are going on a long voyage; you will see great people; you will revolutionize many lives."'

"Heavens!" sighed the parson, "I know that was true, for he simply turned mine topsy-turvy!"

"'And sure enough,' said my business friend, 'I did go a long voyage, though I had no idea of it when I consulted the clairvoyante, and I did meet a lot of great people, and my own life is absolutely changed from what it was, and I believe the whole thing will be a brilliant success.'

"So I bought five hundred shares at par straight away. Curiously enough that very night I went out to dinner with some friends, and later on in the evening I told them what I had done.

"'You were stupid,' said my hostess; 'you ought to have consulted our Planchette first. However, it may not be too late yet. Let's have a try.'

"So the Planchette board was produced. My host and hostess sat down. They were not in the least psychic or mystical people; they were just ordinary Society people, particularly well bred and well connected, with an absolutely fanatical horror of anything *outré* or eccentric or anything approaching spiritualism—very common-sense, and he, in particular, was, if anything, rather ultra-sceptical than not; just thoroughly nice, ordinary people, but all the same with a fixed belief in Planchette.

"So we started the old thing going, and it answered every question for all the world like a human being. In fact, it went out of its province altogether several times, and got so excited and so emphatic and so joyously optimistic that we could scarcely contain ourselves.

"'Is this company going to be a success?'

"'Greatest on earth,' was the reply, spelt out swiftly and eagerly upon the board.

"One thing in its favour was it didn't drop any 'aitches,' which so many of these kind of machines and people, or whatever you call them, are in the habit of doing, and it used no lurid language.

"'How will the shares go?' I asked.

"'They'll be £200 a share before Christmas,' was the immediate answer.

"Well, putting that and my friend's old gloves together, what more *could* I ask?"

"And what are the shares to-day?" said our hostess.

"You can have mine at 3d. a share," gloomily replied the parson, "and welcome, and I'll be glad of the money."

"So you don't believe in crystals and clairvoyantes and planchettes at all?" continued the lady of the house.

"No, I confess I don't," replied the parson; "but I've enjoyed our conversation enormously, and I am sorry if I've damped any one's enthusiasm or endangered their simple faith."

As we rose from the table I went up to the clergyman and I said: "Do you know, I was in the court last year when you were in the witness-box and gave that evidence about Planchette. I never heard a judge laugh so much in my life."

The parson smiled. "Yes, and wasn't he funny about it too? Weren't you sitting near the solicitors' table? I seem to remember your face."

"Yes," I replied. "I was there with Mortimer Menpes the artist. But what the papers missed! I don't think there was a single reporter in the court."

"Well, you see, luckily for me, it was a Chancery case, and I dare say they thought an order for winding-up wouldn't afford much scope for copy."

"Did you get your case?" I asked.

"Well, so far that the judge wouldn't allow the company to be wound up, as he thought there was a chance of everything coming right when the war was over. I don't think he is quite such a convinced optimist as Planchette, for instance, but we have to appear again six months after peace has been declared. Perhaps that isn't saying much. I think, however, the court enjoyed itself enormously that day."

Closely allied to these mysteries of the crystal and the dual personalities and all the many mystic phases of human life is the subject of mesmerism, of which I have had only one experience in my life, but it was so remarkable that I think I may well record it here. A friend and myself were members of a large house-party at Haverholme Priory a good many years ago, during the lifetime of the late Lord Winchelsea. Staying in the house also was Colonel Edgar Larking, a younger brother of Colonel Cuthbert Larking, a well-known Court official in the days of Queen Victoria. One evening at dinner the conversation turned upon mesmerism and hypnotism, and my friend Alaricus Delmard and Colonel Larking had a great argument about it. At last Larking said—

"Well, Delmard, I will engage to throw you into a mesmeric trance, and you shall do everything I wish you to. Will you accept the challenge?"

"Very good," replied Delmard; "but I think you will fail."

I must mention that neither Lord nor Lady Winchelsea, being at another table, knew anything of what had taken place. At ten o'clock, the hour of a cotillion dance which Delmard had got up, he and Larking and myself went into Lord Winchelsea's study, and in two minutes or so Colonel Larking had actually thrown Delmard into a deep trance.

"Now get up," he said, "go into the ballroom and select your partner, dance with her, and at the end of the cotillion distribute the presents and prizes."

Rather dreamily, but still not noticeably so to any one who was not in the secret, Delmard did exactly as he was told. He went through a number of extremely intricate figures in the dance, then he distributed the favours and presents and prizes to those who had won them, and then he began to get a little vague. So Larking went up to him and said, quite casually—

"Come and have a drink in the smoking room, Delmard."

Delmard accompanied the Colonel to the smoking-room, and then Larking tried to bring him back to earth again, and for a time his efforts were in vain.

Just at that moment Lord Winchelsea came in. He was rather annoyed.

"I wish you hadn't done this, Larking," he said. "If

I had known of it I should not have permitted it. I don't like these queer dodges."

And then he left the room, and Larking made some vigorous passes. Delmard, to our great relief, slowly and dreamily came back to full consciousness, and expressed the greatest surprise to learn the cotillion was over, and absolutely refused to believe us when we told him of the leading part he had taken in the evening's proceedings.

It was interesting to me mainly because it was purely spiritual and mental; there were no tangible or visible or material aids and paraphernalia as in the case of crystals and old gloves and the like.

As I walked home from that luncheon party I turned over in my mind the interesting conversation that had taken place, and I found myself wondering concerning the curious tendency of the human mind to associate the spiritual with the material, its apparent inability to grasp the one without the assistance, as it were, of the other—the crystal, the old, well-worn glove, the board and pencil of Planchette. It appeared to me to be so closely associated, as it were, with the Ju-ju of the West African forest. You stick a cock's feather into the ground and no native dare remove it or pass within the tabooed and, therefore, consecrated ground under pain of wasting away, disease, and death. You try to get out of it by saying that it is only a form of government, an order of the police as it were. Yes, but how about Ju-ju being placed on a white man who refuses to believe in its superstition, and who defiantly removes the cock's feather, and who is overtaken by all the horrors it symbolizes and threatens! and I am credibly informed this has often happened.

What is this curious relation between the appallingly and momentously spiritual and the ludicrously trivial and unimportant material?

You find this connection, in one form and another, worked out in almost all religions, in all ages, and among all people.

May I not suggest, in all reverence, that you find a hint of it, a kind of parallel, a survival of it, as it were, in the Sacraments and mysteries of the Christian religion: the water in baptism, the bread and wine in the Holy Communion, the ring in marriage.

It appears almost impossible for the human mind to grasp the purely spiritual without the aid, as it were, of the material. And of what nature is the otherwise common-sense, very material, and commercial mind of the British Stock Exchange merchant, or the keen, hard-headed soldier, or the quick-witted barrister and ordinarily unsentimental man of affairs that he should be affected by or should attach importance to such superstitious trivialities?

CHAPTER XXII

THE THINGS WE REMEMBER BEST

ONE of the most charming and enduring memories of my life centres round a fluffy little white toy rabbit which beat a drum and which I always took to bed with me. I loved that rabbit more than anything else on earth—at the time—but, then, I was only two and a half years old. That is my first memory; it may quite possibly be my last. That was a great event in my life, but quite frequently I have discovered that in later life it is the comparatively unimportant thing that lingers delightfully on when the most important events of life or travel have faded into the world of oblivion. And this has brought me to a realization of the great fact that there is no such thing as the unimportant in a man's life; we can never tell what apparently small occurrence may not eventuate in great results. And one discovers this kind of thing in travel more frequently and directly than in any other way. The thing which we have most eagerly anticipated is dissipated in nothingness almost before realized, whilst that unimportant thing of which we may never even have heard, materializes with vast results or lingers in the mind when all else has long been forgotten.

And these unexpected and delightfully lingering memories constitute with me a kind of cinematographic record of the most interesting portions of my wandering life. Take Japan, for instance, which I visited twenty years ago, and my chief memory of the Land of the Rising Sun does not centre round the great maker of modern Japan, Prince Ito, the Premier, of whom I saw a good deal, so much as it is concerned with a Japanese travelling valet whom my companion, a well-known artist, and myself had engaged in the innocent expectation that he would confine his services to buying our railway tickets and looking after our wardrobe and generally attending to our comfort and well-being. Vain hope!

We had engaged him, at a high price, as our valet and our guide; he employed us as his unpaid and overworked tutors in the art, the languages, the literature, and the science of modern Europe. He was, I can quite honestly declare, the most relentlessly discouraging and remorselessly disconcerting person I ever met, or my friend either. He could make hopeless fools of us at a moment's notice. Let me give an instance. At the hotel in Tokyo we English and American visitors were in the habit of gathering together after dinner in the reading-room, where we used to sit in dead silence and read the papers. One evening—I recall it well, and I can actually see the people round the table busy reading—the following amusing incident occurred. There sat the two Bishops, one of Osaka, Dr. Awdry, and one of South Tokyo, Dr. Bickersteth; next to them the present Lord Islington and Lord Grimthorpe (then Mr. Ernest Beckett), who were travelling together and making vast purchases of the most exquisite curios; there, too, was Mr. Herbert Raphael and his wife; old Lord Dormer, a frequent visitor to Japan in the nineties; Canon Pleydell Bouverie; several very pretty American girls; altogether a notable assemblage. Silence reigned supreme, so deep that you might have heard the proverbial pin drop. I was standing by the fireplace, lost in delightful contemplation of my wonderful tour and what was to come, when suddenly there rang out, clear and loud and wholly unabashed, the remorseless voice I dreaded most on earth. At once every head was raised in joyous expectancy, for only too well known, alas! were the disconcerting results of that voice among our travelling companions. The two bishops especially appeared to revel in my attitude of torture.

"My lord," said my guide and valet—he always called me "my lord," it was the only thing I liked about him—"My lord, this morning before breakfast I reading Herbert Spencer's 'First Principles.'"

"Well, I wasn't!" I angrily replied, for well did I know what the insufferable prig was going to say.

"No, my lord, you reading silly stories; your friend not reading at all, only sleeping. Your friend always sleeping; both of you always wasting time. My lord, when your friend going Nikko?"

"I don't know," I nervously replied. "He is of age, ask him." (My friend, I may observe, was sitting at his very side, trembling more than I was!)

"My lord, I have ask him ten times; he no decisions answer giving."

I then fled the room, amid the joyous chuckles of the bishops and the rest of the company. On the following day I said to him, "Haru-Mitsu, to-day we will go Miyanoshita."

"No, my lord, to-day we going Nikko. I have there new book by Herbert Spencer; I go and fetch it." And to Nikko, I grieve to relate, we went. I will not weary you with further memories of Haru-Mitsu. I will only say that all the romance and all the beauty and all the feudal interest of Japan—yes, even the exquisite temples of Nikko and the tinkling waterfalls of lovely Miyanoshita—fade into insignificance beside the all-pervading memory of that calm, patient, irresistible, imperturbable and relentless personality of my Japanese guide and valet.

And another cinematographic memory of Japan rises to my mind even as I write.

We were in a railway carriage, a few of us, returning from a great naval ceremony at Yokohama, in which our own Fleet, under the command of gallant old Sir Alexander Buller, who was very kind to me during the whole time I was in the Far East, the Japanese, the French, Russian, and German battleships had taken part, a review given in honour of a whilom British First Lord of the Admiralty who was visiting Japan at the time, the late Lord Spencer, with his beautiful wife. Prince Ito asked me to travel back with him and Lord and Lady Spencer and one or two others, one of the party being, if I remember rightly, that wonderful Japanese scholar and really great *littérateur*, Sir Ernest Satow, the British Minister at the Imperial Court. I stood regretfully gazing out at old Japan slipping by the window and Prince Ito stood at my side. "Ah!" I said to the Prince, "I prefer the old Japan to the new."

He pointed to his frightful top-hat and appalling badly fitting frock-coat, of both of which he was inordinately proud. "Oh!" he said, "this very good coat, very good hat. What you like better?"

"Ah, Prince," observed Lord Spencer, "the civilization that is coming upon you is not to be compared with the civilization that is passing away from you." And as he spoke I caught a glimpse of the sunset glow upon the snowy cap of Fuji-Yama, and a long line of exquisitely coloured kites, crimson dragons, and many-hued fishes and wide-winged birds fluttered in the evening breeze, and the tolling of a temple bell stole in through the window, and for the moment the romance and the undefinable charm and the undying glory of old Japan imprinted themselves for ever on my mind.

Old Lord Dormer rushed into my bedroom in Tokyo one glorious April morning and said: "Look at my top-hat which I brought out specially from England to go to the Mikado's garden-party to-day." And I looked. It was overgrown with mushrooms or some awful fungi gendered by the heat and damp of Singapore and the Indian Ocean. An hour's hard work and the hat was just barely presentable. I must tell you that the Emperor's annual garden-party to see the blossoms in the Palace Gardens is the one great event in Japan to which foreigners, who must be introduced by their Ambassadors, specially look forward. Two other qualifications only are necessary: you must wear a frock-coat and a top-hat.

One famous English artist, the late Sir Alfred East, had neglected to bring his silk hat with him. Nothing daunted, however, he set to work on the very morning of the party and manufactured one for himself out of cardboard, painted it black, varnished it, and then, having let it dry in the sun all the morning, he made a triumphant if somewhat ridiculous appearance at this, which is perhaps the most romantic and picturesque and beautiful Court function that you can see in the whole world, and one that very few Europeans have ever seen. The gardens are quite lovely and the cherry and apple blossoms the most exquisite conglomeration of colour that it is possible to conceive. And then at a given moment all the guests, consisting of Ambassadors from every country in the world, naval officers in harbour of all nationalities and glittering in silver and gold, well-accredited tourists from England, America, France, Russia, Germany, Italy, Spain ; bright little British middies, Japanese officials, all form a lane through which a few moments afterwards the royal and Imperial party, preceded by Baron Sanomyia, the Court Chamberlain, closely followed by my friend Prince Ito, the Premier, both clad in shocking frock-coats and top-hats and walking backwards, slowly passed, whilst the Band of the Imperial Guard played the wailing, rather haunting, and charming strains of the Japanese National Anthem. The Emperor, an impassive, impressive figure dressed in a European Field-Marshal's uniform, walked beside the Empress, who, with all the ladies of the Court, greatly to our disappointment, was clad in European costume, which did not suit one of them in the slightest degree.

And that permits of a slight digression. We talk much of the unchanging East, but I am sometimes inclined to think that we Westerners—we English, at all events—would be far more conservative and unchanging than the Oriental who has come, or been thrown, into contact with Western civilization. I have been inclined now and then to blame British Imperialism and French and American enterprise for the sadly inartistic innovations which are rapidly destroying the exquisite artistic charms of the Eastern world and reducing it to the commonplace horror of Tottenham Court Road on a Saturday afternoon. But I begin to think quite seriously that it is the Oriental himself who is to blame for this state of things and not the Westerner. An engineer who was working on the great dam at Assouan, where they employed upwards of fifteen thousand Egyptian fellaheen and Arabs, told me that one of the most amusing experiences of his life was the manner in which, imitating the English navvies, the native employees used to go in for tea and eggs and bacon for breakfast, instead of the simple bread and figs that they had used, unchanged and unchanging, for the past fifteen or twenty thousand years. The truth of the matter is that the Oriental, left alone, would go on for ever in his old routine—which is why Palestine under the rule of the unprogressive Turk has retained its nameless charm undisturbed for countless thousands of years—but once you introduce or suggest, ever so remotely, a new régime, he will go in heart and soul for the new mode of life. And those Arab workmen would learn English, too. But catch the British carpenter and plumber and navvy changing his food or his dress or his tongue for any other than that to which he and his forbears had been accustomed! No, thank you! And if ever an Oriental nation, say a thousand years from now, conquered and occupied Great Britain, we should die sooner than adopt their costume, as almost universally, I grieve to say, they are adopting our most hideous of all national dresses—trousers, frock-coat, and billycock hat!

One day Prince Ito said to me, "Would you like to see something of our Army?"

And quite innocently, never dreaming of what he had in his mind, I replied, "I should like nothing better," supposing that he meant I should go and see the soldiers drilling one morning. However, one morning a smart carriage and pair dashed up to my hotel door and the Prince's A.D.C. got out of it and asked for me. He had come, he said, to take me to see the soldiers. I thought it seemed rather an unnecessary trouble on his part; however, still supposing I was going to see them at their ordinary drill, I drove with him down to the barracks of the three regiments of the Imperial Guards, corresponding to our Household troops.

There, gathered together at the great front entrance of the officers' quarters, were the Colonel-in-Chief of the Guards, and behind him stood about fifty officers. I very nearly collapsed when I realized that I was the only European present and that a grand parade of these magnificent regiments had been arranged for my special entertainment. The Colonel led me into the mess-room, upon the glittering table of which stood champagne glasses, cakes, and cigars. The officers trooped in behind us, and then the Colonel, stepping forward, addressed me in a long Japanese speech of which, of course, I did not understand one single, solitary word, but which the Secretary translated for me, sentence by sentence; a most kindly and flattering speech which filled me with confusion and gave me a most uncomfortable feeling of being a regular, unconvicted impostor, for I need scarcely say I had no right to such honours. My health was then most solemnly drunk by all the officers present, and I rose to reply—which I did in the most halting and nervous fashion it is possible to conceive. We then all filed out on to the parade-ground, the Colonel, Viscount Somebody-or-other, leading the way, with my unworthy and guilty self walking along at his side. Upon the parade-ground were drawn up the three regiments of the Imperial Guard, some three thousand strong, and up and down the lines of those splendid soldiers, many of whom were destined to fall in the dreadful Russo-Japanese War eight years later, I marched with the Colonel. And really splendid soldiers they were: stocky and smart and well-set-up and superbly armed and accoutred. A remarkable and unforgettable experience for a quandom East End curate, was it not? and yet, curiously enough, it was not my first experience of the kind. The other occurred in India, and I may as well relate it here.

During the course of a long conversation with Sir George White when he was Commander-in-Chief in India, he asked me if I would like to see a really typical Sikh regiment on parade and I replied I should.

"All right," he replied, "as you are staying with Colonel Massey, the Commissioner at Delhi, I will ask him to arrange it." Sure enough, a few days after I had another earth-shaking experience, more alarming even than that of Japan. I quitted Sir George in Simla and travelled from there to Delhi. About six o'clock one burning morning I woke to find the train running into Delhi station. Now, as it chanced, I had been travelling for twenty-four hours, eight or ten hours in a tonga, rattling down through the dust and heat of a burning May morning in the Himalayas to Kalka, where I entered the train for Delhi. When I quitted Simla I was a sight for the gods to revel in : a most beautiful snowy white suit, with a sea-green cummerbund about my waist, clean-shaven, fresh, and smart-looking. But the dust of the tonga journey and the smoke and ashes and blacks of the long night in the railway train had reduced me to a spectacle so unbelievably filthy and horrible, that, unbathed and unshaven as I was, a music-hall or an American cinematograph tramp would have scorned to have been seen in my company. Well, as I say, I woke to find the train running into Delhi, and I thought, "Well, I'll take a ticca-gharry and drive straight to the Commissioner's and get a shave and a bath and a change all round and I shall be myself again."

As the train ran along the crowded station platform I caught a dazzling glimpse of what appeared to be a General officer in helmet and plumes accompanied by two very smart A.D.C.'s. "Ah," I thought, "I wonder who they are here for. A native prince, or perhaps the General of the District." And I didn't give the matter another thought, but began to get my things together. As I stepped out of the carriage I caught a glimpse of the uniformed demi-deities I had espied a moment before hurrying towards my carriage. Even then the full horror of the moment hadn't begun to dawn upon me, until—oh, ghastly moment !—a voice said : "How do you do, Mr. Blathwayt. I got his Excellency's wire and I have *chota-hazri* ready for you in the waiting-room, and then we'll drive straight to the parade-ground. You are lucky in arriving on the Queen's birthday, for there will be a splendid parade of all the troops in Delhi, and after the *feu-de-joie* you can inspect the 32nd Sikhs."

I replied, "But, Colonel Massey, I can't possibly go to a parade like this. Why, I'll get taken up ! "

Colonel Massey, a tall, very smart, very handsome, and splendidly set-up man, whose position of Commissioner of such a place as Delhi was almost regal in its glittering circumstance and dignity, laughed heartily. "Oh, that doesn't matter. Every one looks like a tramp off such a journey as you've just come. But come and have your tea, for there isn't a moment to spare," and he introduced me to his A.D.C. and to another officer, and we all went to the waiting-room, where I had a very welcome cup of hot tea—and no one who hasn't spent a May night on an Indian railway even begins to know how comforting tea can be under such circumstances—and then Colonel Massey led the way to his carriage. And do you know what those magnificent carriages, perched high on C-springs, in India are like, with a gorgeous native coachman driving a superb pair of horses, and two equally gorgeous native servants standing up behind? And in this case, as soon as we had taken our seats, a cavalry escort fell into line behind us, and we clattered magnificently away to the parade-ground. How all that glittering scene comes back to me as I write: the burning Indian sun, the magnificent parade-ground, the lances of the long lines of cavalry flashing in the brilliant sunshine, the splendid uniforms, the white rings of smoke as they soared away from the cannon's mouth into the blue ether, the strains of the National Anthem borne upon the morning breeze, the myriad colours and costumes of the native crowd gathered to witness the impressive spectacle. Whilst the general parade was held and the *feu-de-joie* was fired, I sat alone in the carriage, Colonel Massey having gone on to the parade-ground to take the salute. As soon as that was over and the European troops were being marched off the ground, the Commissioner, accompanied by the Colonel of the regiment, marched up to where I, grubby beyond all description, was miserably seated, and I was introduced. Well, there was nothing to do but put a good face on the matter, though, to make matters worse, as I jumped down from the carriage one of my braces broke, and I had to keep hitching my once white trousers up to prevent them falling down altogether, as, with the

Colonel at my side and followed by a whole bevy of officers, I marched up and down between the lines of those superb Sikh soldiers, the finest, I suppose, that the world has ever seen.

There is one little memory of India that will never fade from my mind. I always recall a great train clanking into the wide, echoing station at Umballa one burning Indian night. We had to stop there twenty minutes, and I employed them in walking up and down the platform and studying the multitudinous colours of the myriad crowd by which I was surrounded—fierce Afghans down from the hills, eagle-faced Pathans and Sikhs, the snaky, oily Bengali-baboo, Tommy Atkins, smoking here and there in easy, laughing, unconcerned groups. And in the middle of them all, with his head upon his knapsack, fast asleep and absolutely unconscious of all the whirl and tumult round him, lay a little English drummer-boy. Suddenly the bell rang. A British officer, with a general's plumes nodding in his white helmet, passed by. Bending down, he gently touched the boy on the shoulder, and the little lad sprang startled to his feet. Somehow or another there flashed upon me, in a moment, the wonderful might and majesty of the British Empire, in whose all-protecting arms, as it were, that child had slept safe and unconscious amid a horde of all the wildest tribes in all the wild land of our vast and surging Indian Empire.

And of Tunis, what is my most lingering memory? Certainly not of the dead-and-gone glories of old Carthage, around which, even as a child, one used to weave to oneself such fascinating memories, but which so sadly and disappointingly fade into nothingness on the actual spot; nor even of those deathlessly unforgettable and immemorial native streets; or of those dim bazaars of which one's memory is a vision here and there of scarlet cloths and the glitter of old brass-work and the splashes of golden sunlight upon the carpets hanging there in such prodigal confusion. No; my memory of Tunis is centred round the quiet isolation of a little Sister of Mercy who stood by the staircase in the hotel where our merry party off the ship lunched at midday. I watched that charming, patient face, upon which was imprinted for ever the peace that passeth all understanding. In a way the stately aloofness of that figure in the midst of the careless, hurrying, hungry British crowd of tourists was the finest thing I ever saw. For me she stood as the very personification of the visionary and the ideal in the midst of all that was crudely and vulgarly material, so much so that I absolutely hated my own personality in the presence of everything that I was not.

I recall one very amusing incident in Pretoria. I was roaming round the beautiful Zoological Gardens there with the custodian, and I happened upon a rather charming lion. "Ah! there's a story attached to that lion," said my companion. "Just before the Boer War broke out President Krüger received a wire saying, 'Look out. The British lion will arrive by the seven o'clock train to-morrow night.' When the train rolled into the station at Pretoria the following evening the guard handed out a beautiful little baby lion which he had been instructed to give to the President as a present from Mr. Cecil Rhodes.

"But the old gentleman was in a great fury. 'I am not going to have any British lions running about Pretoria,' said he, and so the lion was shipped back to Cape Town. At the end of the war it was sent here, and it has been in these gardens ever since."

I have a delightful memory of a race-meeting in Jamaica. Somehow or another a colonial race-meeting possesses far more of an interest for me than anything we ever see in England of the same kind. There always appears to me to be more of real sport in it than we get at home: less of the purely betting element, more of the horses, more of the sport of the whole thing. On this occasion Miss Dolf Wyllarde and I sat together on the grand stand and watched the assembling of the picturesque throng; for negroes are generally keen sportsmen. The crowd grew apace as we sat and ate our sandwiches, and presently the band struck up the

National Anthem as Sir Sidney Olivier, the Governor, and his party drove up and took their places in the royal enclosure. The racing itself was a spirited performance, and some of the little West Indian horses made good running. And behind all, bathed in the glory of the tropic sunshine, the Blue Mountains splendidly dominated the whole sparkling scene.

And a companion picture rises to my mind of a polo-meeting on the racecourse at Durban: the clouds of red dust upon which the rays of the South African sun fell with a brilliant effect of illumination, through which one caught glimpses of the ponies and their riders dashing here and there, twisting and turning, and the ball flashing by like lightning and the enthusiasm of that delightful colonial gathering, the eager faces of the Zulu boys scattered about the course, the sparkle of the uniforms here and there, the dainty costumes of the pretty South African women, the kindly, friendly spirit of the cosmopolitan crowd, the utter absence of English reserve and stiffness, the indefinable hanging together of the handful of white people, behind whom always towers as a sort of menace the thundercloud of the great black peril—a cloud which may burst at any moment for all that any one can tell. And it all forms a vast cameo, as it were, of that vast and unimagined and but little realized mystery which we know as the British Empire.

I have alluded to Miss Dolf Wyllarde, a charming personality, with keen vision and insight and a quite remarkable faculty, for a woman especially, of discerning the curious inner meaning of Empire and for realizing and depicting the multi-coloured characters and personalities of those who are called upon to administer the Imperial rule in far-off and little-known portions of our vast and widespreading Empire. I remember one day she and I drove to Montego Bay, in Jamaica, and there in a little hotel, overlooking the Caribbean Sea, beneath the palm-trees, clashing in the strong sea-breeze, with the ceaseless murmur of the foam-tipped waves in our ears, we sat and discussed the romance of an Empire upon which the sun never sets and the farthest limits of which she and I each knew so well and the points of contact or of difference which we were so well able to institute: the curious effect of climate and of racial differences upon the stolid and upright English character, the constraining influences which are so unflinchingly and so undeviatingly brought to bear upon the coloured men of many races, equally and relentlessly from Tuticorin to Table Bay, from Port Royal to Singapore.

In a way Miss Wyllarde has done almost as much to make known to the untravelled Englishman the romance, and mystery even, of the Crown Colonies of the British Empire as Mr. Kipling has done regarding the vast Empire of India itself. And I have a memory of a certain Cabinet luncheon that was once given to Mr. Michael Davitt and myself many, many years ago by the Premier of a great Australian State, and how much both he and I were impressed by the wide vision, the practical common sense, the splendid humanity of our host, behind whom there stretched a lifetime of effort and accomplishment on behalf of a great colony. And after the luncheon the Premier and the chief members of his Cabinet and Mr. Davitt and myself went out on to the veranda to drink our coffee and we were unexpectedly joined by a number of the Labour Members of the Parliament House, within the walls of which we were seated at the moment, and nothing would satisfy them but that the Premier should sing them a comic song, which he accordingly did with admirable verve and spirit and a sense of humour which would have delighted a music-hall audience here in London. I shall never forget the scene: the tall, stalwart figure of the Premier, with his golden beard tossing in the light afternoon breeze, as he swayed to and fro and loudly demanded—

> "Where *did* you buy that hat,
> Where *did* you get that tile?"

I tried to picture Mr. Gladstone or Lord Salisbury under similar circumstances. And the very next time I saw this same Premier he was solemnly driving down

Piccadilly, cheered to the echo by the London public, in that glorious procession of the Queen's Diamond Jubilee.

Late in life I met Horatio Bottomley, and I am very glad I did. He is a delightful experience, and in his way very typical. He is much detested by a certain class of politician, why I don't quite know, but mainly, I suspect, for his outspoken hatred of cant and shams, though, curiously enough, it is for that very reason some of them profess to detest him. He is frequently denounced by people of this sort, and I dare-say quite sincerely, as a humbug. Well, as a matter of fact—and I know him fairly intimately—he is no more of a humbug than the majority of his Majesty's lieges. The sturdy Briton, for some reason or other, is traditionally credited with a definite hatred for anything in the shape of humbug or hypocrisy; and yet, compared with the men of almost any other nation, the typical Briton is more hypocritical, unconsciously so, in his attitude towards the facts of life than any one else on earth. Bottomley faces things pretty straight as a rule, except when he tries to humbug himself into the belief that things are really better than they appear to be. He is an optimist to the world at large, with a lot of the cynic in the snug shelter of his study. I don't think any one of his keenly acute mental calibre could possibly be as optimistic as he displays himself in his weekly pronouncements to his myriads of admirers. And yet he does the nation—nay, the Empire—real good service by these same articles of his. As to the sincerity of his views upon religion, I believe they are the most really sincere thing about him. He is so astonished and delighted and "intrigued" at discovering certain religious truths, familiar from our cradles to most of us, and exploiting certain theological theories—not dogmas, which he detests—that he gives expression to them with an enthusiasm and a zest which entirely do away with all possibility of humbug or self-deception. And when people say to me, "What a humbug the man is!" I just think of an incident which occurred in the early part of last year, or towards the end of the year before. I paid him a very early call one morning, and I found him sitting up in bed, surrounded by MSS. and documents and newspapers of every description, and the tears raining down his cheeks. "I've got such an infernal cold," he said a little shamefacedly, "I can hardly see out of my eyes!" And then he looked at me and tossed me the sheets he had just written—"The Ghosts of Gallipoli." "It's no good," he said. "Writing that article has broken me up altogether. It's more than I can stand to think of all those dear boys going so splendidly to their deaths in order that old fellows like you and me shall be comfortable in our beds o' night. I mean to devote my life to helping those chaps who come back, and God do so to me and more also if I fail!"

And for this he is denounced by some as a hypocrite, by others as a bloodthirsty Jingo, whereas all the time he has more fervidly at heart than any one else I know the welfare of the England he loves as few people have ever loved it. I shall always carry that vision of Bottomley in my mind, for I had caught him in that one moment when a man is true to himself as he never can be in the sight of the ordinary callous everyday world. And he possesses a delightful sense of humour. He is bubbling over with it; it is spontaneous, irresistible, and inescapable.

His story of two opposing teams of cricketers in India—one an English regiment, the other of youthful Calcutta baboos—is delightful. Somebody said to the coloured team, "Well, boys, you'll have to play your best to-day." "Oh," said they, "that is all right; we've raised fifteen rupees, and we've given it all to the umpire!" And his story of the parson and the bullying barrister also is good. It was a horse-dealing case. "Do you know the difference between a horse and a cow?" shouted the barrister. "I hardly know the difference between a horse and a cow or the difference between a bully and a bull," gently replied the clergyman; "only a bull, I am told, has horns, whilst a bully," he continued, with a courteous bow to his persecutor, "luckily for me, has none."

He has a fondness for wandering about old churchyards and looking for quaint epitaphs, and he told me of several. One related to the tombstone erected over a missionary in India who had been accidentally killed by his native servant—

> Sacred to the memory of the Rev. John Dash.
> Accidentally shot by his khitmutgar,
>
> Well done! thou good and faithful servant!

As a matter of fact I believe that text has been lately deleted.

A memory that often comes to my mind is of Cardinal Manning at eighty-three years of age, a beautiful and a stately figure, with his clean-cut, ascetic features——ascetic to the point of emaciation—his beautifully modelled hands, and his shabby old cassock, trimmed with red, standing at the window of his great study in Westminster, looking down at a group of street arabs playing cricket. "That little chap shapes well," he said as one of the children very prettily "cut" a ball across the yard. "What a pity he has no one to take him in hand and train him properly."

I observed, "You are fond of cricket, your Eminence?"

"Indeed I am," replied the doughty old ecclesiastic. "I was in the Eleven at Harrow. Why, it's only a few years ago that I went up to St. Charles's Monastery, in Bayswater, and I found the Fathers and Brothers having a game of cricket. And one of the young men asked me to join them, and, in consideration, I suppose, for the poor old clergyman, he started bowling me slow underhand lobs. So I said, 'Look here, my lad, you take the bat and I'll bowl you a few overs.' And I did—good, swift roundhand that he couldn't tackle a bit. They didn't catch the old soldier so easily as they had thought to do," chuckled the dear old Cardinal.

And then his light midday meal was brought in, I sitting apart the while he talked with much spirit, though very slowly, and at times sniffing vigorously, as was his habit when expressing dissent or disapproval. "What's your favourite pudding?" he said to me as the servant placed a "trifle" before him. "This is mine," he said. "I love trifle-pudding, but being a total abstainer I take good care not to ask what it's made of." He began to discuss a brother prelate. "He's too tactful," he said. "I hate a tactful man, Mr. Blathwayt. I can never trust him. Still, tact has its uses—in moderation," he continued. And then, with a smile, he said: "Indeed, sometimes it's absolutely essential. Archbishop Sumner used to tell a good story. One day he received a letter from a country vicar, begging him to use his influence to present him to a new living he much desired. And here is how he began the letter—

"'MY LORD ARCHBISHOP,

Conscious as I am of your Grace's many physical ailments and your rapidly failing powers of mind, I,' etc.

I hate tact, but I think I should have hated that letter even more."

CHAPTER XXIII

THE THINGS THAT MATTER IN THE END

WHAT has struck me most in my passage through life, and it is more in evidence to-day than ever it has been in the past, is the swift turn of the kaleidoscope in the diorama of human thought. Athwart the intricate woof and web of the patterns shuttled to and fro in the brain of man, are shot never-ending and dazzlingly brilliant iridescences which, however irrelevant they may appear to be to the original design, yet tend in the end to give it its chief colour, value, and meaning. Beneath the bewildering perplexities of modern theories and speculations induced by and evolved out of modern points of view and angles of vision there ever exist the solid foundations of the thought of the ages, even though for a moment, as it were, the newest gleams and flashes appear to dazzle and blind our vision.

And that is our salvation.

I am not attempting to preach; I am but drawing attention to a curious but an obvious fact. For many years past it has struck me that this English nation is undergoing a spiritual and an intellectual revolution of which it is only just beginning to be conscious. We are, as a rule, a curiously unspiritual people, which is probably a geographical phenomenon mainly owing to our distance from the equator, for the nearer you are to the equator the nearer, it has been said by thoughtful people, you are to God.

Spirituality is a faculty in which as a nation we are conspicuously lacking, but it has yet to be demonstrated that we are therefore lacking either in vision or ideals, or that we are more markedly degenerate than are nations more easily susceptible to those things and influences which are not seen but which are eternal. I had begun to think three years ago or so that the English people were becoming too hopelessly frivolous to be touched by any appeal, to be pointed to any ideal, to be able to appreciate anything above and beyond the hopelessly material and commonplace. And yet they have proved themselves, at once and quite naturally and spontaneously, capable of the noblest self-sacrifice, the most splendid courage, and they have in their own personalities set up the loftiest ideals ; whilst nevertheless beneath it all, and most contradictorily, remains, more absolutely visible and evident than ever, that extraordinary capacity for frivolity and light-mindedness of which I had accused them in my heart in the piping days of peace, a frivolity that really, in some curiously perverse manner, appears to illuminate and glorify, rather than to dim, a capacity for heroism and self-sacrifice for which neither secular history nor sacred legend can find a parallel. The very thing that I had dreaded as inevitably and scientifically bound to result in enfeebled demoralization of character, namely, the extreme laxity or total absence of all sense of discipline and self-control, no less in the Mayfair drawing-room than in the Whitechapel slum, in the Public School boy as much as in the lad out of the County Council schools, has demonstrated itself as being, so far as we can judge, absolutely harmless, and without evil or deteriorating effect, in the hour of trial. Which proves that the human soul is grander than we know.

And one would wish to know to what it is that this innate nobility of national character is really due, and whence in truth it is derived. It can hardly be attributed to an overwhelming love for and devotion to the teachings and traditions of conventional theology, because the nation is quite confessedly, as a nation, not religious—not conventionally so, at all events. The larger proportion of the community, right through all classes, practically make no profession of religion at all, and those who do comply with the demands or expectations of the ultra-respectable frequently do so with the idea of propitiating ideals and deities with which they have but slight sympathy, and in which even their belief is fast decaying into the dust.

I often wonder which, in the end, with the greatest number of people, exercises the most actively restraining influence—principle, priest, or policeman!

One of the most curious and obvious changes in the community is the social evolution which is the outcome of the far greater sympathy and interchange of thought and opinion, and the freer intercourse, that exists between all classes of society to-day. In my young days the lines of demarcation were far more clearly defined than they are now, and snobbery reigned supreme in all classes. To-day those lines of demarcation are rapidly becoming obliterated, and the little commissioned officer from behind the draper's counter is demonstrating to a delighted world that he possesses as much magnificent courage, and is inspired by as lofty ideals and traditions of chivalry, as the *preux chevalier* Bayard himself, *sans peur et sans reproche*.

Snobbery, so-called, will never altogether die down in the English breast, or, indeed, in the breast of humanity generally; it is innate in the whole lot of us; and I have never met more than two people in my whole life who, I should say, were absolutely incapable of it. Our Bible, which stands literally as the foundation of the race, is, as it were, a compendium of humanity, it is a mirror of the human soul, and therefore, while at one moment it is violently socialistic, it is at another—and I say it in all deep reverence—the very essence of what we call snobbery, but which perhaps is not snobbery after all; whilst as for the Anglican Church Catechism, it is nothing more nor less than a compendium of snobbery. At the same time there are those—and I am quite sincerely conscious that I am one of them—whom it is indeed well that the cataclysm through which we are still passing has shaken into a new attitude and state of being in which there is no room for snobbery at all, and in which we gladly and frankly and thankfully recognize and realize the splendid qualities that exist in other people, of the lack of which and the impossibility of attaining to which we are sadly conscious so far as we personally are concerned. In a word, we have learned humility, which always brings with it, not only a sense of proportion but also a common-sense depreciation of our own poor endeavours and achievements, and a far more generously appreciative recognition of what other people, whom we would have been inclined to ignore in the days of old, are easily capable. And that feeling, engendered first in the shell-stormed trenches of Northern France and upon the tortured hills of Gallipoli, is gradually revolutionizing the whole social point of view.

And again, we are beginning to realize the extraordinary importance of the apparently unimportant; we are beginning to understand that there is, in good truth, no such thing at all as the unimportant.

Let me try and illustrate it by a homely and perfectly possible incident. We are at the War Office, let us say. A great council of statesmen, admirals, and generals is assembled to consider the proposition by a famous inventor concerning a new gun; a gun of such terrific power that the possession of half a hundred of them would place their owner in the position of being the conqueror of the whole world. And the inventor says: "Place one of these guns upon an ordinary P. and O. liner, and that liner could not only defy, but she could sink, a whole enemy fleet before that fleet could get near her; she could shell Paris from London and Paris could make no reply." (This, of course, sounds absurd, and I am not concerned to defend it; though I may say that two articles upon such a gun actually appeared in a great monthly review some eight or ten years ago.) And just at that moment the Prime Minister says: "We will discuss the secret of this at luncheon, which has been waiting for the past half-hour, and as I have had no breakfast I am too famished to wait any longer." And so to luncheon they go. The inventor, in his eager haste, chokes himself with a prosaic piece of beefsteak, and his secret dies with him. In a moment of time he has exchanged Downing Street for the other world, materialism for spirituality, time for eternity ; and while the piece of steak is still sticking in his throat he confronts either chaos and annihilation or absolute nothingness, or else perchance a world and a life immeasurably vaster and more exquisite than the one he has just quitted ; at the same time he leaves behind two continents sunk in unutterable woe, and all because a little piece of beefsteak prevented the revealing of a secret which would have meant the salvation of a hundred millions of human beings. Out of so small a cause can such inconceivably vast effects and issues result.

I was seated this morning (November 8, 1916) in the Old English rooms at the National Gallery, and my glance fell upon Sir Joshua Reynolds' fine portrait of Lord Ligonier seated on horseback in the middle of a typical eighteenth-century battle, and I began to reflect upon the extraordinary difference between the warfare of that far-off period and that which is being waged upon the Somme to-day. I noticed too the date of the picture, 1760, the year in which my own grandfather was born, and the world as it then was and all its charm and romance surged across my mind. Japan in the depths of its feudal system and with all its marvellous art untouched, untainted, unspoilt by, and all unknown to, European and American civilization ; Cairo still reminiscent of the Arabian Nights and exquisitely mediæval ; the South Sea Islands with their fiercely painted warriors prancing about the battlefield, and who have now given place to white-chokered dissenting ministers and deacons, and over whose palm-lined avenues the trail of Tottenham Court Road lies uglily and prosaically in evidence. And then came to me the quaint thought how the portrait of that comparatively unknown nobleman, Lord Ligonier, had entered into and interwoven itself with and made a part, however infinitesimal, of my own life—for we are a part of all we have ever known or met—and of the lives of countless thousands of people who also had witnessed it and thought over it and admired it since the day it was first on view ; how unconsciously everything we see is interwoven into our lives, and how everything helps to link every other thing and every other person not only together but with the whole universe, the whole hereafter, the palpable with the impalpable, the seen with the unseen, the unimagined with the proven, body, soul, and spirit all together.

I caught a glimpse of myself the other day in a mirror that had once reflected back the merry *riante* face of Nell Gwynne ; and looking over her dainty shoulder, I pictured to myself the swarthy countenance of her royal admirer, the jealous glances of Castlemaine or Louise de Querouaille, the smiles and frowns of Rochester, Sedley, or quaint Samuel Pepys himself, or even of the gloomy Duke of York or the sad-faced, ill-fated Monmouth ; all summarized and visualized within that quaint, old-fashioned circular mirror of a dead king's dead mistress.

It is not possible to do more than hint at these curious fantasies of the brain, and yet which are in sober truth among the most real things of which we are conscious, for they all go towards the compilation, or they are the serious and deliberate outcome, of human thought, which, when all is said and done, is the chief thing in the universe—is, indeed, the main thing by which we are drawn into harmonious relationship and correspondence with that universe. And it is the manner in which we apprehend and appreciate these ideas that gives us our standing among our fellows, that constitutes our right to our place in the world.

It is in such crises as the present that we begin faintly to apprehend the meaning of much that has but vaguely appealed to us in the dead and dreamy past, for in such ways and by such unexpected issues is built up that mysterious and yet all-important quality commonly known as character. It is these things and the putting of them right that really matter in the end ; for the rest one is thankfully conscious that a new standpoint altogether, an immeasurably clearer and more steadfast angle of vision, is taking the place of the old and easy-going and fast-dimming points of view so characteristic of those now far-off and dreamland days of universal peace. But what appears to me to be most necessary, next to a complete revolution of our methods of education and character-building, is a realization of, and scientific instruction in, the things that really matter, the apprehending of those things that really give its chief value and its dominant colour to human life—in a word, the subversion of all our false ideals and our monstrously silly and rotten conventions. We all want to get back to an immeasurably simpler condition of existence. To realize that the shimmer upon the wing of the seagull, hovering over the translucent curve of the wave breaking in a sunlit mist of foam and spume upon a beach of silver sand, is really more beautiful and soul-satisfying than Piccadilly upon a crowded June afternoon, is to gain a vision into life which, universally and consistently acted upon, will eventually revolutionize the whole of human existence, because it means a realization of the things that most matter in the end. It means, as Algernon Blackwood puts it, getting back to the primal state in which only true happiness is to be found. I trust this isn't high falutin', though I am rather doubtful if it isn't a little crude and obvious; I can only plead that at all events it is sincere. The highest happiness in life, and that which never palls, is invariably to be found in the simplest and most natural things. And it is just possible that this much to be desired simplicity of existence may be one of the outcomes of this tremendous world upheaval, though I doubt if even that is capable of digging down deep enough into the foundations of the human soul.

To come down a little more to detail in one's speculations as to the manner in which the community has changed during the last fifty years or so, I should say it is, to begin with, infinitely more introspective and sensitive than it was capable of being in the older days. Like a highly sensitized photographic plate, it is far more alive to external impressions than it was in the days when the singularly simple-minded and non-mentally complex heroes of Waterloo and the Crimea strode the world. And to a certain shallow extent it is perhaps better educated. It certainly knows more; it can scarcely help doing so, for the influence that of old mind was held to exercise upon matter has been equalled, if, indeed, it has not been actually surpassed of late years, by the influence, the undoubted influence, that matter, especially in the shape of mechanism, can exercise upon mind. And yet, with it all, the modern mind always strikes me as being on the whole far more superficial than the mind of fifty years ago and more; it is certainly less deeply, if, possibly, more widely read than in the sober days of the early and mid-Victorian era; at the same time, I cannot help thinking it is more delicately sensitive and more susceptible to the appeal of the really spiritual, if that appeal is made in the right manner and if it proceeds from the right quarter. To give a concrete illustration of what I am driving at. It is a commonplace to say, for instance, that Shakespeare has lost his hold upon and his power of appeal to the nation. And yet, though the sturdy Londoner of Wellington's and George IV's day revelled in Kean and Macready's presentations in the great plays of the national bard, I doubt if a man among them could even have begun to appreciate the marvellous delicacy of Mr. Martin Harvey's production of "Hamlet" last spring at His Majesty's Theatre. His wonderfully subtle insight into the complexity of the poor distraught prince's brain, his beautiful vision of the inner spirit of Shakespeare's wisest and most human—and sometimes most boring—play, his absolutely human and natural and everyday envisagement of the most perplexing character ever placed upon the stage, the extremely subtle and yet exquisitely artistic staging of the drama, the reticence and restraint and yet perfect harmony of his scheme of colour, his absolute realization of every single possibility and potentiality in the play, whilst they thrilled into delighted silence a vast assemblage of Londoners, of whom a large number were wounded Tommies from the trenches, would have been absolutely above and beyond the heads and hearts of an Early Victorian audience. So it is difficult to say definitely and finally whether either intellectually or spiritually England really is as much upon the down grade as, before the war, some of us felt ourselves justified in declaring she was. In many respects, in modern war-shaken England, the people really are beginning to appreciate the things that most matter in the end.

That the war is exercising a vast influence upon the mind and soul of the people is evidenced, according to the universal testimony of many of my Society friends, by the remarkable craze that has seized hold upon all sorts and conditions of men and women of that particular class to pry into the mystic secrets and sources of human existence. Not even in all the early fervour engendered by Blackwood in his fine study of "John Silence" and by Richard and Isabella Ingalese in their subtle and intricate essays upon mysticism, was there such a feverish desire to get into communication with the world of spirits as there almost universally is to-day. And whilst I quite agree with my old friend R. J. Campbell that the heart of England is essentially irreligious, I am convinced that it is only so from the orthodoxically theological point of view, and that the man who is impatient of and who wholly refuses to put his faith in mediaeval dogma and outworn creeds is beginning at heart to realize more than ever he did before the crying need for the deep, soul-satisfying religion of the immortal spirit of humanity. And that is the secret of the whole thing. An enormous hope for and belief in the immortality of the individual soul of man is springing up alike in the minds and hearts of the modern man, and that must inevitably result in a revolution of the whole social scheme. Though science may not, so far at all events, have been able to give them much assurance of the going on after death, yet heart and hope and a certain sweet reasonableness of things and a certain arguing from primal analogies are beginning to work in the minds and intellects of people who have seen the flower of their beloved land cut off in all its pristine youth and beauty. And this, though hopelessly unscientific, is gradually swaying the community towards a more spiritual, and perchance a clearer and more justified, vision of the problems of existence.

than has ever before been possible in this very material England of ours. And when it comes to the heart of things it is not unlikely that the appeal of sentiment may outweigh the more solid claims of science, the more so that when we give ourselves up to quiet reflection we realize that even the foundations themselves of science are rooted in the very shifting sands of ever-changing human research and inquiry.

Some of my readers may be wondering why this lengthy dissertation on matters so abstruse ; to which my own reply is that most of life is thought, and that these thoughts, however wandering and disconnected they may be, form, after all, the main burden and are the most abiding outcome of my journeyings through life and round the world. England and the Empire—the long, long story of the one and the building up and fashioning of the other—are the two great facts in the history of humanity which, I suppose, most appeal to me. I find it impossible to dissever my own insignificant personality and individuality from that of my country, and I am deeply interested in the attempt to discern those qualities in my fellow-Englishmen which have resulted in such a magnificent culmination. And, as a student in a very casual and amateur fashion of the metaphysical conditions which go to the formation of human personality, I am vastly "intrigued," as the French put it, as to why and how this curious tendency—I might say this absolute abandonment—of the whole nation to the frivolous regard of the overwhelming mystery of life, should nevertheless almost unfailingly eventuate in such a magnificent and stately confrontation of that mystery when suddenly it looms up at them out of the darkness of the unknown. The French arrive at precisely the same glorious consummation by way of sheer grimness of nature ; our men meet death, and such tragedy of death ! with the words of a music-hall song upon their lips, and one wonders wherein consists that depth of soul which must be theirs, or they would never be able to confront the grisly horrors they are called upon to encounter, as they do. And one realizes that

that in truth is the great spirit of Empire. It is the splendid, unconscious faculty of just taking everything as it comes. "What is life?" asked the tutor. "One d——d thing after another," replied the pupil, and that is the secret of the English nation, which finishes a game of bowls on the Hoe and then "finishes" an Armada on the sea, which plays football sandwiched in between the most appalling battles that earth has ever seen. That is the kind of thing that knocks the bottom out of pedantry and that blows theory, and dogma too, for the matter of that, sky high. I am, however, greatly puzzled to know when we, as a nation, developed this extraordinary frivolity of spirit, this light-hearted habit of sauntering through life, this debonair confrontation of tragedy and death. Have we always been so, un-unconsciously? or is it one of the many outcomes and developments of the great Board School movement in 1870? For centuries the English have been regarded as the embodiment of grim and taciturn determination, the French as the very essence of light-hearted irresponsibility. Ten years ago or more some of us realized that we had, as a nation, literally exchanged our traditional characteristics with one another, and ten months ago the English nation as a whole began to realize it too.

But none of us, not even those of us saturated with the memories of Agincourt and Elizabeth and Trafalgar, Waterloo, and Balaclava, even began to imagine the unbelievable, the miraculous heroism of the Cockney and colonial lads in Flanders and Gallipoli, the undying daring and accomplishment of the boys of the Flying Corps, instituted a couple of years ago, if so much, whose main spirit, whose chief attitude towards life, death, and the great hereafter is almost entirely that of the unthinking, unconscious frivoller. Such a revelation absolutely "puts the lid" on the solemnity and the dogmatism of the pedant, shaking his head over the decadence of the present generation.

And a good thing too.

I am quite willing to own that a lot of things are all

wrong, as the Bishop of London, a very acute if somewhat emotional man of the world, is at such continual pains to point out to us; but I cannot help feeling that the spirit of magnificent daring and doing, the spirit of such utter self-abnegation and self-sacrifice and self-forgetfulness which is almost universal to-day, in all classes of the community, must eventually result in a supremely fine people. Though I quite agree with the Bishop that the plague-spots in our midst must be done away with as speedily as possible ere the whole nation become tainted, on the whole I should think that there is more cause for thankfulness than for despair concerning the general character of our happy-go-lucky nation; and that is a noteworthy admission from one whose best friends have never accused him of the very slightest tendency to undue optimism. As a matter of fact it is an opinion arrived at only because it is forged out of one by the irrefutable evidence of one's own daily experience. We are saved by our inconsistencies just as we are frequently imperilled by the defects of our qualities. Just as the Bible, which, as I say, is the epitome of the British race, and the Church of England Catechism, which has helped in days gone by to form the very backbone of the British people, are at one moment, the one almost savagely anarchical and the other crudely snobbish, so is the English nation so contradictory that it is a mystery to itself and a marvel to the rest of the world. The one great thing is that it should never lose its appreciation of the value of tradition and long descent—even in this matter of all that is new and horrible.

I can remember a curious and somewhat pregnant incident. I was seated in an upper chamber, far above the nave of the magnificent new cathedral at Westminster, looking down upon the wonderful scene beneath me. At my side sat an artist busily engaged upon a huge altar-piece, representing the Virgin and Child, and beside him was his beautiful and singularly clever wife. Gazing down upon the tesselated pavement far beneath me, athwart which the westering sun sent a stray shaft of flickering golden light, and taking in at the same moment the exquisite proportions of this wonderful and as yet unfinished building, I happened to say to Mrs. Nico Jungman, the lady in question, "What this building lacks so much are memories and history and associations." And she replied: "And somehow or another that gives it its chief interest for me. To begin with, I think this scene right up here in this little gallery is so mediaeval. Nico might be a Florentine artist in the days of the Medici, and he is painting exactly the same picture, the same subject, the same poetry and art, with the same identical idea and intention as they would have painted. And hundreds of years hence people will come and look at this great altar-piece and wonder what kind of man the artist was. And another thing: it is the history that this place *will* have that makes it so interesting to me; it is making its own history. Look at those tombs of the two Cardinals—Manning and Vaughan. They are the first of the Archbishops to be buried here. Who will be the last? And think of all the splendid processions that will pass before that altar all through the long centuries to come, and all the different costumes one will see in this church: we may even get back to the dresses of the Middle Ages. And this church may help to make history just as the Abbey has done; it is sure, at all events, to have history made in it. Anyway, it's a bit of England, and may one day be a very big bit."

And I thought of that remark one day last winter when I saw a wonderful crowd of Gallipoli heroes from Australasia pouring through the great door of the cathedral in order that they might take part in that historic requiem over their glorious comrades. It is in this manner that every great building, every single department of life, the individualities and personalities and idiosyncrasies of every single person in the community are gradually and irresistibly absorbed and incorporated into the making and composition of the whole Empire, of the whole world, of the whole of human life.

And so I come to the conclusion of the whole matter

so far as these special memories and reflections are concerned. Like Lord Bellomont, a little farther back in this book, I have writ myself almost dead—and I should fear my readers too, who must be saying to themselves that if life is half as complicated and involved an affair as this chapter, it must be a thing too terrible to contemplate. But I cannot conclude without an expression of real gratitude and thanks for the many friends I have made during my pilgrimage through the world, and my regret that I have not deserved them so well as I fear I have on occasion deserved the enemies that are the lot of every man constituted as I am; for I feel quite sincerely that it is the rarest thing in life to make an enemy and not to deserve him.

However, when all's said and done and when one realizes that, so far, at all events, as oneself is concerned, this great round world and all that is therein is passing from one's gaze and knowledge, I think the only true view of it all to take is that hinted at by my little friend upon the Canadian prairie, and so finely expressed by Dora Sigerson—

> The seas that shake and thunder will close our mouths one day,
> The storms that shriek and whistle will blow our breaths away,
> The dust that flies and whitens will mark not where we trod.
> What matters then our judging? We are face to face with God!

And that last word, I have learned with Mr. Britling, embraces *the* Thing that will, in the end, matter most of all.

INDEX